THEANDRIC AND TRIUNE

T&T Clark Studies in Systematic Theology

Edited by

Ian A. McFarland
Ivor Davidson
Philip G. Ziegler
John Webster†

Volume 40

THEANDRIC AND TRIUNE

John Owen and Christological Agency

Ty Kieser

LONDON • NEW YORK • OXFORD • NEW DELHI • SYDNEY

T&T CLARK

Bloomsbury Publishing Plc, 50 Bedford Square, London, WC1B 3DP, UK
Bloomsbury Publishing Inc, 1359 Broadway, New York, NY 10018, USA
Bloomsbury Publishing Ireland, 29 Earlsfort Terrace, Dublin 2, D02 AY28, Ireland

BLOOMSBURY, T&T CLARK and the T&T Clark logo are trademarks
of Bloomsbury Publishing Plc

First published in Great Britain 2024
Paperback edition published 2025

Copyright © Ty Kieser, 2024

Ty Kieser has asserted his right under the Copyright, Designs and
Patents Act, 1988, to be identified as Author of this work.

For legal purposes the Acknowledgments on pp. xi–xii constitute an
extension of this copyright page.

All rights reserved. No part of this publication may be: i) reproduced or transmitted in any form, electronic or mechanical, including photocopying, recording or by means of any information storage or retrieval system without prior permission in writing from the publishers; or ii) used or reproduced in any way for the training, development or operation of artificial intelligence (AI) technologies, including generative AI technologies. The rights holders expressly reserve this publication from the text and data mining exception as per Article 4(3) of the Digital Single Market Directive (EU) 2019/790.

Bloomsbury Publishing Plc does not have any control over, or responsibility for, any third-party websites referred to or in this book. All internet addresses given in this book were correct at the time of going to press. The author and publisher regret any inconvenience caused if addresses have changed or sites have ceased to exist, but can accept no responsibility for any such changes.

A catalogue record for this book is available from the British Library.

Library of Congress Cataloging-in-Publication Data
Names: Kieser, Ty, author.
Title: Theandric and triune : John Owen and Christological agency / by Ty Kieser.
Description: New York : T&T Clark, 2024. |
Series: T&t Clark studies in systematic theology |
Includes bibliographical references and index.
Identifiers: LCCN 2023036109 (print) | LCCN 2023036110 (ebook) |
ISBN 9780567713735 (hardback) | ISBN 9780567713711 (paperback) |
ISBN 9780567713704 (epub) | ISBN 9780567713742 (pdf)
Subjects: LCSH: Owen, John, 1616–1683. | Act (Philosophy) | Jesus
Christ–Person and offices. | Jesus Christ–History of doctrines.
Classification: LCC BX5207.O88 K54 2024 (print) | LCC BX5207.O88 (ebook) |
DDC 128/.4–dc23/eng/20231102
LC record available at https://lccn.loc.gov/2023036109
LC ebook record available at https://lccn.loc.gov/2023036110

ISBN:	HB:	978-0-5677-1373-5
	PB:	978-0-5677-1371-1
	ePDF:	978-0-5677-1374-2
	eBook:	978-0-5677-1370-4

Series: T&T Clark Studies in Systematic Theology, volume 40

Typeset by Integra Software Services Pvt. Ltd.

For product safety related questions contact productsafety@bloomsbury.com.

To find out more about our authors and books visit www.bloomsbury.com
and sign up for our newsletters.

To Kate, my best friend, lifelong teammate, and undeserved wife

He was born—but He had been begotten …
He was wrapped in swaddling clothes—but He took off the swathing bands of the grave …
He was laid in a manger—but He was glorified by Angels …
He hungered—but He fed thousands …
He was wearied, but He is the Rest of them that are weary and heavy laden …
He prays, but He hears prayer …
He weeps, but He causes tears to cease …
He asks where Lazarus was laid, for He was Man; but He raises Lazarus, for He was God …
He is sold, and very cheap; but He redeems the world, and that at a great price …
He is bruised and wounded; but He healeth every disease and every infirmity …
He lays down His life, but He has power to take it again …
He dies, but He gives life …
He is buried, but He rises again …
If the one give you a starting point for your error, let the others put an end to it.

—Gregory Nazianzen

CONTENTS

Acknowledgments	xi
List of Abbreviations	xiii
List of Short Titles in *The Works of John Owen*	xvi

Chapter 1
INTRODUCING THE CASE FOR CHRISTOLOGICAL AGENCY 1
   I. Introduction 1
   II. Agency's Case 3
      A. The Prominence and Promise of Agency 4
         1. The Prominence of Agency Language and the Need for Clarity 4
         2. The Promise of Agency Language 7
      B. The Premises and Parameters of Agency 8
         1. The Premises and Theological Commitments 9
         2. Definitional Parameters 11
   III. Classical and Reformed Christological Commitments 17
      A. Classical Conciliar Affirmations 18
         1. Unity of Identity 19
         2. Distinct Capacities 20
      B. Classical Trinitarianism 22
      C. Reformed: Integrity of Christ's Human Nature 24
      D. Reformed: *Sola Scriptura* 26
      E. John Owen (1616–83) as Representative and Principal Witness 27
         1. The Historical Location of Owen as a Witness 27
         2. The Form of His Testimony 28
         3. Material Attention to Trinitarian and Christological Action (esp. in Terms of Agency) 30
         4. The Contemporary Significance of His Testimony 31
   IV. Contemporary Christology and *Prima Facie* Liabilities 33
      A. Social Trinitarianism and Three Independent Agents 34
      B. Spirit Christology and the Holy Spirit as Executing Agent 36
      C. Divine Passibility and Divine Limitation 37
      D. Parallelism and Two Christological Agents 38
      E. Strong Instrumentality and Lack of Human Activity 40
   V. Conclusion 42

Chapter 2
THE EVIDENCE OF TRINITARIAN ACTION FROM JOHN OWEN 43
   I. The Ontology of the Triune God 44
      A. The Essential Unity of the Triune God 45

       1. Simplicity and Pure Act   45
       2. Divine Attributes (Especially Impassibility)   46
       3. One Will   47
    B. The Distinction of Triune Persons   48
       1. Divine Relations and Persons   49
       2. Begotten of the Father   50
       3. From the Father and the Son (*Filioque*)   50
    C. Summary   51
  II. The Operations of the Triune God   52
    A. The Unity of Divine Agency   53
       1. Singular Agency   53
       2. Principle of Operation   54
       3. Indivisible Operations   55
       4. The Triune Agent (Singular)   57
    B. The Distinctions of the Divine Agents-in-Relation   58
       1. Operations *Ad Extra* Mirroring Relations *Ad Intra*   59
       2. Divine Missions   61
       3. Appropriations   62
       4. The Dogmatic Necessity of Three Distinct Agents-in-Relation (Plural)   64
    C. Summary   65

Chapter 3
THE EVIDENCE OF CHRISTOLOGICAL AGENCY FROM JOHN OWEN   67
  I. The Ontology of the Mediator   68
    A. One Person   69
       1. Assumption and Hypostatic Union   69
       2. The Triune Shape of the Son's Assumption   70
       3. The Role of the Spirit in the Assumption   71
       4. *An/Enhypostatic* Union   72
       5. Communication of Attributes   74
    B. Two Natures   75
       1. Humanity Not Divinized (*Extra Calvinisticum*)   75
       2. Divinity Not Humanized   77
       3. Two Essential Properties (Dyothelitism)   78
  II. The Operations of the Mediator   79
    A. Single Agent   80
       1. Acts of One Theandric Agent   80
       2. The Son, the Mediator   85
       3. *Principium Quo/Quod*   86
    B. Distinct Agencies   89
       1. Two Principles of Operation   90
       2. Immediacy   92
       3. Human Agency and the Holy Spirit   96
  III. Summary   98

Chapter 4
DIVINE AGENCY: COHERENCE AND PRUDENCE — 101
- I. Trinitarian, Divine Agency — 103
  - A. Causal Acts: God as Single Agent with Singular Agency — 103
  - B. Proper Actions and Personal Modes of Acting — 106
  - C. Appropriated Actions — 109
- II. Simple, Divine Agency — 114
  - A. Simple Agency — 115
  - B. Constant Agency — 118
- III. Divine Agency in Scripture: Romans 5:8 — 122
  - A. Singular Divine Agency — 124
  - B. Filial, Shared Divine Agency — 127
  - C. Distinctly Divine Agency — 129
- IV. Theological and Pastoral Prudence — 131
- V. Summary — 133

Chapter 5
HUMAN AGENCY: COHERENCE AND PRUDENCE — 135
- I. Ordinary, Distinct Human Agency — 135
  - A. Belief: Finite Knowledge — 136
  - B. Desire: Christ's Human Will — 141
  - C. Anointed by the Spirit — 148
- II. Dependent — 150
  - A. Agency and Dependence: Instrumentality — 151
  - B. Perspectives on Agency — 154
- III. Human Agency in Scripture: Hebrews 5:7-10 — 157
  - A. Rhetorical Structure and Pastoral Function of Heb. 5:7-10 — 158
  - B. The One That Had Days without Flesh Who Prays (5:7) — 160
  - C. The Forever-Priest Who Dies (5:6, 7d, 10) — 161
  - D. The Son Who Learns Obedience (5:8) — 162
  - E. The Source of Eternal Salvation Who Is Perfected (5:9) — 163
  - F. Summary — 164
- IV. Theological and Pastoral Prudence — 165
  - A. Christ as a Sympathetic Model to Imitate — 165
  - B. Christ's Obedience as Human — 166
- V. Conclusion — 170

Chapter 6
THE THEANDRIC AGENT: UNITY AND DISTINCTION — 173
- I. The Theandric Unity of the Agent — 173
  - A. Christ, the Theandric Mediator in Reformed Christology — 173
  - B. Precedents for Theandric Unity: Historic and Contemporary — 178
  - C. Historic Analogy of Theandric Action — 182
- II. Distinct Agencies and Distinct Effects — 183
  - A. Distinct Effects — 184

    B. Simultaneous Operations   192
  III. Objection! The Charge of Nestorianism   198
    A. Do Two Agencies Imply Two Agents?   198
    B. Four Agents of Divine Action?   201
  IV. Pastoral and Theological Significance: Theandric Priestly Action   205
  V. Summary   207

Chapter 7
CONCLUSION   209
  I. Summary   209
  II. Liabilities and Proximate Positions   212
  III. Future Research   213
  IV. Closing Statement   214

Bibliography   216
Index   239

ACKNOWLEDGMENTS

The title page bears only one author's name, but countless people have contributed to this project, and they have done so in a wide variety of ways—from pizza nights to editing footnotes. I have been the recipient of their tremendous kindness throughout my time writing this project. As a small attempt to recognize their efforts, I want to specifically thank a few of those people.

My PhD supervisors deserve a lot of credit for their help, patience, and effort during my time at Wheaton. Dan Treier has patiently attended to all of my academic and personal idiosyncrasies with grace and humor. He has gone above and beyond any reasonable expectations of a supervisor, and I am certainly a better thinker and better acquainted with Jesus because of him. My mom chuckled when I first told her that my two supervisors were named Marc Cortez and Dan Treier because "Mark" and "Dan" are also the names of her two brothers. Looking back on this project and program, "theological uncles" is probably the best way I could describe these two men. Like prototypical uncles, they were often simultaneously serious and funny; they brought laughter, shared wisdom and insight, pushed me toward faithfulness, and gave immensely helpful feedback. I am tremendously grateful for my *Doktor-onkels*. This project is better because of their input, and my approach to theological engagement will forever be shaped by their influence.

Our church family has been instrumental to our relational and spiritual wellbeing throughout our time here. Particularly encouraging was my men's group, the pastoral staff, and our small group with the friendships therein (Ekstrands, LaRussos, Somboonsiris, Kims, Yoos, Eric, Justin, Sophie, and Ryan). Bethany Baptist Church's support (financially and relationally) was also monumental in getting us to the place we are at now.

I owe a lot of gratitude to the professors on the PhD committee (many of whom read and commented on versions of this project) and the other professors at Wheaton who provided me with opportunities and guidance throughout my time there (esp. Amy Peeler, Keith Johnson, George Kalantzis, Beth Jones, and David Capes). Likewise, to my mentors/friends across the country whose prodigious kindness has formed me academically, spiritually, and relationally. Kyle Strobel, Matthew Levering, and Kevin Hector deserve special recognition here for the time that they have graciously offered to me over the past ten, eight, and five years (respectively) and for reading portions of this project. Finally, to Kelly Kapic, who served as my examiner, for his thoughtful questions, a careful reading, and buoying encouragement.

My friends at Wheaton and beyond have shaped, supported, and challenged me throughout the program. I am especially grateful for the members of my cohort at Wheaton (Dustyn, Josh, Justin, Keiko, and Mason) and the Treier'ites (Craig, Jeremy, Dustyn, Gerardo, and David) who colabored with me and suffered through reading a good portion of my research. Likewise, to the rest of the at Wheaton have made this program what it was, I am thankful for each one of you. If I named any one person, I would have to name you all. So much of what I have learned in the program came through conversations at the lunch table or leaning against a cubicle doorframe. My friends in theology at other institutions have likewise contributed to my theological formation. Daniel Lee Hill, David Moser, the Cleveland brothers, Fellipe do Vale, Will Bankston, Emily Vindas, Luke Kieser, and Jenny-Lyn de Klerk especially contributed much to this project through their careful editing and insightful conversations.

The institutional support that I have received has also been tremendous. I never quite understood why authors thanked librarians, but then I met Greg, Cheryl, and Linda. Likewise, Linda, Krista, and Courtney were huge administrative helps throughout. The Theological University Kampen provided me with a study fellowship in the summer of 2019, which gave me time and space to sketch out parts of what is now Chapter 4. Between the administrative support of Koos, Klaas, and Jos, the friendships with other fellows, and the feedback of Hans Burger, Dolf te Velde, and Wolter Rose, the time was as academically helpful as it was enjoyable. Most recently, Criswell College has been exceedingly gracious to my family and me.

Thanks also to the publishers involved in the process. IJST and SJT provided permission to use portions of my earlier work[1] and the T&T Clark series editors, reviewers, and editorial staff provided helpful feedback that improved the manuscript. Given the timing of review processes and early career job moves, I have not attempted to comprehensively update the bibliography from its earlier life as a dissertation.

Finally, I want to thank my family. Both my parents and my wife's mom and dad have been tremendously kind to us. Their support, along with the kindness and care of our many siblings, greatly contributed to the completion of this project and our happiness in the process. My wife and kids deserve the most credit and gratitude. My kids (Jaycee, Arawen, Tellan, BrenLea, Skyler, and Kirklyn) have kept me sane over the past several years of theological education. They bring laughter to my days and purpose to my time. I pray that they learn half as much about life and the Lord from me as I have learned from them. My wife, Kate, painstakingly read through multiple versions of this project. Yet more importantly, she has brought daily joy, encouragement, and love. I could not ask for a better best friend and teammate in life. She continues to point me to the goodness of the Lord and encourage me in this journey of a long obedience in the same direction, of which the project and program are a small part.

Soli Deo gloria
Ty Kieser

Quotes from chapters 2 and 3 used with permission from: "John Owen as ProtoSocial Trinitarian? Reinterpreting Owen and Resisting a Recent Trend," *Scottish Journal of Theology* 74 (2021): 222–34; The Holy Spirit and the Humanity of Christ in John Owen: A Re-Examination," *International Journal of Systematic Theology* 25 (2023): 93–113.

ABBREVIATIONS

AB	Anchor Bible
ABD	*Anchor Bible Dictionary*. Edited by D. N. Freedman. 6 vols. New York, 1992
ANCTRTBSS	Ashgate New Critical Thinking in Religion, Theology and Biblical Studies Series
ANF	*Ante-Nicene Fathers*. Edited by A. Roberts and J. Donaldson. Buffalo, 1885–96. Reprint, Grand Rapids, 1975
ASBT	Acadia Studies in Bible and Theology
ASTIA	Ashgate Studies in Theology, Imagination and the Arts
ATR	*Anglican Theological Review*
BACBS	Bloomsbury Academic Collections: Biblical Studies
BCCT	Brill's Companions to the Christian Tradition
BDF	Blass, F., A. Debrunner, and R. W. Funk. *A Greek Grammar of the New Testament and Other Early Christian Literature*. Chicago, 1961
BECNT	Baker Exegetical Commentary on the New Testament
BETL	Bibliotheca ephemeridum theologicarum lovaniensium
BGP	Bloomsbury Guides for the Perplexed
BIS	Biblical Interpretation Series
CBI	Counterpoints: Bible & Theology
CBQ	*Catholic Biblical Quarterly*
CCT	Challenges in Contemporary Theology
CIT	Current Issues in Theology
CPHST	Changing Paradigms in Historical and Systematic Theology
CSCD	Cambridge Studies in Christian Doctrine
CTJ	*Calvin Theological Journal*
CWBL	Collected Works of Bernard Lonergan
DLGTT	*Dictionary of Latin and Greek Theological Terms: Drawn Principally from Protestant Scholastic Theology*. Richard Muller. 2nd ed. Grand Rapids, 2017
EETR	Edinburgh Edition of Thomas Reid
EGGNT	Exegetical Guide to the Greek New Testament
EJPR	*European Journal for Philosophy of Religion*
EKK	Evangelisch-Katholishcer Kommentar
ES	*Ecumenical Studies*
F&P	*Faith and Philosophy*
FET	Foundations of Evangelical Theology
FRSCTP	Faith and Reason: Studies in Catholic Theology and Philosophy
HTANT	Historisch theologische Auslegung: Neues Testament
IJST	*International Journal of Systematic Theology*
IST	Issues in Systematic Theology

ITQ	*Irish Theological Quarterly*
JAT	*Journal of Analytic Theology*
JEH	*The Journal of Ecclesiastical History*
JES	*Jonathan Edwards Studies*
JETS	*Journal of the Evangelical Theological Society*
JP	*Journal of Philosophy*
JRT	*Journal of Reformed Theology*
JTS	*Journal of Theological Studies*
LATC	Los Angeles Theology Conference
LCC	Library of Christian Classics
LCL	Loeb Classical Library
LNTS	The Library of New Testament Studies
LW	*Luther's Works.* Edited by J. Pelikan and H.T. Lehmann. 55 vols. St. Louis, MO, 1955–86
MM	Medieval Mediterranean
NIB	*The New Interpreter's Bible*
NICNT	New International Commentary on the New Testament
NIGTC	New International Greek Testament Commentary
NovTSup	Novum Testamentum Supplements
NPNF[1]	*Nicene and Post-Nicene Fathers,* Series 1. Edited by Philip Schaff. New York, 1886–90. Reprint, Peabody, MA, 1994
NPNF[2]	*Nicene and Post-Nicene Fathers,* Series 2. Edited by Philip Schaff and Henry Wace. New York, 1890. Reprint, Peabody, MA, 1994
NSBT	New Studies in Biblical Theology
NSD	New Studies in Dogmatics
NTM	New Testament Monographs
NTS	*New Testament Studies*
NZSTP	*Neue Zeitschrift für Systematische Theologie und Religionsphilosophie*
ODNB	*Oxford Dictionary of National Biography*
OECS	Oxford Early Christian Studies
OECT	Oxford Early Christian Texts
OSAT	Oxford Studies in Analytic Theology
OSHT	Oxford Studies in Historical Theology
OWC	Oxford World's Classics
PG	*Patrologia Graeca.* Edited by J.-P. Migne. 162 vols. Paris, 1857–66
PL	*Patrologia Latina.* Edited by J.-P. Migne. 217 vols. Paris, 1844–64
PML	The Peter Martyr Library
PNTC	Pillar New Testament Commentary
PPS	Popular Patristics Series
PRRD	*Post-Reformation Reformed Dogmatics.* Richard A. Muller. 4 vols. Grand Rapids, 2003
PTMS	Princeton Theological Monograph Series
RHT	Reformed Historical Theology
RIPS	Royal Institute of Philosophy Supplement
SBJT	*The Southern Baptist Journal of Theology*
SBLRBS	SBL Resources for Biblical Studies
SCDS	Studies in Christian Doctrine and Scripture

SCES	Sixteenth Century Essays and Studies
SCG	*The Summa contra Gentiles*. Translated by the English Dominican Fathers. 4 vols. London, 1924–9
SCHT	Studies in Christian History and Thought
SECT	Sources of Early Christian Thought
SJT	*Scottish Journal of Theology*
SMRT	Studies in Medieval and Reformation Thought
SMRTTS	Studies in Medieval and Reformation Traditions: Texts and Sources
SNTSMS	Society for New Testament Studies Monograph Series
SPR	Studies in Philosophy and Religion
SPT	Studies in Philosophical Theology
SRT	Studies in Reformed Theology
ST	*Summa Theologiæ*
TDNT	*Theological Dictionary of the New Testament*. Edited by G. Kittel and G. Friedrich. Translated by G. W. Bromiley. 10 vols. Grand Rapids, 1964–76
TJ	*Trinity Journal*
TNTC	Tyndale New Testament Commentaries
TS	*Theological Studies*
TSRPRT	Texts and Studies in Reformation and Post-Reformation Thought
TTCBS	T&T Clark Biblical Studies
TTCCRBS	T&T Clark Critical Readings in Biblical Studies
TTCSET	T&T Clark Studies in English Theology
TTCSST	T&T Clark Studies in Systematic Theology
WA	*Luthers Werke: Kritische Gesamtausgabe*. Weimar, 1883–2009
WCF	*Westminster Confession of Faith*
WJE	Works of Jonathan Edwards
WMANT	Wissenschaftliche Monographien zum Alten und Neuen Testament
WTJ	*Westminster Theological Journal*
WUNT	Wissenschaftliche Untersuchungen zum Neuen Testament
ZECNT	Zondervan Exegetical Commentary on the New Testament
ZNWKK	*Zeitschrift für die Neutestamentliche Wissenschaft und die Kunde der älteren Kirche*

LIST OF SHORT TITLES IN *THE WORKS OF JOHN OWEN*

All Owen citations are from *The Works of John Owen*. Edited by William H. Goold. 24 vols. Edinburgh: Johnston & Hunter 1850–5.

In order to make the literary context of Owen's theological claims more explicit, short titles are provided in the text and listed in WJO order below (with a parenthetical indication of their page range within their WJO volume). Citations of Owen throughout the project follow this format: WJO, *Short Title*, volume:page.

Christologia	Χριστολογια: Or, a Declaration of the Glorious Mystery of the Person of Christ—God and Man (1:1–273)
Glory of Christ	Meditations and Discourses on the Glory of Christ, in His Person, Office, and Grace (1:274–417)
Glory of Christ Applied	Meditations and Discourses Concerning the Glory of Christ Applied unto Unconverted Sinners and Saints under Spiritual Decays (1:418–63)
Catechism	The Greater Catechism (1:470–93)
Communion	Of Communion with God (2:1–274)
Vindication of the Preceding Discourse	A Vindication of Some Passages in a Discourse Concerning Communion with God (2:275–364)
Vindication	A Brief Declaration and Vindication of the Doctrine of the Trinity (2:365–440)
Pneumatologia	Πνευματοαογια: Or, a Discourse Concerning the Holy Spirit (3:1–651)
The Reason of Faith	The Reason of Faith (4:4–117)
Understanding the Mind of God	Συνεσις Πνευματικη: Or, the Causes, Ways, and Means of Understanding the Mind of God as Revealed in His Word, With Assurance Therein (4:118–234)
Spirit as Comforter	A Discourse of the Holy Spirit as a Comforter (4:352–419)
Justification	The Doctrine of Justification by Faith, through the Imputation of the Righteousness of Christ (5:1–400)
Evidence	Gospel Grounds and Evidences or the Faith of God's Elect (5:401–56)
Mortification	Of the Mortification of Sin in Believers; The Necessity, Nature, and Means of It (6:1–86)
Temptation	Of Temptation: The Nature and Power of It; The Danger of Entering into It; and the Means of Preventing That Danger with a Resolution of Sundry Cases Thereunto Belonging (6:87–152)
Indwelling Sin	The Nature, Power, Deceit, and Prevalency of the Remainders of Indwelling Sin in Believers (6:153–322)
Exposition of Psalm 130	A Practical Exposition upon Psalm 130 (6:323–648)

Spiritual Mindedness	Φρονημα του Πνευματος: Or, the Grace and Duty of Being Spiritually Minded Declared and Practically Improved (7:261–498)
Righteous Zeal	Righteous Zeal Encouraged by Divine Protection (8:127–206)
Branch of the Lord	The Branch of the Lord the Beauty of Zion (8:281–311)
Gospel Worship	The Nature and Beauty of Gospel Worship (9:53–69)
Sermon VII	Sermon VIII (9:476–484)
Arminianism	Θεομαχια Αυτεξουσιαστικη: Or, a Display of Arminianism (10:1–138)
Death of Death	Salus Electorum, Sanguis Jesu; Or, the Death of Death in the Death of Christ (10:139–428)
Death of Christ	Of the Death of Christ, the Price He Paid, and the Purchase He Made (10:429–80)
Divine Justice	A Dissertation on Divine Justice (10:481–624)
Perseverance	The Doctrine of the Saints' Perseverance Explained and Confirmed (11:1–666)
Vindiciæ Evangelicæ	Vindiciæ Evangelicæ; Or, the Mystery of the Gospel Vindicated and Socinianism Examined (12:1–590)
Evangelical Love	Discourse Concerning Evangelical Love, Church Peace, and Unity. (15:56–186)
Divine Original	Of the Divine Original Authority, Self-Evidencing Light, and Power of the Scriptures (16:295–344)
Condescension of Christ	The Humiliation and Condescension of Christ (17:561–69)
Theologoumena	Θεολογούμενα Παντοδαπά (17:1–481)
BT	Biblical Theology: The History of Theology from Adam to Christ. Translated by William Goold and Stephen P. Westcott. Grand Rapids, 1994.
Sacerdotal Office of Christ	Concerning the Sacerdotal Office of Christ (19:3–262)
Observations	Summary of Doctrinal and Practical Observations (19:461–546)
Exposition of Hebrews	An Exposition of the Epistle to the Hebrews (vols 20–24)

Chapter 1

INTRODUCING THE CASE FOR CHRISTOLOGICAL AGENCY

I. Introduction

The gospel of John portrays the one and only Son of God as the singular actor who accomplishes actions that seem to be both absolutely divine (1:3; 5:19) and ordinarily human (4:6; 11:33–35; 19:28).[1] Likewise, the ecumenical councils of Chalcedon (451) and Constantinople II (553) embrace the distinct claims that the one "who works miracles is ... identical with the Christ who suffered,"[2] while also confessing that "it does not belong to the same nature to weep out of deep-felt pity for a dead friend, and to call him back to life again."[3]

Understanding the acts of Christ, a single subject, according to his divine and human natures has been called a "mighty conundrum" and a "riddle" (Rätsel) of "severity" (Härte) by some of the most notable contributors to modern Christology.[4] One prominent (yet often opaque) approach to the question of action is the concept of "agency" (i.e., minimally defined as the capacity for action) and its corresponding term "agent" (i.e., minimally, a performer of actions). Yet, even in the mid-twentieth century, Hans Urs von Balthasar lamented that "a sufficiently concrete delineation of Jesus' distinctively human agency is a task that remains

---

1. See Richard Bauckham, *Gospel of Glory: Major Themes in Johannine Theology* (Grand Rapids: Baker Academic, 2015), 239–52.
2. This is a positive framing of the anathema of canon three of Constantinople II (Norman P. Tanner, ed., *Decrees of the Ecumenical Councils* [Washington, DC: Georgetown University Press, 1990], 1:114; hereafter, *Degrees* followed by volume and page number).
3. This is from Leo's letter to Flavian, in ibid., 1:80.
4. The former is from Kathryn Tanner, *Jesus, Humanity and the Trinity* (Minneapolis: Fortress, 2001), 22; the latter is Karl Barth, *Die kirchliche Dogmatik* (Zürich: Theologischer, 1980), IV/2, 388; hereafter, *KD*. Likewise, Ivor Davidson says that the question of human and divine distinction in a "single ethical agent" is a field in which "a variety of pitfall lurk" ("'Not My Will but Yours Be Done': The Ontological Dynamics of Incarnational Intention," *IJST* 7 [2005]: 197).

with the church to this day as *unfinished business*."⁵ Participating in this unfinished business, the project that unfolds in the following pages seeks to investigate this "mighty conundrum" and help to further order speech regarding the divine and human agency of Christ.

The theological method throughout this project might be illustrated through an analogy from civil government. For this project, the proper task of theology is not to create new principles, or laws, about God (as the legislative branch does), nor to enforce preexisting laws (like the executive branch), but instead the task of theology resembles the responsibilities of the judicial branch: interpreting the authoritative law (of Scripture), considering the historical precedent of previous courts (i.e., the tradition), and settling contemporary disputes accordingly.⁶ Therefore, this project will not seek to create a new model of christological action, nor mandate certain conclusions, but will seek to adjudicate claims of christological agency within a particular theological jurisdiction: classical and Reformed Christology.⁷ This will serve as a local court case that adjudicates between the contemporary language of christological agency, on the one hand, and classical and Reformed Christology, on the other (with John Owen as its key witness). The goal of this project is to provide an internally coherent and theologically prudent account of divine and human agency in classical and Reformed Christology with its commitment to Scripture, the ecumenical councils, a classical doctrine of the triune God, and Reformed christological emphases.⁸

---

5. Hans Urs von Balthasar, *The Dramatis Personae: Persons in Christ*, trans. Graham Harrison, vol. 3 of *Theo-Drama: Theological Dramatic Theory* (San Francisco: Ignatius, 1993), 215–16, emphasis mine. William J. Abraham, *Divine Agency and Divine Action, Volume II: Soundings in the Christian Tradition* (New York: Oxford University Press, 2018), 112, likewise notes the absence and difficulty of such an account.

6. The framework of this analogy comes from Kevin W. Hector, "Barth and Theological Method," in *Blackwell Companion to Karl Barth*, ed. George Hunsinger, Keith L. Johnson, 2 vols (Oxford: Blackwell, 2020), 1:87. As with all analogies (especially extended ones), this image will fail to correspond to the target domain in several ways. For example, my role (as the author) might be conceived of as resembling that of a defense attorney; however, there is no obvious analogy to the role of the "prosecutor." Further, the "judge" of this case could be conceived of as every reader, or all readers collectively, or the church (1 Cor. 6:2), or simply the Lord (Jn 5:22).

7. When I use the phrase "christological agency" I am using "agency" generically to mean the topic and surrounding questions regarding agents, agency, and action. So, while I will later argue that Christ has multiple "agencies" (technically defined), I do not consider it incompatible with the singular use of the generic phrase "christological agency" here. Similarly, we could discuss the topic of trinitarian "personhood" (singular) or the "being of Christ" and no one would assume that we meant to communicate that there is a single person in God or one nature in Christ.

8. Internal coherence refers to the maintenance of all four core commitments throughout the project.

The goal of coherence—rather than veracity or superiority—ought to indicate the delimited character of this project. The project is not suggesting that the following is the only plausible way to conceive of christological action in terms of agency, but that it is a logically coherent way of doing so given a certain set of Reformed commitments. Further, this project is not seeking knowledge for the sake of curiosity (knowing for knowing's sake) or vanity (knowing in order to become known) but prudence (knowing for the formative value) that leads to charity.[9] So the conclusions that follow will be measured not only by their logical viability but also their ability to foster "right reason in action,"[10] specifically the possible pastoral implications of these conclusions for the Christian life.

Toward that goal, this chapter will establish the parameters of the case: articulating the prominence and propriety of agency as a theological concept (§II); mapping the criteria for classical and Reformed Christology (§III); and presenting the *prima facie* challenges that classical and Reformed christological agency is liable to and the contemporary positions that are most proximate to its conclusions (§IV).

II. Agency's Case

The question of Christ's divine and human action is *present* in patristic and medieval Christologies. However, on the heels of the modern "turn to the subject,"[11] which emphasizes beings *in act*[12] and is often suspicious of metaphysics,[13] action and agency have become *prominent* in modern Christology.[14] This section will articulate the employment of agency language in contemporary Christology and its need for

---

9. This use of prudence and contrast with curiosity and vanity is drawn from Bernard of Clairvaux, *On the Song of Songs*, 4 vols. Cistercian Fathers, trans. K. Walsh, I. M. Edmonds (Kalamazoo, MI: Cistercian, 1971–80), sermon 36: 3.

10. Thomas Aquinas, *ST* II–II, Q. 47, A.2.

11. As traced in Charles Taylor, *Sources of the Self: The Making of the Modern Identity* (New York: Cambridge University Press, 1989), 3.

12. See Wolfhart Pannenberg, *Jesus: God and Man*, trans. Lewis L. Wilkins and Duane A. Priebe (Philadelphia: Westminster, 1968), 298 for the turn toward christological activity (specifically) and divine/human distinction in modernity.

13. Simon Gathercole specifically says of Christology, "A good deal of twentieth-century exegesis focused more on agency or function, that is, on Jesus' execution of divine action at the expense of making claims about his nature" ("The Trinity in the Synoptic Gospels and Acts," in *The Oxford Handbook of the Trinity*, ed. Gilles Emery and Matthew Levering [New York: Oxford University Press, 2011], 58).

14. Elizabeth A. Johnson attributes this post-Kantian trend with rising interest in humanity of Christ and his human operations (*Consider Jesus: Waves of Renewal in Christology* [New York: Crossroad, 1990], 12).

clarity (§A), then briefly present a theology of agency (§B), which will provide the terminological foundation for the duration of the project (esp. Chs. 4–6).

A. *The Prominence and Promise of Agency*

Over the past fifty years "agency" language has gained a prominent place in philosophical discussions of ethics (e.g., moral responsibility), legality/criminality (e.g., legal responsibility), and human autonomy (e.g., free will).[15] Most notably for our purposes, it is also widely used in various theological discussions.

1. The Prominence of Agency Language and the Need for Clarity Agency language is employed in nearly every theological locus, from the doctrine of providence and the doctrine of God to sacramental theology and speech act theory.[16] Additionally, in biblical studies, particularly in Pauline studies, agency language is employed for the sake of soteriological discussions.[17] Perhaps most illustrative of this phenomenon is William Abraham's ongoing tetralogy, *Divine Agency and Divine Action*, with its broad philosophical, historical, and dogmatic coverage.

Even amid the constant usage of the language in discussions of Christian theology, there is frequently a high degree of confusion about what the concept means and how to use it. Speaking of the discussions of divine agency in philosophy and theology, William Abraham says that "there is little consensus as to how best to identify the core issues to be addressed. Worse still, there is no agreement on the most promising way to address them."[18] Likewise emphasizing the opaque

---

15. Hyman and Steward say that it "occupies a central position in ethics, metaphysics and jurisprudence" (*Agency and Action*, RIPS 55 [New York: Cambridge University Press, 2004], vi). One of the best representations of this phenomenon is the six-volume series *Oxford Studies in Agency and Responsibility* (New York: Oxford University Press, 2013–19).

16. E.g., Hans W. Frei, *The Identity of Jesus Christ: The Hermeneutical Bases of Dogmatic Theology*, expanded and updated ed. (Eugene, OR: Cascade, 2013); Michaela Kušnieriková, *Acting for Others: Trinitarian Communion and Christological Agency*, Emerging Scholars (Minneapolis: Fortress, 2017); Kevin Timpe, "Cooperative Grace, Cooperative Agency," *EJPR* 7 (2015): 223–45; W. Travis McMaken, "Definitive, Defective or Deft?: Reassessing Barth's Doctrine of Baptism in Church Dogmatics IV/4," *IJST* 17 (2015): 89–114; Philip Clayton, *Adventures in the Spirit: God, World, Divine Action* (Minneapolis: Fortress, 2008); Kevin J. Vanhoozer, *Remythologizing Theology: Divine Action, Passion, and Authorship*, CSCD (New York: Cambridge University Press, 2010).

17. John M. G. Barclay and Simon J. Gathercole, eds., *Divine and Human Agency in Paul and His Cultural Environment*, TTCBS (New York: T&T Clark, 2008); Jason Maston, *Divine and Human Agency in Second Temple Judaism and Paul: A Comparative Study*, WUNT 2/297 (Tübingen: Mohr Siebeck, 2010); Preston M. Sprinkle, *Paul and Judaism Revisited: A Study of Divine and Human Agency in Salvation* (Downers Grove, IL: IVP Academic, 2013).

18. William J. Abraham, *Divine Agency and Divine Action, Volume I: Exploring and Evaluating the Debate* (New York: Oxford University Press, 2018), 2.

nature of the discussion, Christoph Schwöbel says, "Discourse about divine action is as fundamental in Christian faith as it is fundamentally unclear in Christian theology."[19]

The opacity of the "agency" word-group (i.e., "agency"; "agencies"; "agent[s]") is perhaps most evident in the primary locus of this project: Christology. There is, minimally, an assumed and implicit definition in much of contemporary literature. This assumption is probably most glaring in the constant use of the language of "agency" without definition in discussions of "Early High Christology," defending that the claim that Christ is a divine "agent" and shares in "divine agency."[20] This is also evidenced by the invocation of the language without explicit definitions in contemporary dogmatic accounts.[21] Further, the lack of definitional clarity contributes to inconsistency throughout the literature in the attribution of the labels of agent and agency in Christology. For example, Brian Daley's work *God Visible* states that an affirmation of the "one real, living agent, the Word" is a staple of orthodoxy (i.e., Cyril and Gregory's Christology), while Theodore's Nestorian Christology considered Christ's two natures as "two agents."[22] Yet Robert Jenson claims that the councils affirm that "each nature is agent to" distinct kinds of actions.[23] Likewise, Bruce McCormack suggests that a literal reading of Chalcedon requires that the "eternal Son and the man Jesus" be understood as "two agents of the one history of God."[24] Finally, Thomas Flint states that considering Christ's humanity as "an agent with morally significant freedom" has "historically been

---

19. Christoph Schwöbel, *God: Action and Revelation*, SPT (Kampen: Kok Pharos, 1992), 23.

20. Larry W. Hurtado, *One God, One Lord: Early Christian Devotion and Ancient Jewish Monotheism* (Philadelphia: Fortress, 1988); Larry Joseph Kreitzer, *Jesus and God in Paul's Eschatology*, BACBS 19 (New York: Bloomsbury Academic, 2015), 90; David B. Capes, *The Divine Christ: Paul, the Lord Jesus, and the Scriptures of Israel*, ASBT (Grand Rapids: Baker, 2018), 166–7.

21. E.g., the prominence of agent/agency language in Bruce Lindley McCormack, *The Humility of the Eternal Son: Reformed Kenoticism and the Repair of Chalcedon*, Current Issues in Theology (New York: Cambridge University Press, 2021), 11–13, 31; 48–9, 159, 210–11, 224–5, 258, 269–70, 281–2. Additionally, Stephen Wellum uses the language of "agent" in his definition of "person" and nowhere defines "agent" (*God the Son Incarnate: The Doctrine of Christ*, FET [Wheaton, IL: Crossway, 2016], 378). R. Michael Allen, *The Christ's Faith: A Dogmatic Account*, TTCSST (New York: T&T Clark, 2009), 113, 119.

22. Brian E. Daley, *God Visible: Patristic Christology Reconsidered*, CPHST (New York: Oxford University Press, 2018), 184–5, 191.

23. Robert W. Jenson, *Systematic Theology: Volume 1: The Triune God* (New York: Oxford University Press, 2001), 131.

24. Mc Cormack, *Humility of the Eternal Son*, 13; cf. 261.

the dominant position."[25] Sometimes these assertions of two agents in orthodox Christology are explicit, yet other times they are implicit (and potentially unwitting). Examples of the implicit affirmation or allusions to two agents include Charles Hodge's description of the *soul* of Christ as "a self-conscious, intelligent, voluntary agent"[26] (presumably alongside the Son who is a second voluntary agent) and, more recently, Rowan Williams' statement that Jesus is the "supremely and perfectly human agent … [and] is also the perfectly divine agent."[27] Another discrepancy in the literature around the usage of "agency" is evident in (on the one hand) Stephen Wellum's claim that Chalcedonian Christology "rules out any idea of dual agency,"[28] while others argue that "double agency" is a valuable and Chalcedonian category.[29] Additionally, there is rarely explicit attention devoted to a consistent "reverse proportionality" of trinitarian and christological grammars in terms of agents and agency.[30] That is, rarely is there attention to the trinitarian implications of christological claims regarding agency (e.g., calling Christ a single agent, naming each nature an agent, or denying double agency), or the christological implications of trinitarian claims regarding agency (e.g., speaking of the Son's unique agency or singular trinitarian agency).[31] Finally, there is not much explication of the connection between the language of "agency" and "agents" (e.g., does distinct agency require/imply distinct agents?). To illustrate this last point,

---

25. Thomas P. Flint, "Should Concretists Part with Mereological Models of the Incarnation," in *The Metaphysics of the Incarnation*, ed. Anna Marmodoro and Jonathan Hill (New York: Oxford University Press, 2011), 69, similarly, Charles M. Stang, "The Two 'I's of Christ: Revisiting the Christological Controversy," *ATR* 94 (2012): 529–47.

26. Charles Hodge, *Systematic Theology*, 3 vols (Grand Rapids: Eerdmans, 1981), 2: 379.

27. Rowan Williams, *Christ the Heart of Creation* (Bedford Square: Bloomsbury Continuum, 2018), 165.

28. Wellum, *God the Son Incarnate*, 317.

29. This is especially true in Karl Barth and Barthians (Karl Barth, *The Church Dogmatics*, ed. Geoffrey William Bromiley and Thomas Forsyth Torrance, trans. Geoffrey William Bromiley (Edinburgh: T&T Clark: 1958), IV/2, 16; George Hunsinger, *How to Read Karl Barth: The Shape of His Theology* [New York: Oxford University Press, 1993], 189, 223; Paul Dafydd Jones, *The Humanity of Christ: Christology in Karl Barth's Church Dogmatics* [New York: T&T Clark, 2008], 202).

30. This phrase comes from Brian Daley, "The Persons in God and the Person of Christ in Patristic Theology: An Argument for Parallel Development," in *The Mystery of the Holy Trinity in the Fathers of the Church the Proceedings of the Fourth Patristic Conference*, ed. D. Vincent Twomey and Lewis Ayres (Portland: Four Courts, 2007), 32; similarly, Lewis Ayres, *Nicaea and Its Legacy: An Approach to Fourth-Century Trinitarian Theology* (New York: Oxford University Press, 2006), 236.

31. An interesting example of this last category is Thomas H. McCall's commitment to "genuine personal distinction and even agency of the Father, Son, and Holy Spirit" (*Analytic Christology and the Theological Interpretation of the New Testament*, OSAT [New York: Oxford University Press, 2021], 173; cf. 124, 148–9, 156, 170).

Kathryn Tanner speaks of three divine persons and three "agencies" so that Jesus "has his own agency" (indicating that agency maps onto persons), yet she also speaks of "divine agency" (presumably singular) in Jesus and in the world.[32]

These examples ought not to be viewed as inherently critical or accusatory, but evidentiary of the language's prominence yet definitional opacity and dogmatic inconsistency. As such there is a need to define terms carefully, to relate them to each other coherently, to align them rightly with conciliar statements, and to locate them rightly within a dogmatic structure (esp. trinitarian theology and Christology). As Adonis Vidu says, of a related issue, the complexity of this question "should at the very least alert us that we must tread very carefully over this sensitive dogmatic terrain."[33]

2. The Promise of Agency Language Admitting that agency language is prominent and in need of clarity, we must also concede that not all prominent yet opaque phenomena are worth clarifying. Some concepts are better left to wallow in their own ambiguity (e.g., I am very content to let most of the slang that junior high kids use remain unclear). So we might ask, what value might clarifying "agency"/"agent" add to discussions of christological action?[34]

First, there is potential contextual purchase in the language of agency that could give a modern voice to conciliar Christology. While some modern theologians may be leery of the metaphysical freight that concepts like "nature" or "soul" bring, agency may be able to gain traction. Evidencing this interest in agency, David Kelsey explains that there has been a shift "from the person as patient or subject of consciousness to the person as agent," and he celebrates the "fertile" possibility of this shift being applied to Christology.[35]

Second, drawing again from Kelsey, agency helps us to appreciate the "concrete material contexts" in which actions are made.[36] That is, agency appreciates the particularity, concrete reality, and embodiment of human actions performed by

---

32. Kathryn Tanner, *Christ the Key*, CIT (New York: Cambridge University Press, 2010), 224; "The Trinity as Christian Teaching," in *The Oxford Handbook of the Trinity*, ed. Gilles Emery and Matthew Levering (New York: Oxford University Press, 2011), 356; *Jesus, Humanity and the Trinity*, 57, 21.

33. Adonis Vidu, "Ascension and Pentecost," in *Being Saved: Explorations in Human Salvation*, ed. Marc Cortez, Joshua R. Farris, and S. Mark Hamilton (London: SCM, 2018), 104–5.

34. This section does not imply that agency is a "better" category than those previously employed (e.g., "nature," "will," and "energy") or a substitute for them, but simply that there are valuable reasons to include agency in christological discussions alongside these categories.

35. David H. Kelsey, "Human Being," in *Christian Theology: An Introduction to Its Traditions and Tasks* (Philadelphia: Fortress, 1982), 166, 167.

36. Ibid., 166.

human creatures.[37] In his defense of the importance of the body, Richard Swinburne appeals to the way in which intentional actions are necessarily both embodied and public acts bringing about change in the world.[38] Here we see agency (i.e., capacity for intentional action) incorporating embodiment in a way that makes human activity necessarily physical and particular. This is especially pertinent and potentially helpful in Christology since so much of the recent discussion on christological action has operated within the sphere of Christ's "consciousness."[39]

Agency also recognizes the inherent storied-ness to Christology and the intimate connection between Christ's person and work by linking Christ's person (i.e., ontology, capacities, and composition) to the history of redemption (i.e., the enacted effects of Christ).[40] Hans Frei, in his chapter on "the enacted intention of Jesus," shows how the story of Jesus in Scripture turns on the enacted intentions of Christ, binding "the individual Jesus" with God's "saving activity" and his intention to "enact the good of humanity on their behalf … in perfect obedience to God."[41] Connecting Christology and agency back to the story of Christ, Frei says that "this narrative sequence of events" enables us to "identify Jesus by an intention and action pattern."[42]

Finally, christological agency appreciates the indissolubly trinitarian character of Christology. By virtue of doctrines like the indivisibility of triune operations, agency discussions can quickly recognize the trinitarian underpinnings of christological action. The agency word-group also appreciates and wrestles with the "reverse proportionality" between Christology and trinitarian theology, whereby whatever is predicated of persons, Christ has one of and God has three of and whatever is predicated of natures, Christ has two and God has one.

B. The Premises and Parameters of Agency

So, if agency is a category that is in need of clarification and such an attempt would be beneficial to Christian thought and life, this attempt will do so in a "theological" way. That is, we begin not with a definition of action and agency

---

37. Sarah Coakley, *Powers and Submissions: Spirituality, Philosophy and Gender*, CCT (Oxford: Blackwell, 2002), 27, suggests that this is a failure of many recent defenses of "Chalcedonian orthodoxy."

38. Richard G. Swinburne, "What Is So Good about Having a Body?," in *Comparative Theology: Essays for Keith Ward*, ed. T. W. Bartel (London: SPCK, 2003), 139.

39. Andrew Ter Ern Loke names over a dozen modern theologians who have entered this discussion of consciousness in the past decades ("On the Use of Psychological Models in Christology," *Heythrop Journal* 58 [2017]: 44).

40. See Barth's understanding of Christ's "active person or his personal work" (*CD* IV/1, 128). Thomas Weinandy spends much of his recent book appreciating the "centrality of divine and human actions in the gospels" (*Jesus Becoming Jesus: A Theological Interpretation of the Synoptic Gospels* [Washington, DC: Catholic University of America Press, 2018], xix).

41. Frei, *Identity of Jesus Christ*, 109; cf. 109–12.

42. Ibid., 111.

that we superimpose onto God but instead with the revealed truth that "God ... acts" (Isa. 64:4), and particularly that "he worked in Christ" (Eph. 1:20).[43] While the material content and formal shape of this theological account will be unfolded throughout the book, this section will provide the fundamental theological premises of our definitions of the agency word-group and establish definitional parameters in the project-long attempt to provide clarity for the concept. So, as we will see in the coming chapters, agent/agency is a semi-open concept that permits various criteria and conditions in various contexts. Therefore, it is not until after these contexts are named that we can more fully understand and organize these conditions and, thereby, definitions. However, the parameters designated here represent the definitions and their criteria for the most common contexts in our understanding of agents/agency.

1. The Premises and Theological Commitments As such, this section begins by noting the methodological premises upon which a theological account of agency might be established as it seeks to be consistent with classical and Reformed theology. From there, it will follow an "agent-causation" paradigm of action in order to define the foundational designations of the pertinent concepts related to actions, agents, and agencies.

For classical and Reformed theology God is simple and not composed of parts or pieces.[44] As creatures of the eternal Creator, we can "describe" God, yet we must also be aware of the qualitative distinction between God the Creator and ourselves

---

43. The twentieth century hosted an active discussion over whether or not God could be considered an "agent" (at pains of claiming that God was just an agent like/among other agents). See Abraham, *Divine Agency*, 1:165–86 for a summary and affirmation of God as an agent without making God a creature.

44. If God is "simple/pure act" (see Ch. 2 §I.A.1), then "God does one thing, and that is to be God—perfectly, eternally, and incomprehensibly" (Stephen R. Holmes, "'Something Much Too Plain to Say': Towards a Defence of the Doctrine of Divine Simplicity," *NZSTR* 43 [2001]: 139). This does not mean that the one "simple action" of God excludes distinct effects and therefore "acts" of God in creation. The promise that God makes to Abraham is a distinct act from the promise he makes to Isaac. Similar to the way that divine simplicity means that God's attributes are identical with his own being yet not identical to one another (i.e., "all identical in references but different in sense"), so too God's acts in history are distinct manifestations and effects in time of the pure actuality of God. They are thereby the "temporal effects of the single eternal act identical with God, God's action in the strict sense" (Eleonore Stump and Norman Kretzmann, "Absolute Simplicity," *F&P* 2 [1985]: 356–7; see also Thomas G. Weinandy, *Does God Suffer?* [Notre Dame: University of Notre Dame Press, 2000], 132; Adonis Vidu, *Atonement, Law, and Justice: The Cross in Historical and Cultural Contexts* [Grand Rapids: Baker Academic, 2014], 249–56; Will Bankston, "The Responsiveness of Pure Actuality: Unmediated Agency, Linguistic Potentiality and the Divine Accommodation of Speech Acts," *IJST* 21 [2019]: 290–313).

as creatures. This distinction is particularly pertinent when it comes to the way we use language about God and God's actions (e.g., the divine nature does not have a body to move, vocal cords, or brain neurons). Adonis Vidu argues that the doctrine of divine simplicity ought to qualify our theological language about divine action.[45] Based on this qualified language and distinction between the Creator and his creatures, our affirmations about divine agency must be understood to be analogous to human agency.[46]

The doctrine of divine simplicity further influences our understanding of agency insofar as the "God of the 'classical' Christian tradition differs far more radically from all creation than any difference we may find within the created order."[47] Consequently, William Abraham argues that agency is an "open" concept. For Abraham, "agency" differs from the concept "knowledge" (and concepts like it) in which there are necessary and sufficient conditions (e.g., justified true belief) that are applicable across contexts. Instead agency is much more like the concepts "quality" and "thing" with a "great variety of context-dependent criteria."[48] As such, we cannot universalize an account of human agency across all human and divine contexts, nor can we insist on one kind of divine action (e.g., the act of creating) and establish that as paradigmatic for all divine actions.[49] Extending beyond Abraham, this project seeks to understand agency not as a "purely open concept" (i.e., one that is incapable of ever having conditions and criteria) but as a "semi-open concept": one whose conditions and criteria differ from context to context, yet the greater precision and clarity that one provides in delineating the specific context, the greater precision and clarity one can have in establishing conditions and criteria within that context. So, for example, we could consider the word "thing" in a semi-open way if we establish a particular context with particular consistency of reference within that context and, thereby, provide greater clarity and precision on the conditions and criteria for a "thing." In the context of me baking with my

---

45. Vidu, *Atonement, Law, and Justice*, 253–6.

46. This is in contrast to William Alston's (and what is likely the default lay-Christian's) univocal account of divine and human agency ("Divine and Human Action," in *Divine and Human Action: Essays in the Metaphysics of Theism*, ed. Thomas Morris [Ithaca: Cornell University Press, 1988], 273).

47. Abraham, *Divine Agency*, 1:63.

48. Ibid., 1:1.

49. Ibid., 1:4. In addition to the semi-open extension that I make of Abraham here. Our projects also differ in that Abraham finds the most basic agency claims (i.e., someone did something in some way) to be unilluminating and of little value (*Divine Agency*, 2:1–2, 14), seeking instead to answer "how," "why," and "so what" questions of distinct divine actions. Yet, this project focuses upon these prior claims and finds them meaningful. So this project can ask of Christ's actions: Who did what in what way? That is, is the agent of the acts of Christ a divine person (and if so, which one?) or a divine-human person? What did that agent do (e.g., were they human acts? divine acts?)? How did he do that (e.g., by human intention? By emptying his divine capacities? By alternating between capacities?)?

wife in our kitchen under careful usage, "thing" may mean: "a cooking utensil that is owned by the Kieser family, yet is infrequently used by Ty." While this hardly obtains to the level of precise necessary and sufficient conditions of a concept like "knowledge," it does provide greater specificity such that a set of criteria can be used to rule out some referents and include others. So, in this context, when I ask my wife where she put that "thing," she can use those criteria to understand that I do *not* mean the car key (since it is not a kitchen utensil) or cast-iron skillet (since I frequently use it), but I might mean the immersion blender or potato masher.

With the semi-open concept and nature of God sketched, we can gesture toward theological premises that will influence the definition of the agency word-group throughout the project. Specifically, there are trinitarian and christological premises that will influence classical and Reformed Christology's understanding of agency. Classical and Reformed Christology's view of the triune God (as we will see below) holds that God is one essence in pure act, without potency. So divine and human "capacities" are very different (e.g., God is not able to suffer).[50] Likewise, the distinction between the persons as relations of origin indicates that God's activity toward creation is unified and indivisible. Therefore, in our definition of an act, we must be able to attribute singular divine acts to all three divine persons. However, as we will see, particular effects can fittingly be appropriated to particular divine persons (i.e., the Holy Spirit) without constituting an independent action, implying the possibility of individuated predication to divine persons and the constitution of multiple effects in a single act. Likewise, classical and Reformed Christology holds to the conciliar affirmation that all the acts of Christ (regardless of how seemingly human or divine) are to be predicated to the Son, while affirming that the Son does not cease to act in the indivisibly triune acts of God during his incarnation. Additionally, the conciliar affirmation of Christ's multiple wills and multiple energies (or operations) indicates the distinct "operations" of Christ. So classical and Reformed Christology affirms that Jesus acted as a human being with human operations. Because of this last point ordinary human definitions and articulations for the agency word-group within ordinary human contexts can be instructive for our purposes (even if they are not universalizable). Especially built upon the human nature and operations of Christ and the analogical nature of human language, this project follows an accepted articulation of human agency as a valid understanding within a particular context as a core component to classical and Reformed theology's definition of the agency word-group.

2. *Definitional Parameters* This project follows the work of preceding Christian theologians and philosophers (esp. William Abraham, Timothy O'Connor, and Thomas Reid) in its acceptance of an "agent-causality" model in order to articulate definitions and concepts that are consistent with Christian theology in general

---

50. I'm here taking "capacities" in general to include both causal power (the capacity to cause changes in external objects) and causal liabilities (the capacity to be the object of change or action).

and classical and Reformed Christology in particular.[51] Agent-causation (as distinct from event-causation) claims that the cause of an action is primarily and fundamentally "an agent."[52] On agent-causation the "purpose the agent is acting for" might be called an intention,[53] minimally defined as (A) a desire for some end and (B) the belief that a particular movement will bring about the said desired end.[54] As agents execute these intentions, they do so according to their "causal capacities," or "active powers."[55]

"*Action*" While it is common to understand an "action" as a particular kind (e.g., intentional) of event (i.e., as a species of the *genus* "event") that agents cause,[56]

---

51. While general divine and human action (i.e., providence) is not the subject (or context) of this project, it might be objected that the number of libertarians influencing this section (i.e., O'Connor, Abrahams, Reid) indicates an inconsistency with the compatibilism common within classical and Reformed theology. My response would be multidimensional: (1) There are various meanings of compatibilism and the Reformed tradition contains various versions (Richard A. Muller, *Divine Will and Human Choice: Freedom, Contingency, and Necessity in Early Modern Reformed Thought* [Grand Rapids: Baker Academic, 2017]); (2) the content of what is affirmed in this section is (in my view) consistent with most versions of compatibilism. For example, few compatibilists would describe divine providence as bringing about events that are the "outcome of priorly determined factors" apart from the action of a human agent; (3) the semi-openness of agency means that human actions can require a different definition of agency if set in a different context.

52. For a summary of the debate and a defense of agent-causality, see Jennifer Hornsby, "Agency and Action," in *Agency and Action*, ed. John Hyman and Helen Steward, RIPS 55 (New York: Cambridge University Press, 2004), 1–24.

53. Timothy O'Connor, "Reasons and Causes," in *A Companion to the Philosophy of Action*, ed. Timothy O'Connor and Constantine Sandis (Malden: Blackwell, 2010), 130.

54. For this as a basic claim in the literature, see Robert Audi, "Intending," *JP* 70 (1973): 395; Alfred R. Mele, "Intention," in *A Companion to the Philosophy of Action*, ed. Timothy O'Connor and Constantine Sandis (Malden: Blackwell, 2010), 109. This contrasts with the view that "states of affairs" provide the reasons or purpose for acting (as in E. J. Lowe, *Personal Agency: The Metaphysics of Mind and Action* [New York: Oxford University Press, 2008], 10–11; Jonathan Dancy, *Practical Reality* [New York: Oxford University Press, 2000], 114–15). For example, it is not the existence of the puddle that provides a purpose for my daughter's jumping high into the air but her *belief* that there is a puddle there, since she would have jumped even if that puddle were a mirage or an elaborate chalk drawing and she would have had a reason to do so.

55. Thomas Reid, *Essays on the Active Powers of Man*, ed. Knud Haakonssen and James A. Harris, EETR 7 (University Park: Penn State University Press, 2010); Timothy O'Connor, *Persons and Causes: The Metaphysics of Free Will* (New York: Oxford University Press, 2000), xiv; Abraham, *Divine Agency*, 1:219–20, likewise affirms the theological value of "active powers" on the basis of the image of God in creatures.

56. Events are nearly unanimously treated as something like "changes in the world" which are comprised of causes and effects (i.e., the consequences of the cause).

I follow Alvarez and Hyman in departing from this trend and instead define an "action" as the intentional "causing of an event by an agent."[57] Therefore, it is *not* the case that the "event is the agent's action, or that an action is itself an event."[58] Rather, as they say,

> An action, although the phrase is a clumsy one, is a causing of an event by an agent .... Thus, a killing is a causing of a death .... Hence, an action is of such and such a kind if and only if its result is of the corresponding kind: [e.g.,] an action is a killing if and only if its result is a death.[59]

"Actions" and "Effects" (Distinguishing and Individuating Actions) When we consider actions, we are left to wonder how we individuate and distinguish them from one another.[60] Taking a famous example, we might ask, are "moving my finger," "flipping a switch," "turning the lights on," and "illuminating the room" distinct *acts* or distinct *descriptions* of the same act? There are two theories for understanding the relationship of actions to one another. Coarse-grained (or austere) theory understands these as four descriptions of the s*ame act*.[61] Fine-grained (or prolific) theory understands these as four distinct acts.[62]

We may take speech acts as a means of illustrating the fine- and coarse-grained theories of action. For a coarse-grained understanding, the basic action is the utterance of the mother's locution: "Only two more days until Christmas." Now, this single utterance, or causing of an event by the agent (i.e., action), can have multiple

---

57. One primary reason for this is the infinite regress that occurs if actions are events caused by agents (i.e., if agents cause actions, then it seems that the causing of that action is itself another action, and *ad infinitum*).

58. Maria Alvarez and John Hyman, "Agents and Their Actions," *Philosophy* 73 (1998): 224.

59. Ibid., 233.

60. It is important to keep in mind that there is an inherent difficulty in "counting acts" and we often have an easier time "distinguishing acts." This is similar to "counting things" and "distinguishing things." For example, I recently told my six-year-old son that he had to pick up ten things in the living room before he could eat dessert. He walked into the living room, picked up a book, put it on the bookshelf, and said (with an honest look on his face), "I'm done, I even picked up more than ten things—that book has like fifty pages." His confidence in meeting the qualifications evidences that it is hard to "count" things (e.g., is that one book, fifty pages, or a thousand words?) but it is easier to distinguish things. That is, those fifty pages are identified with the one book. Likewise, our task here will be distinguishing actions, rather than counting them.

61. Donald Davidson, "Actions, Reasons, and Causes (1963)," in *Essays on Actions and Events* (New York: Oxford University Press, 2001), 3–20; G. E. M. Anscombe, *Intention* (Cambridge: Harvard University Press, 1957) are classic examples of this position.

62. Alvin I. Goldman, *Theory of Human Action* (Englewood Cliffs, NJ: Prentice-Hall, 1970) is a prominent example of this theory.

effects and multiple intentions within the singularity of the event. For example, she may be "informing" her children with the effect of excited anticipation, while simultaneously warning her husband with the intended effect of motivating him to finish buying presents. A fine-grained theorist would see these distinct effects and call them distinct actions, while a coarse-grained theorist would see these as distinct effects/consequences of a single action.[63]

While both theories are useful (and plausible) in this understanding of action, I favor coarse-grained theory. This is in part due to some of the difficulties of fine-grained theory when taken as the fundamental understanding of action. For example, since an action is the intentional causing of an event, a fine-grained understanding of action could seemingly identify an action at every intentionally caused fine-grained-effect. Taken to the extreme, we could consider Bill's raising his arm to be thirty fine-grained actions (or more) since we could consider every half inch of arm movement to be a distinct effect (i.e., thirty effects brought about by thirty fine-grained actions). Additionally, when we consider the quantity of distinct descriptions, we encounter a similar *ad absurdum* argument. For example, I might describe my current action as any of the following: "writing a book," or "typing on my laptop," or "inserting words on a screen," or "word-vomiting," or "voluntarily torturing myself," yet anyone observing me would be hard-pressed to call my current activity "five+ actions." While I consider this evidence against fine-grained understandings as fundamental, I do think that the fine-grained account adds value in that it notes the distinct perspectives of this action. So "writing a book" takes the perspective of the action's teleological effect (i.e., to complete a project); "inserting words on a screen" takes the perspective of a technological effect; "voluntarily torturing myself" takes the perspective of the effects on my psychological state. Therefore, while I favor coarse-grained understandings of actions, I appreciate fine-grained theories and seek to incorporate the goods they add by including "distinct perspectives" (a designation that will become important later). In order to incorporate and appreciate the fine-grained distinctions, I will refer throughout the project to distinct fine-grained actions (yet the same coarse-grained action) as "operations." So "writing a book," "typing on my laptop," and "inserting words on a screen" are all one action (coarse-grained), yet distinct "operations" (fine-grained).

On a coarse-grained understanding, we can come to see that actions with distinct effects still have the same intentional "causing" and therefore ought to be identified as the same action. We might consider (a less-than-purely-hypothetical) sixteen-year-old-version of myself in the backyard at my parents' rural home involving two fireworks. Let's say I set off the first firework and immediately afterward my mother threatens, "If you do that again, I'm grounding you for life." The consequences of a second "kaboom" would be drastically different if scenario A) the wick that I lit

---

63. While not applied in a fine/coarse-grain discussion, this analogy comes from Nicholas Wolterstorff, *Divine Discourse: Philosophical Reflections on the Claim That God Speaks* (New York: Cambridge University Press, 1995), 55.

(before the maternal decree) was connected to both fireworks that were set to go off in a prolonged sequence, as opposed to (scenario B) lighting a second firework after I received the threat.

This example helps us understand some key components of coarse-grained action theory. First, new actions require additional effort and intention on the agent's part.[64] In the first scenario, I did not exert any additional effort to cause the additional effects nor did I intend anything new. However, in the second scenario, I put in extra effort to light the additional wick and intended to disobey my mother, making those distinct actions. Second, it evidences that we can speak of distinct "effects" in a single "event." In scenario A the "event" refers to the change in the world by virtue of both the cause and the multiple effects. An event is said to be "discrete" when it may reasonably be said that the immediately related changes have run their course. Contrastingly, an effect can be understood as an intentionally caused change in any object at a certain point in time. Since there are multiple objects and durations of time in events, there may be multiple effects in one action. Therefore, in scenario A the wick that I lit was connected to two fireworks, so each explosion was its own distinct effect, yet together they constitute the event of "setting off fireworks" and it was intentionally caused by me (the agent) as an "action."

These distinct effects are often linked to one another as means toward an end in the event. This connection is often referred to as the "accordion effect."[65] Donald Davidson depicts actions as accordions, squeezing and stretching, sometimes giving additional details, sometimes elliptically shortening the sentence. However, the accordion itself remains the same instrument regardless of its shape—i.e., the same event—just under different descriptions. Yet, even at its widest point, the longest descriptions often entail the shorter ones.[66] So the event of "setting off fireworks" is like the accordion resting untouched, yet the same event (i.e., same instrument) may be stretched to be "I moved my hand next to the wick, lit the wick on fire, made a loud noise, and scared my mom with an explosion outside her window." Both of these descriptions name one action, but the latter description includes several effects.

"Agent" On the basis of the definition and support above, if an action is the intentional causing of an event by an agent, then an agent is someone who intentionally causes events. Herein, we recognize that being someone who intentionally causes events requires that person to have particular capacities and requires them to be causally determinative of that event. If a creature lacks the capacity to bring about an event, then they cannot be called the agent of that event.

---

64. David-Hillel Ruben, "Cambridge Actions," in *A Companion to the Philosophy of Action*, ed. Timothy O'Connor and Constantine Sandis (Malden: Blackwell, 2010), 87.
65. Donald Davidson, "Agency (1971)," in *Essays on Actions and Events* (New York: Oxford University Press, 2001), 58–9.
66. Ibid.

So the rooster is not the agent of a sunrise and Daniel is not the agent of shutting the mouths of the lions. For this project I will adopt (and slightly modify) Timothy O'Connor's suggestion that someone is not the agent of any given event if that event is the necessary "outcome of prior determined [human] factors" (e.g., my son is not the agent of the act "getting in bed" if I carry him up the stairs and place him in his bed; my daughter is not the agent of her sneezing while grinding pepper over her food).[67] Likewise, E. J. Lowe says that on agent causality a person is the agent of an action if "those actions do not have sufficient causes in the form of antecedent events."[68] Therefore, for someone to be the agent of an action they must possess certain capacities to bring that event about (i.e., my sleeping son does not have the capacity to get into bed, nor does my daughter have the capacity to sneeze at will) and act in a causally determinative way (i.e., my son did not causally bring about the event, even if he had the capacities of being awake and able to walk).

"*Agency*" The agent's possession of this power to operate in a particular way, their capacities and dispositions, is articulated here as "agency." Thomas Reid, an advocate of agent-causality, articulates efficient causality in a way that is helpful for our understanding of agency. He says, "I take an efficient cause to be a being who had power to produce the effect, and exerted that power for a purpose."[69] Likewise, an agent acts according to its agency (i.e., capacity to produce an effect) for a purpose (or intention). Reid elaborates upon these capacities according to the language of "active power." An active power includes the capacity to produce an effect, but also the power "not to act." "Otherwise," he says, "it is not power but necessity."[70] Therefore, acid may have a kind of power (i.e., capacity to oxidize), yet it does not have "agency" (i.e., the capacity to produce or not to produce effects). This closely links the agent to their capacities. For example, Alvarez and Hyman say that for an agent to act "is to exercise a causal power—to cause, bring about or effect an event."[71]

---

67. The adjective "human" is added here in order to recognize the possibility of version of theological compatibilism—the language of "prior" here and "antecedent event" below may accomplish something similar also. So if "all things come to pass immutably, and infallibly" (WCF 5.2) this does not exclude any action from acting "according to the nature of second causes" (WCF 5.2) because God's primary causation in providence does not constitute an "antecedent event" that sufficiently determines actions apart from involvement of secondary causes. This would, however, exclude things like biological or psychological determinism. So, if I was fully hypnotized or mind controlled, then I would not be the agent of my action.

68. Lowe, *Personal Agency*, 6.

69. Thomas Reid, "93. To James Gregory," in *The Correspondence of Thomas Reid*, ed. Paul Wood, EETR 4 (Edinburgh: Edinburgh University Press, 2002), 174. While some equate agent and efficient cause (e.g., Edward Feser, *Scholastic Metaphysics: A Contemporary Introduction* [Heusenstamm: Editions Scholasticae, 2014], 88), I will not do so here for reasons that will become apparent later.

70. Reid, "93. To James Gregory," 174.

71. Alvarez and Hyman, "Agents and Their Actions," 233.

These capacities are, as O'Connor says, "grounded in a property or set of properties."[72] Here we see the foreshadowing of a constant affirmation throughout this project that ontology grounds activity.[73] Particularly in agent-causation, this means that these capacities (in conjunction with appropriate circumstances) "make possible the agent's producing the effect" as "choice-enabling properties."[74] Therefore, agency is the capacity for intentional action on the basis of "choice-enabling properties."[75] For example, I do not possess the being of a bird; therefore, I do not have the choice of whether or not I will fly right now. By contrast, most birds (having avian being and avian agency) have the power to choose whether or not they will fly.

These designations and definitions of action, effect, event, agent, and agency will be engaged throughout the project. Yet this section establishes a foundation that is accessible for common contexts and therefore serves as the fundamental designation of the terms throughout the project. With the terms of the case established, we turn to delineate the commitments of the classical and Reformed side of the case.

III. Classical and Reformed Christological Commitments

This project seeks to address the question of christological agency from a "classical and Reformed" perspective, which I take to include a combination of specific material claims: (§A) classical conciliar affirmations of the ecumenical councils,[76] (§B) classical trinitarianism, (§C) distinct emphases of Reformed Christology, and (§D) a Reformed commitment to *Sola Scriptura*. Therefore, the conjunction in "classical and Reformed" is essential for understanding the location of this discussion. To say "classical and Reformed" does not mean that

---

72. O'Connor, *Persons and Causes*, 73.

73. See Ch. 2 §II.B.1.

74. O'Connor, *Persons and Causes*, 73.

75. It might be objected that an account of divine agency would imply strong occasionalism. Namely, if God is to have agency, then he must have the capacity to choose or not to choose any given thing. Therefore, God must have the capacity to do good or to do evil. However, active power need not mean the capacity to choose a given thing (e.g., good) and its opposite (e.g., evil) but the capacity to act (e.g., create a good creation) or not to act (e.g., not create). Additionally, the divine acts are not arbitrary if there is in God a natural orientation toward goodness. Yet, even if this orientation is perfectly directed toward goodness, it is not required that he exercise this goodness in a particular way.

76. These councils retain a "ministerial authority" for classical and Reformed theology because of the subsequent commitment to the "magisterial" authority of Scripture (see Kevin J. Vanhoozer, *Biblical Authority after Babel* [Grand Rapids: Brazos, 2016], 109–47).

all classical positions are Reformed, or that all Reformed positions are classical.[77] Instead my focus is on exploring the position which seeks to sit at the overlapping intersection of the Venn diagram representing classical commitments and Reformed commitments.

However, rather than being overly myopic or idiosyncratic, this overlap of classical and Reformed represents a populated and growing region of contemporary Christian theology.[78] Further, I take the combination of "classical and Reformed" to be a natural paring in regard to Christology specifically because of the Reformed tradition's "old roots" with a concern to "anchor their arguments in the authority of Scripture as heard by an ecumenical tradition," seeking to be "faithful not only to Chalcedon, but to its later conciliar expansion."[79]

The material claims within each of these commitments will be important for establishing the internal coherence of classical and Reformed christological agency. That is, if a claim about Christ as an agent with particular kinds of agency violates any of the material claims herein, then classical and Reformed Christology fails to maintain coherence.

A. Classical Conciliar Affirmations

In order to understand more clearly the good news of God-made-flesh, classical theology turns to the christological definitions, expositions, canons, and anathemas of the seven ecumenical councils: Nicaea (325), Constantinople (381), Ephesus (431), Chalcedon (451), Constantinople II (553), Constantinople III (680–1),

---

77. As such, there are contemporary Catholic theologians who are "classical" but not Reformed (see many of the Catholic figures below) and there are modern theologians who are Reformed but not classical (see Kevin Hector, "Friedrich Schleiermacher," in *The Cambridge Companion to Reformed Theology*, ed. David Fergusson and Paul Nimmo [New York: Cambridge University Press, 2015], 163–78).

78. This is probably most evidently seen in those Reformed and Calvinistic theologians who follow (consciously or unconsciously) in the wake of John Webster. For example, note the acknowledgment of Webster in Michael Allen and Scott R. Swain, *Reformed Catholicity: The Promise of Retrieval for Theology and Biblical Interpretation* (Grand Rapids: Baker Academic, 2015), viii; and Craig A. Carter, *Contemplating God with the Great Tradition: Recovering Trinitarian Classical Theism* (Grand Rapids: Baker Academic, 2021), 1; and note the prominence of Reformed and classical themes in Michael Allen and R. David Nelson, eds., *A Companion to the Theology of John Webster* (Grand Rapids: Eerdmans, 2021).

79. Ivor J. Davidson, "Christ," in *The Oxford Handbook of Reformed Theology*, ed. Michael Allen and Scott R. Swain (New York: Oxford University Press, 2020), 446, 458. See the importance of the councils and the role of Christ's mediation in the definition of Reformed Christology in Stefan Lindholm, *Jerome Zanchi (1516–90) and the Analysis of Reformed Scholastic Christology*, RHT 37 (Göttingen: Vandenhoeck & Ruprecht, 2016), 48–9, 54 n. 62. Hodge suggests, "The Reformed taught what the first six general councils taught, and what the Church universal received,—neither more nor less" (Hodge, *Systematic Theology*, III.3, §6).

and Nicaea II (787).[80] The ecumenical councils provide the church today with a consistent christological "boundary" involving affirmations and negations of various christological claims.[81] Here we are most interested in the councils' affirmations and negations on *the unity of Christ's identity* and the *diversity of Christ's capacities*.[82] First, the unity of Christ's identity is presented through the thought of Cyril of Alexandria and his influence on the councils of Ephesus and Constantinople II. Second, we will note the conciliar construction of the diversity of capacities as seen in Leo the Great and Maximus the Confessor through their influence on the councils of Chalcedon and Constantinople III.

1. Unity of Identity The councils' claims on the unity of identity in Christ are largely seen as the result of Cyril's victory over Nestorius and the early Nestorians (who divided Christ's two natures into two subjects [and therefore two identities]) as codified in the councils of Ephesus (anathematizing Nestorius) and Constantinople II (anathematizing Theodore of Mopsuestia, Theodoret of Cyrus, Ibas of Edessa). For Nestorianism, the Word takes up a complete human being and bestows upon him favor in such a way that both the humanity and divinity accomplish independent acts as two distinct subjects of actions, yet they do so in agreement, association, and a unified appearance (or "face" [*prosopon*]).[83] On this account, Christ is not personally identified with the Word (nor vice versa), but Christ is

---

80. For the classical and Reformed view of the ministerial authority of the seven ecumenical councils, see Calvin, *Institutes*, IV.ix; Herman Bavinck, *Reformed Dogmatics*, ed. John Bolt, trans. John Vriend (Grand Rapids: Baker Academic, 2003), 1:86, 3:255; hereafter, *RD* followed by volume: page. On the inclusion of the entire content of these councils (rather than merely the definitions/creeds) see Timothy Pawl, *In Defense of Conciliar Christology: A Philosophical Essay*, OSAT (New York: Oxford University Press, 2016), 1–14. On the use of the adjective "conciliar" rather than "creedal," see Tanner, *Decrees*, 1:38, 65.

81. For the "negative," "minimalist," or "boundary" nature of the councils, see Sarah Coakley, "What Does Chalcedon Solve and What Does It Not? Some Reflections on the Status and Meaning of the Chalcedonian 'Definition,'" in *The Incarnation: An Interdisciplinary Symposium on the Incarnation of the Son of God*, ed. C. Stephen Davis, Daniel Kendall, and Gerald O'Collins (New York: Oxford University Press, 2002), 143–63.

82. By "identity" throughout this project I mean to suggest the "who" of an action. For example, the woman who married me and the woman who taught my son to read are the same "who" and are identified as "my wife." For a more theological treatment of identity, see Bruce D. Marshall, "Christ and the Cultures: The Jewish People and Christian Theology," in *The Cambridge Companion to Christian Doctrine*, ed. Colin E. Gunton (New York: Cambridge University Press, 1997), 95–6; cf. see Kevin W. Hector, *The Theological Project of Modernism: Faith and the Conditions of Mineness*, OSAT (New York: Oxford University Press, 2015), 3–5 for his account of intention, identity, and "mineness."

83. Daley, *God Visible*, 184–5.

still able to reveal a common form (e.g., sonship).[84] On the basis of this refusal to personally identify Christ with the Word, Nestorianism denies that Mary was the "mother of God" (or the "bearer of God" [*theotokos*]) and instead chooses to call Mary the "bearer of Christ."[85]

For Cyril and the conciliar response, salvation itself was dependent upon the personal identity of Christ as a single subject. For Cyril, the story of the gospel of Christ's birth, death, and resurrection was *not* a testimony of some "formal relationship" but the acts of God himself (i.e., God the Son) in history.[86] Gregory of Nazianzus' christological claim reflects that which is accepted and solidified in the councils when he says that "the constituents of our savior are different 'whats' (ἄλλο καὶ ἄλλο) … but not different 'whos' (ἄλλος καὶ ἄλλος)."[87]

At Ephesus, these considerations came together and the doctrine of Mary as *theotokos* becomes accepted ecumenically.[88] Likewise, the third canon of Constantinople II says, "If anyone declares that the [Word] of God who works miracles is not identical with the Christ who suffered … [or] that our Lord Jesus Christ was not one and the same, the Word of God incarnate and made man … let him be anathema."[89] Most famously, the tenth canon of Constantinople II provides the *theopaschite* formula, "one of the Trinity suffered in the flesh," while affirming that God the Son is personally identified with the Christ who suffers.[90]

2. Distinct Capacities Affirming Christ's distinct human ontology, in opposition to Apollinarianism, Gregory of Nazianzus issued his famous dictum: "That which Christ has not assumed he has not healed."[91] This soteriological principle contributes to the Chalcedonian definition whereby the church ecumenically

---

84. Brian E. Daley, "Christ and Christologies," in *Oxford Handbook of Early Christian Studies*, ed. Susan Ashbrook Harvey and David G. Hunter (New York: Oxford University Press, 2008), 896; Stephen W. Need, *Truly Divine and Truly Human: The Story of Christ and the Seven Ecumenical Councils* (Peabody: Hendrickson, 2008), 83.

85. See, for example, Richard A. Norris, ed., *The Christological Controversy*, SECT (Minneapolis: Fortress, 1980), 124–5.

86. Daley, "Christ and Christologies," 897; cf. Edward T. Oakes S.J., *Infinity Dwindled to Infancy: A Catholic and Evangelical Christology* (Grand Rapids: Eerdmans, 2011), 147–8.

87. St. Gregory of Nazianzus, *On God and Christ: The Five Theological Orations and Two Letters to Cledonius*, trans. Lionel Wickham, PPS 23 (Crestwood, NY: St. Vladimir's, 2002), 157; revised according to *PG* 37:180A. See Andrew Hofer O.P., *Christ in the Life and Teaching of Gregory of Nazianzus*, OECS (New York: Oxford University Press, 2013), 135–6.

88. Tanner, *Decrees*, 1:69.

89. Ibid., 1:114.

90. Ibid., 1:118. For the background and explanation of this formula, see John Meyendorff, *Christ in Eastern Christian Thought* (Crestwood, NY: St. Vladimir's, 1987), 69–89; Cyril Hovorun, *Will, Action and Freedom: Christological Controversies in the Seventh Century*, MM 77 (Boston: Brill, 2008), 42–50.

91. Nazianzus, *On God and Christ*, 23:158; revised on basis of *PG* 37:181C–184A.

agrees that Jesus is "perfect in divinity and perfect in humanity, the same truly God and truly man, of a rational soul and a body."[92] The Pope at the time of the council, Leo the Great, contributed to its content through his "Tome."[93] Of Christ's operations he says that each nature in Christ works "what is proper to it" such that as Christ stands before Lazarus' tomb, "it does not belong to the same nature to weep out of deep-felt pity for a dead friend, and to call him back to life again."[94] Here we see that each nature has distinct capacities (e.g., the capacity to cry and another to raise the dead), yet even Leo's bold claims of distinction are not divided into two subjects but are always accomplished "in communion" with both natures and are executed by the one person as the ultimate single subject of the actions.[95]

Yet Chalcedon does not settle all christological controversies, and it may have even ignited more.[96] Specifically, the Monenergists (advocates of one energy in Christ) and Monothelites (one will) attempted to protect Christ from corruption (which they thought was the logical entailment of a human will) and described Christ's activities as coming exclusively from divine capacities through the human as a "vehicle of the divine flow of will."[97]

Against this position, and at the end of a winding and tumultuous political road, stands the sixth ecumenical council (680-1). This council "proclaims ... two natural volitions or wills (θελήματα) in him and two natural principles of

---

92. Tanner, *Decrees*, 1:86.

93. There has been a suspicion of Leo and historical diminishment of his influence upon the council in recent historical accounts; see John Anthony McGuckin, *Saint Cyril of Alexandria and the Christological Controversy* (Crestwood, NY: St. Vladimir's, 2010), 236. I need not take a stance on this historical question other than to observe that the Tome of Leo is considered "support we have in common" (Tanner, *Decrees*, 1:85) by the fathers and is included in the Chalcedonian documents accepted as authoritative (1:127).

94. Tanner, *Decrees*, 1:79-80.

95. This is following Hovorun, *Will, Action and Freedom*, 122, 141-2; contrary to Grillmeier, *Christ in the Christian Tradition*, 1:536. See Demetrios Bathrellos, *The Byzantine Christ: Person, Nature, and Will in the Christology of St. Maximus the Confessor*, OECS (New York: Oxford University Press, 2004), 205-8 for the historical and logical difficulty of this phrase in Leo.

96. Daley, "Christ and Christologies," 898; Grillmeier, *Christ in the Christian Tradition*, 1:555-7; see Karl Rahner, "Chalkedon—Ende oder Anfang," in *Das Konzil von Chalkedon: Geschichte und Gegenwart*, ed. Aloys Grillmeier and Heinrich Bacht, 3 vols (Würzburg: Echter Verlang, 1954), 3-49.

97. Aloys Grillmeier, *Christ in the Christian Tradition: From the Council of Chalcedon (451) to Gregory the Great (590-604)*, trans. John Cawte and Pauline Allen (Louisville: Westminster John Knox), 2:164.

action (ενέργειας)."⁹⁸ This Dyenergist and Dyothelite conclusion was significantly influenced by the theology of Maximus the Confessor. For Maximus, the person of Christ is a single subject, yet this single subject acts according to his two wills and two operations.⁹⁹ Maximus sees the activity of a nature corresponding to its effects (αποτέλεσμα) such that different activities produce different effects.¹⁰⁰ He gives the example of a sword which is placed in an oven so that the iron starts on fire. In this *one* sword we see two capacities for action (i.e., the capacity to cut [according to the sword's iron nature], and the capacity to burn [according to the sword's fire nature]), and when this one sword is brought down on a piece of wood, it brings about distinct, yet simultaneous and concurrent, effects—the effect of cutting the wood and the effect of burning the wood.¹⁰¹ Similar to the way that these two effects are the consequence of the two capacities which belong to the sword's two natures, Christ brings about distinct effects according to distinct capacities, accomplished in communion with one another by the single agent.

B. Classical Trinitarianism

Classical Christology is rooted in and consistent with the classical tradition's claims of trinitarian theology.¹⁰² The sketch that follows articulates these affirmations through patristic, medieval, and Reformed thinkers (esp. Augustine, Thomas Aquinas, John Calvin, Francis Turretin, and Herman Bavinck) as representatives of classical Trinitarianism,¹⁰³ especially as it is received in the Reformed tradition.

The doctrine of divine simplicity played an important early role in the Augustinian tradition, but one significant version of the doctrine solidifies in

---

98. Tanner, *Decrees*, 1:128. For a summary of the theological difficulties of Monothelitism, see Bathrellos, *The Byzantine Christ*, 131–2; one other difficulty of this position may have been the failure of one advocate of Monothelitism to raise the dead after placing a published defense of Monothelitism on top of a corpse, as he was convinced it would produce a miracle (Hovorun, *Will, Action and Freedom*, 90).

99. St. Maximus the Confessor, *On the Cosmic Mystery of Jesus Christ*, trans. Paul M. Blowers and Robert Louis Wilken, PPS 25 (Crestwood, NY: St. Vladimir's, 2003), 173.

100. Maximus, "Disputatio" (PG 91:341b); Hovorun, *Will, Action and Freedom*, 119.

101. Hovorun, *Will, Action and Freedom*, 119.

102. See Christoph Schwöbel, "Reformed Traditions," in *The Cambridge Companion to the Summa Theologiae*, ed. Philip McCosker and Denys Turner (New York: Cambridge University Press), 329–30 for the reliance of the Reformed tradition (and Owen in particular) on Thomas, particularly on questions of the doctrine of God.

103. The singular use of the phrase need not imply univocity or unanimity of the tradition (as though there were only one doctrine of God), but a consistent set of affirmations that exist across the breadth of Christian history.

Thomas Aquinas' doctrine of God.[104] Thomas' doctrine of simplicity has been summarized in terms of three key components: (1) It is impossible that God could have any *spatial or temporal parts* that could be distinguished from one another (i.e., here or there; now or then) and so God cannot be a physical entity. (2) It is impossible that God could have any accidental properties. (3) All that can be intrinsically attributed to God simply *is* his essence.[105] So we do not say God *has* goodness, but that God *is* goodness.[106] Bavinck relies explicitly on Thomas in his account of divine simplicity, which he draws from Exod. 3:14 and the divine name YHWH,[107] maintaining that "in God all his attributes are identical with his being."[108] Likewise, Calvin and Turretin affirm that the "essence of God is simple"; the attributes of God exist within him perfectly and infinitely.[109]

Also relevant for our purposes are the doctrines of divine impassibility and immutability (i.e., that God does not suffer or change). The Westminster Confession connects the truth of simplicity and impassibility, affirming that God is "without body, parts, or passions."[110] Bavinck states that the first "natural implication" of aseity and simplicity is the doctrine of immutability because God "remains who he is."[111] Bavinck claims, "If God were not immutable, he would not be God …. All that changes ceases to be what it was …. That which truly is remains."[112]

Additionally, classical Trinitarianism affirms the unity of one will in one divine essence. On the basis of divine simplicity, Calvin refers to God's will as "one and simple."[113] Likewise, Turretin says that "the will in God is only one and most simply, by which he comprehends all things by a single and most simple act."[114]

---

104. For the doctrine's historical rootedness, see Gavin Ortlund, "Divine Simplicity in Historical Perspective: Resourcing a Contemporary Discussion," *IJST* 16 (2014): 436–53; Steven J. Duby, *Divine Simplicity: A Dogmatic Account*, TTCSST (New York: T&T Clark, 2014), 7–53; Lewis Ayres, *Augustine and the Trinity* (New York: Cambridge University Press, 2010), 208–17.

105. Eleonore Stump, *Aquinas* (London: Routledge, 2005), 96–7; S *T* I, Q.3, A.4.

106. *PRRD*, 4:53.

107. Bavinck, *RD*, 2:150–1.

108. Bavinck, *RD*, 2:118; cf. 2:173–7.

109. Calvin, *Institutes*, I.xiii.2; Francis Turretin, *Institutes of Elenctic Theology*, ed. James T. Dennison, trans. George Musgrave Giger, 3 vols (Phillipsburg: P&R, 1992), III:9.19; I:3.vii.3 (hereafter, *Institutes*, Volume:topic.question.paragraph).

110. *WCF*, 2.1.

111. Bavinck, *RD*, 2:153. A century later David Bentley Hart calls impassibility one of the two "metaphysical implications" of divine simplicity (*The Experience of God: Being, Consciousness, Bliss* [New Haven: Yale University Press, 2013], 137).

112. Bavinck, *RD*, 2:154.

113. Calvin, *Institutes*, I.xviii.3.

114. Turretin, *Institutes*, I:3.xv.1.

Yet simplicity in essence does not exclude distinction in the relations of the divine persons to one another.[115] For example, in Thomas Aquinas the scriptural affirmation of three divine persons indicates that "there must be a real distinction in God," not in essence (because God's essence is "supreme unity and simplicity") but according to "that which [is] relative."[116] Thomas sees four relations within God—paternity, filiation, spiration, and procession—and the two opposite relations (paternity: filiation; spiration: procession) must refer to three distinct subsisting relations.[117] Since whatever is in God must *be* God, each of these three subsisting relations—paternity, filiation, and procession—is a distinct divine person: Father, Son, Holy Spirit.[118] Therefore, there is the One who begets (Father), the One who is begotten (Son), and they together spirate the One who proceeds (the Holy Spirit). Likewise, Turretin affirms that there are "three distinct persons subsisting in but one, undivided essence."[119]

On the basis of the ontological unity of the divine essence and the relations of origin as the distinguishing factor, the classical tradition understands God's acts toward creation to be indivisible. That is, every triune person is involved in every act of God toward creation. Yet, this does not mean that the divine persons are indistinguishable in their economic acts. Instead, particular acts can be "appropriated" to particular divine persons on the basis of the act's fittingness to the divine person's relation of origin.[120]

C. Reformed: Integrity of Christ's Human Nature

Dependent upon the councils and thinkers before them, Reformed Christology stresses continuity with the broader, classical and conciliar, Christian tradition regarding Christology.[121] However, it also bears distinctive christological emphasis,

---

115. Augustine of Hippo, "On Christian Doctrine," 1.5.5 (*NPNF¹* 2:524); cf. Turretin, *Institutes*, I:3.vii.16.

116. Aquinas, *ST* I, Q.28, A.3.

117. Aquinas, *ST* I, Q.30, A.2.

118. Thomas says, "Several persons are the several subsisting relations really distinct from each other" (*ST* I, 30, ii). Cf. I, 41, vi; Bruce D. Marshall, "Ex Occidente Lux? Aquinas and Eastern Orthodox Theology," *Modern Theology* 20 (2004): 45–6.

119. Turretin, *Institutes*, I:3.xxv.3; cf. I:3.xxvii.10; cf. Calvin, *Institutes*, I.xiii.2.

120. For the historicity of this idea and its affirmation in Augustine, Abelard, and Thomas Aquinas, see O. P. Gilles Emery, *The Trinitarian Theology of Saint Thomas Aquinas* (New York: Oxford University Press, 2010), 312–37.

121. E.g., Calvin, who says that in Christology the "church's definition stands firm" (*Institutes*, II.xiv.5); for Owen's commitment to Chalcedon see Sinclair B. Ferguson, "John Owen and the Doctrine of the Person of Christ," in *John Owen: The Man and His Theology*, ed. Robert W. Oliver (Phillipsburg: P&R, 2002), 90.

especially in contradistinction to Lutheran and Anabaptist Christologies.[122] While each tradition affirms Christ's genuine human nature, Reformed Christology places a unique emphasis on the integrity of the human nature of Christ as it preserves human properties and capacities.[123] This is seen concretely in the tradition's denial of the ubiquity of Christ's human nature (i.e., *extra Calvinisticum*)[124] and in the tradition's explicit focus on the one Christ as the one "mediator" in both his divine and human natures.[125]

Based on these distinctive affirmations and emphases, there is a supposition (at least within the Reformed tradition) that a Reformed Christology is well equipped to appreciate the human activity of Christ without jettisoning classical divine properties or the respective activity of the Son and Spirit when addressing

---

122. See Stephen R. Holmes, "Reformed Varieties of the Communicatio Idiomatum," in *The Person of Christ*, ed. Stephen R. Holmes and Murray A. Rae (New York: T&T Clark, 2005), 70–86.

123. Michael Allen claims, "Along with the claim that the incarnate Son enjoys full human integrity, Reformed theologians have also been among the first to insist on the fully active humanity of Jesus" (*Reformed Theology*, 10, cf. 68–9). Additionally, William B. Evans suggests that "the desire to safeguard the integrity of Christ's incarnate humanity" is one of the two main concerns "prominent in Reformed Christology since the sixteenth century" ("Doctrine of Christ," in *The Oxford Handbook of Presbyterianism*, ed. Gary Scott Smith and P. C. Kemeny [New York: Oxford University Press, 2019], 333). Likewise, Bruce McCormack says, "What is essential to any genuinely Reformed Christology is (again) the emphasis placed upon the integrity of the divine and human elements in their uniting" (*Humility of the Eternal Son*, 252).

124. For the history of this distinction, see the classic study, E. David Willis, *Calvin's Catholic Christology: The Function of the So-Called Extra Calvinisticum in Calvin's Theology*, SMRT (Leiden: Brill, 1966), 8–100. More recently see the Pre-Reformation affirmations of this position in Andrew M. McGinnis, *The Son of God beyond the Flesh: A Historical and Theological Study of the Extra Calvinisticum*, TTCSST (London: T&T Clark, 2014) and see K. J. Drake's works for the extra's "fundamental" character in the Reformation debates around the Eucharist and Christology (*The Flesh of the Word: The extra Calvinisticum from Zwingli to Early Orthodoxy*, OSHT [New York: Oxford University Press, 2021], 11). Drake calls the "concern to preserve the integrity of Christ's human nature" a "distinctive character of Reformed christology" (*Flesh of the Word*, 17).

125. For the Reformed emphasis on Christ as "mediator," see, for example, Heiko Oberman, "Extra Dimension in the Theology of Calvin," *JEH* 21 (1970): 60; R. Michael Allen, *Reformed Theology*, Doing Theology (New York: T&T Clark, 2010), 70–1. For the role of "mediator" in the book of Hebrews from a Reformed christological perspective, see Daniel J. Treier, "'Mediator of a New Covenant': Atonement and Christology in Hebrews," in *So Great a Salvation: A Dialogue on the Atonement in Hebrews*, ed. Jon C. Laansma, George H. Guthrie, Cynthia Long Westfall, LNT 516 (New York: T&T Clark, 2019), 105–19.

the question of christological activity.[126] Supporting this claim, Herman Bavinck argues that concern for the genuine humanity of Christ is upheld by the Reformed tradition better "than any other."[127] There are also several Reformed theologians who have sought to incorporate the Holy Spirit into their accounts of the genuine humanity of Christ in significant ways. Historically, we might look especially to John Owen, Jonathan Edwards, and Edward Irving;[128] more recently, Colin Gunton, Michael Horton, and Alan Spence have provided Reformed accounts of the role of the Holy Spirit in Christ's life.[129]

D. *Reformed:* Sola Scriptura

The Supreme Court of Reformed theology is the canon of Scripture, the Word of God.[130] That is, Scripture is the ultimate authority and norming norm of Protestant theology in general and Reformed theology in particular. This is historically most prominent in the formal principle of the Reformation: *sola Scriptura*. *Sola Scriptura* means that Scripture is the ultimate instrument of God to exercise his authority over his church as it is living, active, powerful, and fruitful (Isa. 40:8; 55:11; Heb. 4:12).[131]

Particularly pertinent to this study is the affirmation that, as Calvin says, God's Word expresses his nature and character: "For just as [human] speech is called the expression of the thoughts, so it is not inappropriate to apply this to God and say that he expresses himself to us by his Speech or Word."[132] Therefore, as the church, we receive the revelation of God's Word as the ultimate and final authority.

---

126. For this pattern in Reformed Christology, see Ty Kieser, "Is the Filioque an Obstacle to a Pneumatologically Robust Christology? A Response from Reformed Resources," *JRT* 12 (2018): 394–412; see the argument for "classical Reformed Christology" being "congenial" to explicit pneumatological attention in McCormack, *Humility of the Eternal Son*, 250–2.

127. Bavinck, *RD*, 3:310.

128. For Irving, see Colin Gunton, "Two Dogmas Revisited: Edward Irving's Christology," *SJT* 41 (1988): 359–76 for Edwards see Oliver D. Crisp and Kyle C. Strobel, *Jonathan Edwards: An Introduction to His Thought* (Grand Rapids: Eerdmans, 2018), 155–9 for Owen see Alan J. Spence, *Incarnation and Inspiration: John Owen and the Coherence of Christology* (New York: T&T Clark, 2007).

129. Colin Gunton, *Father, Son and Holy Spirit: Toward a Fully Trinitarian Theology* (New York: T&T Clark, 2003); Michael S. Horton, *Lord and Servant: A Covenant Christology* (Louisville: Westminster John Knox, 2005); Spence, *Incarnation and Inspiration*.

130. This need not imply that *Sola Scriptura* is exclusively affirmed by the Reformed tradition but that it is a prominent distinctive of it (especially, in contrast to other classical Catholic accounts).

131. John Webster, *Holy Scripture*, CIT (New York: Cambridge University Press, 2006), 42–67.

132. John Calvin, *The Gospel According to St. John 1–10*, ed. David W. Torrance and Thomas Torrance, trans. T. H. L. Parker (Grand Rapids: Eerdmans, 1959), 7.

As it pertains to Christology, this means that the christological conclusions must submit to the conclusions of Scripture, but also to the underlying assumptions of Scripture's claims.[133] That is, what must be true of Jesus from the truth of the text and what must be true of Jesus for the text to be true.

Sola Scriptura does not, however, mean "Scripture exclusively" (i.e., *solo scriptura*). Instead there are "ministerial authorities" (such as church tradition) which interpret Scripture and from it derive valid (albeit, lesser) authority.[134] Therefore, it is fully keeping with Reformed thought to turn to the tradition of the church and hear the voices of our brothers and sisters in Christ as we seek faithful articulation of the realities of Christ under the Word of God.

E. John Owen (1616–83) as Representative and Principal Witness

As this project seeks to articulate a classical and Reformed Christology under the authority of Scripture, founded upon a classical doctrine of the triune God, consistent with the ecumenical councils, and upholding Reformed christological emphases, it will draw from a theologian who attempted to locate himself within each of these spheres: John Owen. Owen is not the only theologian who would fit in such categories, nor will he be the only witness to classical and Reformed Christology. However, Owen will serve as the prime witness because he represents a faithful representation of the tradition, while also standing in a unique historical location, providing a unique theological articulation, and bearing unique contemporary significance in distinction from others within the tradition.

So other theologians may have a similar historical location, but may not have the same commitments (e.g., Baxter, Bunyan), or they may not have the same contemporary significance (e.g., à Brakel, Boston, Charnock, Goodwin); and yet others lack the same extended attention to the topic at hand (e.g., Bavinck, Ames, Sibbes, Witsius). Therefore, while Reformed theologians such as those mentioned above (esp. Calvin, Bavinck, and Turretin) will play important roles in later discussions of classical and Reformed Christology, the cumulative value of Owen's testimony for these reasons gives him pride of place in such an account.

1. The Historical Location of Owen as a Witness John Owen (1616–83) was a Reformed theologian, pastor, army chaplain, vice-chancellor at Oxford University, and statesman in England during the tumultuous seventeenth century. Owen's work joins in the seventeenth century's "struggle to articulate, codify, and confessionalize the doctrine of the Trinity."[135] This task also evidences something

---

133. B. B. Warfield, *The Person and Work of Christ* (Philadelphia: P&R, 1950), 237.

134. Kevin J. Vanhoozer and Daniel J. Treier, *Theology and the Mirror of Scripture: A Mere Evangelical Account*, SCDS (Downers Grove, IL: IVP Academic, 2015), 117; J. V. Fesko, "The Doctrine of Scripture in Reformed Orthodoxy," in *A Companion to Reformed Orthodoxy*, ed. Herman J. Selderhuis, BCCT 40 (Boston: Brill, 2013), 249–64.

135. Lim, *Mystery Unveiled*, 2.

of his historical location in the Reformed tradition, specifically what is considered "High Orthodoxy"—where polemics drove toward further clarification of theological questions "for and in the church."[136]

Owen finds himself as the recipient of the great classical tradition and yet also is sitting on the cutting edge of what will become "modern" thought. As such, he not only looks backward at the tradition but also foreshadows particularly modern theological moves.[137] As such Owen typifies what James Eglinton describes as a core move of Reformed theology: looking back to the Scripture and tradition and looking forward to contemporary questions and discussions.[138] Insofar as the topic at hand likewise exists in a position that straddles both the classical tradition and modern developments, drawing from a figure in Owen's position is a logical decision.

2. The Form of His Testimony As a theologian in the Reformed Orthodox tradition, Owen places significant weight on the creeds, councils, church fathers, medieval scholastics, and early Reformers. Owen does not see tradition as entirely separate from Scripture as an "ancillary authority," but as the "context for the correct interpretation of the Scripture."[139] Owen claims to have constructed his Christology without indulging in speculation, and that he "not only diligently attended unto the doctrine of the Scripture, our only infallible rule and guide, but also expressly

---

136. Willem J. Van Asselt and Eef Dekker, "Introduction," in *Reformation and Scholasticism: An Ecumenical Enterprise*, ed. Willem J. Van Asselt and Eef Dekker, TSRPRT (Grand Rapids: Baker Academic, 2001), 13; Suzanne McDonald, *Re-Imaging Election: Divine Election as Representing God to Others and Others to God* (Grand Rapids: Eerdmans, 2010), 6 Muller, *PRRD*, 30–2. It is at this point that Owen is often inserted into the (now well-trodden) "Calvin and the Calvinist" debate. For helpful recent survey of the debate as it intersects with Owen, see Willem van Vlastuin and Kelly M. Kapic, "Introduction, Overview and Epilogue," in *John Owen between Orthodoxy and Modernity*, ed. Willem van Vlastuin and Kelly M. Kapic, SRT 39 (Boston: Brill, 2018), 8–10.

137. This is the underlying thesis in the collection of essays, Willem van Vlastuin and Kelly Kapic, eds., *John Owen between Orthodoxy and Modernity*, SRT 39 (Boston: Brill, 2019).

138. James Eglinton, *Bavinck: A Critical Biography* (Grand Rapids: Baker Academic, forthcoming).

139. Philip Dixon, *Nice and Hot Disputes: The Doctrine of the Trinity in the Seventeenth Century* (New York: T&T Clark, 2003), 61; citing WJO, *Vindiciæ Evangelicæ*, 12:46, 60. Likewise, Robert Letham, "John Owen's Doctrine of the Trinity in Its Catholic Context," in *The Ashgate Research Companion to John Owen's Theology*, ed. Kelly Kapic and Mark Jones (Burlington: Ashgate, 2012), 191.

considered what was taught and believed in the ancient church in this matter, from which I know that I have not departed."[140]

Beyond the councils and creeds, Owen was thoroughly Augustinian, scholastic, and Reformed.[141] Owen says of Augustine, "There is none among the ancient or modern divines ... [who] have equalled, much less outgone him, in an accurate search and observation of all the secret actings of the Spirit of God on the minds and souls of men."[142] He draws from the scholastics, especially Thomas Aquinas and Duns Scotus, throughout his life.[143] Of the Reformed, Owen audaciously claims to "have no singular opinion of my own, but embrace the common, known doctrine of the reformed churches."[144] Trueman rightly summarizes Owen's dependence upon the tradition: "His thought represents in many ways the attempt of a seventeenth-century theologian to work out the implications of Reformed theology in terms set by the classic Trinitarian and Christological formulations of the early church .... His theology is constructed with self-conscious reference to the catholic patristic tradition."[145]

Owen not only shares the formal commitments of the project but also employs them in associative and expansive ways. That is, Owen addresses the questions of trinitarian and christological action expansively (spending thousands of pages

---

140. WJO, *Pneumatologia*, 3:7. Significantly, this quote comes from *Pneumatologia*, the volume which several interpreters believe contains Owen's most inventive Christology. It should be noted that Owen's commitment to the historic confessions is less than entirely straightforward throughout his life (Gribben, *Experiences of Defeat*, 222), yet Owen's commitment to a classical doctrine of God and conciliar Christology remained firm (see Rehnman, *Divine Discourse*, 45–6, 179–81).

141. For Augustine's influence, see Carl R. Trueman, "Patristics and Reformed Orthodoxy: Some Brief Notes and Proposals,"*SBJT* 12 (2008): 52–60.

142. WJO, *Pneumatologia*, 3:349.

143. For Thomas' influence, see Christopher Cleveland, *Thomism in John Owen* (Burlington: Ashgate, 2013); cf. Rehnman, *Divine Discourse*, 34; likewise, Trueman says that "compared to say, Calvin or Bullinger, Owen exhibited just as great a knowledge of the patristic tradition, a better understanding of medieval theology and philosophy" (*John Owen: Reformed Catholic, Renaissance Man* [Burlington: Routledge, 2007], 22, 24, 127). For the influence of Scotus, see Timothy Robert Baylor, "A Great King Above All Gods: Dominion and Divine Government in the Theology of John Owen" (PhD diss., University of St Andrews, 2016), 30–78.

144. WJO, *Vindiciæ Evangelicæ*, 12:595. Richard A. Muller, "Sources of Reformed Orthodoxy: The Symmetrical Unity of Exegesis and Synthesis," in *A Confessing Theology for Postmodern Times*, ed. Michael S. Horton (Wheaton: Crossway, 2000), 45–6; Sinclair Ferguson cites Calvin as tremendously influential in *John Owen on the Christian Life* (Carlisle: Banner of Truth, 1987), 224.

145. Carl R. Trueman, *The Claims of Truth: John Owen's Trinitarian Theology* (Carlisle: Paternoster, 1998), 29.

addressing the topic [see below])[146] and associatively (i.e., allowing his prior theological conclusions to influence his later argumentation).[147] These virtues are evidenced not only within Owen's corpus but also in the reception of Owen's thought on these issues. For example, Owen plays a prominent role in Richard Muller's articulation of Reformed Scholastic trinitarian theology.[148]

3. Material Attention to Trinitarian and Christological Action (esp. in Terms of Agency) One aspect of the expansiveness of Owen's trinitarian theology is his attention to the topics of trinitarian and christological action. Part of Owen's quantitative superiority to other thinkers on this front likely has to do with the occasional nature of Owen's work. Owen did not, like Turretin, Witsius, à Brakel, and Ames, attempt to write (what we would today call) a systematic theology. So while thinkers such as Witsius are limited by space on a topic (i.e., he only spends twenty-four pages on God's triunity) due to the genre, Owen can engage in extended discussions that revolve around trinitarian action for multiple volumes.[149] The occasional nature of Owen's thought inclined itself toward the topics at hand because of the polemics he engaged in. Against Catholics he argued for the two-natured mediation of Christ (especially in Christ's priestly office); against Arminians and Amyraldians he argued for the efficacy of divine actions; with Quakers he disputed the nature of the Spirit's actions; against Socinians he argued for the divinity and supremacy of Christ from his actions, and the personhood and deity of the Holy Spirit on the basis of his divine acts.[150] In addition to the topical attention that Owen devotes, he also often does so frequently within the linguistic key of agency. While counting occurrences is hardly fool-proof guide, a cursory glance at Owen's works and their tables of contents will produce several uses of

---

146. Veli-Matti Kärkkäinen calls Owen's pneumatology "one of the most comprehensive treatises into the Spirit ever written" (*Holy Spirit and Salvation: Sources of Christian Theology* [Louisville: Westminster John Knox Press, 2010], 197).

147. This associative mode is evident throughout the extended articulation of Owen's thought.

148. E.g., Muller, *PRRD*, 4:113–15; 259–73; 349–53;

149. Herman Witsius, *Sacred Dissertations on What Is Commonly Called the Apostles' Creed*, trans. Donald Fraser (Edinburgh: Fullarton & Co., 1823), 1:121–45.

150. On the polemical context of Owen's theology see Trueman, *Claims of Truth*, 21–4; Trueman, *John Owen*, 29–31; Spence, *Incarnation and Inspiration*, 45; Richard Muller, "Diversity in the Reformed Tradition: A Historiographical Introduction," in *Drawn into Controversie: Reformed Theological Diversity and Debates Within Seventeenth-Century British Puritanism* (Oakville, CT: Vandenhoeck & Ruprecht, 2011), 29–30; Lim *Mystery Unveiled*, 214–15; Glynne Lloyd, "The Life and Work of the Reverend John Owen D. D., the Puritan Divine, with Special Reference to the Socinian Controversies of the Seventeenth Century" (PhD diss., The University of Edinburgh, 1942). Michael A. G. Haykin, "John Owen and the Challenge of the Quakers," in *John Owen: The Man and His Theology*, ed. Robert W. Oliver (Phillipsburg: P & R, 2002), 131–55.

the language of agent and agency.[151] Even in contrast to someone like Jonathan Edwards, who uses the language frequently, Owen's attention to divine agents and agency is notable against Edwards' expression of human freedom and faculties through these terms.[152]

4. *The Contemporary Significance of His Testimony* Owen's testimony is valuable not only because of his location within the classical and Reformed traditions and his formal and material articulation of that tradition on this topic—helping this project to assess the coherence of classical and Reformed christological agency—but also because he plays an important role in contemporary discussions of christological agency, especially as they address Reformed accounts—helping this project to assess the prudence of such a proposal. Owen's account stands prominent in contemporary discussions of christological agency and in a potentially controversial way. So if another figure (who fulfills the above conditions to various degrees [e.g., Vermigli or Bavinck]) were chosen as the principal witness, then that account would run the risk of presenting classical and Reformed christological agency in a way that (1) has already been accomplished by Owen (and contemporary theologians' employment of him) or (2) contradict Owen's account of Reformed Christology, making Owen an important counterexample—i.e., someone may say, "sure Bavinck gives an example of classical and Reformed Christology, but Owen's influential account diverges from Bavinck at several key points, so how can Bavinck's be considered representative and superior?" By choosing Owen—a thinker who is considered novel by many—and reading him in continuity with the classical and Reformed traditions, this account can address those proposals of christological agency which purport to be Reformed and unique insofar as they are rooted in Owen's thought and it can do so in a way that evidences the coherence of Owen with the rest of the Reformed tradition.

---

151. In reading through Owen's works I have counted almost 300 uses of "agent" or "agency." This is in contrast to the fewer than ten occurrences that I found in each of Kuyper's nearly 700-page *Pneumatology*, Ames's *Marrow of Theology*, Flavel's over 550-page account of Christ's mediation, and Goodwin's 430-page treatise on Christ the Mediator. Abraham Kuyper, *The Work of the Holy Spirit*, trans. Henri de Vrie (Grand Rapids: Eerdmans, 1946); William Ames, *The Marrow of Theology*, trans. John Dykstra Eusden (Grand Rapids: Baker, 1997); John Flavel, *The Fountain of Life Opened Up: Or, A Display of Christ in His Essential and Mediatorial Glory*, The Works of Rev. Mr. John Flavel, vol. 1 (London: Baynes and Son, 1820); Thomas Goodwin, *Of Christ the Mediator*, The Works of Thomas Goodwin, vol. 5 (London: James Nisbet and Co., 1763).

152. A brief search on the Yale database shows more than 700 uses of agent and agency, many of which occur in *Freedom of the Will*, Works of Jonathan Edwards, vol. 1, ed. Paul Ramsey (Yale: Yale University Press, 2009) and many others occur in editorial introductions. Cumulatively they indicate a high degree of attention to human action.

Once called the "forgotten man of English theology," Owen has recently elicited "a busy-bee cottage industry" of scholarship.[153] Not only has Owen been engaged by those interested in Puritan studies in general but Owen has also contributed to broader theological discussions by Reformed constructive theologians (e.g., Colin Gunton, Bruce McCormack, George Hunsinger, Kevin Vanhoozer, and John Webster).[154] This attention is often centered on Owen's contribution to trinitarian and christological discussions.

Owen's thought permeates discussions of christological agency in contemporary Reformed literature. For example, Colin Gunton employs Owen's understanding of trinitarian operations, and one of Gunton's students, Alan Spence, has published multiple pieces that present Owen on trinitarian and christological operations. Often on the basis of Spence's reading, others have engaged Owen in discussions of trinitarian and christological operations.[155] Additionally, others (especially in analytic theology circles) have engaged Owen's thought in order to advance

---

153. J. I. Packer, "Forward," in *From Heaven He Came and Sought Her: Definite Atonement in Historical, Biblical, Theological, and Pastoral Perspective*, ed. David Gibson and Jonathan Gibson (Wheaton, IL: Crossway, 2013), 14; Trueman, *Claims*, 1. Joel Beeke and Mark Jones likewise lament the dearth of literature on post-Reformation Reformed Christology (*A Puritan Theology: Doctrine for Life* [Grand Rapids: Reformation Heritage, 2012], 336); see Vlastuin and Kapic, "Introduction," 8–13 on reasons for the recent interest in Owen.

154. Colin E. Gunton, *Theology through the Theologians: Selected Essays 1972–1995* (New York: T&T Clark, 2003), 187–205; Bruce L. McCormack, "'With Loud Cries and Tears': The Humanity of the Son in the Epistle to the Hebrews," in *The Epistle to the Hebrews and Christian Theology*, ed. Richard Bauckham et al. (Grand Rapids: Eerdmans, 2009), 37–68; George Hunsinger, "Justification and Mystical Union with Christ: Where Does Owen Stand?," in *The Ashgate Research Companion to John Owen's Theology* (Burlington: Ashgate, 2012), 199–214; John Webster, *God without Measure: Working Papers in Christian Theology: Volume 1: God and the Works of God* (New York: Bloomsbury, 2016), 50–1; Kevin J. Vanhoozer, "The Spirit of Light After the Age of Enlightenment: Reforming/Renewing Pneumatic Hermeneutics via the Economy of Illumination," in *Spirit of God: Christian Renewal in the Community of Faith*, ed. Jeffrey W. Barbeau and Beth Felker Jones (Downers Grove, IL: IVP Academic, 2015), 149–67. Insofar as Crawford Gribben's claim is correct that Owen made "no distinctive and enduring contribution to English or Reformed theology" (*John Owen and English Puritanism: Experiences of Defeat*, OSHT [New York: Oxford University Press, 2016], 270) there is a need to recover and retrieve Owen and these thinkers have already made strides in that direction.

155. McCormack, "With Loud Cries"; Horton, *Lord and Servant*, 159–77; Myk Habets, "Spirit Christology: The Future of Christology," in *Third Article Theology: A Pneumatological Dogmatics*, ed. Myk Habets (Minneapolis: Fortress, 2016), 207–32; Oliver D. Crisp, *Revisioning Christology: Theology in the Reformed Tradition* (Burlington: Routledge, 2011), 91–110; Lucy Peppiatt, "Life in the Spirit: Christ's and Ours," in *The Christian Doctrine of Humanity: Explorations in Constructive Dogmatics*, ed. Oliver Crisp and Fred Sanders, LATC (Grand Rapids: Zondervan, 2018), 165–81.

and locate their own claims about trinitarian operations (especially indivisible operations).[156]

This contemporary interest, especially on the topic at hand, does not make Owen the only plausible option, but because of this preexisting dialogue, he is recognizably a valuable guide through this web of theological connections. Yet, he too must be held accountable by the authoritative sources he held to (i.e., Scripture, tradition, and coherence). In this sense, the following project follows Christopher Cleveland's assessment that "John Owen's use of Thomism is part of a strongly Western and catholic theological synthesis that builds upon patristic and medieval formulations .... It is such a usage that allows Owen's theological formulations to transcend their seventeenth-century context and retain relevance for any theological program that seeks to build upon a Western catholic framework."[157] As such this project will view Owen as a reliable witness to classical and Reformed theology and a valuable guide and theological model in engagements with contemporary theology.[158] As the key witness of the case, however, it is not Owen who is primarily or exclusively on trial. The project will draw from his thought throughout (esp. in Chs. 2 and 3), yet Chapters 4–6 will add additional classical and Reformed voices to Owen's testimony in order to articulate a well-rounded account of classical and Reformed Christology.

IV. Contemporary Christology and Prima Facie Liabilities

The commitments of classical and Reformed Christology run into some *prima facie* liabilities as we start to articulate it in terms of agencies. That is, there are some classical and Reformed conclusions on christological agency that would superficially seem to be incoherent with other claims within its core commitments. For example, if Jesus is the Son of God and is said to be one agent, then (by virtue of reverse proportionality) it would seem that the Father is an agent and the Spirit is an agent, in addition to the Son. However, this conclusion of three agents in God seems superficially inconsistent with the classical and Reformed commitment to a classical doctrine of God wherein the one God acts as a single and unified actor in history.

---

156. Keith E. Johnson, "The Work of the Holy Spirit in the Ministry of Jesus Christ: A Trinitarian Perspective," *TJ* 38 (2017): 147–67; Adonis Vidu, "Trinitarian Inseparable Operations and the Incarnation," *JAT* 4 (2016): 106–27.

157. Cleveland, *Thomism*, 7.

158. Vlastuin and Kapic say that Owen "modeled an early modern attempt to present a Protestant theology which was intentionally historic, 'catholic,' and yet stood under Scripture abiding voice for his own day" ("Introduction," 12); Bruce McCormack says that Owen was "the most formidable Reformed theologian of his time" and the "most intriguing" example of orthodox Christology ("With Loud Cries," 38–9); see also Horton, *Lord and Servant*, 167.

For each of these conclusions that classical and Reformed Christology is potentially liable to, there is a corresponding contemporary position that is closest to those conclusions. These positions do not necessarily fall victim to the liability in question, but represent the most proximate position to that conclusion.[159] So for each seemingly incoherent conclusion, we must ask how vulnerable classical and Reformed Christology is to the *prima facie* liability and how it relates to the contemporary position most proximate to that conclusion. For example, the contemporary position that is most proximate to the conclusion that the triune God acts as three agents is social Trinitarianism. By the end of the project, the coherence of classical and Reformed christological agency will be determined by its ability to coherently address each of these *prima facie* liabilities and its prudence will be evidenced, in part, by its relation to the contemporary proximate positions. We will focus on five positions and liabilities in question, beginning with those focused on trinitarian action in Christ and then those focused on the relation of the divine and human.

A. Social Trinitarianism and Three Independent Agents

As stated above, there is a *prima facie* inclination toward social Trinitarianism and (further) three independent triune agents.[160] This conclusion is reached on the basis of the "reverse proportion" of predicates to natures and persons in trinitarian and christological thought.[161] Since the councils affirm that Christ is God the Son, a single person and subject of predicates (as evidenced by the *theotokos* formula) and an actor whose actions are all predicated of God the Son (as evidenced by the *theopaschite* formula), then it would seem that persons are "agents" and that God is three "agents," which is a conclusion reached nearly exclusively by

---

159. To illustrate this, I can continue the example of social Trinitarianism: I agree with Thomas McCall that social Trinitarianism is often associated with positing three agents, but also that there is a sense in which each divine person is a distinct agent for any orthodox account of the Trinity (*Analytic Christology*, 149). The particular sense in which I can make this affirmation will be made clear below.

160. Even if the affirmation of three independent agents is not sufficient for a definition of social Trinitarianism (per McCall, *Analytic Christology*, 148–9), I would consider it a constitutive feature and emphasis of social Trinitarianism. This is evident in the following, but it is also evident in McCall's affirmative use of Scott Williams (*Analytic Christology*, 172). Williams articulates a trinitarian theology that seeks to be both social and Latin, and he suggests that the "social" element is composed of an affirmation of mutual love between divine persons and of the three persons as "three metaphysical agents" ("Indexicals and the Trinity: Two Non-Social Models," *Journal of Analytic Theology* 1 [2013]: 84).

161. See especially Daley, "Persons in God," 12–13.

social Trinitarianism, and is part and parcel of the definitional clarity of social Trinitarianism.[162]

For example, agent and "subject" language have played central roles in Jürgen Moltmann's understanding of the "social Trinity."[163] For Moltmann, the three divine persons are distinct and interrelating subjects, willing persons who act and bring about effects (i.e., agents).[164] More recently, social Trinitarianism has been defined as a theory in which the Father, Son, and Holy Spirit have "distinct centers of knowledge, will, love, and action."[165] As distinct centers of knowledge and will, it would seem that social Trinitarianism would freely label the three persons as three agents. Additionally, as "distinct centers of ... action," they would also likely be willing to attribute the causation of distinct actions to distinct agents. To illustrate the social Trinitarian commitment to three agents, we may note one of the position's most ardent counterparts, Karl Barth, who claims that there is "only one Willer and *Doer* that the Bible calls God."[166] He likewise insists that the "Christian faith and the Christian confession has one Subject, not three."[167] Therefore, insofar as Barth and Moltmann represent the two sides of the modern trinitarian discussion, the claim of "three agents" seems to belong uniquely on the social Trinitarian side. So classical and Reformed theology must ask if its commitment to Christ as a single agent leads to three independent agents and how such a conclusion relates to social Trinitarianism.

---

162. Carl Mosser suggests that at the "center" of social Trinitarianism is the claim that "Each [divine person] is a distinct agent who possesses all the necessary attributes of divinity as well as his own center of consciousness, thought, will, and love" ("Fully Social Trinitarianism," in *Philosophical and Theological Essays on the Trinity*, ed. Thomas McCall and Michael Rea [New York: Oxford University Press, 2009], 133; cf. 145). Further, see Thomas McCall's definition of a person as an "agent" and his appeal to Jesus as an "agent who is distinct and discrete from his Father" as putatively self-evident support for social Trinitarianism (*Which Trinity? Whose Monotheism? Philosophical and Systematic Theologians on the Metaphysics of Trinitarian Theology* [Grand Rapids: Eerdmans, 2010], 14, 58–9, 85).

163. Moltmann's significance in modern theology can hardly be stated any stronger than John Cooper's claim that he is "the most widely known and popular contemporary Protestant theologian" (*Panentheism: The Other God of the Philosophers: From Plato to the Present* [Grand Rapids: Baker Academic, 2006], 237).

164. For this definition, see Jürgen Moltmann, *The Spirit of Life: A Universal Affirmation*, trans. Margaret Kohl (Minneapolis: Fortress, 1992), 11.

165. Cornelius Plantinga Jr., "Social Trinity and Tritheism," in *Trinity, Incarnation, & Atonement: Philosophical & Theological Essays*, ed. Ronald J. Feenstra and Cornelius Plantinga Jr. (Notre Dame: University of Notre Dame Press, 1989), 22.

166. Barth, *CD* I/1, 351, emphasis mine.

167. Barth, *CD* IV/1, 205. Elsewhere he says, "The notion of a 'Social Trinity' is fantastic!" (*Karl Barth's Table Talk*, ed. John D. Godsey [Richmond: John Knox, 1962], 50). Likewise, see Karl Rahner, *The Trinity*, trans. Joseph Donceel, Milestones in Catholic Theology (New York: The Crossroad, 1997), 106–7.

B. Spirit Christology and the Holy Spirit as Executing Agent

The second position, likewise, presupposes that Christ is a single agent. This position then takes into account the biblical testimony of the activity of the Spirit in Christ's work (Mt. 1:18, 20; 4:1; 12:18; Lk. 4:18; Isa. 61:1; Heb. 9:4), as well as the reinvigorated interest in the Holy Spirit on the heels of the explosion of Pentecostalism and the "renewal of Trinitarian theology" in the twentieth century.[168] Additionally, the classical trinitarian appropriation of the Holy Spirit as the power and efficacy of the triune God (see Ch. 2 §II.B.3) has led some to a *prima facie* conclusion that the divine agent to whom we attribute the execution of the acts of Christ is the Holy Spirit as it empowers the humanity of Christ. This attribution of the activity (and even primacy of activity) to the Holy Spirit is seen most prominently in a contemporary movement (or a conglomerate of movements) called Spirit Christology.[169]

Spirit Christology often presents a narrative of "pneuma neglect," whereby the church has supposedly overlooked the Spirit and sold the biblical account of Christ as the Spirit-anointed One for a bowl of "Logos Christology" porridge.[170] According to the narrative, "Logos Christology," in which "the identity of Jesus is formulated in terms of the Word and … determined by the agency of the logos,"[171] was solidified by Chalcedon in 451 and has dominated the church's understanding

---

168. For the history of the revival of trinitarian theology and a (rather critical) assessment, see Stephen R. Holmes, *The Quest for the Trinity: The Doctrine of God in Scripture, History and Modernity* (Downers Grove, IL: IVP Academic, 2012). For the Pentecostal explosion and its implications for Spirit Christology, see Sammy Alfaro, *Divino Compañero: Toward a Hispanic Pentecostal Christology* (Eugene, OR: Wipf & Stock, 2010).

169. Spirit Christology is notoriously difficult to define (Ralph Del Colle, *Christ and the Spirit: Spirit-Christology in Trinitarian Perspective* [New York: Oxford University Press, 1994], 5), yet I am here defining it as "a sustained account of Christ's person and work explicated with direct reference to the Spirit and oriented toward the significance of the Spirit, often by appreciating themes and texts in Scripture regarding the Spirit" (Kieser, "Is the Filioque an Obstacle," 395).

170. E.g., Robert W. Jenson, "You Wonder Where the Spirit Went," *Pro Ecclesia* 2 (1993): 296–304. More recently, a similar claim is made by Alister E. McGrath, *Christian Theology: An Introduction*, 5th ed. (Malden: Wiley-Blackwell, 2011), 307.

171. Cornelis Van Der Kooi, "On the Identity of Jesus Christ: Spirit Christology and Logos Christology in Converse," in *Third Article Theology: A Pneumatological Dogmatics*, ed. Myk Habets (Minneapolis: Fortress, 2016), 194–5. I owe the label "pneuma neglect" to conversations with Kyle Claunch.

of Christ ever since.¹⁷² On many accounts of broadly orthodox Spirit Christology, the empowerment of the Spirit bestows an independence and priority on Christ's (Spirit-enabled) human activity so that Veli-Matti Kärkkäinen comments, "Jesus' ministry was the function of the Holy Spirit."¹⁷³ There is much to appreciate in various accounts of Spirit Christology because of the biblical testimony of the Spirit and because of the indivisibility of triune operations. So Michael Allen rightly says, "Even ardent critics of flawed versions of Spirit-Christology must affirm the need to extend the classical affirmation of the Spirit's significance in the life of Jesus dogmatically."¹⁷⁴

Yet, the claim that the Spirit is the divine person responsible for accomplishing Christ's acts seems to be superficially inconsistent with the conciliar affirmation that the "Word of God" (i.e., the Son) suffered and worked miracles, with the biblical testimony (e.g., Jn 1:18; Rom. 5:8; Gal. 4:4-5), and with the nature of Christ's filial revelation (whereby Christ's activities manifest the glory of the Son of the Father [Jn 1:14]).¹⁷⁵ Therefore, classical and Reformed Christology must consider how the attribution of christological activity to the Holy Spirit relates coherently with the predication of Christ's acts to the Son and it must ask itself if such a conclusion constitutes a Spirit Christology.

C. Divine Passibility and Divine Limitation

The third *prima facie* liability is the doctrine of divine passibility, considered the "new orthodoxy" of modern theology, yet excluded by conciliar and classical theology.¹⁷⁶ Again, this position supposes that the Christ who suffers on the cross is the divine Son and is a single agent. Such a commitment is said by some to imply that the divine agent must suffer and, thereby, that divinity must suffer. Bruce McCormack highlights the concerns of christological agency when he suggests that if we are to hold to the Son as a single subject, then it necessarily implies

---

172. Myk Habets, *The Anointed Son: A Trinitarian Spirit Christology* (Eugene, OR: Wipf & Stock, 2010), 55. Some accounts of Spirit Christology leverage the Bauer thesis and suggest that Logos Christology was imposed upon early Christian communities by the institutionalized church and Spirit Christology represents an attempt to revolt against this coercion (e.g., Rosemary Radford Ruether, *Sexism and God-Talk: Toward a Feminist Theology* [Boston: Beacon, 1983], 131). The strong Spirit Christology versus Logos Christology narrative has, however, been questioned recently (e.g., Christopher R. J. Holmes, *The Holy Spirit*, NSD [Grand Rapids: Zondervan, 2015], 123–33).

173. Veli-Matti Kärkkäinen, "The Spirit of Life: Moltmann's Pneumatology," in *Jürgen Moltmann and Evangelical Theology: A Critical Engagement* (Eugene, OR: Pickwick, 2012), 133.

174. Allen, *Christ's Faith*, 14.

175. See the third canon of Constantinople III (Tanner, *Decrees*, 1:114).

176. The origin of this phrase is often attributed to Ronald Goetz, "The Suffering God: The Rise of a New Orthodoxy," *Christian Century* 103 (1986): 385.

that he suffers in his divine nature.[177] The only alternative is to introduce a second passible "subject in its own right," with the consequence of dividing Christ like a Nestorian. He claims that as long as Christ is a single agent of all his action, then impassibility is "completely untenable." He calls for a distancing from the conciliar account of God if modern Christology is to overcome the "problems resident in the nexus of ideas which made the Chalcedonian Formula possible."[178]

Kenotic Christology, although present in the tradition as far back as the nineteenth century, has made a contemporary resurgence (esp. within the Reformed tradition) and seeks to resolve this tension by providing an account "that explains the incarnation in terms of the Logos temporarily 'giving up' or 'laying aside' or 'divesting itself of' or 'emptying itself of' certain properties."[179] This is particularly true of divine impassibility. So the Son may have been impassible prior to his kenotic self-emptying, but in the incarnation the one agent allows himself to suffer as a human.

Classical and Reformed Christology wants to deny Nestorianism (like McCormack and Kenoticism) and to affirm the *theopaschite* formula, yet it must ask if it can accomplish both of these tasks without violating the impassibility of classical trinitarian theology.

D. Parallelism and Two Christological Agents

The next position also seeks to advocate for, and work from, the "basic assumption of contemporary Christology" (i.e., the humanity of Christ) by preserving the strong distinction between Christ's divine and human natures.[180] This assumption

---

177. McCormack, "With Loud Cries," 45.

178. Bruce L. McCormack, "The Actuality of God: Karl Barth in Conversation with Open Theism," in *Engaging the Doctrine of God: Contemporary Protestant Perspectives* (Grand Rapids: Baker Academic, 2008), 221; on the incoherence of the incarnation and classical impassibility, see also Stephen T. Davis, "Is Kenosis Orthodox?," in *Exploring Kenotic Christology: The Self-Emptying of God*, ed. C. Stephen Evans (New York: Oxford University Press, 2006), 115.

179. Davis, "Metaphysics of Kenosis," 118. For early Kenotic Christology, see David R. Law, "Le kénotisme luthérien et anglican: les christologies de Gottfried Thomasius et Frank Weston," *Études théologiques et religieuses* 89 (2014): 313–40.

180. The quote comes from Don Schweitzer, *Contemporary Christologies: A Fortress Introduction* (Minneapolis: Fortress, 2010), 128. Claims which prioritize the significance of Christ's humanity over his divinity may be seen in Pannenberg, *Jesus*, 189; John Knox, *The Humanity and Divinity of Christ: A Study of Pattern in Christology* (New York: Cambridge University Press, 1967), 73–4. For commentary on the centrality of the humanity of Christ in contemporary Christology, see Tanner, *Jesus, Humanity and the Trinity*, 7–10; Johnson, *Consider Jesus*, 19–34. Moltmann says that "humanity" has "become the main question about Christ." *The Crucified God: The Cross of Christ as the Foundation and Criticism of Christian Theology*, trans. R. A. Wilson and John Bowden (Minneapolis: Fortress, 1993), 92.

has led to complaints about classic Christology's tendency toward Apollinarianism, "cryptomonophysitism," and a "naive docetism."[181] That is, critics suspect that in traditional Christology the divinity of Christ "overshadows" his humanity, such that in "the Catholic, Orthodox, and Reformation traditions" the humanity of Christ tends to be "marginalized."[182] These concerns about "space suit Christology" are often evident and significant in terms of christological action.[183] The starting point here is the distinct principles of operation and, presumably, "agency."

The position most proximate to this commitment might be called christological "parallelism."[184] On this account, often by making use of the doctrine of *concursus*, advocates view Christ's activity to be fully human alongside activity that is fully divine. The transcendence of God, they argue, implies that God is not competing for causal space with creatures in a zero-sum game. Applying this position to Christology, they posit a noncompetitive relationship between the human and divine natures of Christ.[185] The employment of *concursus* as a christologically plausible doctrine often takes shape in what is called the "Chalcedonian pattern" (i.e., divine and human action are without separation, without division, without mixture, and without confusion) summarized by the labels "unity, differentiation, and asymmetry."[186] Presupposing this model of divine action and infusing it with notions of freedom, Elizabeth Johnson, following Karl Rahner, says that by virtue of the union Christ's humanity has with divinity, his humanity is "more human, more free, more alive, more his own person than any of us."[187] This intuition to attribute autonomy to Christ's humanity has led some theologians to claim that

---

181. Karl Rahner, "Current Problems in Christology," in *TI* 1:185–200, esp. 188; see also Coakley, *Powers and Submissions*, 15.

182. Ian A. McFarland, *The Word Made Flesh: A Theology of the Incarnation* (Louisville: Westminster John Knox, 2019), 3. McFarland, however, does not think we need to move beyond the councils and creeds these traditions are built on but need a "Chalcedonianism without reserve."

183. R. P. C. Hanson, *The Search for the Christian Doctrine of God: The Arian Controversy, 318-81* (Grand Rapids: Baker Academic, 2006), 448.

184. The language of parallelism and instrumentality are borrowed from McMaken's discussion of divine and human action in baptism ("Definitive, Defective or Deft?").

185. Tanner, *Jesus, Humanity and the Trinity*, esp. 4–9; Kathryn Tanner, *God and Creation in Christian Theology* (Minneapolis: Fortress, 2005), 90–104, 152.

186. Hunsinger, *How to Read Karl Barth*, 185–224; cf. this pattern is called the "master key" to Barth's theology by Deborah van Deusen Hunsinger, "The Master Key: Unlocking the Relationship of Theology and Psychology," *Inspire* 5 (2001): 22.

187. Johnson, *Consider Jesus*, 29. She is here following Rahner's claim that the nearer a creature is to God the greater autonomy they possess (*Foundations of Christian Faith: An Introduction to the Idea of Christianity*, trans. William V. Dych [New York: Seabury, 1978], 78).

Christ's humanity is "autokinetic," minimally meaning "self-moved."[188] That is, the free activity of God is in parallel (and nonconvergent) with the free activity of humanity. For some theologians, the parallelism present here constitutes dual agency.[189]

However, if we attend to the christological implications of this agency language, dual agency may imply two agents. For example, in Patrick Patterson's account of "dual agency" in modern Christologies, he appeals to "the distinctive dynamic of human nature that makes for uniquely human freedom, willingness, intention, purpose, and *act*. The willingness and freedom, the *activity* and *agency* of Jesus Christ are authentically human" such that Christ's humanity had a "created autonomy" so that "it exercised in time a true human freedom."[190]

Again there is much to parallelism that classical and Reformed Christology appreciates (i.e., genuine human action, strong distinction between divinity and humanity), yet the question remains whether (and how) classical and Reformed Christology can maintain its commitment to the integrity of Christ's humanity coherently with the conciliar affirmation of a single agent and the conciliar denial of two agents. If classical and Reformed Christology can remain internally coherent, it must also ask how it relates to contemporary accounts of parallelism.

E. Strong Instrumentality and Lack of Human Activity

The converse position of the above also laments current directions in modern Christology. Yet this position fears that modern theology has attributed *too much* priority and independence to the humanity of Christ at the cost of christological unity. Some of the critiques of the above modern trend suggest that "very many modern theologians are Nestorian" and that there is a "tendency toward Nestorianism in modern Christology" which, when fully grown, leads to an inability to identify the Christ as the Word of God.[191] Therefore, especially in terms

---

188. This affirmation can be seen in more recent Reformed theologians (see below), but it is also evident in Helmut Thielicke, who claims that the humanity of Christ possesses "supreme originality and autonomy" and is an "autokineton" as our "representative before God" (*The Evangelical Faith* [Edinburgh: T&T Clark, 1978], 2:321, 320).

189. E.g., Tanner, *Jesus, Humanity and Trinity*, 90–8. For others, like James McClendon, "two narratives" is more appropriate, yet materially similar in terms of christological activity (Doctrine, *Systematic Theology* [Nashville: Abingdon, 1986], 2:276).

190. Patrick D. M. Patterson, "By Thine Agony and Bloody Sweat: A Dogmatic Description of the Double Agencies of Christ—A Modest Proposal" (PhD diss., University of Toronto, 2013), 55–6, 23; cf. 75, emphasis mine.

191. Richard Swinburne, *The Christian God* (New York: Oxford University Press, 1994), 228; Thomas Joseph White, *The Incarnate Lord: A Thomistic Study in Christology* (Washington, DC: Catholic University of America Press, 2015), 113, cf. 112–13. For a survey of the "persistent temptation" of contemporary Christology in this direction, see Aaron Riches, *Ecce Homo: On the Divine Unity of Christ*, Interventions (Grand Rapids: Eerdmans, 2016), 9.

of activity, this position worries that contemporary Christology's penchant toward distinction may be unable to describe Jesus' acts on earth as revelatory of God or to attribute Christ's salvific work to God. In order to combat this trend, there is an insistence that the agent of the incarnate acts of Christ is the divine Word who operates in his human nature as an instrument of the divine person to the degree that the humanity participates in the power of the divine nature.

These claims may be best represented by a contemporary position which I call "strong instrumentality."[192] Often propounded today by contemporary Thomists, this position seeks to solidify the unity of Christ's acts, particularly insofar as Christ's incarnate acts are his "filial mode of action" that shows us the Father.[193] This position insists that for the unity of this instrumental action to be possible, the humanity of Christ must participate in the divine energy such that Christ's humanity receives maximal knowledge of all facts and experiences the beatific vision (i.e., immediately beholding the divine essence) throughout his life. This strong instrumentality is theologically necessary if Christ's human acts are to reveal who Christ is as the Son of God.[194]

This position, positively, maintains the classical and conciliar commitments in its strong affirmation of the unity of Christ's acts and the *an/enhypostatic* character of the hypostatic union. It is therefore well equipped to affirm the revelatory significance of Christ's acts so that we know that, having seen Christ, we have seen the Father (Jn 14:9). Yet, it is not clear that such a position on maximal knowledge, the beatific vision, and participation in divine energy by Christ's human nature is compatible with the classical and Reformed commitment to the ontological and operational distinction of his human nature.[195]

---

192. See Gilles Emery, "Le Christ médiateur: L'unicité et l'universalité de la médiation salvifique du Christ Jésus suivant Thomas d'Aquin," in *Christus, Gottes schöpferisches Wort: Festschrift für Christoph Kardinal Schönborn*, ed. George Augustin et al. (Freiburg: Herder, 2010), 337–55. The adjective "strong" will be contrasted with another version of instrumentality in Chapter 5. Degrees of instrumentality are evident in discussions such as McCormack, *Humility of the Eternal Son*, 29, 39—with Apollinarius representing "complete instrumentalization."

193. See Dominic Legge O.P., *The Trinitarian Christology of St Thomas Aquinas* (New York: Oxford University Press, 2017), 187–220.

194. See Aquinas *ST* III, Q.6, A5; Q.64, A.3–4 for instrumentality. See White, *Incarnate Lord*, 254–7 for a summary of the necessity of the beatific vision by virtue of the doctrine of revelation.

195. Gunton's critique of Athanasius' Christology, in which the Son "wields his body" like an instrument illustrates the modern concern with this position (*Theology through the Theologians*, 151).

V. Conclusion

This chapter has introduced the prominence and promise of the language of agency for contemporary accounts of christological action. It introduced the complexity of defining the agency word-group and provided definitions for several key terms considered under an ordinary human context. Next it articulated the assets of classical and Reformed Christology and defended the selection of John Owen as the key witness to the position. Finally, it presented five points at which classical and Reformed Christology must attend to possible internal incoherence and five contemporary proximate positions.

From the foundation established in this chapter, the project will present the material commitments of classical and Reformed theology through the testimony of John Owen by surveying his account of trinitarian (Ch. 2) and christological (Ch. 3) action. Then it will assess the coherence and prudence of classical and Reformed christological agency in conversation with its *prima facie* liabilities and contemporary positions in contemporary Christology in terms of Christ's divine agency (Ch. 4), and human agency (Ch. 5), and theandric unity (Ch. 6).

The ultimate goal will be to provide an internally coherent and theologically prudent account of divine and human agency in classical and Reformed christology, one that is committed to Scripture, the ecumenical councils, a classical doctrine of the triune God, and Reformed christological emphases. As such, it will seek to demonstrate the way that these commitments can coherently hang together and thereby contribute to contemporary discussions of christological action.

Materially, this project will argue that classical and Reformed Christology primarily considers Christ as a single theandric agent acting according to two distinct (i.e., divine and human) agencies by which he brings about distinct immediate effects. In the words of Owen, then, this project seeks to defend the claim that Christ's acts should "not be considered as the act of this or that nature" because they are works of the "whole person."[196] Christ's two natures are "distinct principles of Christ's operations," united in one person, and therefore "his person is the principle or only agent" of these operations.[197] Put differently, this project is functionally a defense and elaboration of Barth's passing comment that redemption "is in fact accomplished through the coincidence of two agencies, divine and human, possessed and exercised by one and the same agent, the God-man, Jesus Christ."[198]

---

196. WJO, *Christologia*, 1:234.

197. WJO, *Communion*, 2:329.

198. Barth, *CD* IV/1, 204. As we will see below, "coincidence" (minimally) ought not to be taken technically here.

Chapter 2

THE EVIDENCE OF TRINITARIAN
ACTION FROM JOHN OWEN

The primary objective of this chapter and the following is to articulate the material commitments of classical and Reformed christological agency through the testimony of the Reformed Scholastic John Owen. These two chapters will express Owen's commitment to classical and Reformed theology while specifically attending to the theological location and material formulation of his account of trinitarian and christological action. The goal here is not to present Owen as the indefectible champion of classical and Reformed theology but to articulate Owen's testimony regarding trinitarian and christological action as the foundational framework from which the internal coherence and theological prudence of a classical and Reformed account of christological agency will be evaluated. As such, the following two chapters freely note Owen's occasional lack of technical terminology consistency,[1] yet depend upon previous scholarship in Owen studies to defend Owen as a viable and valuable advocate for classical and Reformed thought. It will do so through attention to Owen's treatment on trinitarian and christological action as it sprawls through multiple volumes (especially, *Communion*, *Vindiciæ Evangelicæ*, *Pnuematologia*, and *Christologia*). This chapter will seek to appreciate the expansive and associative engagement with the topic of agency in Owen while arguing for an understanding of his trinitarian thought that aligns him with the commitments of classical trinitarian theology.

The fundamental assumption of this chapter is that Christology is an inherently trinitarian doctrine—as we see in the early Johannine introduction to the λόγος, who *is* God (Jn 1:1), acts with God (Jn 1:3), and reveals God

---

1. The inconsistencies that follow could simply be the product of Owen's employment of the "popular" and "scholastic" distinction (see Donald Sinnema, "The Distinction between Scholastic and Popular: Andreas Hyperius and Reformed Scholasticism" in *Protestant Scholasticism: Essays in Reassessment*, ed. Carl R. Trueman and R. Scott Clark [Eugene, OR: Wipf and Stock, 2005], 127–43). Special thanks to Joshua R. Tollett for drawing my attention to this possibility.

(Jn 1:18).² So the prudent predication of agency language in classical and Reformed Christology requires first understanding the trinitarian agency of God as Father, Son, and Holy Spirit.³

In order to highlight this trinitarian foundation for christological operations, this chapter will articulate Owen's understanding of divine agency. As the primary witness of classical and Reformed theology, this chapter will argue that Owen insists on the unity of divine agency, the triune God as a single agent (from the perspective of causality), and the triune persons as distinct agents-in-relation (from the perspective of an act's *terminus*).⁴ This articulation of the tenets of classical and Reformed theology will begin with the unity and diversity of the triune ontology (§I) before turning to the unity and diversity of triune operations (§II).

I. The Ontology of the Triune God

Owen's account of christological action is rooted in his understanding of trinitarian unity and distinction, which finds its own rooting in the essence of who God is. So in order to establish the ontological foundation of his account of triune operations, we begin with a presentation of the triune God in himself (*ad intra*). This section presents Owen's understanding of the divine nature, attributes, and persons.⁵

---

2. This is simply a recognition that the Trinity is the first "distributed doctrine" in Christian dogmatics (John Webster, *God without Measure: Working Papers in Christian Theology, Volume I, God and the Works of God* [London, Oxford, New York, New Delhi, Sydney: Bloomsbury, 2016], 117).

3. Trueman says that Owen's theology "demands that his Christology be understood within the larger Trinitarian context" (*Claims*, 151).

4. These chapters on Owen will operate from broader and more general definitions of agency/agents and gradually provide more clarity as they move into contemporary engagement in Chapters 4–6. Therefore, the later chapters will employ the definitions in Chapter 1, while this chapter and the following will use something of a minimal definition of agent as "doer of an action" and agency as "ability/capacity to act" (see WJO, *Vindication*, 2:401).

5. Trueman argues (from WJO, *Vindiciæ Evangelicæ*, 12:170–7) that Owen employs a distinction between divine "substance" and "essence" in which "essence" indicates the "whatness" of a thing, while "substance" indicates the concretization or actual being of a thing (*John Owen*, 49). While this position finds support in the text Trueman cites (and others), Owen also places the terms together in apposition. For example, five times in one paragraph Owen appositionally lists "substance" and "essence" together, as in "the nature, being, substance, or essence of God" (*Vindication*, 2:407). Therefore, I will not make a practice of technically distinguishing the terms, yet I am not denying the genuineness of the distinction everywhere in Owen, especially in *Vindiciæ Evangelicæ*, where it seems most prominent.

Starting with the unity of the one divine essence (§A), we move to distinguishing between divine persons based on their subsisting relations (§B).

A. *The Essential Unity of the Triune God*

In order to ground the unity of God conceptually, Owen looks to the one essence of the Father, Son, and Holy Spirit. For Owen the biblical testimony clearly reveals that the Father, Son, and Spirit are the one God, from which it "necessarily and unavoidably follows" that they are "one in essence."[6]

1. Simplicity and Pure Act As the one God and Creator of all, God is qualitatively distinct from creatures, antecedent and superior to all, without composition of parts or accidents. Owen appeals to God's revelation of himself to Moses as the great "I AM—that is, a simple being, existing in and of itself."[7] This affirmation from Scripture is the foundation for Owen's commitment to "the simplicity of the nature of God, and his being a simple act. The Scripture tells us he [God] is eternal, I AM, always the same, and so never what he was not ever."[8] As God's essence is synonymous with his existence ("I *am*"), God cannot "become" anything different than what he "is." This claim is integral in Owen's insistence that God is "pure act," a classical and scholastic commonplace, which means that God's being is fully actualized and contains no potentiality.[9] That is, God does not have the potential to be more loving than he eternally is, since he *is* perfectly and infinitely love.[10] Consequently, Owen insists that God is immutable (i.e., without change), perfect (cannot be improved), and all-sufficient (requiring nothing else to be who he is).[11] For Owen, God as "simple act" means that he is not composed or compounded of parts or pieces; his being is "existing in and of itself" and can never be what "he was not ever." That is, God is one in *essence* (not merely united in activity or agreement), such that the Father, Son, and Holy Spirit are God "by virtue of this

---

6. WJO, *Vindication*, 2:379.

7. WJO, *Vindiciæ Evangelicæ*, 12:71–2.

8. Ibid., 12:70; see Trueman, *John Owen*, 38 for Owen's definition of simplicity. See also Owen's treatment of Exod. 3:14 in *Glory of Christ*, 1:368. D. Stephen Long says that Owen "has one of the more in-depth accounts of simplicity found among Reformed theologians" (*The Perfectly Simple Triune God: Aquinas and His Legacy* [Minneapolis: Fortress, 2016], 154).

9. Christopher Cleveland says that Owen's doctrine is "identical to the Thomistic notion of divine simplicity" (*Thomism in John Owen* [Burlington: Ashgate, 2013], 34). See also Trueman (*John Owen*, 23) and his connection between Owen's doctrine of simplicity and Thomas Aquinas' understanding.

10. See WJO, *Arminianism*, 10:19–20; see also Turretin, *Institutes* I.3.vii; Trueman, *Claims*, 111–12.

11. WJO, *Vindiciæ Evangelicæ*, 12:72.

divine nature or being."[12] Because this divine essence is not compounded and does not possess any potency to be that which God is not, "whatever is so *in* God *is* God."[13]

Owen believed that the doctrine of simplicity is not driven by speculative Greek metaphysics, but by Scripture.[14] He says that the doctrine "is manifest from his [i.e., God's] absolute independence and firstness in being and operation, which God often insists upon in the revelation of himself," then quotes at length Isa. 44:6 and Rev. 1:8 (also noting Rev. 21:6, 22:13).[15] Since God is simple, God's being exists "in and of itself" and is without cause or dependence. For Owen, this doctrine solidifies a strong distinction and dissimilitude between God the Creator, "who dwells in unapproachable light" (1 Tim. 6:16), and ourselves as creatures.[16] Likewise, the doctrine solidifies the unity of the divine nature and grounds any claims about the divine attributes.

2. Divine Attributes (Especially Impassibility) Based on divine simplicity, whereby all that is in God *is* God, Owen considers the attributes of God to be "the same with the essence of God itself" and therefore, "essentially the same with one another."[17] Owen's classical commitment to the divine attributes will be sketched through a brief examination of one divine perfection: impassibility.[18]

Against his Socinian opponents, especially John Biddle, who claims that "the affections mentioned are really and properly in him [God] as they are in us," Owen insists that the God of the Bible is impassible; he does not suffer nor is he susceptible to the coercion of creatures.[19] However, Owen is very aware that Scripture seems

---

12. WJO, *Vindication*, 2:407; *Arminianism*, 10:44; see also *Vindiciæ Evangelicæ*, 12:72, quoting Deut. 6:4, Ps. 102:27, Exod. 3:14-15, and Rev. 1:8.

13. WJO, *Death of Death*, 10:275, emphasis mine.

14. For this point, see Christopher Cleveland's chapter on pure act in Owen and the "underlying biblical grounding" of pure act (*Thomism*, 27–68, esp. 53).

15. WJO, *Vindiciæ Evangelicæ*, 12:71.

16. WJO, *Christologia*, 1:45; *Pneumatologia*, 3:69; see also 3:38; for the "radical Creator–creature distinction" in Owen see Lim, *Mystery Unveiled*, 45; see also Kapic, *Communion*, 69–73.

17. WJO, *Vindiciæ Evangelicæ*, 12:72. Note that Owen says "essentially the same" (i.e., same in essence); therefore this text does not exclude either logical or virtual distinctions.

18. I have chosen impassibility for several reasons: (1) impassibility will be a present in multiple places later in the project; (2) it is definitively a classically trinitarian doctrine; (3) it is closely related to Owen's doctrine of simplicity and divine unity; (4) it incorporates divine acts toward creation.

19. Owen is so adamantly opposed to the attribution of passibility and (thereby mutability) to God that he avers, "A mutable god is of the dunghill" (WJO, *Death of Death*, 10:452).

to attribute emotions/passions to God (Ps. 7:11; Judg. 2:18).[20] Although making a passing note about anthropopathisms of God in *Vindiciæ Evangelicæ*,[21] Owen's primary solution to the attribution of passions to God emphasizes the Creator-creature distinction with a christological orientation.[22]

Owen locates the "pathos" attributed to God in Scripture within the incarnation of the Son of God in a passible human nature. That is, the biblical accounts of a seemingly "passionate" God are true by virtue of the hypostatic union of the divine Son, wherein his human nature is capable of suffering. He says, "The whole Old Testament, wherein God perpetually treats with men by an assumption of human affections unto himself ... proceeded from the person of the Son, in a preparation for, and prospect of, his future incarnation."[23] That is, the passions of God in the Old Testament are true on account of the "future" assumption of a human nature (and human passions) by God the Son.[24] Owen goes so far as to say that it would be "absurd" to attribute "anthropopathies, [such] as grieving, repenting, being angry, well pleased, and the like, were it not but that the divine person intended [i.e., the Son] was to take on him the nature wherein such affections do dwell."[25]

Owen's rather unique account of divine impassibility provides us with further evidence that orients his theology of the unity of the divine nature christologically. Beyond the attribute of impassibility, Owen says that Christ is the object in whom "we may contemplate and adore, all divine perfections."[26] In Christ we see the God of classical Trinitarianism embodied. This christological orientation allows Owen to insist on the classical position that God is impassible by reading the Scriptures and articulating classical theology with an eye toward the incarnation.

3. *One Will* Affirming another pillar of classical and Reformed theology, Owen states that the triune God has one will. He does so because of the Scripture's testimony regarding a singular essence of the triune God and the will's location in the essence. Owen claims that the triune God is "one ... in nature, *will*, and

---

20. On the relation and definition of affections and passions in God, see Muller, *PRRD*, 3:33.

21. WJO, *Vindiciæ Evangelicæ*, 12:109; see also *Communion*, 2:265 for "grieving the Holy Spirit"; *Vindiciæ Evangelicæ*, 12:111–12 and *Divine Justice*, 10:543 for examples of divine anger; see Trueman, *John Owen*, 45.

22. WJO, *Vindiciæ Evangelicæ*, 12:109.

23. WJO, *Christologia*, 1:89; see also *Communion*, 2:82.

24. As shown below (I.A.4), Owen's claims here are based on an understanding of the *Logos Incarnandus* that avoids the potential for eternal incarnation or the temporalization of the divine nature.

25. WJO, *Glory of Christ*, 1:350.

26. WJO, *Christologia*, 1:73; see also 1:166. Christopher Cleveland rightly says that the divine attributes describe "the manner in which God acts toward believers in Christ" (*Thomism*, 56–7).

essential properties."²⁷ Connecting the singularity of the divine will to the doctrine of divine simplicity, Owen says, "The essence of God, then, being a most absolute, pure, simple act or substance, his will consequently can be but simply one; whereof we ought to make neither division nor distinction."²⁸

Owen carefully delineates the way in which each divine person possesses the one will, wisdom, and understanding of God, stating, "The wisdom, the understanding of God, the will of God, the immensity of God, is in that person, not as that person, but as the person is God."²⁹ That is, each divine person possesses the singular divine will "as the person is God" and subsists in the one divine essence. This is true of Jesus in his divine nature "as he was the eternal Word and Wisdom of the Father … [he] had an omnisciency of the whole nature and will of God, as the Father himself hath, … their will and wisdom being the same."³⁰ Likewise, the Spirit can be said to "will," "move," and "determine" (e.g., Acts 2:4; 1 Cor. 12:11; Jn 3:8). Owen summarizes:

> The *will* is a natural property, and therefore in the divine essence it is but one. The Father, Son, and Spirit, have not distinct wills. They are one God, and God's will is one, as being an essential property of his nature; and therefore are there two wills in the one person of Christ, whereas there is but one will in the three persons of the Trinity.³¹

In Owen's insistence on the singularity and unity of the divine will, we see both the significance of the one divine essence and a foreshadowing of the subsistent relations of the divine persons.³² Owen, thus, supports a united divine essence, yet not incongruently with his support of the three divine persons as subsistent relations in the one essence.

B. The Distinction of Triune Persons

Based on Owen's understanding of the unity of the divine essence within a classical framework, we turn to Owen's understanding of distinction between trinitarian persons. This subsection will argue that Owen's doctrine of trinitarian relations

---

27. WJO, *Catechism*, 1:472.

28. WJO, *Arminianism*, 10:44. There is significant discussion on how the divine decrees and execution of the divine will relate to the divine essence (see Baylor, "Great King," 11, 13; Cleveland, *Thomism*, 39–46; Long, *The Perfectly Simple Triune God*, 150–7).

29. WJO, *Vindication*, 2:404–7.

30. WJO, *Exposition of Hebrews*, 20:30.

31. WJO, *Sacerdotal Office of Christ*, 19:87.

32. There is a lingering objection regarding God's one divine will in relation to Owen's account of the covenant of redemption (Barth, *CD* IV/1, 65). I address this objection in "John Owen as Proto-Social Trinitarian?" 225, 228–9.

2. The Evidence of Trinitarian Action

maintains continuity with the classical tradition and provides the foundation for his classical and Reformed account of trinitarian action.[33]

1. Divine Relations and Persons Owen's doctrine of the distinction of the persons in the divine essence is defined by the relations of origin and their order of subsistence. That is, the triunity of God is not to be conceived of primarily as a "unity of three" distinct persons but instead as three subsistent relations "in the same essence."[34] That is, the unity of the essence logically establishes the oneness of God, not the intimacy of their relationship (e.g., *perichoresis*).[35] Based on his doctrine of divine simplicity (whereby everything in God *is* God), Owen claims that a divine person is "*nothing but* the divine essence, upon the account of an especial Property, subsisting in an especial manner."[36] That is, rather than prioritizing an individuated consciousness or existence, a divine person is a distinct manner of subsistence in the divine essence and this distinct manner is determined by "an especial Property," a relational property (e.g., begetting the Son; being begotten of the Father).[37] As such, "In the person of the Father there is the divine essence and being, with its property of begetting the Son, subsisting in an especial manner as the Father."[38] Owen clarifies, "Because this person hath the whole divine nature, all the essential properties of that nature are in that person."[39] The relations of

---

33. As Richard Daniels rightly says, "Given the catholic character of his theology, Owen's statement of the doctrine of the Trinity is not at all unique" (*The Christology of John Owen* [Grand Rapids: Reformation Heritage, 2004], 96).

34. WJO, *Divine Original*, 16:340.

35. McGraw claims that *perichoresis* is the "foundation of the opera trinitatis principle" (*A Heavenly Directory*, 54), the "order and unity of divine operations" (68), and "mutuality of worship" (73). In addition to the evidence below for the unity of the three persons in the one essence, it ought to be noted that Owen explicitly denies the usefulness of this "barbarous term" since it communicates a "disjunction" of the three persons in "their nature and being" (WJO, *Vindiciæ Evangelicæ*, 12:73). Significantly, this claim immediately follows after Owen's presentation of divine simplicity (12:70-2) and the definition of persons according to subsistent relations (12:72-3). The best support for *perichoresis* in Owen that I have seen comes from *Exposition of Hebrews*, 20:30, yet even here (where Owen uses "συμπεριχώρησις, or in-being of each person" in a positive manner) he suggests that this mutual indwelling is "by virtue of their oneness in the same nature." Further and more specifically related to McGraw's claim, Owen connects the worship of Christ primarily to his subsistence in the divine nature (WJO, *Christologia*, 1:23-4), not his mutual indwelling with the Father.

36. WJO, *Vindication*, 2:407, emphasis mine; see also *Vindiciæ Evangelicæ*, 12:73; *Pneumatologia*, 3:77-80.

37. Contrary to Robert Letham ("John Owen's Doctrine of the Trinity in Its Catholic Context," 191).

38. WJO, *Vindication*, 2:407.

39. Ibid., 2:407.

origin (e.g., begetting, being begotten) are not "essential properties" (properties that belong to the divine essence) but "personal properties" (properties of each particular person). Therefore, for Owen the relations of origin define and constitute the divine persons.

2. *Begotten of the Father* Owen's understanding of the Son's filiation is particularly evident in his polemics against the Socinians, who claim that Christ *becomes* the Son of God and is the "son" according to office (rather than by nature). Amid this polemic, Owen's "Christological concerns," particularly his christologically oriented doctrine of God as it attends to the deity of the Son, "drive his trinitarian theology."[40] Against the Socinian claim that Christ is the Son because of his conception by the Holy Spirit, and therefore "son" as the one commissioned by God, Owen says that Christ is the Son of God "on the account of his being begotten of the essence of his Father from eternity" and "solely on this account."[41]

Defending the eternal begottenness of the Son against the biblicist Socinians, Owen often appeals to Scripture. For example, Owen appeals to Jn 5:26 ("As the Father has life in himself, so he has granted the Son also to have life in himself") and says that this life "was by the Father's communication of life unto him, and his living essence or substance; for the life that is in God differs not from his being."[42] That is, because of the doctrine of divine simplicity, the Son receives all that the Father is, yet does so as the begotten Son. Additionally, Owen sees Jn 1:1 as a summary claim of Christ's shared essence with, yet distinction from, the Father. He says, "Herein is he said to be with the Father, in respect of his distinct personal subsistence, who was one with the Father as to his nature and essence ... God by nature, and with God in his personal distinction."[43]

3. *From the Father and the Son (Filioque)* As the Son is the one who is begotten of the Father, the Holy Spirit also receives both "his substance and personality" from the Father *and* the Son, eternally proceeding from both—*filioque* (lit: "and the son").[44] Owen claims, "In the order of subsistence, he is the third person in the holy Trinity."[45] This does not mean that the Spirit partakes of the divine

---

40. Lim, *Mystery Unveiled*, 184.
41. WJO, *Vindiciæ Evangelicæ*, 12:190; see also 185; *Vindication*, 2:381–2, 407; see *The Racovian Catechism* Q.55–6 and Owen's response in WJO, *Vindiciæ Evangelicæ*, 12:178.
42. WJO, *Vindiciæ Evangelicæ*, 12:189; see also Owen's argument for the begottenness of the Son from Christ as the "essential image of the Father" in Hebrews 1; *Vindiciæ Evangelicæ*, 12:189; see also *Christologia*, 1:294–5; *Exposition of Hebrews*, 20:84–121.
43. WJO, *Vindiciæ Evangelicæ*, 12:203; see also 12:73–4, where Owen defends the eternal begottenness of the Son from Hebrews 1, Micah 5, and John 17.
44. WJO, *Communion*, 2:227.
45. WJO, *Pneumatologia*, 3:91.

nature any less, but that he proceeds from the Father and Son in his relations of origin.[46]

In order to support the divinity of the person of the Holy Spirit, Owen appeals to the biblical titles "Spirit of God" and "Spirit of Christ" as indications of the Spirit's substantial unity with the Father and the Son. Owen says that as the Son is called the Son of God "upon the account of the order and nature of personal subsistence and distinction in the holy Trinity," so also is the "person of the Holy Spirit from him [the Father] by eternal procession or emanation …. And he [the Holy Spirit] is not only called Πνεῦμα τοῦ Θεοῦ, the 'Spirit of God,' but Πνεῦμα τὸ ἐκ τοῦ Θεοῦ, 'the Spirit that is of God,' which proceedeth from him as a distinct person."[47] Similarly, the Spirit is called the "Spirit of the Son" because he proceeds from the Son.[48] Owen concludes, "For the order of the dispensation of the divine persons towards us ariseth from the order of their own subsistence in the same divine essence; and if the Spirit did proceed only from the person of the Father, he could not be promised, sent, or given by the Son."[49] This further evidences the importance of the intra-trinitarian relations and hints at the relationship between trinitarian relations *ad intra* and trinitarian actions *ad extra*.

Owen provides the metaphor of a human breath to illustrate the unity and distinction of the Spirit with (and from) the Father and the Son: "For as the vital breath of a man hath a continual emanation from him, and yet is never separated utterly from his person or forsaketh him, so doth the Spirit of the Father and the Son proceed from them by a continual divine emanation, still abiding one with them."[50] For Owen, the Spirit is a distinct subsistent relation in the one divine essence insofar as the Spirit is spirated by the Father and Son, yet equal in power and glory.

C. Summary

This section sought to confirm Carl Trueman's claim that regarding "the basic contours and substance of his doctrine of God," Owen is a "rather typical figure" who builds "on a long-standing Christian heritage."[51] For Owen, the unity of the triune God is founded upon the unity of the one divine essence within which the subsisting relations (i.e., persons) are thereby distinguished. Owen's account of

---

46. See Trueman, *John Owen*, 57 for an elaboration on the *filioque* in Owen. See also his insistence that "the Western order of procession is integral to the whole scheme" of Owen's thought (*Claims*, 120).

47. WJO, *Pneumatologia*, 3:59–60; see also 3:66–7.

48. On the doctrine of the *filioque* in Owen as it relates to trinitarian and christological action, see Kieser, "Is the Filioque an Obstacle," 399–402.

49. WJO, *Pneumatologia*, 3:61. For more on the theological and biblical justification for the *filioque*, see *Vindiciæ Evangelicæ*, 12:74; *Communion*, 2:175, 226.

50. WJO, *Pneumatologia*, 3:55.

51. Trueman, *John Owen*, 46.

unity and distinction is rooted not in three distinctly existing agents but in the one essence, within which the three persons subsist in relation to one another. Owen summarizes his understanding of the unity and distinction of the divine persons in his *Vindication of the Doctrine of the Trinity*: "Our conclusion from the whole is,—that there is nothing more fully expressed in the Scripture than this sacred truth, that there is one God, Father, Son, and Holy Ghost."[52] Owen then elaborates on this claim, starting with the unity of the divine essence. He denies that agreement, or mutual actions, of the three persons constitute their oneness in the Godhead. Instead, he insists that the one nature of the Father, Son, and Holy Spirit is "one and the same absolutely in and unto each of them … [and] herein consists the unity of the Godhead."[53] That is, each of the divine persons is fully God because each person subsists in the one divine essence. From there, he summarizes the distinctions between the persons, reminding the reader that "a divine person is nothing but the divine essence, upon the account of an especial Property, subsisting in an especial manner."[54] The distinction between the divine persons, then, "lieth in this,—that the Father begetteth the Son, and the Son is begotten of the Father, and the Holy Spirit proceedeth from both of them"; Owen insists that these "distinctions named are clearly revealed in the Scripture."[55] Articulating the unity of the divine essence, the distinction of subsistent relations, and the doctrine of divine simplicity, Owen avers, "Because this person hath the whole divine nature, all the essential properties of that nature are in that person. The wisdom, the understanding of God, the will of God, the immensity of God, is in that person, not as that person, but as the person is God."[56] Owen continues, "Now, as the nature of this distinction lies in their mutual relation one to another, so it is the foundation of those distinct actings and operations whereby the distinction itself is clearly manifested and confirmed."[57] That is, Owen builds his account of trinitarian action upon this unity of the divine essence and subsisting relations of the divine persons. The unity and distinction of his account of trinitarian operations do not depart from, but are built off this understanding of divine unity.

II. The Operations of the Triune God

Upon the ontological foundation of the above, this section will argue that Owen provides an account of unified and singular triune "agency" (i.e., capacity and ability for intentional action), yet is able to distinguish between the actions of three divine "agents-in-relation" (i.e., three persons who intentionally act according to

---

52. WJO, *Vindication*, 2:406.
53. Ibid., 2:407.
54. Ibid., 2:407.
55. Ibid., 2:405.
56. Ibid., 2:407.
57. Ibid., 2:406.

2. The Evidence of Trinitarian Action

their own modes of relating). As we will see, "The order of operation in the blessed Trinity, as unto outward works, answereth unto and followeth the order of their subsistence."[58] That is, fundamental to this section is the claim that the external acts of God mirror the internal nature and relations in God. Consequently, the following two sections will defend the unity of divine agency and the distinction of the divine agents-in-relation. These affirmations allow Owen to maintain the unity of divine agency and action yet predicate specific actions (utilizing appropriations) to specific divine persons in a way that solidifies Owen's continuity with classical Trinitarianism and, thereby, classical and Reformed theology.[59]

A. The Unity of Divine Agency

Owen roots the acts of the one God toward creation so strongly in the essence and relations of the one God in himself that he claims the economic unity and ordering "necessarily follows" and is "directly included" in Scripture's revelation of "God and his subsistence."[60] Because of this ontological foundation, the one God acts as one in everything he does in creation.

1. Singular Agency Based on the simple divine nature, the triune God's agency is singular. That is, each of the divine persons (based on their subsistence in the same essence) shares the same capacity and ability for intentional action. This includes the same will, power, and knowledge while it necessarily *excludes* three independent capacities for intentional action or naturally subordinated capacities of one person under another. Owen asserts that, by virtue of the oneness in the divine nature, the Son "had an omnisciency of the whole nature and will of God, as the Father himself hath, … their will and wisdom being the same."[61]

As the unity of agency is derived from the unity of the divine essence, Owen employed the unity of divine agency in order to defend the deity of the Spirit and reject the ontological subordination of the Son. Commenting on 1 Cor. 2:10, Owen claims that the capacity to know all things (which he determines to be the meaning of "to search everything") is to be omniscient, and "he that is omniscient is God."[62] He argues that the Spirit, like the spirit of a human person, knows the things of that person because of its sharing in the understanding, will, and power of them, "so it is with the Spirit of God: being God, and having the same understanding,

---

58. WJO, *Sacerdotal Office of Christ*, 19:34.

59. See my narration of those who suggest that Owen, by contrast, radically distinguishes operations of divine persons in "John Owen as Proto-Social Trinitarian?" 225-6 and my response in ibid., 229-31.

60. WJO, *Vindication*, 2:407.

61. WJO, *Exposition of Hebrews*, 20:30.

62. WJO, *Vindiciæ Evangelicæ*, 12:335.

and will, and power, with God the Father and Son."⁶³ Likewise, the Son's sharing of the same essence, power, and glory with the Father indicates that "absolutely, therefore, and naturally, in that respect he is capable of no subordination to the Father or exaltation by him."⁶⁴ Owen concludes by reassuring the reader that any subordination of the Son to the Father is "official" (i.e., belonging to his *office* as the mediator) and not essential to the Son as he is God. He claims, "We confess that as Christ is equal with his Father as to his nature, wherein he is God, so as he is the Son in office, he was the servant of the Father."⁶⁵

The claim of singular agency, as it is rooted in the one divine nature, positions Owen's doctrine of triune operations in terms of the unity of the triune God and continuity within the classical and Reformed tradition.

2. Principle of Operation To solidify further the unity and singular agency of God, Owen employs the concept of a single "principle of action." In order to show the impossibility of dividing actions between divine persons to the exclusion of the others, Owen contends, "The nature of God, which is the principle of all divine operations, is one and the same, undivided in them all."⁶⁶

Like the conciliar conclusions of Constantinople III, Owen treats "principles of operation" as capacities and abilities that are inherent to natures and therefore predicated of natures rather than persons.⁶⁷ He glosses the "principle of operation" as the "principle by which [agents] work."⁶⁸ Owen notes this in the natural world, whereby it is the "principles of their operations" that enable the sun to produce

---

63. Ibid., 12:335.

64. WJO, *Exposition of Hebrews*, 20:224. Contra John Starke, "Augustine and His Interpreters," in *One God in Three Persons: Unity of Essence, Distinction of Persons, Implications for Life*, ed. Bruce A. Ware and John Starke (Wheaton: Crossway, 2015), 164. Owen claims that it is the relation of origin alone (i.e., not submission) which distinguishes the Father from the Son. See Stephen R. Holmes, "Classical Trinitarianism and Eternal Functional Subordination: Some Historical and Dogmatic Reflections,"*SBET* 35 (2017): 90–104, esp. 100–1; *Sacerdotal Office of Christ*, 19:88. In Owen, see *Communion*, 2:235; *Vindiciæ Evangelicæ*, 12:497; *Sacerdotal Office of Christ*, 19:77–89 in order to see his use of the divine will in the triune acts of God.

65. WJO, *Vindiciæ Evangelicæ*, 12:326; see also 12:188, 292–9, 420; *Communion*, 2:229. For supporting interpretations, see Lim, *Mystery*, 185; Kay, *Trinitarian Spirituality*, 34; Muller, *DLGTT*, 308; Baylor, "Great King," 168–9.

66. WJO, *Pneumatologia*, 3:162; contrary to Spence (*Incarnation and Inspiration*, 129), who says that there are distinct principles of operations in the distinct persons; unfortunately, Spence does not connect this claim to Christology or the claims of Constantinople III.

67. WJO, *Pneumatologia*, 3:221, 447, where he says "a nature is the principle of all operations." See also 3:386; *Arminianism*, 10:35; *Justification*, 5:255.

68. WJO, *Righteous Zeal*, 8:156; see *Vindiciæ Evangelicæ*, 12:71 for his connection between a singular principle of operation and divine simplicity.

the "effects of light and heat," of "fire to burn," of "wind to blow."[69] This is true of both "natural" subjects (e.g., wind, water) and "intentional" subjects of actions (i.e., divine and human agents). In human capacities, Owen connects the ability to bring some effect about with the principle of operation in the subject of that action.[70] Since a principle of operation is defined as the capacity/ability by which a subject of intentionally accomplishes any action, it maps onto the concept of agency. Therefore, the singular principle of operation in the triune God indicates that the agency of the triune God is singular.[71]

3. Indivisible Operations Owen's account of the triune acts of God further mirrors the unity of the divine essence in his claim that "the Lord Christ and the Holy Spirit are one in nature, essence, will, and power ... as his works were the works of the Father, and the works of the Father were his, all the operations of the holy Trinity, as to things external unto their divine subsistence, being undivided."[72] For Owen and much of the classical and Reformed traditions, the voluntary acts of the triune God (who is one in essence, power, and will) *ad extra* (i.e., toward

---

69. WJO, *Exposition of Hebrews*, 20:106.

70. For Owen's treatment of the corruption of human nature by sin and its consequential fallen principles of operation, see WJO, *Righteous Zeal*, 8:157; *Perseverance*, 11:512–13, 590; *Pneumatologia*, 3:483; *Indwelling Sin*, 6:170–1; *Spiritual Mindedness*, 7:279; *Exposition of Hebrews*, 21:25.

71. As potential evidence to the contrary, Owen does state, "There is one God, Father, Son, and Holy Ghost; which are divine, distinct, intelligent, voluntary, omnipotent *principles* of operation and working" (WJO, *Vindication*, 2:406; as picked up by Spence, *Incarnation and Inspiration*, 128 and Tyler R. Wittman, "The End of the Incarnation: John Owen, Trinitarian Agency and Christology," *IJST* 15 [2013]: 292). However, Owen clarifies earlier that the three persons are "distinct, living, divine, intelligent, voluntary *principles of operation or working*" primarily "in and by internal acts one towards another" such that "this distinction originally lieth in this,—that the Father begetteth the Son, and the Son is begotten of the Father, and the Holy Spirit proceedeth from both of them" (2:405). These clarifications of the "internal acts" and the relations of origins locate this discussion of distinct principles of operation within the context of relations *ad intra* and distinguished by their "mutual relation one to another." Within this context, Owen can claim that "one of them is the object of another's actings" (2:406). Just a few pages later, Owen regards a "principle of ... acts and operations" to be a predicate of natures (2:433). Therefore, the distinction here between "principles" ought not imply that each person has a different capacity or ability to act any more than this sentence ought to be taken to mean that the persons have different intellects or wills. Therefore, this plural use of "principles" is due to Owen's concern about the *ad intra* acts of the persons toward one another, rather than the *ad extra* works of the triune God and an unfortunate inconsistency in his corpus. For more on internal and external acts, see WJO, *Pneumatologia*, 3:158; see also 3:66–7; Cleveland, "Covenant," 74–8.

72. WJO, *Exposition of Psalm 130*, 4:358.

creation) are indivisibly acts of all three persons.[73] Owen boldly claims, "There is, indeed, no gracious influence from above, no illapse of light, life, love, or grace upon our hearts, but proceedeth in such a dispensation" (i.e., through the indivisible operations of the triune God).[74] Owen recognizes indivisible operations as revealed in Scripture and firmly held in the tradition, such that interpreters rightly say that Owen implements it as the "regulative principle in his theological thinking" and the foundational "axiom" for his thought.[75] Owen says, "Now, the works that outwardly are of God (called '*Trinitatis ad extra*'), which are commonly said to be common and undivided," comprise "a concurrence of the actings and operations of the whole Deity in that dispensation, wherein each person concurs to the work of our salvation."[76] The unity of the indivisible works is rooted in the unity of the divine essence and the distinct predication of these works to distinct divine persons is rooted in the order of their subsistence in the divine nature. Trueman says that the doctrine of indivisible operations of the triune God "is an obvious implication of belief in the consubstantiality of the three persons of the Godhead" and that "the Western order of procession is integral to the whole scheme."[77]

This doctrine is especially significant in Owen's work on the Holy Spirit, *Pneumatologia*, where he begins by affirming that the acts of God are attributed to "God absolutely" (i.e., the triune God) because of the indivisibility of triune operations. Owen says, "The several persons are undivided in their operations, acting all by the same will, the same wisdom, the same power. Every person, therefore, is the author of every work of God, because each person is God, and the divine nature is the same undivided principle of all divine operations; and this ariseth from the unity of the persons in the same essence."[78] Here we see the singularity of the divine will and agency, the indivisibility of divine action and its basis in the indivisibility of the divine nature, and the unity of the singular "undivided principle" of divine operations. Owen continues, "In the undivided operation of the divine nature, each person doth the same work in the order of their subsistence ... as one common principle of authority, wisdom, love, and power."[79] Each person shares in the agency of God by virtue of their common principle of "authority, wisdom, love, and power." As such, the acts of God are considered to be acts of the entire Godhead. It is not as though "one person succeeded unto another in their operation, or as though where one ceased and gave over a work,

---

73. See Muller, *DLGTT*, 213.

74. WJO, *Communion*, 2:15.

75. Quotes from Daniels, *Christology of John Owen*, 101 and Paul Lim, *Mystery*, 202, respectively. See WJO, *Vindication*, 2:407; *Christologia*, 1:162, where he calls this the "generally admitted principle" throughout the tradition up to his own day.

76. WJO, *Communion*, 2:18. See also 2:268–9.

77. Trueman, *Claims*, 120.

78. WJO, *Pneumatologia*, 3:93.

79. Ibid., 3:93–4.

the other took it up and carried it on"; instead, "every divine work, and every part of every divine work, is the work of God, that is, of the whole Trinity, inseparably and undividedly."[80]

4. *The Triune Agent (Singular)* Based on the single agency of the triune God (which is itself rooted in the single divine will and power of the divine nature), and the indivisible operations of God (likewise rooted in the simplicity and unity of the divine nature), Owen sometimes calls the triune God himself an "agent." Owen particularly takes note of the freedom, and therefore intentional action, of God in his description of the Trinity as an agent. He says, "God [is] a free agent, and acts freely in what he doth, which is a necessary mode of all divine actings *ad extra*."[81] Based on Scripture's testimony, Owen states, "God being a most perfect, and therefore *a most free agent*, all his actings towards mankind ... are to be resolved into his own sovereign will and pleasure."[82]

Even more explicitly, in the *Death of Death*, Owen considers the triune God a singular agent in the act of redemption. Emphasizing the unity of the external operations and the equity of capacity in the divine persons, Owen says, "The *agent* in, and chief author of, this great work of our redemption is the whole blessed Trinity; for all the works which outwardly are of the Deity are undivided and belong equally to each person."[83] Here Owen links the indivisibility of operations, based on the one divine essence, and the predication of the triune God as a singular agent.

When Owen speaks of the triune God as a single agent, he is speaking from (what I will call) the "perspective of causality." So while Owen is insistent on the singularity of the action and the singularity of the cause, he recognizes the involvement of all three persons in every divine action. I might borrow the analogy of a magnet in order to illustrate the indivisibility of triune operations, the singularity of the triune agent, and the possibility of distinct actions by the Father, Son, and Holy Spirit.[84] When we consider a magnet, we recognize the entire magnet as causing the attraction of a paperclip to itself. Nevertheless, the paperclip is attracted to only one pole. So the magnet is like the singular triune agent and yet acts can *terminate* on one person or another like a paperclip can attach to one pole or the other. From this analogy we can see how Owen speaks of one agent from the perspective of causality, yet recognizes that we might also speak

---

80. Ibid., 3:94–5. For additional defenses of Owen's classical account of indivisible operations, see Wittman, "The End of the Incarnation;" Johnson, "The Work of the Holy Spirit in the Ministry of Jesus Christ," 160–6; Vidu, "Trinitarian Inseparable Operations and the Incarnation," 112.

81. WJO, *Sacerdotal Office of Christ*, 19:106.

82. WJO, *Justification*, 5:240.

83. WJO, *Death of Death*, 10:163, emphasis mine.

84. Vidu, "Ascension and Pentecost," 107; however, Vidu does not explicitly connect this to the triune God as a "single agent."

of distinction from the perspective of the *terminus* of the action. By observing the resulting effect upon the paperclip, we might distinguish between the two poles of the magnet in the action and rightly appropriate the *terminus* of that action to one pole, not the other. Accordingly, Owen expands on the singularity of the triune agent by clarifying that when the "distinct manner of subsistence and order" of the three persons is observed, we might rightly predicate the label "agent" to each of the divine persons in their orderly relations to the other divine persons (what I will call agents-in-relation throughout the project). He is, therefore, basing the possibility of distinction *ad extra* on the relations of origin *ad intra*.

So while the singular "*agent* in ... our redemption is the whole blessed Trinity," Owen goes on in the same treatise to attribute the label "agent" to each divine person and describe the three persons as "these three blessed agents."[85] He claims that the Son "was an *agent* in this great work [of redemption]" and, similarly, "we may consider the actions of that *agent*, who in order is the third in that blessed One, ... the Holy Spirit."[86] The criteria for this distinction, while not yet fully evident, are necessarily based on the unity of the divine nature and the distinction of the relations of origin insofar as they are reflected in the acts of the triune God *ad extra*. Nevertheless, this does not mean that the distinctions indicate discrete actions or parts of actions. Indeed, Owen says, "Every divine work, and every part of every divine work, is the work of God, that is, of the whole Trinity, inseparably and undividedly."[87] So the triune God is a single agent who causes every act, yet this causing agent subsists in three persons.

B. The Distinctions of the Divine Agents-in-Relation

The Death of Death presents both the unity and diversity of the triune God in the work of redemption. This is made evident even by the table of contents, which lists the chapter headings of Book 1:

> III.—Of the *agent* or chief author of the work of our redemption, and of the first thing distinctly ascribed to the person of the Father
> IV.—Of those things which in the work of redemption are peculiarly ascribed to the person of the Son

---

85. WJO, *Death of Death*, 10:175, emphasis mine. This might be compared to Owen's willingness to use both the singular pronoun "he" for God and "they" for the Father, Son, and Holy Spirit (Kapic, *Communion*, 159); cf. Tay, *Priesthood of Christ*, 57.

86. WJO, *Death of Death*, 10:174, 178, emphases mine.

87. WJO, *Pneumatologia*, 3:94; likewise, Polanus, *Syntagma*, VI.xiii (p. 364); found in Muller, *PRRD* 4:272. For a similar affirmation in the medieval scholastic tradition, see Gilles Emery, "The Personal Mode of Trinitarian Action in Saint Thomas Aquinas," *The Thomist* 69 (2005): 42.

V.—The peculiar actions of the Holy Spirit in this business
VI.—The means used by the fore-recounted *agents* in this work.[88]

The above subsection (§II.A) articulated the unity of the triune operations, essentially the content of chapter III in *The Death of Death in the Death of Christ* Book 1. This subsection will investigate the nature of the distinction of the divine persons in their actions—how it is that we can predicate actions to different divine persons, rightly predicating the title "agent" to each,[89] without violating the preceding discussion of divine unity.

Materially this subsection argues that from the perspective of an act's *terminus* Owen can name the divine persons as three distinct agents-in-relation, three personal subsistences of the one divine substance who enact the one divine will modally (e.g., the Son enacts the divine will in a filial way).[90] This is based on (rather than despite) the unity of the simple nature of God, divine persons as subsistent relations, and a classical account of divine relations (i.e., *filioque*). Ultimately, this modal ascription will be employed in the following chapter on Christology so that we might understand how we can predicate the accomplishment of Christ's actions to the Son while still providing a triune account of christological action.

1. Operations Ad Extra *Mirroring Relations* Ad Intra Introduced above through Owen's connection between the ontological and operational, this subsection articulates the viability of understanding the external acts of God as founded upon, and mirroring, the essence and subsisting relations. For Owen, the unity and simplicity of the divine essence determine the unity of the operations *ad extra*. Likewise, the relations *ad intra* determine the order and distinction of operations *ad extra*.[91] As Owen says, "The order of operation in the blessed Trinity, as unto

---

88. WJO, *Death of Death*, 10:iv, emphasis mine; I am here assuming that the chapter titles are original to Owen on the basis of the conventions of editorial additions that these headings lack (see WJO, *General Preface*, 1:xiii–xiv). However, as we will see, Owen uses this language throughout. So even if they are editorial additions, they are accurate.

89. This seems to be the referent of agent that Owen has in mind when he defines an agent as "personal subsistence, that hath being, life, and will" (WJO, *Vindication*, 2:401).

90. When I use the phrase "agents-in-relation" each component is pertinent to its meaning such that I mean to (a) emphasize distinct "agents," that each divine person is intentionally producing an effect and is within this action distinguishable from the other divine persons (from the perspective of an act's *terminus*); (b) emphasize "in relation," that multiple distinguishable agents do not indicate distinct "agency," independent agents, or distinct intentions; and (c) avoid confusion or connotations of univocal language (such as merely using "agent"). On this last point, see Johnson, "The Work of the Holy Spirit in the Ministry of Jesus Christ," 152 n. 28.

91. For this principle in the Augustinian tradition, see Keith Johnson, *Rethinking the Trinity and Religious Pluralism: An Augustinian Assessment* (Downers Grove, IL: InterVarsity, 2011), 102.

outward works, answereth unto and followeth the order of their subsistence," such that "they have the same dependence on each other in their operations as they have in their subsistence."[92]

In God's acts toward creation, the order of divine relations is made visible. Owen says as much in *Communion with God*, "And this relation *ad extra* (as they call it) of the Spirit unto the Father and the Son, in respect of operation, proves his relation *ad intra*, in respect of personal procession."[93] Not only do the divine actions toward creation make visible the relations *ad intra* but these actions are founded upon or, as Owen says, "answer to" the relations *ad intra*.[94] Trueman calls this a "basic axiom" of Owen's theology.[95] As Richard Muller says, this mirroring did not separate the acts of the distinct persons, but allows us to understand the acts of the triune God according to the "modes of operation in the ultimately undivided work of the Godhead."[96] This "rule," for Owen, articulates that (epistemologically) the acts of God in history reveal who God is in himself and that the nature of God in himself (ontologically) grounds God's actions in history.[97] Therefore, we come to know God insofar as God has made himself known "by creation, redemption, and sanctification."[98] God's being is "made known" (not "determined" or "constituted") by these acts because his triune nature undergirds and establishes them.[99]

Unity and distinction *ad intra*, thereby, establish (and are revealed by) the indivisibility and appropriated distinction of acts *ad extra*. On this point, explicitly citing Owen, Muller says, "Just as there is a single divine essence, there is a single *ad extra* divine work—so also, just as there are three persons or modes of subsistence in the Godhead, each distinguished by personal properties and a

---

92. WJO, *Sacerdotal Office of Christ*, 19:34; see also *Pneumatologia*, 3:92. Earlier on this same page he claims, "This constitutes the natural order between the persons, which is unalterable. On this depends the order of his operation; for his working is a consequent of the order of his subsistence." Elsewhere Owen says that unity and distinction of external triune acts "necessarily follow" from the unity of the divine nature and subsistent relations of the persons (*Vindication*, 2:407).

93. WJO, *Communion*, 2:226–7.

94. Ibid., 2:229; cf. *Pneumatologia*, 3:107, where Owen says that "the economy of the blessed Trinity in the work of our redemption and salvation is respected in this order of things" (i.e., "The order of the subsistence of the three persons in the divine nature is regarded").

95. Trueman, *Claims*, 132; see also Daniels, *Christology of John Owen*, 105.

96. Muller, *PRRD*, 4:268; e.g., Turretin, *Institutes*, I:3.xxii.20.

97. Trueman says of the eternal relations and the acts of God in time: "The former [is] the ontic ground for the latter, and the latter the noetic ground for the former" (*John Owen*, 50).

98. WJO, *Catechism*, 1:473.

99. This is contra Letham, who postulates that the relations of origin are not sufficient to distinguish between divine persons and that we must also include their economic activity (*Holy Trinity*, 418).

specific operation, there are also three modes of working in the single *ad extra* divine work."[100]

2. Divine Missions Further evidencing Owen's rule of triune acts mirroring the triune essence, we turn to the beginning of *Pneumatologia*, where Owen says that God appointed two means for the "great and glorious work of recovering fallen man and the saving of sinners" and "two heads of the promise of God," the missions of the Son and Spirit.[101] These trinitarian acts of redemption reveal the character of the triune God to the glory of the triune God. Owen says,

> Hereby were the love, grace, and wisdom of the Father, in the design and projection of the whole; the love, grace, and condescension of the Son, in the execution, purchase, and procurement of grace and salvation for sinners; with the love, grace, and power of the Holy Spirit, in the effectual application of all unto the souls of men,—made gloriously conspicuous.[102]

These divine missions, the condescension of the Son and the sending of the Spirit, are the pinnacle of all divine work and the means of human salvation.[103]

Founded on the principle of external acts mirroring internal relations, we see that these divine missions are brought about according to the order of subsistence. Owen claims that the mission of the Holy Spirit by the Father and the Son "answers the order of the persons' subsistence in the blessed Trinity, and his procession from them both" and upon this "unalterable" order of the processions "depends the order of his operation; for his working is a consequent of the order of his subsistence."[104]

As such, Owen aligns himself with the classical tradition, especially Thomas Aquinas. Thomas claims that a divine mission is simply the procession of a divine person plus a created effect in the creature, what Owen calls an "especial impression."[105] Lodging this affirmation in the created effect protects against the possibility of introducing a change in God, reinforcing his immutability.[106] Further, in each act there is an "especial impression of the order of the operation, with

---

100. Muller, *PRRD*, 4:268; he cites WJO, *Communion*, 2:209.

101. Owen does not use the language of "mission" as frequently as some of his theological forebears, but he does employ it occasionally (e.g., WJO, *Communion*, 2:222, 226, 229). For Augustine's treatment of the divine missions, see Augustine, *Trinity*, ii.2; iv.5; for Thomas see *ST* I, Q.43; I–II, Q.110.

102. WJO, *Pneumatologia*, 3:23.

103. Owen says, "To these heads may all the promises of God be reduced" (ibid., 3:23).

104. WJO, *Communion*, 2:229; *Pneumatologia*, 3:92.

105. Aquinas, *ST* I, Q.43, A.1. For the importance of the impression of a relation in the created effects, see WJO, *Communion*, 2:234.

106. For example, the Son being "sent" does not imply local motion for the divine person as it would for a human (WJO, *Pneumatologia*, 3:111; cf. *ST* I, Q.43, A.1, ad.2).

respect unto their natural and necessary subsistence."[107] This "especial impression" in the creature (i.e., the created effect) corresponds to a relation of the subsistences in God and is thereby predicated of the person who bears that relation of origin. For example, the production of creation (a created effect) is appropriated to the Father insofar as the Father is the one who produces (or, better, begets) another in the triune relations of origin. Likewise, the Son as the one begotten of the Father (the "fount" of divinity *ad intra*) is the "stream" by which "we are led up unto the fountain" and the "beams" of light by which we "see the sun ... of eternal love itself."[108]

3. Appropriations As Owen articulates the distinction between persons in divine action, he bases the distinction on the "manner of subsistence therein, [that] there is distinction, relation, and order between and among them."[109] Moreover, because the external works mirror the *ad intra* relations, Owen concludes: "Hence there is no divine work but is distinctly assigned unto each person, and eminently unto one."[110] That is, each work is rightly said to be caused by all three persons (because of their single agency and principle of operation), yet it may be eminently ascribed to one divine person by virtue of the correspondence of the created effect with the relation of origin. He says, "When any especial impression is made of the especial property of any person on any work; then is that work assigned peculiarly to that person."[111] That is, the correspondence of the created effect to the personal relation justifies the appropriation of a particular action to that divine person. Later, he states that by the divine works *ad extra* "there is an especial impression of the order of the operation of each person, with respect unto their natural and necessary subsistence" in which we are "distinctly taught to know them and adore" each divine person.[112]

As the created effects reflect the relation *ad intra*, we see further support for the mirroring of distinction *ad intra* in the works *ad extra*. Owen clarifies that the "order of operation" among the persons "depends on the order of their subsistence."[113] That is, the acts and ordering *ad extra* mirror the relations *ad intra*. For Owen, this means that the works of "power and authority" belong eminently to the Father, "the procurement of grace" and display of wisdom to the Son, and the "works of God whereby grace is made effectual unto us" to the Spirit.[114] Owen summarizes:

107. WJO, *Pneumatologia*, 3:94–5.
108. WJO, *Communion*, 2:23. These analogies are commonplace in the Fathers (Lim, *Mystery*, 191–2).
109. WJO, *Pneumatologia*, 3:93.
110. Ibid.
111. Ibid., 3:93–4.
112. Ibid., 3:94–5.
113. Ibid., 3:94.
114. Ibid.

2. The Evidence of Trinitarian Action

God plainly declares that the foundation of the whole was laid in the counsel, will, and grace of the Father, chap. 1:3–6 [of Ephesians]; then ... the accomplishing of that counsel of his ... is by the mediation of the Son .... There yet remains the actual application of all to the souls of men, that they may be partakers of the grace designed in the counsel of the Father, and prepared in the mediation of the Son; and herein is the Holy Spirit to be manifested and ... [t]his is the work that he hath undertaken."[115]

Owen elaborates upon this pattern of divine originating (appropriated to the Father), accomplishing/procuring (the Son), and perfecting/applying (the Spirit) throughout his corpus.[116] Owen's designation of the Father as source, Son as wisdom and executer, and Spirit as power and efficacy is not unique to Owen but is a fixture throughout the tradition.[117] Likewise, he is insistent with the tradition that the appropriations and the predication of distinct modes of acting to particular divine persons do not indicate a distinction in causality (i.e., that one person exclusively does an act or that one person does one portion of an act), but that these distinct predications are referring to the "*terminus*" of an action insofar as the possibility of ascribing distinct acts to distinct persons is "on the account of the order of his subsistence in the holy Trinity."[118] For Owen the doctrine of appropriations is not simply a dogmatic consequence but a tool that allows the Christian to understand the work of God in Scripture and her intimate fellowship with the God who is Father, Son, and Holy Spirit.[119]

---

115. Ibid., 3:190.

116. See especially Owen's treatment of Acts 2:24 and 1 Pet. 3:18 in ibid., 3:181–2. I will call this a "perspective of an action" because it seems that the "planning," "executing," and "application" of an action all share the same created effect (e.g., the effectual call of a person), yet they describe different perspectives on the same action. Therefore, we can appropriate different acts to different persons when those acts themselves correspond to a relation (e.g., sanctification to the Holy Spirit), and we can additionally appropriate a particular perspective on that act to a distinct divine person when that perspective corresponds to a relation (e.g., the willing of God's people to be sanctified is attributed to the Father [1 Pet. 1:15]).

117. For example, Basil, "On the Holy Spirit," *NPNF*[2] 8:23–6; Gregory of Nyssa, "An Answer to Ablabius: That We Should Not Think of Saying There Are Three Gods," in *Christology of the Later Fathers*, LCC, ed. Edward R. Hardy (Louisville: Westminster John Knox, 1954), 262. Calvin, *Institutes*, I.xiii.18; Thomas Goodwin, *The Work of the Holy Ghost in Our Salvation*, Works of Thomas Goodwin 6 (Edinburgh: Banner of Truth, 1979), IX.i.405; Hermann Venema, *Translation of Hermann Venema's Inedited Institutes of Theology* (Edinburgh: T&T Clark, 1850), X.222; Henk van den Belt et al., eds., *Synopsis Puioris Theologiae; Synopsis of a Purer Theology: Latin Text and English Translation Volume 2 Disputations 24–2*, trans. Riemer A. Faber, SMRTTS 8 (Boston: Brill, 2016), 2:71; Barth, *CD* I/1, 375.

118. Ibid., 3:162.

119. For the role of appropriations in Owen's devotional treatment of communion with God, see *Communion*, 2:11, 18, 269; cf. Kieser, "John Owen as Proto-Social Trinitarian?" 226, 232–4.

4. The Dogmatic Necessity of Three Distinct Agents-in-Relation (Plural)

By means of appropriation and the predication of distinct action to distinct persons from the perspective of the *terminus* of an action, not only *might* the theologian predicate "agent" (in terms of agents-in-relation) to each divine person but (according to Owen) she *must* make this theological judgment in order to recognize the divinity and personhood of all three.[120] Although it may appear as though this theological move inclines us toward the edge of tri-theism, Owen insists that it is necessary if we are to avoid the other cliffs of modalism and Arianism.

While Owen affirms that each divine person is an agent-in-relation, the necessity of this claim is particularly potent in his polemical engagements with the Socinians over the personhood and divinity of the Holy Spirit (i.e., is the Spirit an agent and, if so, is this agent divine?).[121] In *Pneumatologia*, a publication which Owen says declares the divinity of the Holy Spirit "and his operations" on "almost every page," Owen says that Scripture (e.g., 1 Cor. 2:10; Rom. 8:16, 26) "undeniably denotes a personal action" of the Spirit and "proves him to be an understanding agent."[122] The Spirit is a "voluntary agent" who possesses the divine will as God, and therefore wills to act, even when it is said that he is sent.[123] Elsewhere Owen defends the validity of the Spirit as an "agent" against the supposition that the Spirit is merely a quality of grace or a force in God by appealing to the "personal operations" (i.e., "such acts and actings as are proper to a person only").[124] Based on texts that indicate the Spirit's indwelling believers (e.g., 1 Cor. 3:16; 6:19), Owen says that "qualities ... cannot be said to *dwell*."[125] Instead, "This the Spirit doth [i.e., does dwell in believers], and therefore as a voluntary agent in a habitation, not as a necessary or natural principle in a subject. He exerteth and puts forth his power, and brings forth his grace, in the

---

120. By using the language of "judgment" (drawing from David S. Yeago, "The New Testament and the Nicene Dogma: A Contribution to the Recovery of Theological Exegesis," *Pro Ecclesia* 3 [1994]: 152–64), I am indicating that this claim does not require every theologian to use the label "agent" or "agent-in-relation" of each divine person. Instead, I mean to say that the theological claim to which the attribution of three agents-in-relation points must be affirmed—regardless of the term that any given theologian may use (e.g., person, actor, mode of being).

121. Important for Owen's polemical context is the Racovian Catechism's affirmation that the Spirit is merely a divine power or force (not an agent), and John Biddle's (Owen's most proximate Socinian interlocutor) argument that the Spirit is an agent (but not a fully divine agent) (see Owen's assessment of this reality in WJO, *Vindiciæ Evangelicæ*, 12:343). Notice below how Owen argues for the Spirit as both divine and an agent.

122. WJO, *Pneumatologia*, 3:85.

123. Ibid., 3:112.

124. WJO, *Perseverance*, 11:335.

125. Ibid., 11:336, emphasis mine.

hearts of them with whom he dwells, as he pleaseth."[126] Notice that Owen is distinguishing the Spirit from a "natural" force (like fire or gravity, which would not include intention), and from the "principle" of an agent's action as that by which an agent performs the action (as in the "principle of operations" above). Owen adamantly concludes that the Spirit "is an intelligent, voluntary, divine agent," resolutely proclaiming, "If the Spirit isn't an agent, and therefore person, then the Scriptures were meant to deceive us."[127] So the distinction of the divine persons in the indivisible acts of God is not a mere word-game but biblically and theological significant.

C. Summary

This section has argued for Owen's understanding of the triune God's actions as rooted in the unity and distinction of his essence. Because of the shared and singular essential properties, the three divine persons share a single divine agency, from the singular divine principle of operations. As such every act of the triune God toward creation is indivisibly an act of all three persons. The net effect of this singular agency, principle of operation, and indivisible operations is Owen's consideration of the triune God as a single agent from the perspective of causality. Yet Owen also appreciates the distinction between divine persons insofar as distinct triune action builds upon the foundation of the relational distinctions between divine persons *ad intra*. The acts of God *ad extra* are distinguished by means of appropriation, in which the created effects correspond to the ordering and relations of God *ad intra*, and to each person according to their own manner of action (i.e., the Father acts according to a Fatherly mode, the Son according to a filial mode, the Spirit

---

126. Ibid., 11:336. Owen makes a similar argument about the act of "quickening" and "bearing witness" from Rom. 8:11, 16 in order to support his claim that the Spirit is "an almighty agent" (11:335).

127. WJO, *Vindication*, 2:401, 400; see also 2:399, 404. Andrew Radde-Gallwitz, "The Holy Spirit as Agent, not Activity: Origen's Argument with Modalism and Its Afterlife in Didymus, Eunomius, and Gregory of Nazianzus," *Vigiliae Christianae* 65 (2011): 227–48, makes a similar argument for the necessity of the Holy Spirit as an agent within the historical narrative of Origen's thought and its reception in Didymus, Eunomius, and Nazianzen. This project adamantly affirms Radde-Gallwitz's conclusion about the Holy Spirit as an agent rather than activity, his perception of the connection between substance and activity, and the implications of divine simplicity for the logic of the Holy Spirit as a divine agent. Yet this project departs from Radde-Gallwitz's functional definitions of agent and agency. First, he defines agent as "*source* of intentional action" (288) and thereby implies three "sources" in God—which attributes too much distinction to the divine persons, who (on this account) subsist in the singular source of intentional action. Second, Radde-Gallwitz does not distinguish between "agent" and "agency," thereby attributing a "unique agency" (i.e., distinct from the Father and Son) to the Spirit (248).

according to a pneumatic mode).[128] For Owen, each act is an act of the triune God (according to causality) by means of indivisible operations, yet may be predicated of distinct divine persons (according to *terminus*) by means of appropriation—the predication of an action (or perspective on an action) to a distinct person on the basis of the created effect's fitting correspondence to a divine relation. As such, these distinctions are not distinct causes or independent actions by the distinct persons but distinct ways of understanding the manner of each divine person acting in the one indivisible act of God. The distinctions therein bring about the affirmation that each divine person (while acting unitedly) acts as a distinct agent-in-relation with the other two persons. Owen summarizes the trinitarian acts in the incarnation and their rootedness in the divine essence and relations of origin in *Christologia*. He says, "Wherefore, this work of our redemption and recovery being the especial effect of the authority, love, and power of the Father—it was to be *executed* in and by the person of the Son; as the application of it unto us is made by the Holy Ghost."[129] Owen's account of distinct actions of the divine persons, and its foundation upon the subsistent relations of God, establishes the project's classical and Reformed parameters for the doctrine of God.

---

128. WJO, *Pneumatologia*, 3:93–4.
129. WJO, *Christologia*, 1:219–20.

Chapter 3

THE EVIDENCE OF CHRISTOLOGICAL AGENCY FROM JOHN OWEN

We now turn to a presentation of Owen's evidence for classical and Reformed christological agency. The goal of this chapter is to present Owen's classical and Reformed understanding of Christ's ontology and operations. Specifically, it will argue that Owen's conception of christological agency can be described in terms of one theandric mediator (the agent) operating according to two distinct agencies (divine and human) from the Father and by the Spirit. As such, this chapter builds on the previous not only through its employment of the divine nature and actions of Christ but also insofar as Owen's understanding of the role of the Holy Spirit allows him to appreciate both the trinitarian shape of christological action and the integrity of the humanity of Christ. As in the previous chapter, Owen serves here as a witness for classical and Reformed theology with his Reformed commitments and affirmations. However, here too we see Owen fall short of technical consistency with notable key terms/phrases (esp. *principium quo/ quod* and "principle of operation").[1] Yet, in spite of these inconsistencies, Owen constitutes a reliable witness regarding the structure and content of classical and Reformed christological agency.

Reflecting the structure of the previous chapter, we will consider Christology in Owen both according to Christ's composition (ontologically) and according to the "discharge of his office" of mediator (operationally).[2] As with the last chapter, whereby the ontological reality funded the theology of action, here the ontological claims of Owen's Christology will fund Owen's understanding of christological agency. So this chapter will (§I) articulate the unity and distinction in christological ontology and then (§II) observe the unity and distinction of christological activity.

This argument centers on the ontology and activity of Christ the mediator, a key christological category that Owen employs in his discussion of Christ's person and

---

1. It is, in part, my recognition of Owen's inconsistency at these points that prevents me from elevating Owen from a faithful witness to the level of a "super theologian, leaping quodlibetal questions in a single bound" (Tim Cooper, "The State of the Field: 'John Owen Unleashed: Almost,'" *Conversations in Religion and Theology* 6 [2008]: 237).
2. WJO, *Glory of Christ*, 1:293.

work.³ After the fall, when sin tainted God's good creation and humanity failed to give God the glory due to him, humans were separated from God. The mediator who was needed to reconcile humanity to God could not be merely human, since a finite creature can bring humanity "not one step nearer the essence" of the infinite God "than a worm."⁴ Likewise, the mediator could not be merely divine, since "God is one" and a "mediator is not of one" (Gal. 3:20) but is "taken from among humanity" (Heb. 5:1; Deut. 18:15).⁵ Therefore, God the Son wills to "take on flesh and dwell among us" so that he might be a mediator between God and humanity, as he united both divine and human natures in his one person. As Owen says of the history of redemption, in the fall God says, "Behold, the man is become as one of us" (Gen. 3:22), yet in the incarnation humans gaze upon Christ and can say, "Behold, God is become like one of us" (citing Phil. 2:6-8).⁶

I. The Ontology of the Mediator

Owen's understanding of the mediator's ontology establishes the foundation upon which Owen builds his view of christological action, because action accords with ontology. Christians are not brought near to God in salvation because any given human lived obediently, died on a cross, and was raised from the dead but because it was *this* person, Jesus Christ.⁷

As we examine the ontology of the mediator, we will see that Owen considers the incarnation—the "mystery of godliness" (1 Tim. 3:16) and "the most ineffable and glorious" of all "the effects of the divine excellencies"⁸—to be so majestic that he ardently defers to the classical Christian tradition so that his Christology bears the marks of "catholicity."⁹ This section therefore resists the suggestion that his Christology is so innovative that it had "rarely been tried,"¹⁰ but instead insists that Owen endeavors to "confine" himself to the great tradition, alongside Thomas Aquinas and the "Master of the Sentences," in order to avoid "curious inquiries, bold conjectures, and unwarrantable determinations."¹¹ As Owen says,

---

3. Edwin Tay says that Christ as mediator in his threefold office is "the main category" and the "governing category" of his Christology (Tay, *Priesthood of Christ*, 87, 58).

4. WJO, *Condescension of Christ*, 17:563.

5. Ibid., 17:561-2; cf. Owen's treatment on the nature of Christ's mediation in WJO, *Justification*, 5:117-18; *Vindication of the Preceding Discourse*, 2:311-12; *Vindiciæ Evangelicæ*, 12:301; *Catechism*, 1:479.

6. WJO, *Christologia*, 1:59.

7. See WJO, *Christologia*, 1:86.

8. Ibid., 1:45.

9. Ferguson, "Person of Christ," 84.

10. Bruce L. McCormack, "With Loud Cries," 40.

11. WJO, *Christologia*, 1:224; cf. 1:13; see Entwistle, "John Owen's Doctrine of Christ," 288 on the orthodoxy and lack of originality.

his articulation of these topics corresponds to the way that they are "commonly handled by others" in the Reformed and classical tradition.[12] Owen's account of christological ontology follows closely the conciliar, patristic, medieval, and Reformed traditions preceding him by affirming that Jesus is truly God, truly man, one person in two natures without confusion, change, separation, or division.[13]

A. One Person

Owen calls the single divine personhood of Christ the "foundation of our religion" so that if it were taken away, we would in effect say, "Farewell [to] Christianity, as to the mystery, the glory, the truth, the efficacy of it."[14] Reflecting the classical and Reformed commitments, for Owen it is not only theologically paramount that the incarnation of the Son constitutes one person but it is also biblically and creedally important.[15] If Christ is to be the "umpire" who "lays his hands upon both" parties (Job 9:33), the mediator must represent both parties in one person. This subsection will argue that it was the Son who takes a human nature into his subsistence and constitutes one person (i.e., one *hypostasis*, or individual subsistence of a rational nature). Along the way, it will attend to the triune shape of Owen's articulation of the act of constituting Christ as the person of the mediator. This ontological foundation of hypostatic unity is necessary for Owen's subsequent account of mediatorial operations. Owen tells his readers that "if the divine and human nature of Christ do not constitute one individual person, all that he did for us … would have been altogether insufficient for the salvation of the church."[16]

1. Assumption and Hypostatic Union Owen's account of the being of Christ depends upon his distinction between the "assumption" and the "hypostatic union." The assumption is the initial act "whereby the person of the Son of God assumed our nature, or took it into a personal subsistence with himself," or simply "the divine constitution of the person of Christ as God and man."[17] Subsequently, the "hypostatic union" is the state of affairs and actions of the person of the mediator as an ontological and operational consequence of the assumption.[18] He says that the two are different "in the formal reason of them." (1) "Assumption is the immediate act of the divine nature in the person of the Son on the human; union is mediate, by

---

12. WJO, *Christologia*, 1:13.
13. See Trueman, *Claims*, 154; Cleveland, *Thomism*, 151.
14. WJO, *Glory of Christ*, 1:328.
15. WJO, *Christologia*, 1:226; see Tay, *Priesthood*, 73 for further elaboration on the biblical and creedal context of Owen's claims here.
16. WJO, *Christologia*, 1:40; *Pneumatologia*, 3:164.
17. WJO, *Christologia*, 1:224.
18. Owen draws this distinction from Thomas Aquinas and his definition of the assumption (*ST* III, Q.3, A.1; see Cleveland, *Thomism*, 129–38).

virtue of that assumption."[19] (2) The assumption is an act of constituting a person (a being), whereas the hypostatic union is a relation of "the natures subsisting in that one person."[20] That is, the assumption is unto personhood, an act whereby divine and human natures subsist as one person. Whereas the hypostatic union is an act or relation of the natures subsisting in that one person. (3) Finally, in the assumption, the divine nature is active and the human is passive, while the union "respects the mutual relation of the natures unto each other. Hence the divine nature may be said to be united unto the human, as well as the human unto the divine."[21]

2. The Triune Shape of the Son's Assumption Attending to the triune nature of each divine act (based on the indivisibility of triune operations) means that we must properly locate the act of assumption within its trinitarian framework. Assuming a human nature unto subsistence within himself is an act which terminates upon the Son alone,[22] yet this does not mean that the cause (or "principle") of act of the incarnation was the Son exclusively—i.e., to the exclusion of the Father and the Spirit.[23]

Owen reminds the reader that according to "original efficiency [what I am calling causality], it was the act of the divine nature, and so, consequently, of the Father, Son, and Spirit. For so are all outward acts of God."[24] This act of the divine nature is rooted in Owen's commitment to the agency (i.e., "the wisdom, power, grace, and goodness") exercised therein as derived from the "essential properties of the divine nature."[25] However, according to the terminus of the action, the assumption of the human nature was the "peculiar act of the person of the Son."[26] Like the classical tradition before him, Owen argues that it is fitting that the Son be

---

19. WJO, *Christologia*, 1:225–6.

20. Ibid., 1:226.

21. Ibid. For the active and passive distinction in Thomas Aquinas (see *ST* III, Q.2, A.10). This distinction is present elsewhere in the tradition as well (see Gregory of Nyssa and Theodore of Mopsuestia in J. N. D. Kelly, *Early Christian Doctrines*, rev. ed. [New York: HarperCollins, 1978], 299, 306–7; in Owen see *Exposition of Hebrews*, 20:367–8; Trueman, *Claims*, 156; Daniels, *Christology of John Owen*, 277).

22. See WJO, *Pneumatologia*, 3:160.

23. Here and elsewhere throughout this chapter I will build upon conclusions reached in Ty Kieser, "John Owen as Proto-Social Trinitarian?" and "The Holy Spirit and the Humanity of Christ in John Owen: A Re-Examination." Therefore, please see these for additional argumentation for my reading of Owen and its location in relation to other interpretations of Owen.

24. WJO, *Christologia*, 1:225.

25. WJO, *Christologia*, 1:225. Cleveland states that the person of the Son is both the principle and the *terminus* of the action (Cleveland, *Thomism*, 129, 130). However, it seems more appropriate to say that the divine nature (in which the Son subsists) is the principle of the action, while the person is the *terminus* (see also *ST* III, Q.3, A.2).

26. WJO, *Christologia*, 1:225.

the divine person to take on a human nature.[27] Owen provides several reasons for this fittingness:[28] (1) As the image of the Father, the Son comes to restore the image of God in humans. (2) As the One who is the Son by nature (in his relation *ad intra*), he comes to make believers into sons and daughters by grace. (3) The Son, as the second person of the Trinity in the order of subsistence, accomplishes (or puts into effect) the authority, love, and power of God that originate from the Father and are applied/perfected by the Spirit.[29] On the basis of indivisible operations, Owen says that it "became not the person of the Father" to assume a human nature but the "authority, love, and power whence the whole work proceeded, were his in a peculiar manner."[30] Nor did the act of becoming incarnate belong to the person of the Spirit, "who, in order of divine operation following that of his subsistence, was to perfect the whole work, in making application of it unto the church when it was wrought."[31] Therefore, he concludes that "it was every way suited unto divine wisdom—unto the order of the Holy Persons in their subsistence and operation—that this work should be undertaken and accomplished in the person of the Son."[32]

3. *The Role of the Spirit in the Assumption* The conception of Christ in the womb of Mary is one of the most biblically explicit trinitarian and pneumatological acts (Mt. 1:18, 20; Lk. 1:35) and, as such, is an important touchstone for an account of trinitarian and christological agency which seeks to be biblically faithful. For Owen, it was also an important point of polemical contact against the Socinians, who used this act to argue against the full divinity of Christ.[33]

Owen testifies to the activity of the Holy Spirit in his "coming upon" as being distinguishable in two acts: (1) the Spirit's preparation of Christ's human nature and (2) the Spirit's endowment of grace upon his human nature (Jn 3:34) so that it is "set apart" (sanctified) unto a "sacred purpose."[34] First, the Spirit brings about the "framing, forming, and miraculous conception of the body of Christ in the womb of the blessed Virgin"[35] and protects his human nature from the pollution of

---

27. Ibid., 1:218; cf. *Pneumatologia*, 3:160. With parallels to Owen at multiple points, Dominic Legge appeals to the fittingness of the Son as the incarnate one on the basis of the second person as the image, Son, and author of sanctification (*Trinitarian Christology of St Thomas Aquinas*, 82–102).

28. WJO, *Christologia*, 1:218, 220. See Ferguson, "Person of Christ," 87–8; Kapic, *Communion*, 73–5.

29. Ferguson calls these the reasons for the "extraordinary appropriateness" of the Son as the incarnate divine person ("Person of Christ," 88).

30. WJO, *Christologia*, 1:220.

31. Ibid., 1:220.

32. Ibid.

33. See Trueman, *Claims*, 174; Sarah Mortimer, *Reason and Religion in the English Revolution: The Challenge of Socinianism* (New York: Cambridge University Press, 2014), 147–77.

34. WJO, *Communion*, 2:65.

35. WJO, *Pneumatologia*, 3:162.

sin "from the instant of conception," so that Jesus is not under the federal headship of Adam.[36] Next, the Holy Spirit brings about the sanctification and filling of the humanity of Christ with grace according "to the measure of its receptivity" and this occurs "in the instant of its conception." The Spirit sanctifies the human nature in that he brings "the original infusion of all grace into the human nature of Christ."[37] The act of sanctification does not mean that the humanity of Christ was sinful or fallen (as some suggest)[38] but that every human, "including even prelapsarian Adam, … require[s] the Spirit to enable them to 'live to God.'"[39] The human nature that the Holy Spirit forms and endows with grace is assumed by the Son "into a personal subsistence with himself."[40]

4. An/Enhypostatic Union Owen's doctrine of the hypostatic union builds off of this triune account of the assumption. Owen carefully delineates the doctrine within the conciliar parameters and classical reception of this doctrine throughout the tradition. Owen is particularly cautious here not to posit "two Christs" (i.e., Nestorianism) as the Socinians were charging orthodox Christology of doing.[41]

Owen's primary means of articulating the unity of the person and resisting the multiplication of Christ's two natures into two persons is the tradition's "common prevalent expression" of the humanity of Christ as "*anhypostatic*" (i.e., impersonal) apart from the subsistence of the Son, in whom the humanity of Christ becomes

---

36. Ibid., 3:162–3. Owen is insistent that this ought not to imply that Christ's humanity is temporal antecedent to the assumption (3:165) nor that there is an "independence" in his human nature.

37. Ibid., 3:168; cf. *Christologia*, 1:171. When Owen says, "all grace" he does not mean that Christ's human nature functions at maximal human capacity from the point of conception but that Christ received all "kinds" of grace. Earlier he says, "It was by the Holy Spirit positively endowed with all grace. And hereof it was afterward only capable of farther degrees as to actual exercise, but not of any new kind of grace" (3:168).

38. For example, Hastings, "Honouring the Spirit," 297; Corné Blaauw, "'An Holy and Beautiful Soul': Jonathan Edwards on the Humanity of Christ," *JES* 6 (2016): 27; Spence, *Inspiration and Incarnation*, 53; and Colin E. Gunton, "Forward," in Thomas Weinandy, *In the Likeness of Sinful Flesh: An Essay on the Humanity of Christ*, Scholars' Editions in Theology (New York: T&T Clark, 2006), x.

39. Kapic, *Communion*, 86; citing *Pneumatologia*, 3:168; cf. WJO, *Communion*, 2:65; cf. *Christologia*, 1:170–1, 199, 200.

40. WJO, *Christologia*, 1:224.

41. Thomas Rees, trans., *The Racovian Catechism* (Lexington: American Theological Library Association, 1962), 28. Further, see Cleveland, *Thomism*, 128; Lombard, *Sentences*, III.vi. Cleveland argues that the five criteria Owen uses for Nestorianism also exist in Thomas Aquinas (Cleveland, *Thomism*, 147–8).

"*enhypostatic*" (subsisting in the person of the Son).⁴² Notably, for Owen this union in the one *hypostasis* of the Son means that the humanity of Christ has "no subsistence of its own" (Lk. 1:35; 1 Tim. 3:16) because the Son took this nature "into personal subsistence with himself."⁴³ Owen insists that the Son did not take on "an individual person," but instead, "preventing the personal subsistence of human nature in that flesh which he assumed, he gave it its subsistence in his own person; whence it hath its individuation and distinction from all other persons whatever."⁴⁴ It is because this human nature does not have a subsistence of its own (i.e., it is *anhypostatic*) that it subsists in a "personal union." Owen concludes, "The divine and human nature in Christ have but one personal subsistence; and so are but one Christ."⁴⁵

Employing this distinction to defend against Nestorianism, Owen's account of the hypostatic union presents the two natures as inseparably united in the subsistence of the Son as a distinct kind of union, one that is *sui generis* (i.e., one of a kind).⁴⁶ This union is not merely quantitively more intimate than Christians have with God. Owen avers that nothing "equal to it, or like it, [is] found in any other creatures."⁴⁷

Summarily, we may note Owen's commitment to his Christology as an account that has "not been treating of two, a God and a man; but of one who is God and man"; that is, "he is all this in one person."⁴⁸ We may speak of Jesus Christ as "a man" since Christ possesses all that is necessary to be human (i.e., body and soul). Yet that which made him "that man," and without which he is not "the man" (i.e., a particular subsisting human), was the "subsistence of both [natures] united in the person of the Son of God."⁴⁹

---

42. WJO, *Christologia*, 1:228. Likely originating with Leontius of Byzantium, this category appears in patristic, medieval, and Reformed resources. On the history of the term, see U. M. Lang, "Anhypostatos-Enhypostatos: Church Fathers, Protestant Orthodoxy and Karl Barth," *JTS* 49 (1998): 630–57. Peter Lombard, *Sentences*, 3.5.3; *ST* III, Q.2, A.5; Turretin, *Institutes*, II:13.vi.5; *Synopsis*, 2:79; in Owen see Cleveland, *Thomism*, 134.

43. WJO, *Communion*, 2:51; cf. *Christologia*, 1:228, 233; *Vindiciæ Evangelicæ*, 12:386; *Vindication of the Preceding Discourse*, 2:233; *Glory of Christ*, 1:325.

44. WJO, *Vindication*, 2:418; cf. *Christologia*, 1:233.

45. WJO, *Vindication*, 2:418. In conjunction with Spence's claim that the function of the *anhypostatic* doctrine was to "safeguard the belief that the Son ... became truly man" (*Incarnation and Inspiration*, 35) (i.e., emphasizing human distinctions from the divine nature), I think that the primary function of this doctrine was to safeguard against too much distinction, emphasizing personal unity in the one subsistence.

46. WJO, *Christologia*, 1:228–9; *Pneumatologia*, 3:160–1; see Matthew Barrett and Michael A. G. Haykin, *Owen on the Christian Life: Living for the Glory of God in Christ* (Wheaton: Crossway, 2015), 98–9; Daniels, *Christology*, 277–8. For Owen's dependence on Scripture here, see his treatment of Isa. 9:6; Gal. 3:16, 4:4; Rom. 1:3; Heb. 2:14; Jn 8:58 (*Christologia*, 1:233).

47. WJO, *Glory of Christ*, 1:281.

48. WJO, *Communion*, 2:66–7.

49. WJO, *Communion*, 2:67.

5. *Communication of Attributes* Based on the Son's assumption of a human nature into a single subsistence, we may predicate the various attributes of Christ's two nature to the mediator (e.g., that Christ is both "God" and a "descendant of the patriarchs" [Rom. 9:5]). This way of understanding the person of Christ's Owen (following the classical and Reformed tradition) calls the "κοινωνία ἰδιωμάτων,— that communication of attributes in the person, whereby the properties of either nature are promiscuously spoken of the person of Christ, under what name soever, of God or man, he be spoken of."[50] While some suggest that Owen distances himself from this doctrine or that he reinterprets it,[51] the communication of attributes is an important feature of Reformed christologies (as well as patristic and medieval christologies), and Owen's Christology is no exception.[52] Owen's commitment to the language of Scripture, the integrity of both natures of Christ, and the subsistence of both natures in the one person motivates his account of the communication of attributes.

Following the Reformed *communicatio idiomatum in concreto*, Owen claims that "whatever may be said of either nature may be said of his whole person" and, by implication, may *not* be said of the other nature.[53] He gives the examples: "So God

50. Ibid., 2:51.

51. The argumentation in this subsection resists Spence's claims that Owen distanced himself from the communication of attributes because, he supposes, through this position "a true appreciation of Christ's humanity was effectively lost" (*Incarnation and Inspiration*, 110; see also "Christ's Humanity and Ours: John Owen," in *Persons, Divine and Human: Kings College Essays in Theological Anthropology*, ed. Christoph Schwöbel and Colin Gunton [Edinburgh: T&T Clark, 1991], 82). Further, Spence admits (without citation) that Owen employs the *communicatio* in some sense (*Incarnation and Inspiration*, 140). Ferguson suggests that Owen's version of this doctrine would be better expressed as the "communion" of two natures in one person ("Person of Christ," 90). Both these thinkers seem to suppose that a "communication of attributes" would imply that the humanity ontologically receives divine properties. If this were true, they have good reason to be suspicious. However, this kind of communication, as we will see, is not what Owen intends by the doctrine. It is true, however, that Owen rarely uses the explicit language of the *communicatio*. Such a move is perhaps attributable to Owen's desire to convince his interlocutors from the language and authority of scripture (WJO, *Vindiciæ Evangelicæ*, 12:84; *Biblical Theology*, 2; Rehnman, *Divine Discourse*, 122–3; Letham, "John Owen's Doctrine of the Trinity in its Catholic Context," 190). Therefore, when Biddle names the "communication of properties" as among those "phrases unheard of in the Scripture" which Biddle's opponents supposedly use to "slily couch false doctrines" (WJO, *Biddle's Preface*, 12:57), Owen's response depends upon the "thing intended by it" [i.e., the phrase], being "clearly delivered in Scripture" (*Vindiciæ Evangelicæ*, 12:75).

52. For a brief history and traditional articulation of the doctrine in patristic, medieval, and Reformation Christologies, see Richard Cross, *Communicatio Idiomatum: Reformation Christological Debates*, CPHST (New York: Oxford University Press, 2019), 1–38.

53. WJO, *Catechism*, 1:478.

may be said to die, but not the Godhead; the man Christ to be everywhere, but not his humanity; for his one person is all this."⁵⁴ As a consequence of this union and the communication of properties, Owen says, "Three things are to be observed, which the Scripture, reason, and the ancient church, do all concur in."⁵⁵ The first is that each nature preserves its essential properties "without mixture, without composition or confusion"; the second is that each nature operates according to its own properties; and the third is that every act is to be considered an act of the whole person. These three points of christological summary will serve as guides throughout the rest of the chapter. They will address the ontological integrity and distinction of each nature (§I.B), then the acts of the whole person (§II.A), and finally, the operations of each nature (§II.B).

B. Two Natures

As was shown above, by taking upon himself a human nature (and not a distinct human person), the Son partakes of both parties in one person. Owen says,

> He lays his hand upon God, by partaking of his nature, Zech 8:7; and he lays his hand upon us, by being partaker of our nature, Heb 2:14, 16: and so becomes a days-man, or umpire, between both. By this means, he fills up all the distance that was made by sin between God and us; and we who were far off are made nigh in him.⁵⁶

The Son's continual mediation in each nature means that each nature must preserve its characteristics. He says, "Each nature doth preserve its own natural, essential properties, entirely unto and in itself."⁵⁷ Since both natures preserve their essential properties, Owen is adamant that neither is Christ's humanity divinized nor is Christ's divinity humanized. Specifically, Owen says, "The divine nature is not made temporary, finite, limited, subject to passion or alteration by this union; nor is the human nature rendered immense, infinite, omnipotent."⁵⁸

1. Humanity Not Divinized (Extra Calvinisticum) Here we will approach this first denial (i.e., that Christ's humanity is divinized) under the category of the "extra Calvinisticum,"⁵⁹ a staple position for the Reformed tradition and, as some have argued, for the classical tradition as a whole.⁶⁰ The "extra" is the claim that the

---

54. Ibid.
55. WJO, *Christologia*, 1:234.
56. WJO, *Communion*, 2:51.
57. WJO, *Christologia*, 1:234; cf. *Catechism*, 1:478.
58. WJO, *Christologia*, 1:234; cf. *Glory of Christ*, 1:309–10.
59. See this affirmed in Owen by Ferguson, "Person of Christ," 92; Trueman, *Claims*, 163; Trueman connects Owen's emphasis on the *extra Calvinisticum* to his "Spirit-Christology" (198).
60. See James R. Gordon, *The Holy One in Our Midst: An Essay on the Flesh of Christ* (Minneapolis: Fortress, 2016), 1. For "the extra" in Calvin, see *Institutes*, IV.xvii.12.

divine presence of the Son is exercised/exists beyond his bodily presence.[61] This concept is most obvious in the discussions of Christ's presence in the Lord's Supper, in which the Reformed tradition denies the Lutheran claim that Christ's humanity is bodily present in favor of an affirmation of Christ's spiritual presence (since his body is spatially located at the right hand of the Father). Because of his conviction that each of Christ's natures retains its essential properties, Owen insists that Christ's corporeal presence in the sacrament is a "monstrous figment" that "fully overthrows our Saviour's human nature."[62] Therefore, Owen understands Christ's claim to be "in heaven" (Jn 3:13) while walking around Jerusalem to imply that "he had another nature, wherein at that time he was in heaven also."[63]

Owen does not limit his explanation of this christological category to spatial locatedness but also includes other essential properties for finite creatures (e.g., finite knowledge). Owen claims, "I do not hereby ascribe the infusion of omniscience, of infinite understanding, wisdom, and knowledge, into the human nature of Christ. It was and is a creature, finite and limited" and, therefore, does not possess infinite knowledge.[64] He insists that if Christ's prayer for glory from the Father (Jn 17:5) implied the communication of omniscience and omnipresence to the human nature of Christ, then he would have been praying "destruction, and not the exaltation" of his humanity since it would "lose all its own essential properties, and consequently its being."[65]

Owen, additionally, draws the reader's attention to the soteriological importance of the affirmation of the *extra Calvinisticum* and the integrity of his human nature. For Owen, if Christ's human nature did not retain its essential properties, then Christ's humanity would be unlike ours so that he would be "a person in whom we are not concerned ... [and] thereof hath no alliance or kindred unto us."[66] To those who deny essential attributes of the humanity of Christ, Owen says, "As they had feigned unto themselves an imaginary Christ, so they should have an imaginary salvation only."[67]

---

61. Oberman, "Extra Dimension in the Theology of Calvin," 48.

62. WJO, *Catechism*, 1:478; see also *Christologia*, 1:233–4; *Exposition of Hebrews* 23:12.

63. WJO, *Vindiciæ Evangelicæ*, 12:358, 228; cf. *Glory of Christ*, 1:326; likewise see his treatments of Jn 6:38 and Mt. 28:20 (*Christologia*, 1:92; *Communion*, 2:224–5). See also, Thomas Watson, *A Body of Divinity* (Carlisle: Banner of Truth, 1983), 163–4.

64. WJO, *Christologia*, 1:93. While he does not elaborate, this claim runs contrary to Ryan McGraw's interpretation of the maximal wisdom of Christ in his human nature ("Seeing Things Owen's Way: John Owen's Trinitarian Theology and Piety in Its Early-Modern Context," 189–99). See also Owen's claim in WJO, Θεολογούμενα Παντοδαπά, 17:38; John Owen, *Biblical Theology: The History of Theology from Adam to Christ*, trans. Stephen Westcott (Grand Rapids: Reformation Heritage, 1994), 18.

65. WJO, *Christologia*, 1:44.

66. WJO, *Glory of Christ*, 1:327.

67. Ibid., 1:329.

2. Divinity Not Humanized While recognizing that Christ's humanity preserves its essential characteristics so that he existed finitely and locally on earth according to his human nature, Owen is equally adamant about the parallel claim: that Christ existed infinitely and omnipresently according to his divine nature. Therefore, Owen denies that the incarnation meant Christ's divinity was transformed or changed into humanity or finitude.[68] Owen says that the biblical claim "God was made man" cannot mean that there is a change of "the divine nature into the human" because it would destroy both his natures, as the water in the miracle at Canaan was destroyed by its transformation into wine.[69] Therefore, Christ did "not cease to be God when he became man."[70] The condescension of the Son did not imply "change or alteration in the divine nature" (e.g., localization or spatial location).[71] Owen says that when "he came down from heaven ... he did so" while he "still continued in heaven."[72]

For Owen the Son's "infinite condescension"[73] and "emptying of himself" (Phil. 2:7) does not imply an ontological change in the divine nature, since God does not suffer change.[74] Instead, Owen contends that the "Word was made flesh ... not by ceasing to be what he was, but by becoming what he was not."[75] Therefore, the "infinite, unspeakable, unconceivable condescension of the Son of God" was not that the Son "ceased to be in the form of God; but continuing so to be, he 'took upon him the form of a servant' in our nature: he became what he was not" (citing Jn 3:13).[76] Of John 1, Owen says, "This Word was made flesh, not by any change of his own nature or essence, not by a transubstantiation of the divine nature into the human, not by ceasing to be what he was, but by becoming what he was not, in taking our nature to his own, to be his own, whereby he dwelt among us."[77]

---

68. Ibid., 1:326.

69. Ibid., 1:327.

70. WJO, *Condescension of Christ*, 17:564.

71. WJO, *Glory of Christ*, 1:327. On the denial of local motion of the divine nature see *Christologia*, 1:92, 93.

72. WJO, *Christologia*, 1:92.

73. Owen seems to love this phrase and uses it repeatedly throughout his lifetime. For example, ibid., 1:105, 169, 173; *Glory of Christ*, 1:323–31; *Glory of Christ Applied*, 1:422, 423; *Exposition of Hebrews*, 23:12, 15, 21, 68, 116, 125.

74. WJO, *Glory of Christ*, 1:327.

75. WJO, *Christologia*, 1:46; *Glory of Christ*, 1:327. This well-known affirmation within the classical and Reformed tradition likely originated with Hilary of Poitiers in the mid-fourth century ("On the Trinity," *NPNF*² 9:66 [III.16]) and was repeated nearly word for word by other patristic theologians (e.g., Gregory of Nazianzus, "Oration XXIX," in *NPNF*² 7:308; Leo, "Sermon XXI: On the Feast of the Nativity," *NPNF*² 12:129). On the importance of this claim for Owen's theology, see Spence, *Incarnation and Inspiration*, 76 and Kapic, *Communion*, 79–80.

76. WJO, *Exposition of Hebrews*, 21:526; *Glory of Christ*, 1:326; cf. *Glory of Christ*, 1:327, 329; *Christologia*, 1:232.

77. WJO, *Christologia*, 1:46–7; cf. *Glory of Christ*, 1:326.

3. *Two Essential Properties (Dyothelitism)* Since both natures retain the essential properties of that nature, Owen says, "All natural properties are double in Christ—as [the] will ... ; [and] all personal [properties], [such] as subsistence, [are] single."[78] Vital for our purposes is the further acknowledgment that "wills" belong to natures. Since God has one will and Christ has two of all natural properties, he has two wills.[79] This affirmation, for Owen, is significant regarding the representation of God by Christ. That is, Christ is the perfect representation "of the nature and will of God" because Christ shares in the one divine will of God according to his divine nature.[80] In addition to possessing the divine will, Owen insists that Christ possesses "the will and understanding of the human nature" as well.[81] Owen affirms the presence of Christ's human "rational faculties and powers of his soul, his understanding, will, and affections ... [since his] divine nature was not unto him in the place of a soul."[82] Owen says that as Christ interacted with people around him, Jesus "was no less a man than any of themselves were."[83]

In addition to the implications of this doctrine for Christ's obedience to the Father and his willing sacrifice on the cross,[84] Owen employs dyothelitism to bolster his claims about the possibility of the covenant of redemption (see Ch. 2 §I.A.4). In his christologically oriented account of the doctrine of God, Owen posits the possibility of agreement between the Father and the Son when we consider the Son "as he was to be incarnate" and "by his own [i.e., human] will."[85] Owen says that when we consider the covenant of redemption and the seeming distinction between the wills of the Father and the Son, we must keep in mind the "supposition of the susception of our human nature into personal union with the Son."[86]

The distinction of Christ's two wills on the basis of the preservation of both his divine and human properties is a soteriologically significant conclusion for Christ's mediation of salvation. As Christopher Cleveland says, "If the integrity of the two natures is diminished in any fashion, then Christ's solidarity with either

---

78. WJO, *Catechism*, 1:478; see the *Racovian Catechism*, 56-7 for the polemical context of Owen's claims on the distinct essential properties.

79. WJO, *Spirit as Comforter*, 4:358; *Catechism*, 1:478. *Glory of Christ*, 1:330; Tweeddale, *John Owen and Hebrews*, 113.

80. WJO, *Glory of Christ*, 1:294-5; cf. *Vindiciæ Evangelicæ*, 12:351 for the polemical significance of this claim in contrast to Socinianism.

81. WJO, *Exposition of Hebrews*, 20:325; cf. *Christologia*, 1:230.

82. WJO, *Pneumatologia*, 3:169; see Kapic on Christ as the "perfect man" insofar as Christ possesses all human faculties (*Communion*, 93, 94 n. 115, 243).

83. WJO, *Condescension of Christ*, 17:566.

84. See WJO, *Vindiciæ Evangelicæ*, 12:431.

85. WJO, *Christologia*, 1:56.

86. WJO, *Sacerdotal Office of Christ*, 19:77. On this point Kendall Cleveland associates Owen's position with the *Logos incarnandus* ("the Logos 'to be incarnate'") ("Covenant," 203).

party in the act of reconciliation is diminished .... [And] his value as a mediator on behalf of humanity is likewise impaired."[87]

II. The Operations of the Mediator

Having surveyed the ontology of the mediator, we now turn to consideration of operations of the mediator. Like the above section, this section seeks to appreciate the mediatorial foundation, the trinitarian shape, and the traditional rootedness of Owen's Christology as it articulates his understanding of christological agency. In contrast to viewing Owen's account of christological action as "novel" or radical,[88] this section will argue for Owen's consistency with the Reformed and classical tradition. Specifically, the section will argue that Owen presents Christ as one theandric agent, acting according to two distinct agencies.[89] This section will present Owen's understanding through his three observations on the implications of the hypostatic union, observations which "the Scripture, reason, and the ancient church, do all concur in": (1) "Each nature doth preserve its own natural, essential properties, entirely unto and in itself; without mixture, without composition or confusion, without such a real communication of the one unto the other" (i.e., the subject of the above subsection); (2) "Each nature operates in him according unto its essential properties;" and yet, (3)

> it is the same person, the same Christ, that acts all these things ... [so that] all that he did and suffered ... is not to be considered as the act of this or that nature in him alone, but it is the act and work of the whole person,—of him that is both God and man in one person[90]

This last point on the unity of Christ's action funds the first subsection (§A) before we turn to the distinct operations and capacities in the second subsection (§B).

---

87. Cleveland, *Thomism*, 152.
88. "What Owen is doing here has rarely been tried .... [It] is rather novel by more modern standards. But it is also novel by early orthodox standards" (McCormack, "With Loud Cries", 40). Stephen Holmes says Owen's claims represent "a radicalization of the basic Reformed position" (*God of Grace and God of Glory*, 136). Habets says that this "formulation stands in stark contrast (but not contradiction) to the long tradition received in the West through Chalcedon" ("Spirit Christology: The Future of Christology," 222).
89. For additional engagement with other interpretations of christological action in Owen, see Kieser, "The Holy Spirit and the Humanity of Christ in John Owen."
90. WJO, *Christologia*, 1:234.

A. Single Agent

This first subsection argues that, for Owen, the "agent" of the accomplishment of Christ's actions is fundamentally the theandric mediator, the God-man.[91] As such, Owen's commitment to the theandric agent resists an understanding of the Logos *simpliciter* or either nature as the agent of christological action. Here we will first look at the unity of the acts of the one mediator as theandric, and examine the way in which the theandric agent relates to the three divine persons, and finally transitions into a discussion of distinct agency through Owen's use of *principium quo/quod* ("principle by which/which") and *apotelesma* ("ultimate effect").

1. Acts of One Theandric Agent This section contends that Owen considers the agent of the acts of Christ to be the theandric mediator.[92] For Owen, it needs to be a singular agent (i.e., the theandric mediator) accomplishing these salvific acts, not only to maintain a conciliar account of christological unity but also in order to secure his theology of salvation. If the acts of Christ are not God's then humans must save themselves, and if the acts of Christ are not human then our side of the covenant is unfulfilled and our righteousness unmerited. According to Owen, this mediator accomplishes salvation for us as God and man. As with the previous section, the concept of "mediator" plays a vital role in christological action.[93] Owen's employment of the concept of Christ the mediator solidifies his location in the Reformed tradition. While this account is in continuity with the councils,[94] it departs from Roman Catholic Christology in that the Reformed hold that Christ is a mediator according to both his divine and human natures, while the traditional

---

91. I am here clarifying the "accomplishment" of these acts because of the Trinitarian pattern of appropriation in which created effects correspond to divine relations, indicating the person to whom that act is appropriated. So, as we will see below, we might also argue that the Holy Spirit is the agent of the perfection of these acts.

92. Sinclair Ferguson, likewise, notes that the acts of Christ are "acts of the whole person" ("Person of Christ," 90). Yet he goes on to gloss this as an affirmation of these acts as of the "totus Christus." While I agree with the material claim he makes, because of the ecclesiological use of *totus Christus* and distinct christological conversation in those terms (e.g., John Webster, *Holiness* [Grand Rapids: Eerdmans, 2003], 71), it seems that the Latinized English "theandric" is more appropriate than "totus Christus."

93. It is by means of Owen's emphasis on the mediatorial action of Christ (i.e., historically and spiritually significant activity) that I think he is able to avoid the charge of building a Christology which is comprised merely of "abstractions," or merely theoretical and static realities (as accused by Lloyd, "Owen and Socinian Controversies," 221).

94. For support of this claim, see Holmes, "Communicatio Idiomatum," 86.

Catholic position is that he only mediates according to his human nature.⁹⁵ As Edwin Tay states, "What distinguishes his view from the medieval tradition is the ... active participation of the Mediator's divine and human natures in its [i.e., his mediatorial office's] accomplishment."⁹⁶

Owen claims, "Whatever acts are ascribed unto him [Christ], however immediately performed, in or by the human nature, or in and by his divine nature, they are all the acts of that one person, in whom are both these natures."⁹⁷ Owen names this reality the "personal operations" of Christ, since these operations "could not have been wrought by him [exclusively] either as God or man" (e.g., raising himself from the dead or redeeming the church with his blood).⁹⁸ Owen recognizes that this is a "maze" which has "bewildered" interpreters, but contends that Scripture testifies to this reality.⁹⁹ Specifically, Owen claims that the properties of the divine nature are divine, and the properties of the human nature are human, yet "all the operations and works of Christ, as mediator, are theandrical."¹⁰⁰ Owen

---

95. See below for more on the history of this controversy (Ch. 6, 4 §I.A). For this affirmation in the Reformed tradition, see Peter Vermigli, *Life, Letters and Sermons*, ed. John Patrick Donnelly, trans. John Patrick Donnelly, PML 5 (Kirksville, MO: Trueman State University Press, 1999), 142–54, 178–222; Ames, *Marrow*, I.xviii–xxiv; Heinrich Heppe, *Reformed Dogmatics*, ed. Ernst Bizer, trans. G. T. Thomson (Eugene, OR: Wipf & Stock, 2007), 410–87; Turretin, *Institutes*, II:14.ii; Calvin, *Institutes*, II.xiv.3; Perkins, *Works*, I.27; Muller, *Christ and the Decree* 31–4; Muller, *DLGTT*, 188–9. In Owen, see Trueman, *Claims*, 165; Trueman, *John Owen*, 81; Cleveland, "Covenant," 10–12; Tay, *Priesthood*, 78–9.

96. Tay, *Priesthood*, 79.

97. WJO, *Vindication*, 2:415. For more on the "immediacy" qualifier, see below.

98. WJO, *Vindication of the Preceding Discourse*, 2:329.

99. Ibid.

100. WJO, *Vindication of the Preceding Discourse*, 2:329. It might be objected that Owen's connection between theandric action and mediation could imply that if Christ performed non-mediatorial actions, then they were non-theandric. Potentially indicating the existence of non-mediatorial acts, Owen suggests that Christ's act of praying for the forgiveness of the people at the foot of the cross (and other operations) "he did in obedience to the law as a private person, [they] were not acts of mediation, nor works of him as mediator" (*Death of Death*, 10:196; cf. 10:249). My response would be based on (1) the constitution of his person, (2) the immediacy of actions, and (3) the comprehensive duration of his mediation. First, immediately after the above claim, Owen recognizes that these putatively

admits that there is "nothing in the person of Christ but his divine and human nature" (with the consequence that "the distinct natures are distinct principles of Christ's operations"), "yet the person of Christ is neither his divine nature nor his human" and instead "his person is the principal or only agent; which being God-man, all the actions thereof, by virtue of the communication of the properties of non-mediatorial acts were "of him who was mediator" (10:196). That is, the mediator is God and man and thereby acts as God and man. On the basis of the first point and as we will see below, (2) particular operations (like praying and obeying) can immediately belong to either nature. Yet, this does not exclude the simultaneous character of theandric action; it only names the focus or perspective on a particular immediate effect. So here he may mean that "praying, forgive them" belongs immediately to the human nature like "obeying" belongs to the human nature. This does not exclude simultaneous divine operations, but it does mean that Christ may not be eternally forgiving these people according to his divinity, like Christ is not obeying according to his divinity. Finally, Owen considers Christ's mediation to persist throughout the entirety of Christ's life. That is, coming to do the will of God (Heb. 10:9) is not punctiliar but continuous throughout Christ's life (*Exposition of Hebrews*, 23:451–2). Likewise, Owen says that mediation consists in intercession (which "continues forever" [Heb. 7:24]) and "oblation," which "compriseth the whole economy and dispensation of God manifested in the flesh and conversing among us, with all those things which he performed in the days of his flesh" (10:176). Notice that this includes both divinity and humanity in the entirety of Christ's life. This comprehensive duration of mediatorial activity seems to indicate that Christ did not cease to act as mediator, only that a particular operation may not have his mediation in view. Today we recognize this most starkly when people in a particular office violate the office. While examples from presidents, professional athletes, and Hollywood stars abound, we may consider a pastor who is watching their child's basketball game at the local high school. While the act of cheering for their daughter does not have the pastoral office in immediate view, if the pastor begins to angrily and unjustly berate the referees, then we recognize this as an unseemly and shameful act of the pastoral office. So while cheering for only one team the pastor can say, "I am cheering as a parent, not a pastor" (i.e., the office is not immediately in view). Yet the pastoral office does not cease to apply nor do they cease to act from it; so after berating the referee, the pastor *cannot* say, "I was not acting as a pastor, I was acting as a parent."

both natures therein, are theandrical."¹⁰¹ That is, there is no third thing in Christ besides the two natures subsisting in the one person, and this one person (who subsists in two natures) is the agent of Christ's actions.

Owen draws his account of theandric activity from Scripture, aiming to interpret Scripture rightly. Commenting on Tit. 2:13—τοῦ μεγάλου θεοῦ καὶ σωτῆρος ἡμῶν Ἰησοῦ Χριστοῦ ("our great God and savior Jesus Christ")—Owen says that the "subject is one; his epithets here two."¹⁰² The first attribute (being God) belongs to Christ according to his divine essence, and the second (being savior) belongs to him as mediator. Likewise, Owen rhetorically asks of Acts 20:28 (where Luke says that God "redeemed the church by his own blood"), "Was not the person of Christ, by the communication of the properties of each nature in it and to it, a principle of such operations as he could not have wrought either as God or man, separately considered? How else did God 'redeem his church with his own blood?'"¹⁰³ Elsewhere Owen comments on Acts 20:28: "The purchase that was made thereby was the work of the person as both God and man."¹⁰⁴ Owen insists that most "enunciations concerning the person of Christ" are said to be "on the account of their [i.e., the two natures'] union in him .... So he is said to be the Head, the King, Priest, and Prophet of the church ... and performs the acts of them, not on the singular account of this or that nature, but of the *hypostatical* union of them both."¹⁰⁵ Therefore, Christ acts not according to one nature at a time, turning the other off like a valve, but he performs the acts of mediation in both his natures.¹⁰⁶

For Owen, the God-man as the singular agent is a consequence of Christ's ontological status as the mediator between God and humanity, what this project calls the operational "mirroring" of the ontological. Based on the union of both natures in one *hypostasis*, "whereby [the] whole Christ was one person," Owen says that "all his mediatory acts were the acts of that one person, of him who was both God and man."¹⁰⁷ As the mediator in both natures, the theandric agent, Christ accomplishes the "salvation of the church" through "those acts of his offices," which "could not be performed in and by" either nature on its own.¹⁰⁸ Likewise, Owen says that since each nature operates according to its own distinct agency, every property and operation of the theandric agent belongs "formally and radically unto one [or the other] of the natures," yet he was "fitted and suited unto his

---

101. WJO, *Vindication of the Preceding Discourse*, 2:329.
102. WJO, *Vindiciæ Evangelicæ*, 12:258.
103. WJO, *Communion*, 2:328.
104. WJO, *Christologia*, 1:235.
105. Ibid., 1:234–5.
106. This is contrary to the view of a "duplex personality" whereby "sometimes Christ acted as a man, sometimes as God" (Lloyd, "Owen and Socinian Controversies," 220–1).
107. WJO, *Christologia*, 1:40.
108. Ibid., 1:87.

mediatory operations, which in neither nature, singly considered, he could have performed."[109]

This operational mirroring of the ontological evidences that the function and operation of Christ are rooted in the being of Christ.[110] These theandric actions and the unity therein are based on the unity of Christ's person; additionally, the distinction of agency is based on the distinct natures as distinct principles of operation. Owen says, "The person of Christ is neither his divine nature nor his human; for the human nature is, and ever was, of itself ἀνυπόστατος; and the divine, to the complete constitution of the person of the Mediator, in and unto its own hypostasis assumed the human."[111] Therefore, neither nature (independently) constitutes the mediator and, thereby, neither nature can be (independently) the agent of Christ's mediatorial actions. Owen articulates how the ontology of the mediator founds Christ's theandrical acts throughout his commentary on Mt. 22:41-46, in which Jesus asks how the Messiah can be both the Lord and son of David. Owen's response is,

> This person of Christ is here spoken unto, not in respect of his divine nature only, which is not capable of exaltation ... nor in respect of his human nature only, which is not the king and head of the church; but with respect unto his whole person ... the principle of those theandrical acts whereby Christ ruleth over all in the kingdom given him of his Father, Rev. 1:17, 18. As he was God, he was David's Lord, but not his son; as he was man, he was David's son, and so absolutely could not be his Lord; in his person, as he was God and man, he was his Lord and his son.[112]

Owen further solidifies the activity of the God-man in his ontology, saying, "The Son of God assumed our nature into personal subsistence with himself—whereby the whole Christ was one person, and all his mediatory acts were the acts of that one person, of him who was both God and man."[113]

---

109. WJO, *Glory of Christ*, 2:331.

110. This close connection between ontology and operation evidences one of the ways that this classical and Reformed account diverges from the innovative reading of Owen. Most articulately, Spence (*Incarnation and Inspiration*, 42, 61) considers Owen's account of Christ's ontology to be indicative of "incarnational" Christology, which primarily regards God the Son, and Christ's functions to be "inspirational" Christology, regarding the Spirit; similarly, Kay, *Trinitarian Spirituality*, 190. While the dialectic of this construal is appealing, a classical and Reformed interpretation of Owen views much more continuity between ontology and operation.

111. WJO, *Vindication of the Preceding Discourse*, 2:329.

112. WJO, *Exposition of Hebrews*, 20:225.

113. WJO, *Christologia*, 1:40.

3. The Evidence of Christological Agency

2. The Son, the Mediator For Owen, since these acts are acts of the theandric mediator (the *God*-man), we must ask how the accomplished acts of the theandric mediator relate to the action of the divine persons, specifically upon whom these acts terminate. Owen's response is that the Son is the one who assumed the human nature unto subsistence with himself and the divine person to whom we must predicate the accomplishment of Christ's actions is the Son (rather than the Spirit or Father).[114] Contrary to those who insist upon differentiating between the Son and the theandric mediator, insisting that the Son is not "the single subject" nor "to be identified without qualification with" Christ,[115] this account insists that Christ's accomplished acts belong to (i.e., terminate upon) the Son uniquely, without implying the acts of God are divisible.

Owen's affirmations of the Son as the divine person upon whom the accomplished acts of Christ terminate can be seen in various places throughout his corpus. For example, he says,

> The person of the Son of God, or the divine nature in the second person, continuing God in his essence and God in his state and dignity, did take "upon" him ... the nature of man, into an individual subsistence in his own person, whereby he became that man; and what was done and acted in it by that man was done and acted by the person of the Son of God.[116]

Notice here that Owen affirms that the person of the Son of God is the one who acts in the incarnation. This is not merely an ontological claim (i.e., that the Son assumed a human nature) but also an operational claim (i.e., that the acts of Christ terminate on the Son). Owen says that because the Son assumed a human nature into subsistence with himself, the "whole Christ was the Son of God."[117] Elsewhere

---

114. Spence's understanding of Christ's ontological constitution as the mediator is similar to the one here in that he argues, "The person of Christ in his role as Mediator is the subject of the saving work accomplished by both his natures" (Spence, *Incarnation and Inspiration*, 70). Yet, how Spence relates the "Son" to the person of Christ and how he understands the human operations will diverge from this reading.

115. Spence, *Christ's Humanity and Ours*, 96; *Incarnation and Inspiration*, 34, cf. 100. This is especially important because Spence employs this distinction between the Son and the mediator (a distinction he considers to be "essential to the gospel" [76]) to provide an exception in the indivisibility of triune operations. That is, he considers the Son (according to his divine nature) to be consistently acting indivisibly with the Father and Spirit, but treats the mediatorial acts of Christ as an exception to this traditional rule (32–3). This claim likely derives from Spence's resistance to the Son as the "cause" of Christ's actions. Yet, notice here that we are discussing the *"terminus,"* of the action. As such, I think the discrepancy here is symptomatic of a distinction on the trinitarian action of the Son and Spirit (see Ch. 2 §II.A.3–B.3; Ch. 3 §II.B.2–3).

116. WJO, *Condescension of Christ*, 17:567.

117. WJO, *Pneumatologia*, 3:165; cf. Tay, *Priesthood*, 69.

he says, "The same person—who before was not flesh, was not man—was made flesh as man, in that he took our human nature to be his own. This ineffable act is the foundation of the divine relation between the Son of God and the man Christ Jesus."[118] Owen is insistent that "denying the Lord Christ to be the eternal Son of God" is a rejection of one of the "few … principal fundamentals of Christian religion."[119]

Connecting the assumption, sonship, and theandric action together, Owen says, "The Son of God assumed our nature into personal subsistence with himself—whereby [the] whole Christ was one person, and all his mediatory acts were the acts of that one person, of him who was both God and man."[120] Commenting on Heb. 1:2 ("his Son, whom he appointed the heir of all things"), Owen says that the "whom" refers to the "Son" as "the revealer of the gospel, Θεάνθρωπος, 'God and man.' … the Lord Christ performed all the acts of his mediatory office in and by the human nature, yet he did them not as man, but as God and man in one person."[121] Therefore, not only does Owen insist on the identification of the theandric mediator with God the Son but he also insists that the accomplishment of the theandric acts terminate upon the Son (i.e., not the Spirit nor the Father). This affirmation need not violate the indivisibility of triune operations either. Owen claims, "Wherefore, this work of our redemption and recovery being the especial effect of the authority, love, and power of the Father—it was to be *executed* in and by the person of the Son; as the application of it unto us is made by the Holy Ghost."[122] That is, it is "in and by" the Son that the theandric acts of Christ are accomplished. As we will see below, this need not exclude the prominent activity of the Holy Spirit nor the operability of the humanity of Christ.

3. *Principium Quo/Quod* We may further elaborate upon Owen's understanding of the theandric acts of the mediator through an investigation of a standard formula in the Reformed tradition of Owen's time. Owen publishes two versions of this same christological formula. While the lack of technical precision in Owen will be evident here, together these texts serve to articulate the single theandric agent and the distinction of divine and human agencies.

---

118. WJO, *Christologia*, 1:225.
119. WJO, *Evangelical Love*, 15:83.
120. WJO, *Christologia*, 1:40.
121. WJO, *Exposition of Hebrews*, 20:40.
122. WJO, *Christologia*, 1:220.

3. The Evidence of Christological Agency

Table 1 Comparing *Communion* and *Vindication* on Christological Action

Communion 2:51 (1657)	*Vindication* 2:433 (1669)
The execution of his office of mediation in his single person, in respect of both natures: wherein is considerable,	The sum is, that in all the mediatory actions of Christ we are to consider—
ὁ ἐνεργῶν—the agent, Christ himself, God and man. He is the principium quo, ἐνεργητικὸν—the principle that gives life and efficacy to the whole work; and then,	(1) The agent; and that is the person of Christ.
2dly, The principium quod—that which operates, which is both natures distinctly considered.	(2) The immediate principle by which and from which the agent worketh; and that is the natures in the person.
3dly. The ἐνέργεια, or δραστικὴ τῆς φύσεως κίνησις—the effectual working itself of each nature.	(3) The actions; which are the effectual operations of either nature.
And, lastly, the ἐνέργημα, or ἀποτέλεσμα—the effect produced, which ariseth from all, and relates to them all: so resolving the excellency I speak of into his personal union.	(4) The effect or work with respect to God and us; and this relates unto the person of the agent, the Lord Christ, God and man.

Both texts claim that (1) there is one agent, the God-man; (2) each nature operates according to its own principle; (3) the operations produce effects according to either nature; and (4) the ultimate effect (i.e., action) relates to the person of the God-man.[123]

The Reformed tradition frequently employs this fourfold affirmation, and a few of those instances will be surveyed in order both to accuse and excuse Owen. For example, Francis Turretin (who claims to be following John of Damascus), Peter van Mastricht, Heinrich Heppe, and Charles Hodge all make this claim.[124] Heppe presents this formula as

> (1) the procuring cause, the *theanthropos* person *energon*. (2) The two principles *energetika* of the producing cause, the two natures in the mediator. (3) The twofold efficacy of the divine and human natures, answer to the number of the two principles, or the twofold *energeia*. Finally (4) the one work, the *energoumenon* or *apotelesma theandrikon*, which the one mediator produces for the two natures through the efficacy peculiar to each.[125]

123. Spence notes the *Communion* text (*Incarnation and Inspiration*, 79, 101) as does Tay (*Priesthood*, 80-1), but neither notices or addresses the potential Nestorian difficulty that we will see below.

124. See below Ch. 6 §I.A. Peter van Mastricht, *Theoretico-Practica Theologia* (Utrecht: W. van de Water, 1724), V.iv.13; Heppe, *Reformed Dogmatics*, 446; Hodge, *Systematic Theology*, 2:458-9; *Synopsis*, 2: 85.

125. Heppe, *Reformed Dogmatics*, 446. See Tay, *Priesthood*, 80-1 for the distinct dogmatic location of the *apotelesma* in Reformed and Lutheran thought.

Likewise, Turretin says,

> (1) He is one that works (*energon*), the agent [*agens*] or principle which [*principium quod*] acts (which is the *suppositum* or person of Christ). (2) The activity (*energetikon*) or formal principle by which [*principium formale quo*] he acts—that by which [*per quod*] the agent or person of Christ works (to wit, the two natures, each of which works without any confusion). (3) The Energy (*energeia*) or operation which depends upon the principle-by-which [*principio quo*] and partakes of the nature of its own principle, so that it is divine if the principle-by-which is the divine nature, but human if it is the humanity. (4) The Effect (*energema*) or accomplishment (*apotelesma*) which depends upon the principle-which [*principio quod*] and is the external work.[126]

This formal and material commonality among Owen and the Reformed who come after him evidence the emphasis on the mediator as the acting agent, the distinct principles of operation, distinct immediate effects, and the single accomplishment of Christ's actions. This aligns with Owen's use of this formula in *Vindication* and articulates the rhetorical effect of both texts. That is, both texts are advocating for the theandric mediator as the single agent, the distinction of agency, and the redemptive effect of that action belonging to the theandric agent.

However, Owen's Latin usage of "*principium quod*" and "*principium quo*" in *Communion with the Triune God* (A) diverges from the historic pattern outlined above, and (B) may be understood to incline toward Nestorianism. Here Owen (unlike Turretin and unlike his *Vindication*) paired the agent with the "*principium quo*" (principle by which) and the two natures with "*principium quod*" (principle which). The problem arises because it seems that if Christ's two natures are "principles which" accomplish acts (akin to agents on other accounts), then Owen has fallen into Nestorianism.[127]

I suggest that while the Latin designations are imprecise (and, therefore, ought not to be followed), there is a way to resolve the problem without relegating Owen to the Nestorian bench for the rest of the theological game. This solution is to

---

126. Turretin, *Institutes*, II:14.ii.3; *Institutio Theologiae Elencticae* (New York: Robert Carter, 1847), 335.

127. A quick dismissal of this expression as a Latin error or an early error that he corrected later in his life is prohibited by the occurrence of the human nature of Christ as the "*principium quod*" in WJO, *Exposition of Hebrews*, 20:30 (1668, just a year before *Vindication*). However, this text seems to be less theologically problematic than the one in *Communion* and a solution in *Communion* would likely apply here also. Here Owen says, "For although the person of Christ, God and man, was our mediator, Acts 20:28, John 1:14, 18, yet his human nature was that wherein he discharged the duties of his office, and the '*principium quod*' of all his mediatory actings, 1 Tim. 2:5." Notice that Owen claims that the "he" who accomplishes the action is the Christ who is "God and man," "our mediator." Likewise, these are "his mediatory actings."

notice that Owen orients this entire paragraph in *Communion with the Triune God* and the consideration therein "in respect of both natures." That is, there is a particular focus in this text on the operations of the natures. This consideration gives the reader a different perspective or focus of the action. Taking my five-year-old daughter as an example: when asked to explain why her brother was crying, she said, "Dad, my hand pushed him and then my foot kicked him." In this story and from her perspective, the "principle which" (quod) is the hand and foot. Likewise, when the natures are in distinct consideration, they can be said to be the "principle which."[128] An understanding that considers Owen's treatment of actions "in respect of both natures" in Communion with the triune God helps make sense of several other factors: (1) the continuity that Owen seems to think he has with the tradition here (i.e., he doesn't indicate a disagreement, maintains the structure and the form), (2) the continuity with his later work, and (3) his connection between "the agent" (which Owen in *Communion* calls the *principium quo*) and the accomplishment (*apotelesma*). On this last point, we might note that Turretin likewise connects the agent and the *apotelesma*, but does so in terms of the *principium quod*. If Owen were changing his view and constructing a Nestorian account of natures as agents, then it seems that Owen also ought to change the connection between the agent and the *apotelesma* (so that the multiple distinct agents bring about multiple distinct *apotelesmata*). Yet, in both texts Owen maintains that the *apotelesma* is connected to the singular agent. Additionally, (4) if Owen were attempting to flip the role of natures and the person (through the flipping of *principium quo* and *principium quod*), then one would expect a standard definition of both terms. But instead he uses an idiosyncratic definition of *principium quo* as "the principle [which] gives life and efficacy to the whole work." This is, minimally, not the standard usage of *principium quo* (a designation that usually connotes ability), evidencing that Owen was not simply attempting to turn natures into agents in a Nestorian way. Finally, (5) Owen's English remains consistent in both texts. Therefore, this text in *Communion with the Triune God* does not successfully convict Owen of Nestorianism, but rather (together with his paragraph in *Vindication*) evidences the singularity of the theandric agent, the distinction of agencies, the immediate effects of the distinct natures, and the redemptive effects of the acts of the mediator (while further reflecting Owen's less-than-consistent use of technical language).

B. Distinct Agencies

The above subsection advocated for an understanding of Christ's actions as theandric and filial insofar as they reflected the ontological foundation of the Son's assumption of a human nature into subsistence with himself. In this subsection, we

---

128. This analogy focuses on the correspondence between the *principium quod* in my daughter's story and in Owen's account. The *principium quo* is not addressed, yet it need not be problematic because Owen is using this phrase in an idiosyncratic way.

will articulate the distinction between human and divine capacities for intentional action (agencies) in christological operations on the basis of the distinct properties of each nature. Significant to this account is the ontological foundation of these distinct capacities (i.e., §II.B mirrors §I.B). The ontological and operational are especially bound together in the conciliar claim of two "principles of operation" in the one mediator, which we will examine first. Then we will address the way in which Owen conceives of these two distinct agencies producing distinct immediate effects. Finally, we will look especially at the way Owen treats the role of the Holy Spirit in Christ's human agency.

1. Two Principles of Operation Ontologically, recalling from §I.B, "All natural properties are double in Christ,—[e.g., the] will."[129] Consequently, Owen often says that natures with their specific properties and capacities are the "principle of operations," meaning that Christ's two natures indicate two principles of operation.[130] Using the burning bush of Exodus 3, Owen illustrates the way in which the infinite Son could become incarnate in a human nature without destroying its human principle of operation.

> This fire was a type or declaration of the presence of God in the person of the Son .... This fire placed itself in a bush, where it burned; but the bush was not consumed .... Thence was God said to dwell in the bush ... Deut 33:16. And this is so spoken, because the being of the fire in the bush for a season was a type of him in whom "the fulness of the Godhead dwelt bodily." ... The eternal fire of the divine nature dwells in the bush of our frail nature, yet is it not consumed thereby.[131]

So, just as the principles of the bush's operation are not destroyed by the addition of the divine fire within the bush, so too are the human capacities and agency of Christ retained in the incarnation of the Son of God.

Based on these distinct natures and natural properties, Owen insists that Christ "acts suitably unto the essential properties and principles of that nature."[132] Therefore, just as his divine nature remained ontologically "immense, omniscient, omnipotent," so too Christ, "as God," "made all things, upholds all things by the word of his power, fills heaven and earth."[133] Moreover, just as his human nature remained "finite [and] limited," so too in Christ's actions "as man, he lived, hungered, suffered, died, rose, ascended into heaven."[134] Likewise, Owen asks the

---

129. WJO, *Catechism*, 1:478; cf. *Vindication*, 2:418.
130. WJO, *Vindication of the Preceding Discourse*, 2:329; *Righteous Zeal*, 8:157; *Death of Death*, 10:35–6, 119–20; *Vindiciæ Evangelicæ*, 12:335; see Ch. 2 §II.A.2.
131. WJO, *Glory of Christ*, 1:311.
132. WJO, *Vindication*, 2:418.
133. Ibid.
134. Ibid.

3. The Evidence of Christological Agency

reader to consider the divine nature and "observe all its essential properties. It acts suitably unto itself; it acts nothing but what becomes it and is proper unto the divine nature …. The divine nature did not act in hungering, and thirsting, and weariness, and bleeding, and dying; it cannot do so."[135] And yet, "All because of the unity of his person" the theandric agent is said to "do all these things."[136]

Recalling the text in *Christologia*, which structured our section, we see the ontological foundation for the affirmation of distinct principles of operation. Owen says, "Each nature operates in him according unto its essential properties. The divine nature knows all things, upholds all things, rules all things, acts by its presence everywhere; the human nature was born, yielded obedience, died, and rose again."[137] This is based on the ontological affirmation that "each nature doth preserve its own natural, essential properties, entirely unto and in itself; without mixture, without composition or confusion."[138] Connecting the ontological properties and operations of each nature, Owen says,

> In the assumption of our nature to be his own, he did not change it into a thing divine and spiritual; but preserved it entire in all its essential properties and *actings*. Hence it really died and suffered, was tried, tempted, and forsaken, as the same nature in any other man might do and be. That nature (as it was peculiarly his, and therefore he, or his person therein) was exposed unto all the temporary evils which the same nature is subject unto in any other person.[139]

Owen is careful not to allow these principles of operation to turn into agents themselves. Thus, in one place, he reinforces his conciliar commitment (i.e., to Constantinople III's affirmation of two energies), yet denies that these two energies, or principles of operation, are themselves agents. He says, "Although every energy or operation be δραστικὴ τῆς φύσεως κίνησις [an active movement of the nature], and so the distinct natures are distinct principles of Christ's operations, yet his person is the principal or only agent; which being God-man, all the actions thereof … are theandrical."[140]

While this above claim from Owen seems abundantly clear and coheres well with the conciliar commitments of classical and Reformed Christology, this phrase "principle of operation" presents a difficulty for understanding Owen

---

135. WJO, "Condescension of Christ," 17:566; cf. Holmes, "Communicatio Idiomatum," 81.
136. WJO, *Vindication*, 2:418–19.
137. WJO, *Christologia*, 1:234; likewise, Bavinck, *RD*, 3:315.
138. WJO, *Christologia*, 1:234.
139. WJO, *Glory of Christ*, 1:329–30, emphasis mine; Owen insists that the incarnation is soteriologically significant for the Christian not only by means of ontological "participation in their nature" but also operational "copartnership with them in their condition" (*Exposition of Hebrews*, 20:468).
140. WJO, *Vindication of the Preceding Discourse*, 2:329.

and evidences, again, his lack of consistency with technical terminology. In christological contexts this phrase is used by Constantinople III and often by Owen in order to defend the distinct capacities of Christ's two natures. However, Owen also uses it in the singular to articulate the singular theandric mediation of Christ.[141] Like the previous chapter, this seems to present conciliar difficulties (since Constantinople III affirms two principles of operation). I will argue that, when understood in context, Owen's imprecise language can be understood in support of his account of theandric action and that it need not violate Constantinople III. One crucial example of Owen's imprecise language is his insistence that by Christ's assumption of flesh the "blessed excellencies of his distinct natures are made most illustriously conspicuous in becoming one entire principle of all his mediatory operations on our behalf."[142] Here Christ in his divine and human natures is "one entire principle" mediating between God and humanity. In order to make sense of this inconsistency in terminology from his earlier usage we might observe: First, this may itself be seen as a judgment of the unity of theandric action as divine and human. Just as Owen considers the person the singular God-man, he considers the agent the theandric mediator. As such, he is denying that nature acts either in isolation or division from the other. If that is the case, then Owen is simply affirming the same judgment as the above through an idiosyncratic and less-than-technical use of "principle of ... operations," meaning something like "single theandric operator." Additionally, Owen's inconsistency could be attributable to his claim that the singular consequence or event (ἀποτέλεσμα) is dependent upon the singular mediatorial agent, who is God and man, as opposed to the immediate effect of either nature.[143] That is, Owen could be so focused on the significance of Christ's singular actions that he is emphasizing these acts as derivative from a singular source (i.e., the theandric agent as something like a source, or "principle" of an "action"). On the viability of these two observations, we need not see Owen's inconsistencies as judgmental contradictions, but less-than-technical usages for the sake of emphasis.

2. *Immediacy* Because of the distinction of these two principles of operation in the acts of the single theandric agent, Owen also distinguishes between distinct immediate effects of these operations. So Owen insists on affirming that the theandric mediator prays, while rejecting that praying is accomplished

---

141. For example, Owen calls the "one Christ" the "one distinct personal principle of all operations, of all that he did or doth as mediator" (WJO, *Vindication*, 2:418; see also *Exposition of Hebrews*, 20:225). Conversely, even in this same text, Owen explicitly denies that the divine and human nature constitutes a "third compound principle of physical acts and operations" (*Vindication*, 2:433), seemingly indicating that principles of action and operation belong to natures.

142. WJO, *Christologia*, 1:158.

143. WJO, *Communion* 2:51; *Vindication* 2:433; *Vindiciæ Evangelicæ*, 12:431; *Justification*, 5:255.

by the divine nature.[144] Likewise, the theandric mediator forgives, yet does not accomplish forgiveness according to his human nature. So, in order to distinguish between the distinct effects of the theandric mediator's operations according to the distinct principles of operation, Owen employs the concept of "immediacy," or direct derivation. This concept allows him to maintain the singularity of the agent who accomplishes the action (i.e., the theandric mediator), affirm the simultaneity of the distinct agencies in all actions, and yet preserve the distinction between the two principles of operation and their effects.

Owen provides an example of the immediate effects of distinct agencies in his narration of Christ's obedience.[145] Beginning with the single agent, the God-man, Owen says, "The obedience we treat of was the obedience of Christ the mediator: but the obedience of Christ as 'the mediator of the covenant,' was the obedience of his person."[146] He then goes on to clarify that this obedience "was performed in the human nature; but the person of Christ was he that performed it."[147] Owen avers that the acts of obedience must not be according to his divine nature, since his divine nature could never be made "under the law." Instead, "He was, indeed, as the apostle witnesseth, made so in his human nature, wherein he performed this obedience: 'Made of a woman, made under the law,' Gal 4:4."[148] Yet this is a theandric act of Christ that was not the "obedience of the human nature abstractedly ... but the obedience of the *person* of the Son of God."[149]

Owen then draws an analogy between the immediacy of ordinary human acts that can belong to either the soul or the body and the acts of Christ, which can immediately belong to either his divine or human natures. Owen says, "As in the person of a man, some of his acts, as to the immediate principle of operation, are acts of the body, and some are so of the soul; yet, in their performance and accomplishment, are they the acts of the person: so the acts of Christ in his mediation."[150] Owen does not further specify or give any examples, but I think we can elaborate on his meaning. For example, we might assume that Owen conceives of "loving God" as an act of the soul. This does not imply that the body is uninvolved (e.g., kneeling, serving others, giving), nor does it mean that the soul is the sole agent (since the agent is the "person" who has both body and soul). Practically, we might think of "ducking down" when a golf ball is

---

144. WJO, *Vindiciæ Evangelicæ*, 12:246.
145. For a helpful survey of the historical and polemical context of Owen's claims on the obedience of Christ, see Tay, *Priesthood*, 84.
146. WJO, *Justification*, 5:255.
147. Ibid.
148. Ibid., 5:256.
149. Ibid., emphasis mine.
150. Ibid., 5:255.

flying at you as an act that belongs to the body as its immediate principle.[151] This does not mean that the body can perform this action exclusively on its own, or that the body is the agent, since the person is the agent. Bringing the analogy back to Christ's actions, Owen says that "as to their ἐνεργήματα, or immediate operation, [these operations] were the actings of his distinct natures,—some of the divine and some of the human, immediately; but as unto their ἀποτελέσματα, and the perfecting efficacy of them, they were the acts of his whole person."[152] Therefore, the agent of these acts is the "whole person," the theandric mediator. Yet the immediate principle of these operations can be either nature. Therefore, the immediate principle of Christ's death on the cross is his human nature and the immediate principle of forgiving sins (Mt. 9:6) is his divine nature. All the while, the agent of both of these operations is the theandric mediator.

This account of immediacy helps to place Owen's significant claim that the soul of Christ acts as "the immediate principle of all his moral operations, even as ours are in us" in its proper theological context.[153] Owen says that this is in contrast to the claim that the "divine nature was … unto him in the place of a soul … [or] did immediately operate the thing which he performed, as some of old vainly imagined."[154] While some suggest that this claim is where "Owen's independence from the tradition is most apparent," I suggest that this claim is indicative of his classical and Reformed account of immediate effects.[155] Spence suggests that this is in contrast to accounts where the Son is "operating as the single subject of all his actions" and instead Christ's humanity is autokinetic, only influenced mediately by the Son's activity through the Holy Spirit.[156] However, I would suggest that Owen is not contrasting his position against those who predicate the actions of Christ to the Son but is instead reiterating his point about the immediate effects of each nature's distinct agencies in the acts of the mediator. Owen's contrast is not with conciliar Christology, but with the Apollinarian (i.e., he describes: "in the place of a soul") and monenergite (i.e., "immediately operate the thing which he performed") heresies that were ruled out at Constantinople III. Owen says, "Christ, as man, did and was to exercise all grace by the rational faculties and powers of his soul, his understanding, will, and affections; for he [en]acted grace as a man,

---

151. There would have to be further discussion on whether (or in what sense) these occurrences are "actions" (the intentional production of an effect) since the effect of the former is not clear and the intentionality of the latter is not clear. However, they serve as a sufficient analogy to the *sui generis* God-man.

152. WJO, *Justification*, 5:255.

153. WJO, *Pneumatologia*, 3:169; notice that (because of the unity of the single agent) this claim does not preclude Owen from claiming that "all the moral operations of that nature are the acts of the person of the Son of God" (*Christologia*, 1:215).

154. WJO, *Pneumatologia*, 3:169.

155. Spence, *Incarnation and Inspiration*, 57.

156. Spence, "Christ's Humanity and Ours," 96; Spence, *Incarnation and Inspiration*, 96.

'made of a woman, made under the law.'"[157] Therefore, the "moral operations" that Owen is referring to are the acts of Christ's obedience, immediately accomplished according to human capacities.[158] So, since these operations are according to human capacities, Christ's human nature is the "immediate principle of all his moral operations." This does not mean that the Son is excluded from this act, but that the operation in view is an immediate effect of the human agency of the theandric mediator.

This construal allows Owen to speak of theandric action in operations that belong immediately to one nature, as well as operations that both are capable of. So the immediacy of the act of dying belongs to the human nature. However, this does not imply that the divine nature is uninvolved in these actions (cf. Rom. 5:8). Owen states that because of divine impassibility there are no Reformed theologians "affirming that Christ died any otherwise than in his human nature, though he who is God died therein."[159] That is, the divine nature did not die, but the theandric mediator who subsists in a divine nature and a human nature did die. Likewise, Owen insisted that it was not proper to the divine nature to pray, so he states, "The Godhead prayed not, but he who was God prayed."[160] Additionally, Owen gives an example that both natures are capable of, yet each in their own distinct way: love. Owen insists that "the love of Christ in his human nature towards his [people] is exceeding, intense, tender, precious, compassionate, abundantly heightened by a sense of our miseries, feeling of our wants, experience of our temptations; all flowing from that rich stock of grace, pity, and compassion."[161] However, if the love of Christ were merely the love of his human nature, it could not be "infinite nor eternal, nor from itself absolutely unchangeable."[162] Thankfully, Christ does possess and exercise divine agency and, therefore, divine love for his church. Of Christ's divine love, Owen says, "But now the love of Christ, being the love of God, is effectual and fruitful in producing all the good things which he willeth unto his beloved."[163] Owen summarizes,

> Wherefore this love of Christ which we inquire after is the love of his person,— that is, which he in his own person acts in and by his distinct natures, according unto their distinct essential properties. And the acts of love in these distinct natures are infinitely distinct and different; yet are they all acts of one and the same person. So, then, whether that act of love in Christ which we would at any

---

157. WJO, *Pneumatologia*, 3:169; for an important clarification of this text, see *Christologia*, 39–40.

158. For this claim in Owen's anthropology in general, see WJO, *Pneumatologia*, 3:326; *Exposition of Hebrews*, 23:460.

159. WJO, *Exposition of Hebrews*, 20:361.

160. WJO, *Vindiciæ Evangelicæ*, 12:246.

161. WJO, *Communion*, 2:62.

162. WJO, *Communion*, 2:62; cf. *Christologia*, 1:169.

163. WJO, *Communion*, 2:63; cf. *Christologia*, 1:166.

time consider, be an eternal act of the divine nature in the person of the Son of God; or whether it be an act of the human, performed in time by the gracious faculties and powers of that nature, it is still the love of one and the selfsame person,—Christ Jesus.[164]

So, in this example of love, we see Owen affirming the simultaneity of human and divine operations accomplished by the single agent and the production of distinct immediate effects according to either nature.

Owen insists that the immediate effect of a particular operation does not constitute that natural agency as a distinct agent. Rather, the agent is the theandric mediator who performs the action according to the agency of both natures. Owen says, "Whatever acts are ascribed unto him, however immediately performed, in or by the human nature, or in and by his divine nature, they are all the acts of that one person, in whom are both these natures. That [is,] this Christ, God and man."[165] Likewise, he claims that while "each nature acts distinctly, according to its own being and properties, yet so as what is the immediate act of either nature is the act of him who is one in both."[166] While Owen adds layers of complexity and bolsters the concept, he claims that the distinction between the immediacy of the distinct natures and unity in the single agent is one of "the common notions of Christian religion—the common principles of our profession, which the Scriptures also abundantly testify unto."[167]

3. Human Agency and the Holy Spirit Having seen the unity of the acts of the theandric mediator and the distinction of the divine and human agencies of that mediator, we now turn to how the Spirit is involved in the activity of Christ. This subsection will argue that the Holy Spirit plays an integral part in Owen's affirmation of distinct agencies, not as the divine person upon whom the accomplished acts of Christ terminate but as the one to whom we predicate the preservation and enablement of genuine humanity and the perfection and application of divine activity.[168] The human nature of Christ is therefore preserved by the Holy Spirit and provided with the necessary grace to accomplish the acts of mediation. While it is particularly this point which some suggest is Owen's point of departure from the classical and Reformed tradition into stream of novelty, I

---

164. WJO, *Glory of Christ*, 1:336; see also Owen's treatment of Christ's personal love according to his divine nature and according to his human nature in the *Glory of Christ*, 1:336.

165. WJO, *Vindication*, 2:415.

166. Ibid., 2:433.

167. Ibid., 2:414–15.

168. For broader treatments on the significance of the Holy Spirit for the integrity of the humanity of Christ, see Spence, "Christ's Humanity and Ours," 75; Cleveland, *Thomism*, 149; Trueman, *John Owen*, 95.

3. The Evidence of Christological Agency

contend that Owen's "pneumachristology" is in service of and in continuity with his classical and Reformed account of christological action.[169]

Much discussion in Owen studies centers on the claims Owen makes in *Pneumatologia* II.3, particularly his claims outlined in the following four points:

1. The only singular immediate *act* of the person of the Son on the human nature was the *assumption* of it into subsistence with himself ....
2. That the only *necessary consequent* of this assumption of the human nature, or the incarnation of the Son of God, is the *personal union of Christ*, ...
3. That all other actings of God in the *person of the Son* towards the human nature were *voluntary*.
4. The Holy Ghost ... is the *immediate, peculiar, efficient cause* of all external divine operations.[170]

I contend that this text evidences that the Spirit infuses sustaining and empowering grace into the human nature incrementally and voluntarily (i.e., not as a necessary or inevitable consequence of the hypostatic union).[171] Therefore, this passage does not indicate that the Spirit is the divine person to whom we attribute Christ's accomplished acts, nor that the divine person of the Son is operationally distant from the actions of Christ.

Further, Owen's account of the Spirit as "the *immediate, peculiar, efficient cause* of all external divine operations"[172] does not mean that the Son is only "indirectly" involved or that the Spirit is "the divine agent in works *ad extra.*"[173] Such construals of the Son and Spirit's action seem to make them sequential or contiguous in their operations. Instead, this account views the whole Trinity as the agent (from the perspective of causality). It is only from the perspective of the terminus that action that we can appropriate acts to distinct persons. So when Owen says that the Spirit is the "efficient cause," he does not mean that the Spirit is the cause of divine actions more or less than the Father or Son, but that the Spirit is the one to whom we predicate the "efficacy" of divine action.[174] So when Owen says, "Whatever the Son of God wrought in, by, or upon the human nature, he did it by the Holy Ghost," it means that the Son is the one who "accomplishes" (i.e., who "wrought" the act),

---

169. This expression comes from Burger, *Being in Christ*, 40.

170. WJO, *Pneumatologia*, 3:160–1.

171. For additional argumentation for my interpretation of Owen and its location within Owen scholarship, see Kieser, "The Holy Spirit and the Humanity of Christ in John Owen."

172. WJO, *Pneumatologia*, 3:160–1.

173. The first quote comes from Spence, *Incarnation and Inspiration*, 142; the second, Trueman, *John Owen*, 69; Trueman, *Claims*, 177; see also, McDonald, *Re-Imaging Election*, 13. This phrase is not clearly elaborated upon in either Trueman or McDonald and both speak rightly about indivisible operations in Owen elsewhere, but it this phraseology reflects a common perception and is therefore worth addressing.

174. WJO, *Pneumatologia*, 3:163.

yet it is the Spirit to whom we predicate the efficacy or application of that act.[175] Just as the Father is active in the work of Christ as the one to whom we appropriate the acts of "designing" (Acts 4:28; Jn 5:20), "willing" (Heb. 10:9), "preparing" (Heb. 10:5), "sending" (Jn 12:49),[176] so the Spirit is the one to whom we appropriate the perfecting, applying, and making efficacious of the acts of the God-man. So the God-man performs miracles "by" the Spirit (Mt. 12:28) not only in the sense that Christ is anointed with the Spirit according to his human nature (Lk. 4:18; Acts 10:38) but also in the sense that the "power of God" is made effectual within creation by the Spirit (i.e., the Spirit is the one upon whom the efficaciousness of the divine acts terminates). Kapic rightly summarizes this subsection when he suggests, "to speak rightly of the incarnation … one must emphasize the Spirit."[177]

III. Summary

This chapter has argued that Owen's treatment of the ontology and operations of the mediator align with the Christology of both "the ancient and modern divines" and is not radically novel in its commitment to the humanity of Christ or the Holy Spirit's activity.[178] Owen's account of ontology and operation allows him to retain the unity of Christ in the single theandric agent who operates according to two distinct principles of operations, bringing about distinct immediate effects. Owen's commitment to the integrity of the two natures and the trinitarian shape of the incarnation allows him to provide a robust account of the work of the Holy Spirit upon the humanity of Christ and in the divine operations of the triune God.

These emphases might be considered a culmination of Owen's classical and Reformed commitments. That is, Owen is here displaying his emphasis on the mediatorial action of Christ, the singularity of the agent, and the distinction of agency. As Edwin Tay states, "Owen clearly follows the Reformed [tradition] … while the distinction of natures and their operations are strictly maintained, there is a conscious attempt to place the emphasis on the person acting."[179]

Owen's account is very much akin to Francis Turretin's claims of Christ as a single person operating in two distinct natures (and, therefore, agencies):

> Our mediator ought to be God-man (*theanthropos*) to accomplish these things: man to suffer, God to overcome; man to receive the punishment we deserved, God to endure and drink it to the dregs; man to acquire salvation for us by dying,

---

175. Contrary to Claunch, "Son and Spirit," 116, who identifies the Son as the agent of "ordinary human activity," but the Spirit is the agent of divine activity (148–52).

176. See *Exposition of Hebrews*, 2:506–8; 6:461–4.

177. Kelly Kapic, "The Spirit as Gift: Explorations in John Owen's Pneumatology," in *The Ashgate Research Companion to John Owen's Theology* (Burlington: Ashgate, 2012), 131.

178. WJO, *Christologia*, 1:223.

179. Tay, *Priesthood of Christ*, 85.

God to apply it to us by overcoming; man to become ours by the assumption of flesh, God to make us like himself by the bestowal of the Spirit. This neither a mere man nor God alone could do.[180]

Following Turretin's attention to the soteriological prudence of Owen's account, we might conclude with a section from *A Vindication of the Doctrine of the Trinity*, in which Owen is addressing the question of how Christ made satisfaction for sin "either as God or as man, or as God and man."[181] Owen responds that Christ does so "as God and man" (citing Acts 20:28; and 1 Jn 3:16, which he glosses, "Hereby perceive we the love of God, because he laid down his life for us"). After citing these texts, he provides two follow-up comments: first he says that this question is only a "pretended difficulty" and "mere effect of ignorance," since it ought to be clear that "all the mediatory acts of Christ being the acts of his person, must of necessity be the acts of him as God and man."[182] Second, he says that this question erroneously presupposes that "satisfaction" is "a real act or operation of one or the other nature in Christ" when it is actually "the *apotelesma* or effect of the actings, the doing and suffering of Christ."[183] Owen clarifies that "the two natures are so united in Christ as not to have a third compound principle of physical acts and operations thence arising; but each nature acts distinctly, according to its own being and properties"[184] (i.e., that each nature retains its distinct agency). "Yet so as what is the immediate act of either nature is the act of him who is one in both; from whence it hath its dignity."[185] That is, each nature retains its own agency that brings about its own immediate effects, yet the agent of every action is the theandric mediator, "who is one in both" natures.

---

180. Turretin, *Institutes*, II:13.iii.19; similarly, Calvin, *Institutes* II.xii.2–3, 465–7; II.xiv.2–3.

181. WJO, *Vindication*, 2:432; cf. Tay, *Priesthood*, 83 for the relation of this passage in Owen to his account of mediatorial satisfaction. Owen's treatment of human and divine love in Glory of Christ, 1:336 could likewise illustrate the summative elements represented here.

182. WJO, *Vindication*, 2:433.

183. Ibid.

184. Ibid.

185. Ibid.

Chapter 4

DIVINE AGENCY: COHERENCE AND PRUDENCE

With Owen's classical and Reformed testimony established, the remainder of the project will seek to build upon Owen and articulate the internal coherence and theological prudence of classical and Reformed christological agency. In order to demonstrate the internal coherence of the position that Owen sketched above, the following chapters reengage the *prima facie* liabilities of classical and Reformed Christology. The prudence of this position will be articulated in relation to other proximate positions, evidencing certain values or benefits that classical and Reformed Christology can offer. My argument for prudence in relation to other contemporary positions need not obliterate the provisional (or provincial) character of the project, whereby its focus is within the boundaries of classical and Reformed Christology.[1]

Owen has provided his testimony as our key witness. The articulation of his account above not only demonstrates the material commitments of classical and Reformed Christology but also exhibits the associative unity of classical and Reformed christological agency (e.g., the coherence of trinitarian action and the Spirit's empowerment of Christ's human nature). Yet Owen is not the sole member of the party on trial. So from this foundation, the case for classical and Reformed Christology will seek to incorporate evidence that clarifies, updates, supports, and extends Owen's treatment. Specifically it will establish greater terminological clarity, engage with recent accounts of christological agency, incorporate other testimonies from the classical and Reformed tradition, and attend to the foundation and implications of many of his christological conclusions. So the task of the remainder of the project is to articulate an account of classical and Reformed Christology in terms of agency that is internally coherent and theologically prudent by attending to the superficial liabilities from the constituent components of the tradition (i.e., *sola Scriptura*, conciliar Christology, classical Trinitarianism, and Reformed christological commitments) and engaging with the corresponding proximate positions raised in Chapter 1. It will unfold in three remaining chapters,

---

1. This is to underscore the modesty of the claim prosecuted here. Specifically, my argument for the prudence of classical and Reformed theology ought not to outright exclude the plausibility of any of these proximate positions.

reflective of the Chalcedonian ordering: perfect in deity, perfect in humanity, "one and the same Christ, Son." Therefore, Chapter 4 will articulate the classical and Reformed understanding of the divine agency of Christ and Chapter 5 will present Christ's human agency. Chapter 6 will provide the concluding principles of unity and distinction in classical and Reformed christological agency. Taken as a whole, the goal is to argue for the coherence and prudence of predominantly understanding Christ as a single theandric agent who operates according to distinct agencies simultaneously.[2]

Demonstrating the coherence of classical and Reformed Christology, this chapter will incorporate the classical trinitarian commitments of Chapter 2 and the biblical testimony of divine agency in Christ. In order to show the theological prudence of such an account, this chapter will position classical and Reformed Christology in relation to other proximate positions on divine agency in Christ. Materially, it will argue that (1) the divine operations of Christ are indivisibly operations of the triune God, the execution of which terminate upon the divine Son, and that (2) Christ's divine operations are executions of simple divine agency. These affirmations allow classical and Reformed Christology to avoid multiple superficial liabilities, namely that (1a) the Father, Son, and Holy Spirit are three independent agents of distinct causation; that (1b) the Spirit is the divine agent of the accomplished acts of Christ; and that (2) the single agent must give up divine properties to suffer and act as a human. The chapter will proceed by demonstrating the coherence of the trinitarian shape of divine agency in Christ (§I), then articulate the coherence of divine simplicity and Christ's divine agency (§II). Next it will engage the testimony of divine agency in Rom. 5:6–11 in order to demonstrate the biblical prudence of classical and Reformed Christology (§III). And finally it will articulate the theological and pastoral prudence of classical and Reformed christological agency (§IV).

The argument for the coherence of this account will depend largely upon the language of "perspectives." This is, in part, dependent upon the philosophy of action distinctions drawn in Chapter 1. Yet, much more than a philosophical imposition or a means of special pleading, my use of distinct perspectives on the same event finds historic precedent in the distinction between the principle and the *terminus* of an action (see Ch. 2 §II.B.3–4). Additionally, it bears similarities to the more recent uses in Gilles Emery (who draws a distinction between two ways of considering trinitarian actions according to their unity and their "dynamism") and in Adonis Vidu's use of the "toggling of agency" in which "the same action is to be ascribed to both the Trinity as a whole, as well as to an individual person."[3]

---

2. The language of "predominantly" is intended to communicate that, because of the semi-openness of the register of "agency," this is the appropriate way of predicating under most common contexts in classical and Reformed christological discussions.

3. Emery, "The Personal Mode of Action," 76; Adonis Vidu, "Opera Trinitatis Ad Extra and Collective Agency," *EJFPR* 7 (2015): 37.

I. Trinitarian, Divine Agency

This section will draw from Owen's testimony of classical Trinitarianism to argue for the coherence and prudence of classical and Reformed Christology's account of divine agency. Specifically, it will argue for the singularity of divine actions (from the perspective of causality), the appropriated distinctions between divine persons in a singular divine act (from the perspective of an act's *terminus*), and the proper predication of particular modes of acting to distinct divine persons (from the perspective of intra-trinitarian relations). These arguments help to uphold the inherent triunity of christological action, appreciate the unity of divine persons, and articulate the necessary activity of the Holy Spirit in Christ. As such, classical and Reformed Christology can adhere to its classical trinitarian commitment and the biblical emphasis on the Holy Spirit without denying the distinct divine person's involvement in every action and particularly the Son's execution of Christ's acts.

A. Causal Acts: God as Single Agent with Singular Agency

With Owen, this section begins by affirming singular divine agency (i.e., singular capacity on the basis of God's singular understanding, power, principle of operation, and will).[4] For Owen, this leads to the conclusion that every divine person acts indivisibly in every divine action. He says, "The several persons are undivided in their operations, acting all by the same will, the same wisdom, the same power. Every person, therefore, is the author of every work of God, because each person is God."[5] Because of the singular agency and the indivisibility of divine actions, Owen can ascribe the predicate "agent" to the triune God.[6]

The prudence and location of classical and Reformed thought in contemporary theology may be viewed in relation to the contemporary theological position that sees the three divine persons acting "in consort as ... [distinct] agents,"[7] social Trinitarianism. Cornelius Plantinga Jr.'s often-cited definition of this position states that "the theory must have Father, Son, and Spirit as distinct centers of consciousness ... [and yet] Father, Son, and Spirit must be tightly enough related to each other so as to render plausible" claims to monotheism.[8] Focusing on the distinctions in actions, Stephen T. Davis adds that the three persons are "distinct centers of consciousness, will, and action ... they have desires, intentions, and

---

4. WJO, *Vindiciæ Evangelicæ*, 12:335.
5. WJO, *Pneumatologia*, 3:93.
6. WJO, *Exposition of Hebrews*, 19:106; *Justification*, 5:240; *Death of Death*, 10:163.
7. Ben Witherington III, "The Trinity in the Johannine Literature," in *The Oxford Handbook of the Trinity*, ed. Gilles Emery and Matthew Levering (New York: Oxford University Press, 2011), 72. See Crawford, *Cyril's Trinitarian Theology of Scripture*, 31 for why "cooperation" is too weak of a term to describe the "necessarily" trinitarian action of the triune God.
8. Plantinga Jr., "Social Trinity and Tritheism," 22.

aims" and have the "ability to act, to do and achieve things."[9] Thomas McCall summarizes the position as holding to three "agents who are (or have) distinct centers of consciousness and will."[10] As such, McCall states, "there is an irreducible distinction in divine action" among the divine persons.[11] The putative value of this position is the distinguishability of the divine persons in their distinct acts. Robert Jenson suggests that the classical trinitarian predication of every triune act as "the work of each person and all" leads to the "bankruptcy of trinitarian meaning."[12]

Yet, in contrast to this the distinctions drawn between the divine persons and their distinct actions in social Trinitarianism, whereby the three persons are three independent agents (and may be said to have distinct agency), the classical and Reformed tradition affirms a single agency that is indivisibly executed in a single act by all three persons. Specifically, this position follows the early church's insistence that "trinitarian monotheism requires the claim that every divine action is equally participated in by all trinitarian persons."[13] Because each divine person participates in the singular agency, each act is caused by each divine person. This includes, but is stronger than, a unity of intention.[14] Instead, it is the indivisible execution of the single intention by the triune God in a single action.

One poignant example that accentuates the single causality of triune operations is the resurrection of Jesus Christ. Contrary to much of modern scholarship, Owen and the classical tradition claim that the Son (according to his divine agency) raises himself from the dead and does so because of the doctrine of indivisible operations.[15] While biblical claims about the resurrection being an act of "God" (Acts 2:24; cf. 2 Cor. 4:14) "by the Spirit" (Rom. 8:11; 1 Pet. 3:18) are commonly referenced and assumed, the resurrection is an act (like all acts of God) of the

---

9. Stephen T. Davis, "Perichoretic Monotheism: A Defense of a Social Theory of the Trinity," in *Trinity: East/West Dialogue*, SPR 24 (Dordrecht: Kluwer Academic, 2003), 42.

10. McCall, *Which Trinity?*, 14.

11. Thomas H. McCall, "Relational Trinity: Creedal Perspective," in *Two Views on the Doctrine of the Trinity*, ed. Jason S. Sexton, CBT (Grand Rapids: Zondervan Academic, 2014), 121.

12. Robert Jenson, *The Triune Identity: God according to the Gospel* (Philadelphia: Fortress Press, 1982), 126–7. Likewise, McCormack suggests that the principle of inseperable operations in the "orthodox dogma of the Trinity" leads to the "unavoidable" step into "practical unitarianism" (*Humility of the Eternal Son*, 23).

13. Michel René Barnes, *The Power of God: Δύναμις in Gregory of Nyssa's Trinitarian Theology* (Washington, DC: Catholic University of America Press, 2001), 303.

14. Contrary to Schwöbel, *God: Action and Revelation*, 43; Moltmann, *The Trinity and the Kingdom*, 149.

15. WJO, *Vindiciæ Evangelicæ*, 12:78; cf. 12:561; *Pneumatologia*, 3:181, 182. The contrary position was held by Socinians in Owen's day (*Racovian Catechism*, 361–4) and today by thinkers like Frei, *Identity of Jesus Christ*, 125–8.

triune God: Father, Son, and Spirit.[16] The inclusion of the Son in the act of the resurrection is biblically attested in Jn 10:18: "No one takes my life from me, but I lay it down on my own accord. I have the authority to lay it down and I have the authority to take it up again" (see also Jn 2:19). Francis Turretin says that it is inherent to orthodoxy to "ascribe the *cause* of the resurrection to Christ himself no less than to the Father. Since the power of the Father and the Son is the same, they think that by the same [power] the Father raised Christ and Christ raised himself"; to deny such a claim is "blasphemous and wicked."[17] From the perspective of causality, every act of the triune God belongs to all three persons, as the triune God is considered a single agent.[18]

The difference between social Trinitarianism and the above position on unity of causality from a single divine agency might be further illustrated through the biblical account of the baptism of Jesus (Mt. 3:13-17). Here we see one of the clearest representations of the three distinct persons in Scripture. For social Trinitarianism, this encounter is representative of "divine persons as distinct agents."[19] So the Father speaks from heaven, the Son ("a divine agent who is distinct and discrete from his Father") walks into the water to be baptized, and the Spirit descends as a dove.[20] Classical and Reformed thought agrees with this insofar as it says that the voice "belongs" to the Father (by means of appropriation), walking into the Jordan River belongs to the Son, and hovering is appropriated to the Spirit. Yet classical and Reformed Christology distinguishes itself from social Trinitarianism in that all of these "belongings" are true only from the perspective of the *terminus* since each of these acts involves the single divine agency and single divine action so that it is caused by all three persons. Augustine says, "The trinity together produced both the

---

16. This theological claim is often overlooked as even a possibility in many modern commentaries. For example, commenting on Jn 10:18 (which seems to be the clearest expression of this reality in Scripture), D. A. Carson appeals to the unity of the Son's "plan" with the Father (*The Gospel According to John*, PNTC [Grand Rapids: Eerdmans, 1991, 389]; J. Ramsey Michaels says that this authority "is not something intrinsically his by nature, but something conferred on him by the Father" (*The Gospel of John*, NICNT [Grand Rapids: Eerdmans, 2010], 591). Conversely, Leon Morris advocates for the Son's role in raising himself, appealing to the "strand of New Testament teaching which says the Son 'rose'" (i.e., actively) (*The Gospel according to John*, NICNT [Grand Rapids: Eerdmans, 1971], 513 n. 49).

17. Turretin, *Institutes*, II:13.xvii.2, 8.

18. McFarland connects this to worship and states, "The classical Trinitarian principle [indivisible operations] ... shored up the claim that God is a single subject, and that Christians have, correspondingly, only a single object of worship" (*Word Made Flesh*, 73).

19. McCall, *Which Trinity?*, 67.

20. Ibid., 64, 58–9.

Father's voice and the Son's flesh and the Holy Spirit's dove, though each of these single things has reference to a single person."[21] That is, each person is responsible for the "production" of every action (i.e., the cause), yet there is a distinction in the *terminus* of that action. So the voice from heaven is caused by all three persons, yet is considered the action of the Father, not as the exclusive agent but as the agent-in-relation to whom the indivisibly triune act terminates. This unity of agency and action distinguishes classical and Reformed christological agency from social Trinitarianism; however, the classical and Reformed attention to the *terminus* of divine acts allows the position to avoid "indifferent" divine action with "no theological difference" as a consequence.[22] Instead, classical and Reformed theology depends upon its coherence with classical Trinitarianism to meaningfully distinguish between divine persons. It is, therefore, because of the commitment to classical Trinitarianism that the classical and Reformed Christology can appreciate the activity of the Holy Spirit and Father in the acts of Christ the Son. So Christ's divine operations need not be considered as "caused" by the Son exclusively (as they would seem to on many social Trinitarian accounts). Instead each of the divine persons is actively and indivisibly involved in causing every divine operation.

B. Proper Actions and Personal Modes of Acting

From the perspective of causality, the single agency of God means that every act is brought about by each of the persons of the Trinity. If this were the only perspective, then it would seem that classical and Reformed theology violates its conciliar commitment by falling into patripassianism (i.e., if every person of the Trinity is involved in every action, then the Father suffers on the cross). Yet the classical and Reformed tradition is committed to the Son being the only one who suffered (in his human nature). Holding the singular causality and the affirmation of theopaschism together, Augustine affirms "This passion happened to one of them, but was brought about by" all three (e.g., Rom. 8:32; Gal. 2:20; Heb. 9:14).[23] The ability of classical Trinitarianism to predicate actions and passions of Christ to the Son will be notable not only for its coherence with the conciliar anathematization of patripassianism but also the prudence of classical and Reformed Christology

---

21. Augustine, *The Trinity*, ed. John E. Rotelle O.S.A., trans. Edmund Hill, O.P., The Works of Saint Augustine: A Translation for the 21st Century I/5 (Hyde Park: New City, 1991), 184; likewise, *ST* III, Q.39, A.8. Likewise, see Turretin, *Institutes*, I:3.xxvii.

22. These critiques come from Jenson, *Triune Identity*, 126–7.

23. Augustine, *Sermons 51–94*, The Works of Saint Augustine. A Translation for the 21st Century, III, trans. Edmund Hill, ed. John E. Rotelle (Hyde Park, NY: New City, 1991), 52.22.

when related to contemporary accounts of Spirit Christology, some of which give the Spirit primacy over the Son in the execution of Christ's acts.[24]

This strong distinction in the suffering of Christ (i.e., the Son not the Father) is possible because of the predication of "proper action" to distinct divine persons (from the perspective of the *terminus* of that action). Ontologically, Owen and classical trinitarian theology can predicate certain properties exclusively of one person as "proper" to that person (i.e., only the Son is begotten) when considering God *ad intra*.[25] Since operations mirror ontology, we can likewise speak of proper actions that terminate exclusively on one divine person.

The clearest example of proper action is the assumption of a human nature terminating properly on the Son. The act of the assumption is an act (like all divine acts) that is caused by all three divine persons. However, the *terminus* of the assumption is uniquely (i.e., properly) the divine Son. Thomas Aquinas distinguishes between the principle of the assumption and the *terminus* of the assumption. He says, "Assuming belongs to the divine nature as such, because the action was accomplished by its power. But to be the term of assumption does not belong to the divine nature as such, but only by reason of the divine person in whom the nature is present."[26] He clarifies that "what belongs to the act of assuming is common to the three persons; but what pertains to the term belongs to one person in such a way that it does not belong to another. For the three persons caused the human nature to be united to one person, the Son."[27] Employing Vidu's analogy of an Elizabethan lord who is dressing for a formal event at the palace with the help of his butler, we see that the cause of "dressing" is predicated to both agents, but "being dressed" applies only to the lord as the terminus.[28] Or, the magnet that acts singularly (i.e., it is not just the act of one pole or the other) upon a metal object and produces a singular effect (e.g., the attraction of a paper clip to the magnet), yet this terminates upon only one pole (e.g., the paper clip attaches to only one pole).[29] Likewise, all three persons of the triune God cause a single action, yet that action terminates upon only the divine Son as the one who assumes the human nature.

Because the assumption of the humanity of Christ and the hypostatic union terminate only upon the Son, the *terminus* of the acts of the hypostatic union is

---

24. While this will be the focus of the following section (§I.C), here it might be worth noting Spence, "Christ's Humanity and Ours," 74–97, who attributes Christ's miraculous work to the Holy Spirit; see also the primary role of the Spirit in Hawthorne, *The Presence and the Power*, 113, 145–6, 208–17; Telford Work, "Jesus' New Relationship with the Holy Spirit," 176.

25. See Bonaventure, *Breviloquium*, ed. Dominic V. Monti, O.F.M., Works of St. Bonaventure 9 (St. Bonaventure, NY: Franciscan Institute, 2005), 45 (1.6.1–2) for the distinction between an appropriated act and a proper act.

26. Aquinas, *ST* III, Q.3, A.2.

27. Aquinas, *ST* III, Q.3, A.4.

28. Vidu, "Inseparable Operations and the Incarnation," 112.

29. Vidu, "Ascension and Pentecost," 108.

proper to the Son. That is, acts that are either (1) directed toward Christ as the object of that action (e.g., being lifted up on the cross) or (2) an effect of Christ's human nature (e.g., writing in dust) terminate properly upon the Son. The first point is true by virtue of the communication of attributes; whatever is true of Christ according to either nature is true of the subsistence (i.e., the Son) because only the Son has united a human nature into subsistence in himself. So Christ's spatial location belongs properly to God the Son by virtue of the communication of attributes; thereby the passion of being lifted up on the cross is true only of God the Son, allowing us to avoid patripassianism. The second point is true by virtue of the humanity of Christ subsisting in the subsistence of the Son who is personally identical to the theandric agent. This does not mean that the Son alone is the cause of the act but the Son alone is the *terminus* of the action. So, for example, the execution of the act "walking on the water" belongs properly to the Son because the action of Christ according to his human nature is true of the Son (in whom the human nature subsists) in a way that is not true of the Father or the Spirit. Yet the operation of "defying the laws of buoyancy" is *caused* by all three persons. The proper acts of the Son through the human nature are like one pole of the magnet that has attracted a paper clip which is holding a picture. We would rightfully say that the one pole of the magnet is "holding a picture" (because that which is attached to it is), while the other is not; yet the magnetic cause is the whole magnet.

However, as Ursinus (and more recently, Gilles Emery) points out, the incarnation is not the only proper action of the divine persons for classical Trinitarianism. Instead, distinct modes of divine actions, when considered from the perspective of the intra-trinitarian relations (i.e., not the *terminus* or the cause, but the way the three persons relate in the single act), can be understood to belong *properly* to one person or another.[30] Most basically and obviously, this means that it is proper to the Father to act "paternally," proper to the Son to act "filially," and proper to the Spirit to act "pneumatically." So only the Father, as the one who begets the Son and together with him spirates the Spirit, acts through the Son and by the Spirit. Only the Son acts from the Father and by the Spirit. Therefore, John's claim that all of creation is made "through him" (Jn 1:3) is proper to the Son. The claim is not that the Son alone creates (since the cause is all three persons), nor that the Son is the exclusive terminus of creating (since it is frequently appropriated also to the Father), but that the mode of creation being from the Father and "through" this agent-in-relation belongs properly to the Son as the one who acts as a "principle from the principle" (begotten of the Father).[31] Emery reiterates, "The action of the Father and the Son is one; the principle of this action is also one (it is the divine nature or essence); the effects of the action are common to the Father and to the Son. But the actors (the subjects of the act: *operantes*)

---

30. Emery does not use the language of "perspective" but does talk about the "side of the relation" (Emery, "The Personal Mode of Action," 53). Zacharias Ursinus, *The Commentary of Dr. Zacharias Ursinus on the Heidelberg Catechism*, trans. G. W. Williard (Columbus: Scott & Bascom, 1851), 120.

31. Aquinas, *ST* I, Q.39, A.8.

are personally distinct and their mode of action is also distinct."[32] Emery is here supporting the claim of this section: the acts of the triune God are indivisible and singular. From the perspective of causality, they are unified; each person produces the same effect upon the creature. Yet, from the perspective of the *terminus* of that action, it can belong to one agent-in-relation. Furthermore, Emery helps us to see that the three triune "agents-in-relation" are best appreciated as distinct "agents" when considered "in-relation." That is, in addition to the perspective of causality (whereby the cause of all divine acts is singular) and the perspective of an act's *terminus* (whereby the *terminus* can belong to one agent-in-relation properly or by appropriation [see below]), the classical tradition helps us to see the perspective of trinitarian relations (whereby a mode of action belongs properly to a divine person).

C. Appropriated Actions

Finally, we can consider the *terminus* of a divine action as *appropriated* to a distinct agent-in-relation. Because operations mirror ontology, the classical Christian tradition has attributed (i.e., appropriated) particular actions to particular divine persons insofar as those actions fittingly reflect something about that agent's relations of origin. Yet this appropriation must not exclude the other divine persons (since all divine acts are produced by all three persons). This theological move does not allow the Father, Son, or Holy Spirit to be the exclusive cause of divine actions, but it ensures the involvement of each in every divine action and the ascription of particular action to particular persons. Therefore, classical and Reformed Christology can relate to much of the contemporary Spirit Christology movement, with its emphasis on the significance of the Holy Spirit in every action throughout the life of Christ. However, because of the above claim of the filial execution of Christ's acts and the following appropriation of perfecting and applying to the Holy Spirit, classical and Reformed Christology does not appropriate the *execution* of christological action primarily to the Spirit.

Owen and the classical and Reformed tradition frequently attribute the origination of an action (i.e., planning, determining) to the Father, the execution of the action (i.e., establishing, performing, revealing) to the Son, and the culmination of that action (i.e., perfecting, applying, making effectual) to the Spirit. Recognizing the operational connection to ontology, Owen says,

> The beginning of divine operations is assigned unto the Father, as he is *fons et origo Deitatis*,—"the fountain of the Deity itself" ... Rom. 11:36. The subsisting, establishing, and "upholding of all things," is ascribed unto the Son: ... Col. 1:17 ... as he is the power and wisdom of the Father .... And the finishing and perfecting of all these works is ascribed to the Holy Spirit.[33]

---

32. Emery, "The Personal Mode of Action," 51.
33. WJO, *Pneumatologia*, 3:94; likewise, *Vindiciæ Evangelicæ*, 12:392.

Owen's claims here are found throughout the classical tradition. For example, Gregory of Nyssa comments, "Every operation which extends from God to creation … has its origin in the Father, proceeds through the Son, and reaches its completion in the Holy Spirit …. There is one motion and disposition of the good will which proceeds from the Father, through the Son, to the Spirit."[34] Calvin likewise says, "To the Father is attributed the beginning of activity, and the fountain and wellspring of all things; to the Son, wisdom, counsel, and the ordered disposition of all things; but to the Sprit is assigned the power and efficacy of that activity."[35] Finally, later Reformed thinkers, like Venema, also employ similar accounts: the Father "begins the work, the Son executes it, and the Holy Spirit perfects it."[36] Yet, we must recognize that this is true insofar as the origination, execution, and culmination reflect the relations of origin in the singular action and do not communicate three stages of a causal sequence as though the three persons are in a three-member relay race.[37]

Appropriations are unlike the proper acts of the magnet and butler analogies because the acts of the magnet (i.e., attracting the paper clip) terminate on one pole to the exclusion of the other. Appropriations may be more similar to three of my daughters buying me clothes to give me as a gift for Christmas. They all decide on the items together, they pay for the items together, and they give me the items together. Yet each aspect of this act corresponds to something unique in each of my daughters' personalities. My oldest is the most conscious of money, my second the most conscious of clothing styles, and my third is the most conscious of gift giving. So when someone compliments my new shirt, I might say, "Thanks, my oldest daughter bought it"; or, "Thanks, my middle daughter picked it out"; or, "Thanks, my youngest daughter gave it to me."[38] Each of those claims would be true, even though my oldest did not pay for it any more than anyone else, my middle daughter did not decide alone, and my youngest did not give it to me apart from her sisters. Now the Father, Son, and Holy Spirit do not have distinct personalities (since they are one in essence, understanding, and will), but they do have distinct

---

34. Gregory of Nyssa, "An Answer to Ablabius," 262.

35. Calvin, *Institutes*, I.xiii.18; also *CD* I/1, 375.

36. Venema, *Institutes of Theology*, X.222; see also Goodwin, *Work of the Holy Ghost*, IX.i.405; *Synopsis*, 2:71.

37. See Ch. 2 §I.B.3; esp. WJO, *Pneumatologia*, 3:94–5.

38. Someone may object: a good dad would never single out one of his daughters without giving the others credit; *mutatis mutandis*, truthful Holy Scripture would never attribute an action to a single divine person if this really were the case. However, I think that we do this kind of thing all the time and, minimally, it is context-dependent. For example, if the person complimenting my clothes was my oldest daughter's teacher, it would be very natural for me to appropriate this action to my oldest. Likewise, if the context of the conversation is the generosity of my youngest daughter, it is very natural for me to attribute the action to my youngest. So too with Scripture: if the context is the supremacy of Christ over all things (Colossians 1), then it is fitting for the act of creation to be appropriated to the Son.

relations of origin (i.e., begetting/spirating, being begotten, and being spirated). Therefore, we often appropriate the act of creation to the Father (even though the Son and Spirit also create [Jn 1:3; Col. 1:16; Ps. 33:6; Job 26:13]) because creation fittingly corresponds to begetting and spirating. The Spirit as the spirated bond of union between the Father and the Son is fittingly the one to whom we appropriate the act of binding us to Christ (1 Cor. 12:13).

This perspective on christological action and predication allows classical and Reformed Christology to appreciate the trinitarian shape of Christ's actions. So, for example, Owen, commenting on Heb. 1:9, names sixteen works regarding the incarnation that are appropriated to the Father. Likewise, commenting on Heb. 2:10 (the ordination of "bringing many sons to glory"), he names ten acts appropriated to the Father (especially in regard to the salvation of humans).[39] Owen's lists indicate that the Father was intimately involved in redemption in Christ from the beginning of time to the culmination of Christ's work. A selection of the appropriated works of the Father toward Christ includes: establishing an eternal council with the Son (Prov. 8:22-31); furnishing the humanity of Christ with the Holy Spirit to enable him to perform his mission (Isa. 11:2-3); giving him up unto death on the cross (Rom. 8:32); raising him from the dead (1 Pet. 1:21); giving all power, authority, and judgment unto him (Jn 5:22); exalting of him to the right hand (Acts 2:33); and crowning him with eternal glory and honor (Heb. 2:9).[40]

The triune character of the incarnate acts of Christ also includes the Spirit. The role of the Spirit has become a prominent discussion in contemporary Christology. While the movement started largely as an alternative to classical Christology, many scholars have more recently offered Spirit Christologies that are complementary with the conclusions of Chalcedon (some even draw from Owen's theology in order to do so).[41] This explicit attention to the role of the Holy Spirit in the life and work of Christ is a helpful and welcome endeavor. However, some of these accounts articulate the work of Christ with the goal of presenting the Spirit as a "personal agent in his own right" so strongly that either (1) they predicate "proper acts" to the Spirit in his acts toward Christ (e.g., the act of sanctification) or (2) they attribute the accomplishment of Christ's actions to the Holy Spirit as the primary divine agent.

---

39. WJO, *Exposition of Hebrews*, 20:379-81.

40. Ibid., 3:194-5.

41. Habets, *The Anointed Son*; G. Liston, "A Chalcedonian Spirit Christology," *ITQ* 81 (2016): 74-93; McFarland, "Spirit and Incarnation"; Lucy Peppiatt, "Life in the Spirit," 165-81; Claunch, "Son and Spirit"; Herschel Odell Bryant, *Spirit Christology in the Christian Tradition: From the Patristic Period to the Rise of Pentecostalism in the Twentieth Century* (Cleveland, TN: CPT, 2015); Sanchez, *Receiver, Bearer, and Giver*; Thomas Weinandy, *The Father's Spirit of Sonship: Reconceiving the Trinity* (Eugene, OR: Wipf & Stock, 2011); Del Colle, *Christ and the Spirit*; Skip Jenkins, *A Spirit Christology*, ES 3 (New York: Peter Lang, 2018); Spence, *Incarnation and Inspiration*; McFarland, *Word Made Flesh*, 133 n. 11.

For some, the activity of the Spirit is placed in contrast to the (often kenotically emptied) agency of the Son. Gerald F. Hawthorne contrasts the Spirit's power with that of the Son, saying that "the Spirit so fully motivated Jesus' speech and action that the miracles he performed and words he spoke, he spoke and performed, not by virtue of his own power; the power of his divine personality [i.e., the Son], but by virtue of the power of the Holy Spirit at work within him and through him."[42] Likewise, Moltmann says, "In the first chapters of the synoptic gospels especially, the Spirit is presented as the divine determining subject of the way [which] Jesus took."[43] Finally, in order to appreciate the biblical ascriptions of the miracles of Christ to the Spirit, Kyle Claunch understands "the super-human and obviously divine actions ... (i.e. Jesus' miracles) as properly terminating on the Holy Spirit," while for "the ordinary human activity performed according to the human nature ... the Son of God is the immediate operator."[44] That is, the divine acts of Christ are proper to the Spirit and the human acts are proper to the Son.

While classical and Reformed Christology wants to appreciate the activity of the Holy Spirit in the life of Christ, it does not want to establish the Spirit as the divine agent to whom we primarily predicate the accomplishment of Christ's acts. Instead, classical and Reformed Christology views the accomplished acts of Christ as filial (see Ch. 3 §II.A.2; Ch. 4 §I.B) and it understands the acts of God in Christ as terminating upon the Spirit in two ways: (1) the Spirit is the *terminus* to whom we *appropriate* the acts of God upon the human nature of Christ and (2) the Spirit is the *terminus* to whom we appropriate the *perfecting and effectual* activity of the divine operations accomplished by the mediator toward other creatures.

First, the Spirit is the one to whom we appropriate the acts of God upon the human nature of Christ. This is seen clearly in the conception of Christ in the womb of Mary, whereby the Spirit is the *terminus* of the divine acts of creating, sanctifying, and uniting humanity to God the Son. These acts of the Spirit are not proper acts, as some suggest, but instead are appropriated to the Spirit as effects of the triune God.[45] The putative parallel between the Son's proper assumption of a human nature and the Spirit's proper sanctification of that human nature has a symmetrical ring, but the biblical testimony attributes the divine act of

---

42. Hawthorne, *The Presence and the Power*, 145–6; likewise, James D. G. Dunn, "Rediscovering the Spirit (1)," in *The Christ and the Spirit Volume 2: Pneumatology* (Grand Rapids: Eerdmans, 1998), 51; James D. G. Dunn, *Jesus and the Spirit: A Study of the Religious and Charismatic Experience of Jesus and the First Christians as Reflected in the New Testament* (Grand Rapids: Eerdmans, 1997), 66.

43. Jürgen Moltmann, *The Way of Jesus Christ: Christology in Messianic Dimensions*, trans. Margaret Kohl (Minneapolis: Fortress, 1995), 92, 93; similarly, Habets, *The Anointed Son*, 214; Ralph Del Colle also describes as the Spirit being the "immediate agent of the incarnation" ("Incarnation and the Holy Spirit," *Spirit and Church* 2 [2000]: 227).

44. Claunch, "Son and Spirit," 148–9.

45. LaCugna, *God for Us*, 100; Sanchez M., *Receiver, Bearer, and Giver*, 32, 96.

sanctification to each divine person and therefore not properly to the Spirit. That is, we can appropriate sanctification to the Holy Spirit as in Rom. 8:13, but Christ is also said to "purify us" (1 Jn 1:9) and to "sanctify himself" (Jn 17:19); further, Isa. 1:18 may be taken as an attribution of cleansing forgiveness to the Father.

Although the Spirit is not the proper agent of acts upon Christ's human nature, the Spirit still does empower and sustain the humanity of Christ in terms of the *terminus* of divine action. Owen notes ten works appropriated to the Holy Spirit regarding the incarnate humanity of Christ in *Pneumatologia*. Among others, the Spirit formed the human nature of Christ in the womb of Mary (Mt. 1:18) and anointed Christ with all the gifts necessary for the exercise of his office (Isa. 61:1). The Spirit sustained Christ's body and soul in death (Acts 2:31) and finally in the ascension the Spirit glorified Christ's human nature (Phil. 3:21).[46]

The Spirit is therefore active in the incarnate Christ, yet the execution of Christ's actions belongs to the Son not the Spirit. In addition to the articulation of proper action and the communication of attributes above (Ch. 4 §I.B), Owen's commitment to the filial acts of Christ in Chapter 3 §II.A.2, and Romans 5 below, we might consider the biblical testimony of Paul, who tells of the "Son of God" (τοῦ υἱοῦ τοῦ θεοῦ) as one who "loved me and gave himself up for me" (τοῦ ἀγαπήσαντός με καὶ παραδόντος ἑαυτὸν ὑπὲρ ἐμοῦ) (Gal. 2:20). Likewise, we also see Jesus' claim that the "Son of Man" does not have anywhere to lay his head (Mt. 8:20), that he will suffer (Mt. 17:12; 20:18), and that he will return (Mt. 24:30; 25:31; 26:64; Mk 14:62). So it is the Son, rather than the Spirit, to whom we predicate the execution of these actions. Yet, like all divine actions, the perfection and application of these acts can be appropriated to the Spirit. Owen summarizes the trinitarian acts in the incarnation and their rootedness in the divine essence and relations of origin:

> The sum of what we can comprehend in this great mystery ariseth from the consideration of the *order* of the holy persons of the blessed Trinity in their operations; for their order herein doth follow that of their subsistence .... The Holy Spirit, who is the third person in order of subsistence, there is made a *perfecting application* of the whole unto all its proper ends. Wherefore, this work of our redemption and recovery being the especial effect of the authority, love, and power of the Father—it was to be *executed* in and by the person of the Son; as the application of it unto us is made by the Holy Ghost.[47]

That is, the Spirit may not be the one on whom the execution of Christ's acts terminates, but that need not dissuade us from appropriating the necessary involvement of the Spirit in every divine action as the one who perfects and applies those divine operations.

---

46. WJO, *Pneumatologia*, 3:162–83.
47. WJO, *Christologia*, 1:219–20.

In summary, classical and Reformed Christology resists the move present in some Spirit Christologies to predicate proper acts of the Spirit upon the humanity of Christ and to predicate the execution of Christ's acts to the Spirit as the determining agent of divine operations. Yet classical and Reformed theology seeks to appreciate the activity of the Spirit by appropriating the divine acts upon the humanity of Christ to the Holy Spirit and appropriating the perfecting of Christ's divine operations to the Spirit as the agent-in-relation upon whom the application and efficacy of divine acts terminates. Indeed, this has pneumatological advantages over even some of the accounts which predicate proper acts or the extraordinary acts primarily to the Spirit (and attribute the rest of Christ's acts to the Son) insofar as classical and Reformed Christology allows each and every act of Christ to include the Holy Spirit (first as equal cause of every divine operation [§I.A.1] and second as the perfecting agent-in-relation of divine action). Rather than being "modalistic" or pejoratively labeled "mere monotheism," a classical Trinitarian account with these distinctions and attention to the Spirit allows the Spirit to be present in every divine act.[48] So rather than indivisible operations acting as the evil step-sister who fights to exclude Cinderella from the ball, indivisible operations is more like the fairy godmother who ensures that the Spirit is included.[49] The proper predication and personal modes of action allow distinctions to be made between the persons in a way that still affirms essential unity. Because of the relations of origin between the divine persons, we may predicate the terminus of human actions and passions properly to the Son as the only one who subsists in a human nature and appropriate the perfection and application of divine operations to the Holy Spirit.

II. Simple, Divine Agency

The doctrine of divine simplicity and the infinite divine attributes of omnipresence, immutability, and impassibility play a pivotal role in classical and Reformed theology (Ch. 2 §I.A.1–2). So as classical and Reformed Christology puts forward an account of a single agent, it must attend to the coherence between these classical affirmations and the singularity of the christological agent. That is, if the agent of christological action is God the Son, how can the agent "suffer" while being

---

48. Jenkins, *A Spirit Christology*, 328 refers to the "originating, executing, perfecting" acts as minimally "modalistic" in its connotations and asks, "How can the eternal Father's love be 'perfected'?" Not only can classical and Reformed theology avoid this critique, it seems that Jenkins bases this critique on the assumption of triune actions as three agents in a causal sequence. The charge of "mere monotheism" is made by Karl Rahner, *The Trinity*, trans. Joseph Donceel, Milestones in Catholic Theology (New York: The Crossroad Publishing Company, 1997), 10–11.

49. McGrath, *Christian Theology*, 307, uses the image of Cinderella to illustrate the Spirit's exclusion in contemporary Christian theology.

impassible? Presenting the classical and Reformed christological position on divine agency, this subsection will address the christological implications of pure act for the fullness and constancy of divine agency. It will do so in conversation with particular versions of contemporary kenotic Christologies in order to show the viable coherence of classical and Reformed theology and its prudence when interjected into these conversations.[50] The section begins with a discussion on the infinite agency of God in relation to ontological and functional kenoticism (§II.A) and then turn to the constant divine agency of Christ in relation to kryptic Christologies (§II.B).

A. Simple Agency

The recent proposals in kenotic Christology are particularly fitting interlocutors because of the affirmation of Christ as a single agent, its influence in Reformed Christology, and its explicit attention to the "activity of Jesus" as described in Scripture.[51] These theologians argue that, if Christology presents us with a single divine agent who acts finitely, spatially, and passibly, then we must acknowledge that this Son "gave up" (ontologically), or restricted the use (functionally) of, certain divine attributes in order to live a genuinely human life.[52]

Articulating the former position, ontological kenoticism posits that "Jesus Christ 'emptied himself' by temporarily giving up those divine properties that are inconsistent with being truly human while retaining sufficient divine properties to remain truly divine."[53] To "give up" a property means that the Son, by his own free choice, does not possess a property in the incarnation that he would otherwise have.[54] This, however, does not mean that the Son ceases to be God, since these attributes are defined as "contingent" divine attributes, not necessary to being

---

50. Brown, *Divine Humanity*, 172, 242 calls kenoticism pervasive in modern theology, much of which would be unrecognizable by the majority of the tradition.

51. Stephen T. Davis and C. Stephen Evans, "Conclusion: The Promise of Kenosis," in *Exploring Kenotic Christology: The Self-Emptying of God*, ed. C. Stephen Evans (New York: Oxford University Press, 2006), 313. For the Reformed participants, see Thomas R. Thompson, "Nineteenth-Century Kenotic Christology: The Waxing, Waning, and Weighing of a Quest for a Coherent Orthodoxy," in *Exploring Kenotic Christology: The Self-Emptying of God*, ed. C. Stephen Evans (New York: Oxford University Press, 2006), 74–111; for the significance of Kenoticism in modern theology, see Kevin J. Vanhoozer, *Remythologizing Theology: Divine Action, Passion, and Authorship*, CSCD (New York: Cambridge University Press, 2010), 105–77.

52. Davis, "Metaphysics of Kenosis," 118.

53. Ibid., 120.

54. Ibid., 121. Richard Cross admits that his method of "trimming" incompatible divine attributes is "an abandonment of a strong form of classical theism" ("The Incarnation," in *The Oxford Handbook of Philosophical Theology*, ed. Thomas P. Flint and Michael C. Rae [New York: Oxford University Press, 2011], 471).

God. So the Son can temporarily give up the contingent attribute of impassibility and remain God, like I can temporarily give up breathing air while swimming under water and remain human.

Relatedly, functional kenoticism/quasi-kenoticism supposes that the Word ontologically retains, but functionally restricts the exercise of, certain divine attributes. According to functional kenoticism, Christ *is* divine (as we usually define divinity), but he does not fully *exercise* his divinity. Adding to the putative trinitarian benefits discussed above, Gerald Hawthorne states that the Son "willed to renounce the exercise of his divine powers, attributes, prerogatives, so that he might live fully within those limitations which inhere in being truly human" by the power of the Holy Spirit.[55] Likewise, Brian Leftow claims that the "Son voluntarily foreswore use of His distinctively divine powers."[56] Oliver Crisp compares ontological kenoticism to Superman encountering kryptonite that disables his superhuman abilities, while functional kenoticism is more like Superman swearing off his hero life and choosing to retire to a life lived only as Clark Kent.[57]

While there are advocates for both these versions of kenoticism in Reformed theology, my contention here is that classical and Reformed christological agency cannot adopt either position if it is to cohere with classical Trinitarianism and the Reformed christological emphases. So this subsection will show how classical and Reformed doctrines (namely, the *extra Calvinisticum* and divine simplicity) have implications which help to distinguish divine and human operations, preserving the impassibility of the divine essence and unity of the single agent.

The first concept that classical and Reformed Christology employs on this front is a touchstone of the tradition: the *extra Calvinisticum*, the claim that the presence of the Son of God is not limited or circumscribed by the flesh of Christ. The *extra Calvinisticum* is particularly relevant to the discussion of kenosis because in both ontological and functional kenoticism, it seems that the Son is no longer engaged in triune operations "beyond the flesh," like the activity of sustaining the world.[58] One defender of kenoticism rhetorically asks and answers the question: "What

---

55. Hawthorne, *The Presence and the Power*, 208.
56. Leftow, "Tempting God," 23.
57. Crisp, *Divinity and Humanity*, 140.
58. A similar charge is levelled against functional kenoticists by Crisp, *Divinity and Humanity*, 142; Wellum, *Son of God Incarnate*, 379. This aspect of kenoticism is vividly depicted by Thomas Senor, who states that the incarnation is analogous to an actor in a "fat suit"—insofar as the fat suit literally circumscribes the person ("Drawing on Many Traditions: An Ecumenical Kenotic Christology," in *The Metaphysics of the Incarnation*, ed. Anna Marmodoro and Jonathan Hill [New York: Oxford University Press, 2011], 100).

happens to the universe with the divine Logos temporarily out of office? [Answer:] Nothing bad: The Father and the Spirit handle things quite competently."[59] Yet, as this quote indicates, the Son not only ceases to be included in the indivisible acts of the triune God but he ceases to be active outside the human actions of Christ. As such, both ontological and functional kenoticism seem untenable for classical and Reformed Christology if it is to cohere with its Reformed emphases. Yet, from the foundation of the *extra Calvinisticum*, classical and Reformed Christology is able to preserve the infinite ontology and omnipresent operations of the divine agency of the theandric mediator. This means that the Son is active in the indivisible triune operations even while he is incarnate in Galilee. Yet, it could be objected that the above critique only works against ontological kenoticism and functional kenoticism could avoid this charge by suggesting something like the position that the *Logos asarkos* remains divine and acts accordingly, while the *Logos ensarkos* restricts his capacities to act as a single human agent with human capacities.

Granting the above proposal, I would suggest that functional kenoticism of this sort is likewise untenable for classical and Reformed Christology because of its commitment to the doctrine of divine simplicity (see Ch. 2 §I.A.1). This is particularly evident when considered with functional kenoticism's assumption of (what I will call) "scalable attributes." That is, it seems that functional kenoticism assumes that divine attributes and human attributes are on the same "scale" such that they can be increased or decreased. For example, if the one agent does not use his omniscience, but instead only uses a finite amount of his knowledge so that his knowledge is human, it presupposes that omniscience is the highest rung on the scale of knowledge. As Davis says, "The whole kenotic scheme depends on there not being any essential divine properties that no human being can have and on there not being any essential human properties that no divine being can have."[60] Davis is here seemingly indicating that these properties exist on a spectrum that is available to various agents to various degrees. David Brown likewise evidences the presupposed scalability of attributes on a kenotic account when he rejects the qualitative distinction between the way that humans hear sound and the way that bats (i.e., the scary animals that live in midwestern attics) hear sound as too disanalogous to the incarnation. Instead he opts for the analogy of kenosis as analogous to method acting, whereby one is to "infuse one's own self with the

---

59. John G. Stackhouse Jr., "Jesus Christ," in *The Oxford Handbook of Evangelical Theology*, ed. Gerald R. Mcdermott (New York: Oxford University Press, 2010), 150. I think this claim evidences the inherently social Trinitarian dimension of kenotic Christology. Thompson and Plantinga Jr. say, "The viability of the kenotic model is dependent on a social understanding of the Trinity—that the success of the former requires the success of the latter" ("Trinity and Kenosis," 166–7).

60. Davis, "Metaphysics of Kenosis," 118.

thoughts, emotions and personality of the character" that they become.[61] Here, the thinking, emoting, and personality are on the same register for both the actor and their character, but the difference is in the degree to which they exercise those.

So, according to Kenoticism, it seems that if the single agent is going to give up, or not exercise, divine attributes, then those attributes must be *quantitatively* distinct from human attributes. Take the ability to jump off the ground as an example: if divine attributes are scalable and quantitatively distinct, then we might depict divine agency (in terms of jumping) as the capacity to jump 50 inches off the ground. So we might imagine someone with the original capacity to jump 50 inches choosing not to exercise their full capacity and instead jumping the average human height of 15 inches off the ground. However, the assumption here is that this capacity can be scaled down to the "human level." In the analogy, the act executed is the same kind of capacity, just to a greater or lesser degree.

However, with the doctrine of divine simplicity, God just *is* his perfections. God does not merely possess a bigger and better version of "goodness" or "love" than humans have.[62] Nor does God merely possess a greater quantity of goodness than humans on the goodness-scale; God *is* goodness itself. Human goodness then is not only quantitatively less than God but it is also qualitatively distinct (i.e., a different, yet analogous, kind). If we accept divine simplicity and its accompanying implication of qualitatively distinct attributes, then attributes are not scalable and the analogy must change. It is no longer a question of the same operation executed to a different degree. Instead, it is a distinct kind of operation. So instead of divine action being equivalent to jumping high and human agency being equivalent to jumping lower, the analogy might now become jumping off of different feet. Jumping off your left foot becomes "left-footed-jumping," while jumping off your right foot becomes "right-footed-jumping." Here, if you are to perform an action (i.e., you jump), you must do so according to one kind or another (or both). Yet you cannot perform "left-footed-jumping" in a way that makes it equal to the kind of "right-footed-jumping."

Because of the classical and Reformed commitment to divine simplicity and the *extra Calvinisticum* neither ontological nor functional Christology is viably coherent with these commitments. Instead, classical and Reformed Christology insists that Jesus possesses simple divine agency.

B. Constant Agency

If the previous subsection argued for the implications of divine simplicity to be applied in terms of agency in particular kinds of actions (i.e., pure activity in any given act), this subsection applies those implications to multiple actions (i.e., constantly throughout Christ's life). That is, since the theandric mediator acts

---

61. Brown, *Divine Humanity*, 252.

62. See Williams, *Christ the Heart of Creation*, 238, *passim*. See his fascinating reading of 1 Cor. 1:18–2:5 on this front (55).

in both natures simultaneously (see Ch. 3 §B.2; 6 §II.B), Christ's divine agency operates in every act of Christ bringing about its proper immediate effects.

The prudence of such a claim may be seen in relation to contemporary "kryptic" Christologies that position themselves adjacent to kenotic Christology. This kind of account is seen most clearly in Andrew Loke and Oliver Crisp.[63] Andrew Loke's account of divine preconsciousness suggests that the Logos, in the incarnation, operates according to "the aspect of his consciousness having human properties," while the aspect of his divine consciousness is hidden (kryptic) as preconscious. That is, he possesses divine memories and items of knowledge but he is not immediately aware of these in his human consciousness.[64] Crisp's account does not employ the same language of consciousness, but instead discusses the restriction of the exercise of certain divine attributes in his human nature. In accordance with the preceding classical and Reformed account, Oliver Crisp argues that the incarnation is not a "giving up" but a "taking on," or "assumption," of a human nature.[65] Crisp then goes on to claim that (contrary to kenotic Christology) there is no restriction of the exercise of the "divine attributes of the word in abstraction of the Incarnation (as per the *extra Calvinisticum*)," but there is instead a "restriction of the exercise of the divine attributes through the human nature of Christ for the period between the virgin conception and death of Christ."[66]

On one reading of these accounts, krypsis is merely another way of suggesting that Christ possesses distinct agencies and Christ brings about immediate human effects according to his human operations. That is, if krypsis means that Christ's divine operations and divine agency are hidden *from our view* and instead supposes that Scripture focuses on those immediate effects which manifest his human operations, then it is a very similar to the classical and Reformed account offered here and is seemingly coherent with classical and Reformed commitments.

However, if krypsis means that the divine agency of Christ is hidden from himself or that he is unable to exercise it, then it seems to be less plausibly coherent with classical and Reformed Christology. Specifically, the potential incoherence of krypsis with classical and Reformed christological agency comes on the basis of classical and Reformed Christology's commitment to divine agency as it is articulated in the (1) conciliar affirmations and (2) the operational implications of the *an/enhypostatic* distinction.

The first point of potential incoherence attends to the statement of "two natural volitions or wills (θελήματα) ... and two natural principles of action

---

63. Andrew Ter Ern Loke, *A Kryptic Model of the Incarnation*, ANCTRTBSS (Burlington: Ashgate, 2014); Crisp, *Divinity and Humanity*, 118–53.

64. Loke, *A Kryptic Model of the Incarnation*, 73. Notice that Spence also proposes a reading like this that emphasizes the Holy Spirit, one which he views to be in continuity with Owen (*Incarnation and Inspiration*, 121).

65. Crisp, *Divinity and Humanity*, 148.

66. Ibid., 150.

(ἐνέργεια)" at the third council of Constantinople (680–1).[67] However, if Christ restricts the exercise of certain properties or hides them in his preconsciousness, then it seems as though Christ is operating with one energy, or principle of operation (i.e., a human one) in most of his actions. This is evidenced by Crisp's claim that Christ restricts the "exercise of divine attributes *through his human nature.*" Such a claim seems to suppose that divine attributes *could* be exercised through his human nature and that Christ chooses not to exercise them; or that they remained in his subconscious without frequently coming into his conscious mind. The krypsists might respond by saying that they affirm two energies, just contiguously (i.e., first divine, then human). However, I do not think that such a response is a viable reading of Constantinople III because the conciliar Exposition of Faith establishes the simultaneous duality of agency (i.e., two principles of operations without confusion, without change …) in parallel with the simultaneous duality of ontology (i.e., two natures without confusion, without change …).[68] Therefore, it would be just as improper to say that the Word had one principle of operation (divine) and then gave up those activities in order to act in another principle of operation (human) as it would be to say that Christ had one nature (divine) and then gave up that nature in order to take on another nature (human).

Even if we grant that it is possible for a "preconscious" or "dormant" divine energy to still qualify as distinct concurrent energy, thereby accounting for the above concern, there is still a lingering question of coherence between kryptic Christology and the *an/enhypostatic* distinction. Specifically, it seems as though krypsis prioritizes Christ's human nature in action, so that the humanity of Christ could be functioning as something like the primary agent (and the divine agency is only occasionally active).[69]

For example, Crisp says that "during the period of his earthly ministry (at least some of) these divine properties are not accessible to the human nature of Christ. Either he is ignorant of possessing them in the hypostatic union, or he does not have access to them per se, for the period of earthly Incarnation."[70] Notice that Crisp says "*he* does not have access." This pronoun and subject of action either refers to "Christ according to his human nature" (i.e., simply a classical and Reformed position) or else this sentence makes the human nature of Christ into the primary agent of the action. If the latter is true, then the "restricted" human nature seems to be the primary principle of action and can itself perform actions

---

67. Tanner, *Decrees*, 1:128. For a summary of the theological difficulties of Monothelitism, see Bathrellos, *The Byzantine Christ*, 131–2.

68. Tanner, *Decrees*, 1:127–8.

69. If the humanity of Christ is the primary agent, then not only does krypsis have some potential concerns in terms of the *an/enhypostatic* distinction, but it also needs to relate Christ to the Son in a way that does not make them distinct agents.

70. Crisp, *Divinity and Humanity*, 150–1.

like "accessing," and presumably acting in light of its access.[71] If Christ's human nature is the primary principle of operation or primary agent, then it seems we have inverted the *an/enhypostatic* distinction as a foundation for our Christology. That is, the fundamental and prior agency is not the divine but human.

Finally, as a modification or elaboration on krypsis, we could consider accounting for kryptic divine agency in Christ through divine permission or "negative actions."[72] So on this version of krypsis we can affirm the two principles of operation and *an/enhypostatic* distinction by stating that Christ possesses two agencies that are constantly operative. His divine agency is logically prior to his human and performs the action of *permitting* the human agency to act. While this would, in some sense, avoid the above critiques, on the basis of the definition of actions as intentionally caused events by an agent, these negative actions do not qualify as genuine "actions." First, some negative actions (e.g., "omitting" and some instances of "allowing") do not include intention. For example, I did not intend to overcook the pasta, but I forgot to set a timer and just let the water keep boiling. Further, negative actions do not cause an actual event (i.e., change in the world). To illustrate this claim, imagine that my wife comes home and asks what I did while she was gone, my response, "I did not vote," "I did not cure cancer," "I did not travel to Mississippi," and "I did not buy our son a dog" would certainly provoke a sideways look and probably a retort, "So what did you do?!" Additionally, negative actions would seem to imply an infinite regress. If "not voting" and "not going to Mississippi" are actions, then there are a nearly infinite numbers of actions you and I perform every day. So, while I would feel much more productive than I often do, negative actions seem to be in a logically tenuous place. So if negative actions are not instances of agency, then negative actions cannot be predicated of the divine nature in a laudatory way. Therefore, the acts of Jesus in which divine agency is merely kryptically/negatively active (e.g., washing the disciples' feet,

---

71. As another, more minor point, it seems odd to call this a "restriction," because a restriction seems to imply the expectation/assumption is greater than the reality. For example, if I normally give my daughter $50 birthday gifts and this year I only gave her a gift that cost $25, then I could honestly say: "I restricted the birthday budget." However, if I normally give her $10 gifts, then it would seem odd for me to say that "I restricted the birthday budget" if I give her a $25 gift, even though the amount given ($25) is the same. Therefore, it seems as though this kind of communication is expected by Crisp, but he does not make clear why it is expected. If anything, his Reformed commitments would seem to incline in the other direction (i.e., expecting less).

72. Kent Bach lists the four most prominent ways to "not do something" as: failing (i.e., trying and not succeeding), refraining (i.e., deciding not to do something), omitting (i.e., unintentionally not doing something), and allowing (i.e., not preventing something from happening) ("Refraining, Omitting, and Negative Acts," in *A Companion to the Philosophy of Action*, ed. Timothy O'Connor and Constantine Sandis [Malden: Wiley-Blackwell, 2010], 53). Yet none of these constitutes an "action" as defined here because they do not intentionally cause an event; likewise, Hyman, *Action, Knowledge, and Will*, 5.

giving himself up on the cross) cannot be laudatory or even positively predicated to God. So God cannot, therefore, be rightly said to reveal himself in Christ on the cross or reconcile us to himself, since God does not actually "do" anything.[73]

This section has considered the possible liability that the affirmation of one christological agent requires the Son to divest himself of divine properties. It considered various versions of this kind of kenoticism and found them to be incoherent with the various commitments of classical and Reformed Christology. Particularly, ontological kenoticism seems to lack coherence with the Reformed commitment to the *extra Calvinisticum*. Functional kenoticism seems to lack coherence with the classical Trinitarian commitment of divine simplicity. Finally, while there is a potential version of krypsis that is compatible with classical and Reformed Christology, there is another understanding of krypsis which seems to lack coherence with the simultaneity of Christ's two principles of operation, the *an/enhypostatic* distinction, or the operative definition of "actions." This section has instead defended the claim that divine agency in classical and Reformed Christology is simple and constant.

III. Divine Agency in Scripture: Romans 5:8

The above has presented the coherence of classical and Reformed christological agency with its commitments to triune and simple divine agency. This section turns to the coherence of a classical and Reformed account of divine agency with its commitment to the ultimate authority of Scripture. As Owen suggests, Scripture testifies to this reality in its ascription of the name of God to Christ without "homonymy or equivocation," whereby "God is said 'to lay down his life for us' [1 Jn 3:16], and to 'purchase his church with his own blood' [Acts 20:24], to come and be 'manifest in the flesh' [1 Tim. 3:16]."[74] Focusing specifically upon Pauline claims of divine action in Romans 5, this section will inquire whether the Bible supports claims of divine agency (i.e., working from the text) and how these

---

73. Even if we consider permitting (i.e., allowing another agent to act) and refraining (i.e., not doing something one ought not do) as acts, both would be problematic. If God "permits" Jesus to reveal him, Jesus is seen as a distinct agent from "God." Likewise, if "permitting an act" can be meritorious, then "permitting sin" would bring culpability to God. Finally, if God "refrains" (i.e., does not do something he ought not to do) then we might ask where this obligation upon God came from and how he is capable of doing something that he *ought* not to do if he is good (i.e., God is not "obligated" not to tempt people because God cannot tempt people [Jas 1:13]). Even if we say that God can obligate himself to refrain from something (like flooding the earth [Gen 9:11]), God is incapable of doing it because God is not capable of going back on his word (Tit. 1:2).

74. Ibid., 1:232, Biblical references are my additions, yet it should be noted that most recent translations of 1 John 3:16 follow an earlier variant that reads "Jesus Christ laid down his life"; cf. *Vindication*, 2:418.

claims help us understand Scripture (i.e., working toward the text). Ultimately, I will argue that Scripture's testimony establishes and coheres with the classical and Reformed position of Christ's filial divine agency.

While "agency" (often understood as "function") has been associated with antimetaphysical readings of Christology and with views of Christ as a less-than-divine messenger of God, it has recently been employed to defend the deity of Christ throughout the New Testament.[75] This section will build on this conversation, yet rather than arguing from first-century or Jewish conceptions of a divine agent, this section will seek to specify the nature of Christ's divine agency as evidenced from his relationship to the activity of God in Rom. 5:6-11. Carrying on the argument of the chapter, the section will specifically argue that Scripture applies "pressure" toward an understanding that Christ filially executes distinct divine agency which he shares with the Father (and Spirit).[76]

In order to investigate the coherence of Scripture with a classical and Reformed account of divine agency, we turn to the relationship between the activity of God (θεός) and Christ (Χριστός) primarily as it is seen in Rom. 5:6-11, one of the most explicit Pauline texts on the divine agency of Christ. This text explicitly links Christ to God in one of the most prototypically divine operations: reconciliation. This section argues that the relationship between the acts of God (θεός) and Christ (Χριστός) implies a shared agency. Fundamentally, this section will argue that if "God shows his love for us in that ... Christ died for us," then Christ's self-sacrifice must be an act of God. If Christ's action is an action of God, then Christ must possess divine agency. This close connection of divine agency in Christ is made even in the midst of the text's focus on the Son's very human act of dying. Given this interpretation, Christ's divine agency is not hidden, turned off, or alternated away from, in these human acts; instead, the single agent executes distinct agencies with distinct immediate effects, and it is the divine Son (rather than the Spirit) to whom we predicate the accomplished actions of Christ. The first subsection argues for the singular divine agency of God in Christ through the rhetorical and grammatical relationship between God and Christ in Rom. 5:6-11 (§A). Then we

---

75. On this narrative, see Gathercole, "The Trinity in the Synoptic Gospels and Acts," 57–8. For employments of defenses of Christ's divine identity from the concept of "agency," see Hurtado, *One God, One Lord*; Richard Bauckham, *God Crucified: Monotheism and Christology in the New Testament* (Grand Rapids: Eerdmans, 1999), 40–2; Paul Owen, "Jesus as God's Chief Agent in Mark's Christology," in *Mark, Manuscripts, and Monotheism: Essays in Honor of Larry W. Hurtado*, ed. Chris Keith and Dieter Roth, LNTS 528 (New York: T&T Clark, 2015), 40–57. These are in contrast, often, with those who advocate for Christ as a merely human figure in much of the New Testament (e.g., James D. G. Dunn, *Christology in the Making: A New Testament Inquiry into the Origins of the Doctrine of the Incarnation* [Grand Rapids: Eerdmans, 1996]; J. R. Daniel Kirk, *A Man Attested by God: The Human Jesus of the Synoptic Gospels* [Grand Rapids: Eerdmans, 2016]).

76. On the language of pressure, see Christopher Kavin Rowe, "Biblical Pressure and Trinitarian Hermeneutics," *Pro Ecclesia* 11 (2002): 308.

turn to an examination of the filial predication of christological action in this text (§B). Finally, we turn to the constant and distinctly divine agency in Christ in this text through the articulation of divine activity amidst Christ's human operations and the distinctly divine prerogative of reconciling humanity.

A. Singular Divine Agency

The first section argues for a strong unity of action and capacity between God and Christ as the foundational premise of Romans 5 (especially verse 8): i.e., it may indicate that God and Christ share a singular divine agency. On such a construction of agency, the divine capacities and activities are so intimately connected that the referent of *theos* and the referent of Christ can either name one agent (i.e., verse 8) or two intimately united agents (i.e., verse 10). Looking specifically at verse 8, we see that the pastoral value and logical coherence of this verse depends upon the unity (even singularity) of divine agency.

The pastoral function of this passage in Romans is to assure the reader of the abundance and magnitude of God's love. The *minori ad maius* (light and heavy) argument that Paul makes in verses 9 and 10 depends on the death of Christ being a remarkably bold act of *God* himself as the "hard part," so that Christians can have confidence today in the love and strength of God, the God who is the same agent as him who demonstrated his love for us on the cross.[77] Doug Moo states that these verses "set Christian hope on the unshakable foundation of the love of God revealed in the cross."[78] On the basis of such a claim, Christians can have hope and need not fear (verse 9) because the same agent who showed us love while we were still sinners (verse 8) has promised to continue to show us love "now that we are reconciled" (verse 10). The pastoral hope depends on the agent of the actions in the death of Christ being the same agent with the same love as the one in whom we hope.[79]

Likewise, the grammar of the text closely links the manifestation of God's love with the action of Christ. The reflexive pronoun (ἑαυτοῦ) further associates the "love" (ἀγάπην) with God (i.e., God's *own* love).[80] This is expounded upon when

---

77. F. F. Bruce, *Romans an Introduction and Commentary*, TNTC (Downers Grove, IL: IVP Academic, 1985), 115. Thomas R. Schreiner, *Romans*, BECNT (Grand Rapids: Baker, 1998), 262.

78. Douglas Moo, *The Letter to the Romans*, 2nd ed., NICNT (Grand Rapids: Eerdmans, 2018), 325; see also 333.

79. It is only when we lose sight of the intimacy and connection between the activity of God and his Son that we can misunderstand the cross as "divine child abuse." This accusation is seen in Rita Nakashima Brock, *Journeys by Heart: A Christology of Erotic Power* (New York: Crossroad, 1988), 56.

80. Eckhard J. Schnabel, *Der Brief des Paulus an die Römer: Kapitel 1–5*, HTANT (Witten: SCM Brockhaus, 2015), 529; unfortunately, Schnabel does not follow the logic of this as far as the below and describes Jesus' act of sacrifice merely as a "God initiated event."

the active verb ἀπέθανεν ("died") in 5:6, 8 (whose subject is Christ) is linked with the active verb συνίστησιν ("demonstrates")—whose subject is God.[81] That is, the subject, God, "demonstrates" his *own* love in the action of Christ. Based on this intimate connection Leon Morris claims, "Paul says that the cross shows us God's *own* love. One might expect him to say that the cross shows us the love of Christ. It does that, of course, but *own* puts the emphasis on the love of the Father."[82] Likewise, F. F. Bruce claims, "So entirely at one are the Father and the Son that the self-sacrifice of the latter can be presented as a token of the love of the former."[83] Even James Dunn (who advocates for an early low Christology in Romans), says, "It is important to note that Paul thinks of *Christ's* death as a demonstration of *God's* love."[84] Dunn then says that the death of "his Son" (5:10) has the "clear implication that this was not simply God's initiative, but God's own action through his Son."[85] Finally, Michael Gorman claims, "This interweaving of God's grace/love and initiative (a theological claim properly speaking) and Christ's grace/love and self-gift (a christological claim) is certainly one of the richest and most profound contributions of Paul to Christian theology .... Indeed this interweaving leads almost inevitably to Trinitarian conclusions."[86] Here I suggest that his interweaving evidences the singular agency of Christ and θεός. As the above scholars indicate, the act of one is credited as the act of the other based on their singular agency.

However, there is ambiguity as to whether the referent of θεός in verse 8 is "the Father" or YHWH (whom we call the triune God). While I believe that either interpretation helps solidify Romans 5 as reliant upon a divine christological premise, this first section will examine the possibility and implications of θεός as a reference to YHWH (i.e., the triune God), while the following will look at the possibility of θεός as a reference to the Father. Operating on the possibility of θεός as a reference to the triune God need not require that Paul have an operative and explicit trinitarian theology that affirms *homoousia*. It only requires that Paul assumes that Jesus is (somehow) included in the identity and name YHWH.

---

81. On the parallel between verses 6 and 8, see Michael Wolter, *Der Brief an die Römer: Teilband 1: Röm 1–8*, EKK VI/1 (Neukirchen-Vluyn: Patmos, 2014), 332. See also Ethelbert Stauffer, "θεός, θεότης, ἄθεος, θεοδίδακτος, θεῖος, θειότης," TDNT 3:103–4.

82. Leon Morris, *The Epistle to the Romans*, PNTC (Grand Rapids: Eerdmans, 1988), 224.

83. Bruce, *Romans*, 115; Morris, *Romans*, 224.

84. James D. G. Dunn, *Romans 1–8*, WBC 38A (Nashville: Thomas Nelson, 1988), 257, emphasis original.

85. Dunn, *Romans 1–8*, 260. Dunn's agreement here evidences either (1) that the "pressure" of Scripture here is not so strong that it demands my conclusion or (2) that Dunn holds the premises he needs to affirm early high Christology in Romans 5 and he does not follow it through to its logical end.

86. Michael J. Gorman, *The Death of the Messiah and the Birth of the New Covenant: A (Not So) New Model of the Atonement* (Eugene, OR: Cascade, 2014), 173.

I argue that if θεός is a reference to YHWH, the triune God, then the text pushes toward viewing the action of Christ as the action of the triune God with a strong identification of agency between them. The text would mean, "the triune God manifests his love for us ... *by* dying for us," since the agent who dies (i.e., the Son) is identified with the agent YHWH. As such, not only does this testify to the fulness of divine agency in Christ but it also pushes us toward understanding divine action as accomplished by the one God, "one agent."

As we will see, taking YHWH (i.e., the Trinity) as the referent of θεός is canonically plausible as well—as such, we ought to not expect θεός to refer exclusively to the Father. This may be most obvious when Jesus is arguably named θεός (e.g., Jn 20:28; Rom. 9:5; Heb. 1:8; Tit. 2:13; 1 Jn 5:20) and thereby is included in the being and identity of God.[87] If any (or all) of these texts include Jesus in the being and identity of God, then it seems that θεός is not used exclusively for the Father in the New Testament and ought not to be expected to refer always to the Father. Furthermore, if we allow this reading to be informed by later trinitarian conclusions, then Paul's appeal to the "will of God" (θέλημα τοῦ θεοῦ; Rom. 12:2) means that θεός is not necessarily referring to the Father any more than the Son or Spirit (who, according to the consensus of the tradition also possess the one will of God). Finally, Romans' numerous appeals to the "judgement of God" (κρίμα τοῦ θεοῦ; Rom. 2:2-3; 14:10-11) might canonically considered (especially according to Jn 5:22-23) be more appropriately predicated to the Son than the Father.

Even if one were to object that a few verses later Rom. 5:10 clearly refers to the Father as θεός (seemingly indicating that the referent of θεός in 5:8 must also refer to the Father), this seems unrequired on the basis of other conical uses. That is, mere proximity does not communicate the continuity of referent. For example, outside of Romans, John 1 has multiple uses of θεὸς in close proximity and yet one refers to "the Father" and the other to the "divine nature" (Jn 1:1b, 1:1c). Summarily, I am saying that if other canonical references to θεὸς include/indicate YHWH as the triune God, then the referent of θεὸς here might also include/indicate YHWH (as the triune God). And if θεὸς here refers to YHWH, then the acts of the agent YHWH can be identified with the acts of the agent Christ—further solidifying Christ's identification with YHWH.

On basis of the pastoral purpose of the text, the grammatical alignment of the subject θεός with the subject Christ, and the potential interpretation of θεός as referring to YHWH we see a strong unity (even singularity) of divine agency here in Romans 5. On such a reading θεός and Christ are taken as identifiable agents possessing singular agency Romans 5 pushes us toward viewing divine agency in Christ as single, even to the point of describing the act of Christ as an act of the one agent θεός (the triune God).

---

87. Karl Rahner, "Theos in the New Testament," in *TI* 1:137-8. For defenses of these texts as valid references to Jesus, see the classic study by Murray J. Harris, *Jesus as God: The New Testament Use of Theos in Reference to Jesus* (Grand Rapids: Baker Academic, 1992); Stauffer, "θεός," 3: 105.

B. Filial, Shared Divine Agency

Yet it may be objected that some of the above arguments overextend the exegetical warrant of the biblical text, especially if we take both uses of θεός here to be references to the Father. Even I (personally) concede that on the basis of this text alone, the above claim is not likely to garner widespread agreement (i.e., I hold to the above conclusion on the basis of other supporting canonical and theological considerations, not the exegesis of this passage alone). However, I believe that there is a plausible yet weaker claim that still meets the threshold of the thesis prosecuted here: i.e., that Romans 5 reflects a divine Christological premise—if we consider Christ as "sharing" divine agency with the Father.

So, here assuming that θεός refers to the person of the Father in verse 8, we have a natural interpretation of the passage's later use of θεός as an obvious reference to the Father in verse 10 (i.e., the Father is the θεός who has a Son). Elsewhere in Romans, Paul speaks of θεοῦ πατρὸς ἡμῶν (God our Father; Rom. 1:7), God who sends his Son (Rom. 8:3), not sparing him (Rom. 8:32), raises him to his right hand (Rom. 8:34), and who is the θεὸν καὶ πατέρα τοῦ κυρίου ἡμῶν Ἰησοῦ Χριστοῦ (God and Father of our Lord Jesus Christ; Rom. 15:6).[88] If this is the case and we have two distinct agents (Father and Son) instead of one (i.e., YHWH, as the above subsection argued), yet I believe that we still have reasons to think that these two agents share in divine agency and divine identity because of their shared "source of action."

Analogously, when two human agents are involved in an action, we can attribute one agent's action to a second agent when they share in a pertinent source of that action. So if I give a message to my oldest daughter and she communicates it to her siblings, her speech counts as my speech because it shares in the relevant source (i.e., my words or the content of my instructions). In the case of the Son and the Father, there is a shared "life" and "love." Here one agent's action (i.e., the Son's act of dying) is credited as the action of another agent. It is my argument that in order for the acts of one agent to be attributed to another agent, both agents must share in the same source of activity (i.e., agency).

To illustrate this, we may take the analogy of a mother and a daughter buying a gift for an elderly neighbor. If the mother sends her daughter to the store to buy a gift which the daughter will deliver, then that action can happen one of a few ways: (1) the daughter does not want to participate, but the mother gives her money and compels her to obey; (2) the daughter wants to (indeed, she initiated the idea) and the daughter pays for the gift with her own money and gives it to the neighbor

---

88. The thematic, linguistic, and structural connection between 5:6-8 and Rom. 8:32 (i.e., giving of the Son to manifest love and foster confidence) is perhaps the most persuasive evidence to me (Christina Eschner, "Die Hingabe des einzigen Sohnes „für" uns alle': Zur Wiederaufnahme des Steben—‚für'-Motivs aus Röm 5,6–8 in Röm 8,32," in *Letter to the Romans*, ed. Udo Schnelle, BETL 226 [Leuven: Peeters, 2009], 659–61).

herself; or (3) the daughter shares the idea, desire, and she pays for the gift from a bank account that she mutually shares with her mom.

If the Son and Father are like the mother and daughter here, and the giving of the gift is the cross, then scenario 1 is not viable because it denies the willingness of the Son in the action of the cross. Scenario 2 makes the act predicable to the Son, but it does not clearly express the Father's love (i.e., he does not accomplish it or fund it in a way that would allow that action to truly be said his own). Scenario 3 is an act of the Son and expresses the love of the Father (i.e., the shared purpose and shared "resources" [capacities]). Therefore, scenario 3 is the only scenario (of the above) in which the action can be accomplished by one agent and attributed to another. So if the act of the Son is going to be predicated of the Father, then the Son and Father must share in the same divine itention, desire, and capacity.

What is further, in the case of Rom. 5:8, the act requires not merely shared words or shared finances but the sharing of life. Unlike voluntarily sharing of communicable sources of action (e.g., money, words, or power), whereby Elijah can speak or heal by the shared power of God and it's credited to both Elijah and God as the agents, "life" must uniquely belong personally and originally to the idenitty of that agent if he/she is to give it up. That is, giving up a life is only significant if there is a shared agency, shared life, between θεὸς and the Son, because the giving of a life is only an act of love if one is giving *one's own* life (cf. Jn 15:13). If one "gives up" the life of another agent apart from shared agency we rightly call that the "taking" of a life (i.e., killing) and we would hardly call it love (e.g., child sacrifices in the Old Testament, Lev. 20:2 5). Even the closest parallel to giving up of life in the Old Testament (i.e., the near-sacrifice of Isaac by Abraham) likewise manifests this point. Abraham's actions manifest his own love. Yet, no one would say that Isaac's actions manifest Abraham's love; because Isaac and Abraham do not possess the same life or source of love.[89] Yet, on the premise that Christ does share in the divine life and love with the Father, Paul can attribute the sacrificial act of the Son to the love of the Father. On this basis we might ask, "Whose love is demonstrated in the reconciling act?" Paul's answers could just as likely be: "Christ's" (5:6) or the "Son's" (5:10) as it is "God's" (5:8). Leon Morris summarizes, "Unless there is a sense in which the Father and Christ are one, it is not the love of God that the cross shows. But because Christ is one with God, Paul can speak of the cross as a demonstration of the love of God."[90]

As an act of the Son that manifests the love of the Father, there is a supposed sharing of life between the two. They are distinct agents whose actions are closely connected to one another on the supposition of a shared life and agency. This shared life and agency reflects the shared identity that Christ with God as divine.

---

89. It is by virtue of this dissimilarity that the sacrifice of Isaac is not a valid parallel here. In Genesis 22, the focus is on the act of the first agent (Abraham) not the second. Genesis 22 might be more similar to Jn 3:16 (which focuses on "sending").

90. Morris, *Romans*, 224.

C. Distinctly Divine Agency

Finally, this last subsection will argue for understanding the divine agency of Christ as distinct from his human agency and indicative of full divine agency that lacks nothing of God's divine power or love, yet it is active in his very human operations at the cross and indicative of full divine agency. As such, this argument from Rom. 5:6-11 pushes toward viewing Christ's divine agency as simple and constant, applying pressure against a self-emptied divine agency or an inactive and hidden divine agency. This argument is made on the basis of (1) the active divine agency in the human operation of Christ's sacrifice, (2) the presupposed full divine agency in the pastoral purpose of the text, and (3) the distinctly divine prerogative of reconciliation.

First, the divine agency of Christ is active in his human operation of his sacrifice. While Romans 5 does not spell out the intricacies of the compatibility of divine and human agency, it does pressure us away from viewing that divine agency as alternating or hiding when human operations are undertaken by Christ (e.g., offering himself unto death).[91] Underscoring the humanity of Christ, the verb ἀποθανεῖν (to die) is located at the end of the Greek sentences in verses 6, 7a, 7b, and 8. This repetition "accentuates the unity of the passage" and thereby accentuates the unity of the claims therein (i.e., the divine agency and the human acts of Christ).[92] Theologically, we might also conclude that the death of Christ is presented as the focal point of the divine act of manifesting love, rather than merely the love of Christ according to his human nature.[93]

However, lest we think that Paul is advocating for a first-century prelude to the death of God movement, we must remember that Christ's death is a "human death." It is likely here that Paul is comparing Christ's work, as a "doom-averting death,"[94] with the "heroic vicarious deaths in the Greco-Roman world (real and literary)."[95] Therefore, we need not conclude that "dying" is a divine capacity and the effect of divine agency; indeed, we must deny this claim because of the eternality (Ps. 90:2), immortality (1 Tim. 6:16), and incorporeality of the divine nature (Jn 4:24).

---

91. David Capes notes that the title Christ is the "most frequent title used by Paul" and "the apostle appears to use it [especially] when discussing the sacrificial death of Jesus" (*Divine Christ*, 55).

92. This quote comes from Moo, *Romans*, 333.

93. On the transcendence of Christ's capacities beyond the Jewish understanding of "what belongs to the nature of humanity" (was zum Wesen des Menschen gehört), see Erik Peterson, *Der Brief an die Römer*, Ausgewählte Schriften 6 (Würzburg: Echter, 1997), 123.

94. Christina Eschner, *Gestorben und hingegeben "für" die Sünder: die griechische Konzeption des Unheil abwendenden Sterbens und deren paulinische Aufnahme für die Deutung des Todes Jesu Christi*, WMANT 122 (Neukirchen-Vluyn: Neukirchener, 2010), 347.

95. Simon J. Gathercole, *Defending Substitution: An Essay on Atonement in Paul*, ASBT (Grand Rapids: Baker Academic, 2015), 90.

Yet the text's insistence on the manifestation of divine love in this act suggests that the divine agency of Christ was actively involved (in some sense) in this operation (perhaps, concurrently). As such, it would not seem to suggest that Christ's divine agency is *hidden* in this human action. To the contrary, his divine agency is actively *manifesting* divine love.

Second, the passage itself presupposes active and distinct divine agency in Christ's action. As mentioned above, the text only provides pastoral comfort if Paul's minori ad maius argument is rooted in the continuity of agency. We should trust God's love toward us "now" because God himself showed us love in the death of God. Because of this rhetorical and pastoral purpose, we might find it odd if the divine agency which Christ executed in his life was a kenotically emptied version of the divine agency that we encounter today. If the love of God in the cross is an exercise of a kenotic capacity, we do not have assurance that that we will continue to meet God with that same love toward us now and in the future.

Finally, we see the divine agency of Christ made manifest in the Pauline concept of "reconciliation" (καταλλαγή) here in Romans 5, and beyond. In the New Testament, the word "reconciliation" (and its word-group καταλάσσω,[96] ἀποκαταλλάσσω,[97] καταλλαγή[98]) is exclusively Pauline.[99] Particularly pertinent for our purposes is Paul's exclusive commitment to employing this word for describing an act of God toward fallen creatures.[100] The relative place of "reconciliation" among the constellation of Pauline concepts has been vigorously disputed,[101] yet there is consensus on the association of reconciliation with the death of Christ and the love of God (e.g., Rom. 5:8, 10; Gal. 2:20; 2 Cor. 5:14-15).[102]

In Rom. 5:10, the reconciliation brought about by the Son "has already been accomplished" (καταλλαγέντες, the aorist passive "having been reconciled") and is not the result of humanity "standing on its own feet."[103] The passivity of people

---

96. Rom. 5:10; 1 Cor. 7:11; 2 Cor. 5:18-20.

97. Col. 1:20, 22; Eph. 1:16.

98. Rom. 5:11; 11:15; 2 Cor. 5:18-19.

99. I. Howard Marshall, "The Meaning of 'Reconciliation,'" in *Unity and Diversity in New Testament Theology: Essays in Honor of George E. Ladd* (Grand Rapids: Eerdmans, 1978), 119–21.

100. *BDAG*, 521; Bruce, *Romans*, 118; Stanley E. Porter, *Καταλλάσσω in Ancient Greek Literature, with Reference to the Pauline Writings*, Estudios de filología Neotestamentaria (Cordoba: Ediciones El Almendro, 1994), 154.

101. See for example the foundational work by Ralph P. Martin, *Reconciliation: A Study of Paul's Theology* (Atlanta: John Knox, 1981), 32–5.

102. Constantineanu, *Social Significance of Reconciliation*, 127; see Adam J. Johnson, *Atonement: A Guide for the Perplexed*, BGP (New York: Bloomsbury, 2015), 37.

103. Schreiner, *Romans*, 264; Dunn, *Romans 1–8*, 268. Likewise, see the aorist in 2 Cor. 5:18 (Harris, *Second Corinthians*, 195). Simon Kistemaker, *Exposition of the Second Epistle to the Corinthians*, NTC (Grand Rapids: Baker, 1997), 195, makes an argument for a strong "past tense" sense.

and the activity of God in reconciliation are also made evident in 2 Cor. 5:19, where "God was in Christ reconciling the world to himself." On the text of 2 Corinthians 5, Mark Seifrid notes this correlation and says, "God's action is thus implicitly identified with Christ's action, and Christ's action is identified with that of God."[104] Noting the active voice in the verb καταλλάσσω ("to reconcile"), Karl Barth says, "Καταλλάσσειν [active] is said only of God, and καταλλαγῆναι [passive] only of humanity."[105] Karl Barth's son, Markus Barth, later says of reconciliation, "God is always presented as the *agent*: he reconciles ... creation to himself ... never the reverse."[106] Again, this text pushes against the divestment of divine agency in Christ and instead suggests the full activity of God in the acts of Christ. Likewise, it pushes against a hiddenness of divine agency and prioritization of human agency. Instead, Christ's activity in the divine act of reconciliation indicates for us the concurrent and operative divine agency even in the midst of his human operations.

IV. Theological and Pastoral Prudence

From the account of reconciliation in Romans 5, we are oriented toward the pastoral prudence of christological divine agency. We affirm divine agency in Christ because we affirm that God is the savior of "all humanity" (1 Tim. 4:10). In the early church, soteriology was the "driving force behind ... reflection on the identity of Christ"; likewise, soteriology drives and is influenced by decisions in the sphere of christological activity.[107] Articulating the significance of divine activity in redemption, P. T. Forsyth states, "The prime doer in Christ's cross was God. Christ was God reconciling. He was God doing the very best for man, and not man doing his very best for God."[108]

Christological divine agency has pastoral and theological benefits pertaining to the locus of revelation as well. On an account of simple and distinct divine

---

104. Mark A. Seifrid, *The Second Letter to the Corinthians*, PNTC (Grand Rapids: Eerdmans, 2014), 257; cf. Gorman, *Death of the Messiah*, 175 for a similar claim about 2 Corinthians 8 and 9.

105. Barth, *CD* IV/1, 74.

106. Markus Barth and Helmut Blanke, *Colossians: A New Translation with Introduction and Commentary*, trans. Astrid B. Beck, AB 34B (New York: Doubleday, 1994), 214.

107. Grillmeier, *Christ in the Christian Tradition*, 1:9. John Webster says, "It is, moreover, properly soteriological in intent, pointing to the place where we might most fittingly begin to answer the questions of the identity of the agent of salvation by attesting to his unity with the gracious Lord of the covenant" (*Word and Church: Essays in Christian Dogmatics*, 144).

108. P. T. Forsyth, *The Cruciality of the Cross* (Eugene, OR: Wipf and Stock, 1997), 17. See also Katherine Sonderegger, "The Sinlessness of Christ," 274; Meyendorff, *Christ in Eastern Christian Thought*, 156–7. Ivor Davidson suggests that this connection between identity and action for us in salvation characterizes the Reformed tradition ("Christ," 451).

agency, we see the fullness of deity dwelling (Col. 1:19) and being made manifest in Jesus, revealing to us the nature of the triune God. On the cross of Christ and his act of sacrifice we see the clarity and comprehensive revelation of the love of God.[109] By contrast, if kenoticism is true, there is a worry that Jesus does not reveal God as he always has been, but of a toned-down version of God. Christ emptied of deity does not reveal deity, Karl Barth complains,[110] and Isaac Dorner laments that a kenotic Christology turns the incarnation into a mere "theophany."[111]

Minimally, ontological and functional kenotic Christology sees the Son exercising a different kind of power in Christ than that which he could, or did, in the Old Testament. Yet a classical and Reformed account can affirm a strong sense of continuity between the acts of YHWH in the Old Testament and Jesus in the New Testament. This is the God who heals those who look to the one is "made sin" (2 Cor. 5:21) and is hoisted up in the wilderness (Num. 21:8-9; Jn 3:14). As N. T. Wright says, "If you start with the God of the Exodus, of Isaiah, of creation and covenant, of the Psalms, and ask what that God might be like, were he to become human, you will find that he might look very much like Jesus of Nazareth, and perhaps never more so than when he dies on a Roman cross."[112]

Accordingly, in Jesus we see the full agency of the *triune* God. Christ is the image of the invisible Father and the exact imprint of his nature (Hebrews 1), only doing what he sees the Father doing (Jn 5:19), thereby manifesting "the glory of God in the face of Jesus Christ" (2 Cor. 4:6). On this account, the acts of Christ are included in the indivisibility of the triune acts of God toward creation. However, if only the Son has emptied himself of attributes, then there seems to be a sense in which Christ's revelation is primarily (or exclusively) true of the Son. By contrast, if Christ exercises a distinct and simple divine agency, then his works reveal the nature of the triune God who is Father, Son, and Holy Spirit.[113] And while there is an affirmation that the divine person to whom we predicate the acts of Christ is the Son, every operation is one of the Father, Son, and Holy Spirit. Therefore, we see in Jesus not a revelation of the "fickleness" of God but a revelation of

---

109. Heiko Krimmer, *Römerbrief*, Bibel-Kommentar 10 (Neuhausen-Stuttgart: Hänssler, 1983), 141.

110. Barth, *CD* I/2, 38–9, 159; IV/2, 40–1.

111. Isaac August Dorner, *History of the Development of the Doctrine of the Person of Christ* (Edinburgh: T&T Clark, 1897), 5: 230.

112. N. T. Wright, "Jesus and the Identity of God," *Ex Auditu* 14 (1998): 54.

113. On the point of works revealing the person and nature of God, see Thomas Aquinas, *Commentary on the Gospel of John*, ed. Daniel Keating and Matthew Levering, trans. Fabian R. Larcher and James A. Weisheipl, Thomas Aquinas in Translation (Washington, DC: Catholic University of America Press, 2010), ch. 5, lect.6, n. 817. Elsewhere he says, "Every action of Christ is a lesson for us" (ch. 11, lect.6, n. 1555).

the fullness of God (Col. 2:9).[114] Finally, connecting the distinct divine agency of Christ to the love of God, Barth reminds us that the act of God in Jesus Christ means that Christians, "with ultimate certainty, know themselves to be beloved of God."[115]

V. Summary

This account of Christ's divine agency has sought to evidence the coherence of classical and Reformed Christology with its biblical, conciliar, and classical commitments. In the first section, classical and Reformed Christology's account of trinitarian action in christological operations was presented. It began by aligning its understanding of triune agency with Owen's claim that "every divine work, and every part of every divine work, is the work of God, that is, of the whole Trinity, inseparably and undividedly."[116] As such, from the perspective of causality there is an appreciation for every one of the divine persons' involvement in divine actions. Yet classical and Reformed theology offers distinctions between the divine persons in the singular divine act by means of appropriations, proper terminating actions, and personal modes of action. Therefore, classical and Reformed Christology is able to account for the significance of the Father and the Spirit in christological operations without attributing independent action to any of the divine persons and without making the Spirit the determinative divine agent in christological acts.

Next this chapter looked at the implications of classical and Reformed Christology's commitment to classical Trinitarianism and Reformed emphases in order to show the incoherencies between classical and Reformed commitment on divine agency and certain kenotic and kryptic accounts. Specifically, it argued that because of divine simplicity the divine attributes are not "scalable," that losing the omnipresence of the Son would imply a violation of the indivisibility of divine operations and the *extra Calvinisticum*, and that Constantinople III requires the distinction between divine and human operations to be constant, not merely contiguous. Furthermore, it argued that an account of krypsis which prioritizes the human nature is at risk of inverting the *an/enhypostatic* distinction.

Finally, this chapter turned to the biblical coherence and the pastoral prudence of divine agency in order to support and illustrate the vital affirmation of divine action in Christ. Romans 5 articulated the necessarily divine operation in Christ's self-sacrifice and the importance of divine initiative in salvation. As such, the

---

114. Evans, "Kenotic Christology and the Nature of God," 210, contrasts the traditional view with his position, which is "an expression of God's lack of fickleness."
115. Barth, *Der Römerbrief 1922—Zweite Fassung* (GA II, 47), 223.
116. WJO, *Pneumatologia*, 3:94.

Christian can look to Christ and be confident in the love of the triune God for his people. With an account of divine agency in classical and Reformed Christology we see that God has revealed himself in Christ as triune and, simply, therein we encounter the God who "acts on behalf" of his people (Isa. 64:4).

Chapter 5

HUMAN AGENCY: COHERENCE AND PRUDENCE

Considered the "main question about Christ" for the last two centuries, the full humanity of Christ has become the primary presupposition and ultimate goal of much of modern Christology.[1] As such, classical models of Christology continue to be considered more "implausible and more incredible."[2] Particularly, accusations against classical Christology have been hurled from various corners based on modern interpretations of biblical texts in which Jesus is seemingly acting in an utterly and exclusively human (e.g., temptation, suffering) way. Brian Daley claims that the human weakness of Christ (e.g., "limitations of his energy" and "ability") raises both the "greatest challenge to the church's proclamation of his lordship and stimulates the most profound theological reflection."[3] This is particularly true for Reformed Christology by virtue of its attention to the integrity of both natures and, especially for Owen, the role of the Holy Spirit in the humanity of Christ.[4] In the midst of this challenge and opportunity, this chapter argues for the coherence and prudence of a classical and Reformed understanding of Christ's human agency by presenting Christ's ordinary and distinct (§I), yet dependent (§II), human agency. Then the chapter moves to display the biblical coherence (§III) and pastoral prudence (§IV) of such a position.

I. Ordinary, Distinct Human Agency

The Reformed commitment to the integrity of Christ's humanity, I will argue, implies a distinction between Christ's two agencies and the integrity of his human

---

1. Moltmann, *Crucified God*, 92; Pannenberg, *Jesus*, 189; Schweitzer, *Contemporary Christologies*, 128; Tanner, *Jesus, Humanity and the Trinity*, 7–10; McFarland, *Word Made Flesh*, 6.

2. Sonderegger, "The Sinlessness of Christ," 272.

3. Brian E. Daley, "The Word and His Flesh: Human Weakness and the Identity of Jesus in Patristic Christology," in *Seeking the Identity of Jesus: A Pilgrimage*, ed. Beverly Roberts Gaventa and Richard B. Hays (Grand Rapids: Eerdmans, 2008), 267.

4. Holmes, "Communicatio Idiomatum," 86.

agency as "ordinary."[5] Part of the distinctiveness of Reformed Christology can be summarized by the Latin phrase *finitum non capax infiniti* (i.e., the finite cannot contain the infinite). Based on this affirmation, classical and Reformed Christology denies the *genus majestaticum* and holds tightly to the finite properties of the humanity of Christ.[6] Following Owen, this project seeks to affirm the "distinctively Reformed emphasis" on the humanity of Christ by utilizing the doctrine of the Holy Spirit and "classical theological categories to achieve Reformation ends."[7] This section will demonstrate the coherence of classical and Reformed Christology with its commitment to the Reformed emphasis on the finitude and integrity of Christ's human nature by arguing for ordinary and distinct human agency. The prudence of such a position will be shown in relation to contemporary suggestions that Christ's human nature necessarily receives the beatific vision and maximal human knowledge throughout his life. The distinct and ordinary human agency will be articulated here in terms of his ordinary human beliefs (i.e., finite knowledge §A) and ordinary human desires (§B). With distinctly human *desires* and *beliefs*, Christ possesses a distinctly human capacity for *intentional* action (i.e., agency).[8] Finally, this section will show the involvement of the Holy Spirit in this ordinary human agency (§C).

A. Belief: Finite Knowledge

The first component of Christ's human agency is his finite human knowledge and faith, stemming from the common Reformed affirmation that Christ

---

5. The language of "ordinary" is not intended to deny the *sui generis* character of the hypostatic union, nor deny his unique sinlessness. Instead, it is a way of specifying the frequent use of "genuine [humanity]" by suggesting that Christ's human agency is recognizably and relatedly human to the ordinary person with ordinary human faculties. It is fundamentally, a way of describing Christ's human actions as those of a pilgrim (*viator*), like every other human while on earth. As shown below, this is not motivated simply by a desire to have a relatable savior but by a desire to properly articulate the sum of the biblical witness.

6. Dorner says that "Reformed theologians have always zealously laid stress on the actuality of the humanity [of Christ]" (*History of the Development of the Doctrine of the Person of Christ*, 5:231).

7. Holmes, "Communicatio Idiomatum," 86; Trueman, *John Owen*, 96. The Reformed position might be summarized as "Christ, in the work of mediation, acts according to both natures, by each nature doing that which is proper to itself" (*WCF*, VIII.7). Likewise, Bavinck says that Reformed theology is "able, better than any other [tradition], to maintain ... his true and genuine humanity" (*RD*, 3:310).

8. Recall that intention is comprised of a *desire* for some end and the *belief* that a particular action will contribute to filling/satisfying that desire.

(pre-resurrection) is a pilgrim or wayfarer (*viator*).[9] This claim resists the most "common opinion" in the early and medieval church, that Christ beheld the divine essence while on earth[10] and that he *necessarily* knew all past, present, and future realities.[11] So this subsection will argue for the common (although not unanimous) Reformed commitment to Christ's finite human knowledge in contrast to claim of Christ's maximal human knowledge and participate on in the beatific vision from his conception.[12]

This affirmation of the beatific vision and complete knowledge of all created realities is largely based on the principle that the closer one is united to God, the more intimately one knows him.[13] Since the humanity of Christ is more intimately united to God than any other creature, Christ (in his humanity) knows (i.e., sees) God more intimately than anyone else.[14] According to defenders of this position, ordinary humans experience a journey of faith before the victory of beholding

---

9. Michael Allen argues that Christ's faith is commonplace in the Reformed tradition and fundamental to Reformed soteriology (*Christ's Faith*, 30 n. 105).

10. The affirmation of the beatific vision is a component of what Timothy Pawl calls "traditional Christology" (Timothy Pawl, *In Defense of Extended Conciliar Christology: A Philosophical Essay*, OSAT [New York: Oxford University Press, 2019], 143). Brown likewise names maximal knowledge from the conception of the standard view before modernity (*Divine Humanity*, 242). However, contemporary Catholicism has its objectors to this position (e.g., Thomas G. Weinandy, "Jesus' Filial Vision of the Father," *Pro Ecclesia* 13 [2004]: 189–201). Gerald O'Collins, *Christology: A Biblical, Historical, and Systematic Study of Jesus*, 2nd ed. (New York: Oxford University Press, 2009), 267.

11. On the consensus holding this position in the early church, see de Aldama and Solano, *Sacrae Theologiae Summa IIIA: On the Incarnate Word, on the Blessed Virgin Mary* (Saddle River, NJ: Keep The Faith, 2014), 142; Timothy W. Bartel, "Like Us in All Things, Apart from Sin?," *Journal of Philosophical Research* 16 (1991): 35—citing Cyril, Athanasius, Gregory of Nazianzus, Basil, and Augustine; Marilyn McCord Adams, *What Sort of Human Nature? Medieval Philosophy and the Systematics of Christology*, The Aquinas Lectures (Milwaukee: Marquette University Press, 1999), 17. John Eck says that "the whole church admits that Christ even according to His human nature is omniscient" and a suggestion to the contrary implies Nestorianism ("Refutation of the Articles of Zwingli," in *On Providence and Other Essays*, ed. Willian John Hinke, trans. Henry Preble [Durham, NC: Labyrinth, 1983], 71).

12. Whether Christ beheld the divine essence while on earth is disputed in the Reformed tradition (Davidson, "Christ," 460). However, rejecting the view that Christ has the uninterrupted beatific vision while on earth seems to be the common (although not unanimous) position (see Suzanne McDonald's, "Beholding the Glory of God in the Face of Jesus Christ: John Owen and the 'Reforming' of the Beatific Vision," in *The Ashgate Research Companion to John Owen's Theology*, ed. Mark Jones and Kelly M. Kapic [Burlington: Ashgate], 152; G. C. Berkouwer, *The Person of Christ* [Grand Rapids: Eerdmans, 1954], 221).

13. Aquinas, *ST* III, Q.10, A.4.

14. Aquinas, *ST* III, Q.10, A.4, ad.3; see also Adams, *Human Nature*, 31.

God in heaven, yet Christ is both the wayfarer and comprehensor while on earth (*simul viator et comprehensor*), beholding the divine essence even in his most extreme moments of agony.[15]

In order to make sense of the biblical witness (e.g., Christ's growth in wisdom, Lk. 2:52), patristic and scholastic (including Reformed) thinkers would distinguish between different kinds of knowledge. Beatific knowledge is the sight of the divine essence, which Christ experiences (according to some) from the moment of his conception through his entire life (including the cross).[16] Infused knowledge is that which God imparts to Christ's human understanding. Because of Christ's beatific and infusion of maximal knowledge by virtue of the intimacy of the hypostatic union Christ knows in his human nature "whatever pertains to human sciences" and divine revelation—i.e., all "truth present, past, and future."[17] Jesus also had "acquired knowledge" that "grew" (Lk. 2:52) as he encountered people, so that he knew a blind man was in front of him not only by virtue of his infused perfect knowledge but also through his senses of sight and touch (i.e., acquired knowledge).[18] Taken together, this position, which is held by many Catholics and some Protestants, guards against the possibility of Christ's failing to know or do something he ought to.[19]

---

15. Aquinas, *ST* III, Q.15, A.10; see Owen's relation to this historical claim in Trueman, *John Owen*, 110. The Reformed tradition affirms that Christ experiences both of these states, but contiguously, not simultaneously (Franciscus Junius, *A Treatise on True Theology with the Life of Franciscus Junius*, trans. David C. Noe [Grand Rapids: Reformation Heritage, 2014], 129–30).

16. For a defense of the instantaneity of the beatific vision from conception, see Legge, *Trinitarian Christology of St Thomas Aquinas*, 173; Pierre-Yves Maillard, *La vision de Dieu chez Thomas d'Aquin: une lecture de l'In Ioannem à la lumière de ses sources augustiniennes*, Bibliothèque Thomiste 53 (Paris: J. Vrin, 2001), 225–54.

17. Aquinas, *ST* III, Q.11, A.1. It is worth noting that Simon Francis Gaine denies the automatic infusion of knowledge, but does go onto affirm that Jesus would be the best mathematician, musician, and quantum physicists on earth (*Did the Saviour See the Father: Christ, Salvation and the Vision of God* [New York: T&T Clark, 2005], 152).

18. Thomas and John of Damascus read this to mean that he "brought more into evidence the wisdom inherent in Him" ("Orthodox Faith," III.22, 326–7; cf. Aquinas, *ST* III, Q.7, A.12, ad.3).

19. Anselm of Canterbury, "Why God Became Man," in *The Major Works*, ed. Brian Davies and G. R. Evans, OWC (New York: Oxford University Press, 1998), II.13. Robert Kolb and Timothy J. Wengert, eds., "Formula of Concord (1577)," in *The Book of Concord: The Confessions of the Evangelical Lutheran Church*, trans. Charles P. Arand et al. (Minneapolis: Fortress, 2000), VIII.74 and is considered viable in Thomas H. McCall, "Son Though He Was, He Learned Obedience: The Submission of Christ in Theological Perspective (in Dialogue with Thomas Aquinas and Karl Barth)," in *Listen, Understand, Obey: Essays on Hebrews in Honor of Gareth Lee Cockerill*, ed. Caleb Friedeman (Eugene, OR: Pickwick, 2017), 148–9; likewise, Thomas H. McCall, *Analytic Christology*, 47–8. This latter McCall text contains a chapter-length treatment of Hebrews 5 and obedience that is functionally identical to the chapter in the collected volume. So for the sake of simplicity I will cite the earlier chapter.

However, Owen and many in the Reformed tradition resist the attribution of the beatific vision and exhaustive infused knowledge to the humanity of Christ during his pilgrimage. Bavinck surveys the "church fathers ... Scholastic, Catholic, as well as Lutheran" regarding this "sentiment" of perfect human knowledge and suggests that "they came into conflict with the clear pronouncements of Scripture."[20] He says, "The reaction of Reformed theologians was, first of all, that Christ's infused and acquired knowledge was not immediately complete but gradually increased; and, second, that Christ on earth was a pilgrim, not a comprehensive knower, that he walked by faith and hope, not by sight, and that he did not yet share the 'beatific knowledge' (*Scientia beata*) here on earth."[21]

Likewise, contrary to the historically Roman Catholic and "some protestant divines" who "outcry against ascribing of ignorance" to the humanity of Christ, Owen says that Christ's human soul is not omniscient, and (we may add) even to the point that Christ may not have known how to read in his human nature.[22] Owen says, "I do not hereby ascribe the infusion of omniscience, of infinite understanding, wisdom, and knowledge, into the human nature of Christ. It was and is a creature, finite and limited" and, therefore, did not possess infinite knowledge.[23]

This human understanding, as Turretin says, necessarily includes some lack of knowledge if he is like us in every way, "truly a partaker of our nature with its guiltless infirmities."[24] This means that the Reformed tradition affirms a literal

---

20. Bavinck, *RD*, 3:312. Owen says that the Roman Catholics of his day "charge with error" those who "affirm no more than what is expressly asserted in ... Scripture" (WJO, *Exposition of Hebrews*, 20:28).

21. Bavinck, *RD*, 3:312; Turretin likewise denies the beatific vision and simultaneity of pilgrim and *comprehensor* (*Institutes*, II:13.xiii.12).

22. WJO, *Communion*, 2:191. For the argument that Jesus may not have been able to read, see Chris Keith, *Jesus' Literacy: Scribal Culture and the Teacher from Galilee*, LNTS (New York: T&T Clark, 2011).

23. WJO, *Christologia*, 1:93; see also Owen's claim in WJO, Θεολογούμενα Παντοδαπά, 17:38; Owen, *Biblical Theology*, 18. This claim runs contrary to Ryan McGraw's interpretation of the maximal wisdom of Christ in his human nature ("Seeing Things Owen's Way: John Owen's Trinitarian Theology and Piety in Its Early-Modern Context," 198–9). For more on the ectypal nature of *theologia unionis*, see Rehnman, *Divine Discourse*, 65–7. However, both Rehnman and McGraw see greater continuity between Owen and Francis Junius (on this point) than I am advocating for here.

24. Turretin, *Institutes*, II:13.xiii.12. Likewise, Rowan Williams suggests that "If the Word is to save humanity by assuming genuine human experience, the Word must assume a subject characterized—like all of us—by limited knowledge and all that goes with it" (*Christ the Heart of Creation*, 19).

growth in knowledge by Christ (Lk. 2:52),[25] and also "in all situations in which Jesus asks about or investigates something (Mark 5:30; 6:38; 9:21; 11:13)."[26] He was the second Adam and created innocent like Adam.[27] Therefore, he did not necessarily behold the divine nature or know all knowable facts in his humanity throughout the entirety of his earthly life.[28] This does not mean that Christ was "ignorant" of things that he ought to know or needed to know in order to fulfill his mission, but he may have been "nescient" of some things that were "unnecessary for that state and time."[29] So Jesus need not have known my (embarrassingly high) golf handicap according to his humanity in order to fulfill "that whole duty which, as a man, he owed unto God."[30]

---

25. See this characterization of the Reformed tradition as an implication of the *extra Calvinisticum* in Drake, *Flesh of the Word*, 278. I want to, like Drake, acknowledge the diversity in the tradition (e.g., Junius), while also appreciating this as a common (albeit, not unanimous) characteristic of Reformed Christology. Yet, unlike Drake, I am disinclined to consider this "ignorance" because of the connotations for culpability. This is especially true when considering Christ's social responsibilities (see Daniel Lee Hill and Ty Kieser, "Social Sin and the Sinless Savior: Delineating Supra-Personal Sin in Continuity with Conciliar Christology," *Modern Theology* 38 [2022]: 568–91).

26. Bavinck, *RD*, 3:312.

27. WJO, *Pneumatologia*, 3:168; *Christologia*, 1:171.

28. This should not imply that Jesus does not partake of the beatific vision after his death and resurrection. While Christ's relation to the object and means of the Christian's beatific vision is contested, multiple views on offer are viable within this account. See McDonald, "Beholding the Glory of God in the Face of Jesus Christ."

29. WJO, *Pneumatologia*, 3:170; Turretin, *Institutes*, 2:351. See also Bernard J. F. Lonergan, *The Incarnate Word*, ed. Robert M. Doran and Jeremy D. Wilkins, trans. Charles C. Hefling, CWBL 8 (Toronto: University of Toronto Press, 2016), 677.

30. WJO, *Exposition of Hebrews*, 20:30. Gaine provides an intriguing account of Christ's beatific knowledge alongside an attempt to straightforwardly understand Mark 13:32 by suggesting that Christ (according to his humanity) genuinely does not know something in the sense that beatific knowledge is not properly expressed in human concepts and images (*Did the Saviour See the Father?*, 151). Therefore, Christ does not know in the sense that he does not yet have knowledge in communicable terms for the day and hour of his return. This is analogous to a professor who is given a complex arithmetic problem by one of her students. She is capable of finding out the answer, but she has not yet worked out the problem. Analogously, Christ knows the date of his return according to the beatific vision, but not in a communicable fashion (157). While Gaine's account retains several of the theological goods desired by Reformed Christology (see 200), in conjunction with the beatific vision, the fundamental difference between his and my accounts can be illustrated through an elaboration on Mark 13. For Gaine, when Jesus (according to his humanity) learns the day or the hour, he can honestly say, "I already knew that humanly" (i.e., it belonged to his beatific knowledge). Yet, for this position, Jesus genuinely learns items of knowledge according to his human nature.

However, one recent Catholic account of the hypostatic union objects to the coherence of the preceding classical and Reformed account of Christ's knowledge and unified christological action. Thomas Joseph White says that Christ's experience of the beatific vision in his humanity is both a necessary consequence of the union and a necessary precondition for the unity of Christ's actions. White says, "If the Son is going to adequately manifest the mystery of the Holy Trinity in his human decisions and choices, then he must be humanly aware of what the Father who sent him wills and of what he wills with the Holy Spirit, so that he can express this in his human actions and choices."[31] White says that Christ's human and divine knowledge must be "epistemologically proportioned."[32] He adds that "without the [beatific] vision … his acts would not stem from an evidential knowledge of this [divine] will …. It would not manifest Christ's certitude of his own divine will received eternally from the Father."[33] Thus, "Only such knowledge will assure the operative unity (in and through two distinct natures) of Christ's personal actions, because this knowledge alone gives the mind of the man Jesus an evidential certitude of the will he shares eternally with the Father."[34]

B. Desire: Christ's Human Will

In order to address this concern about the exercise of Christ's human knowledge as a precondition for unity, we turn to Christ's human desires and his human will (i.e., the faculty by "virtue of which something desires").[35] Based on the previous subsection's articulation of the Reformed commitment to finite knowledge and the doctrine of dyothelitism, this section will argue (contrary to White) that a classical and Reformed account can cohere with the unity of christological action apart from positing the claim that Christ beholds the beatific vision while on earth.

Owen, with the classical and Reformed tradition more broadly, adheres to the conciliar affirmation of the two wills of Christ (dyothelitism).[36] This doctrine has, however, come under suspicion in modern theology, even from within the Reformed tradition.[37] Yet dyothelitism is a crucial component of conciliar

---

31. White, *Incarnate Lord*, 255, 261.
32. Ibid., 261.
33. Ibid., 267.
34. Ibid., 257, see also 246.
35. Pawl, *In Defense of Conciliar Christology*, 214.
36. Crisp, *Divinity and Humanity*, 61 n. 36; see Ch. 3 §I.B.3.
37. Augustus Hopkins Strong, *Systematic Theology: A Compendium* (Valley Forge, PA: Judson, 1907), 695; Jordan Wessling, "Christology and Conciliar Authority: On the Viability of Monothelitism for Protestant Theology," in *Christology, Ancient and Modern: Explorations in Constructive Dogmatics*, ed. Oliver D. Crisp and Fred Sanders, LATC (Grand Rapids: Zondervan Academic, 2013), 151–70; Fredrich Schleiermacher, *A New Translation and Critical Edition*, ed. Catherine L. Kelsey and Terrence N. Tice, trans. Terrence N. Tice, Catherine L. Kelsey, and Edwina Lawler (Louisville: Westminster John Knox, 2016), §96, 586–7.

Christology and of affirming two agencies in Christ. For classical and Reformed Christology, dyothelitism reinforces the affirmation of the genuine humanity of Jesus Christ and thereby the mediatorial activity of Jesus Christ via theandric acts that are accomplished through his distinct natures and the capacities therein.[38] Because of his human will, Calvin says, Christ was not merely "victorious without fighting," but genuinely "felt, without being wounded by them, those temptations which pierce us with their stings."[39]

However, this "fighting" and "feeling" differ from the claim that Christ is simultaneously pilgrim and *comprehensor*. Those affirming the traditionally Catholic stance state that Christ's beatific knowledge meant that he never deliberated over any choice (i.e., considered distinct courses of actions).[40] Yet, I contend that the affirmation of nescience in Christ (i.e., the denial of a beatific vision and comprehensive knowledge) implies the possibility of choice (i.e., between alternatives) and discursive reasoning in Christ according to his humanity, without a Nestorian violation of christological unity (as White charges). As Ivor Davidson suggests, Christ "weighs up possibilities; he intends outcomes; he seeks to put things into effect; he implements his understanding of divine purposes."[41]

The concept of desire is vital for this discussion in particular, and agency (i.e., intention) in general. In order for a temporal agent to possess agency (i.e., capacity for intentional action), they must possess the capacity to bring about that effect

---

38. Edmondson, *Calvin's Christology*, 31; Dolf te Velde, *The Doctrine of God in Reformed Orthodoxy, Karl Barth, and the Utrecht School: A Study in Method and Content*, SRT 25 (Boston: Brill, 2013), 202.

39. Calvin, *A Harmony of the Gospels*, 3:234.

40. See discussions of deliberation in Pawl, *In Defense of Extended Conciliar Christology*, 197–200; Bathrellos, *The Byzantine Christ*, 129; White, *Incarnate Lord*, 254; Andrew Louth, *St. John Damascene: Tradition and Originality in Byzantine Theology*, OECS (New York: Oxford University Press, 2002), 139. I am choosing to use the English language of deliberation and choice because there seems to be a lack of consensus on the meaning and proper usage of the Greek *gnomic*. For some, it is inherently sinful (Daley, *God Visible*, 220); for others, it is inherently Nestorian (Ian A. McFarland, "'Willing Is Not Choosing': Some Anthropological Implications of Dyothelite Christology," *IJST* 9 [2007]: 3–23); yet for still others, it is viably orthodox (Barnes, *Christ's Two Wills*, 178). This ambiguity is reflective of the semantic range of the Greek word with its 28 different uses, as noted by Maximus and the Damascene ("Orthodox Faith," 3.14), and may even be an intentional tension on Maximus' part (Basil Studer, "Zur Soteriologie des Maximus," in *Maximus Confessor: Actes du symposium sur Maxime le Confesseur, Fribourg, 2-5 septembre 1980*, ed. Felix Heinzer and Christoph Schönborn [Fribourg: Éditions Universitaires, 1982], 245–6).

41. Davidson, "'Not My Will but Yours Be Done,'" 191. My agreement with Davidson here and below ought to further suggest my ambivalence toward the historic *gnomic* will discussion insofar as I seek to confirm Davidson's position and Davidson denies a *gnomic* will in Christ. So long as a "weighing possibilities" remains viable, one can affirm or deny a *gnomic* will in Christ.

(i.e., it must be possible) without it being necessary (i.e., it must not be inevitable [recall the way acid that dissolves plastic is loosely and improperly called an "agent" in Ch. 1]). One epistemological aspect included in this capacity is a "desire," or the state of mind which wants a particular event to occur. Taking, for example, my daughter's desires for her life, it seems life for her to have a valid desire this event cannot have (A) already happened (e.g., she cannot "desire" to be born in 2007), (B) nor can it be impossible (e.g., she cannot "desire" to be the first female US senator), (C) nor can she know that it is necessary (e.g., she cannot "desire" to turn thirteen years old in 2020).[42] Applying this distinction to Christ, if Christ is nescient of some things (e.g., some future events), then he can have desires (and, thereby, faith) and he can choose one means to achieve that desire (execute his intention) of his human nature.[43] So, as Davidson says, "The incarnate Son's 'amen' to his Father's purposes is the assent of one who makes a properly human choice .... There is altérité, but not contrariété."[44] Hereby, Christ has ordinary human agency.

With this in mind classical and Reformed Christology can affirm that Christ experiences "fear, sorrow, trouble, [and] perplexity."[45] That is, Christ's acts are "no extravagant behavior such as is seen in us when we strive mightily to control ourselves" when Christ encounters the "great paradox" of his mission "for this hour" and yet has a desire to be saved "from this hour" (Jn 12:27-28).[46] So Christ is nescient of some things and can deliberate in his human nature.

---

42. Tomis Kapitan, "The Incompatibility of Omniscience and Intentional Action: A Reply to David P. Hunt," *Religious Studies* 30 (1994): 55. On the basis of the semi-openness of agency (i.e., definitions of divine and human agency have different criteria), I do not think that this is necessarily true for an atemporal being. Even on a compatibilist view where there is only one possible future (i.e., objectively inevitable events), compatibilism need not deny humans agency because humans do not know those events with certainty, nor does the putative inevitability coercively interfere with their ability to act as they will—such that it is a necessary for them to bring about an action in a certain way whether they want to or not (e.g., WJO, *Pneumatologia*, 3: 225). For a defense of such a position from Scripture, see D. A. Carson, *Divine Sovereignty and Human Responsibility: Biblical Perspective in Tension* (Grand Rapids: Baker, 1994).

43. Advocating for a similar account of the necessity of deliberation in Christ is Karl Rahner, *TI*, 5:202; likewise, Pannenberg, *Jesus*, 333. This need not imply that Christ is peccable (i.e., that Christ's future included sinful options), only that his knowledge of his future included some options (different ways to live sinlessly).

44. Davidson, "'Not My Will but Yours Be Done,'" 196.

45. WJO, *Exposition of Hebrews*, 21:506. Owen doesn't elaborate on what he means by "fear" but minimally he means to affirm whatever it is that Mk 14:33 (Owen translates: "He began to be afraid, and sore amazed") and does not mean that Christ sinned by lacking faith.

46. Calvin, *Institutes*, II.xvi.12.

If we are careless, Christ's human knowledge and intention could imply that the nature is an independent agent (thereby making us vulnerable to White's critique).[47] However, the Reformed tradition avoids this difficulty through the insistence that each nature preserves its natural properties and each operates concurrently in the single acts of the theandric agent. For the Reformed, the singular act suggests a singular "willing" and a single "willer" (Christ, the theandric mediator) according to his two wills.[48] As Bavinck says, Christ the mediator is the "subject … 'which'" operates and his two natures are that "by which" the subject "lives, thinks, wills and acts."[49] Taking the distinction between "willing an end" (which can be distinct without contrariety) and "willing a means" (which is singular),[50] classical and Reformed Christology could affirm that Christ wills two corresponding (yet not identical) ends according to his two natures (e.g., to secure eternal redemption on one hand and obey his Father on the other) and chooses one identical means in the one action (e.g., to go to the cross) by virtue of his two agencies.[51] Since Christ's human beliefs and desires are finite, they are not identical to the divine knowledge of the divine will. Nevertheless, they can correspond without contrariety. Taking a strictly human example, my five-year-old daughter and I both have the intention of vacationing in Florida with our family. However, simply because my desires and beliefs (i.e., willing an end) are more specific (e.g., my will is to travel on a particular route and swim at a particular beach, while she simply wills to "get there" and "play in the sand"), this does not imply contrariety of will. Instead, there is a correspondence that is not identical. Further, we can both choose the same means to accomplish that correspondingly willed end (e.g., both pack clothes and toys in the van).[52]

Therefore, Christ could desire to save the people of God (an end; Jn 10:11) according to his human nature and could desire to save specific people that he omnisciently knows (a corresponding yet not identical end), yet the theandric mediator executes the choice to "go to Jerusalem" (a means to both ends), with each nature bringing about the immediate effects of that choice proper to it (e.g.,

---

47. See, for example, an illustration of how the common terminological imprecision of "agent/agency" language can lead to this conclusion in Paul Blowers's use of the "natural [human] will" as "the *agent* of concurrence with the will of the Father" ("Maximus the Confessor and John of Damascus on Gnomic Will (γνώμη) in Christ: Clarity and Ambiguity," *Union Seminary Quarterly Review* 63 [2012]: 47; emphasis mine).

48. Turretin, *Institutes*, II:13.vii.13.

49. Bavinck, *RD*, 2:306; WJO, *Vindication*, 2:433.

50. This distinction is drawn from Barnes, *Christ's Two Wills*, 138, 161. Although it is used slightly differently.

51. This parallels Blower's use of "commonly willed objective," but with slightly different language ("Maximus the Confessor and John of Damascus on Gnomic Will (γνώμη) in Christ," 49).

52. The obvious incongruity here is that my daughter and I are distinct agents. So, to give an example of a single agent: I might have a desire to "remodel the bathroom" that I indicate by adding the task "replace toilet gaskets" to my to-do list. Even if my desire has narrowed by the weekend to "fix the toilet," I may still choose to execute the choice required ("replace toilet gaskets") as the means to achieve the distinct, yet noncontrary, ends.

he puts one foot in front of the other according to his humanity).⁵³ This is reflective of Maximus' claim that Christ willed "doubly (δυϊκῶς) as God and as man."⁵⁴

This allows for the choice that the theandric mediator accomplishes (as the agent) to be an execution of human capacities. That is, the choice is not accomplished *by* the human nature but accomplished by the theandric agent, who performs every action according to the agencies which operate and bring about the distinct immediate effects that are proper to them. This is particularly pertinent for certain kinds of acts that both natures have the capacity to accomplish (in their own way).⁵⁵ For example, Jesus acts mercifully toward the woman caught in adultery (Jn 8:1-11) according to both natures, since "showing mercy" is a kind of action that both natures have the capacity to accomplish. However, the immediate effects of this singular act of mercy are proper to either nature. Some effects belong immediately to either nature in a way that the other nature cannot immediately bring about. For example, Christ thirsts (i.e., desires a drink) according to his human nature in a way that is not proper to his divine nature, although he can will a corresponding end (e.g., the relief of Christ's human thirst) so that the theandric mediator executes a single choice (a means) that accords with the corresponding will of both natures.

Therefore, classical and Reformed Christology can respond to White's objection with a unified account of action without the beatific vision and perfect knowledge of Christ according to his humanity. The Reformed tradition, like White, wants to affirm a "continual correlation between the divine and human wills" in order to combat the "dual christological errors" of Monophysitism and Nestorianism.⁵⁶ However, classical and Reformed Christology denies White's claim that Christ must have "evidential certitude" (through the beatific vision) in order to avoid an "operational dualism" that results in a "semi-Nestorian quality."⁵⁷ The above classical and Reformed account provides a plausible articulation of christological action and a way around the predication of two agents without the beatific vision. Instead, classical and Reformed Christology can commit to the unity of christological action while still holding that the intimacy of the union does not require the communication of maximal knowledge and beatific vision any more than it requires the divine nature be the recipient of human properties.⁵⁸

Further, White's articulation has premises that do not necessitate his conclusion: (1) that obedience requires certitude and (2) that Christ's wills must be epistemologically proportioned. Regarding the first premise, it seems that Scripture says that Christians can be obedient and reflect the will of God by faith (Jn 20:29), implying that not all obedience requires certitude. Additionally, White's

---

53. This contrasts with Paul J. Griffith's claim that in Christ humanity "had powers and capacities not ordinarily proper to human flesh" (*Christian Flesh* [Stanford, CA: Stanford University Press, 2018], 30).
54. Hovorun, *Will, Action and Freedom*, 144; "Disputatio," (PG 91:289B).
55. Following Owen's account of theandric love, see Ch. 3 §II.B.2; WJO, *Communion*, 2:62.
56. White, *Incarnate Lord*, 256.
57. Ibid., 261; cf. 256–62.
58. WJO, *Exposition of Hebrews*, 23:12.

premise about the proportionality of Christ's human will seems to lack consistent application elsewhere in Christology. That is, if knowing is a human capacity (like strength, energy, feeling, and sensing), then it seems that all of Jesus' human capacities must be identical to his divine capacities if Jesus' actions are to be unified. So, if perfect certitude of the divine will is required in Jesus' knowing in order for Jesus' physical acts to be unified and reveal the will of God, then it seems that Jesus must also have absolute power in his human nature in order to unify his actions with his divine omnipotence if he is going to reveal the power of God. Therefore, if White insists on Christ's two wills being "epistemologically proportioned," why not require Christ's two powers to be "dynamically proportioned?"[59]

Instead, classical and Reformed Christology has advocated for adherence to the conciliar lines of dyothelitism (contrary to some modern accounts) without affirming Christ's possession of the beatific vision or comprehensive knowledge. It was argued that ordinary human agency can cohere with Reformed christological premises and conciliar christological unity. The motivating factors for these Reformed moves undoubtedly include its axiom *finitum non capax infiniti*, yet the constant appeal to the biblical text evidences its strong commitment to *sola Scriptura*. This commitment to both the finitude of Christ's humanity and the preservation of its own properties, along with the affirmation of Scripture, leads the Reformed tradition to focus on the mediator as the anointed messiah, who receives the Spirit without measure (Jn 3:34).

In addition to the related concepts of knowledge and will, recent Christology has frequently trafficked in discussions of consciousness (as noted in Ch. 1). While the primarily goal of this project has been to engage a distinct category (i.e., *what it means* for Christ to be an agent),[60] there are inevitable implications for consciousness and "minds" discussions (i.e., *what it is like* for Christ to be an agent).[61] Yet because the focus of this project is on the proper usage of the language

---

59. Ibid., 261. As a potential response to this objection, McFarland says, "For his earthly actions to be a reliable index of divinity, however, it is not necessary that he be deified in every respect, but only in his will, as the source of those actions" (*Word Made Flesh*, 94). However, it seems that the will still requires the capacity to execute a desire if there is an action that is reflective of the divine character. So it seems unlikely that McFarland would be satisfied with Christ willing something but being unable to execute it. This may be part of the reason some affirm omnipotence in the human nature of Christ (see John of Damascus, "Orthodox Faith," III.19, 322).

60. See Ch. 1 § II.A.2 for the relative value of agency in relation to consciousness discussions.

61. Since the work of Thomas Morris, much of this has revolved around the language of "minds" (Thomas Morris, *The Logic of God Incarnate* [Ithaca: Cornell University Press, 1986], 102–3). The literature on this topic has grown such that the view that "without a distinct human mind, Christ could not have been truly human" has become "especially prominent" in recent accounts (Hill, "Introduction," 14). Yet others are concerned that "two minds" imply "two agents" and "two persons"—therefore, falling into act Nestorianism (Joseph Jedwab, "The Incarnation and Unity of Consciousness," in *The Metaphysics of the Incarnation*, ed. Anna Marmodoro and Jonathan Hill [New York: Oxford University Press], 178–80).

of "agent/agency" in Christology, and because there is similar ambiguity and a lack of consensus around "mind" terminology in the literature, I will only focus on the "minimal" implications of this classical and Reformed account on "minds" discussions. That is, I perceive there to be multiple accounts of "minds" that could be compatible with the classical and Reformed Christology presented here and the affirmations that follow only outline the minimal criteria for a compatible account, but do not exhaust the possibilities. This is primarily because the above account has addressed agency and actions as defined by effects in the external world. It has not dealt with mental acts (if there are such things) or introspective consciousness (which is the aspect of consciousness that frequently stars in "two minds" discussions).[62] So, while the Nestorian objection to this account revolves around actions, the Nestorian objection to two minds revolves around the unity of consciousness.

The first affirmation that classical and Reformed Christology must make is a commitment to the anti-Apollinarian affirmation of a distinctly human "soul." For some, this likewise includes a human "mind."[63] So, I agree with Thomas Senor when he states, "I can't see how any theorist who wants to obey the rules laid down by the creeds and councils can avoid positing a pair of minds in some fashion or other."[64]

The second affirmation extends the distinction between the human "mind" and the divine "mind" beyond the rejection of Apollinarianism to the rejection of maximal human knowledge and the beatific vision. Therefore, insofar as distinct (yet not contradictory) desires and beliefs are constitutive of distinct minds, classical and Reformed Christology is committed to some version of "two minds."

Third, whatever the account of minds/consciousness, if distinct desires and beliefs constitute a distinctly human mind, then that human mind cannot be related to the divine "mind" in an alternating way. That is, the "switch model," "consecutive [i.e., contiguous] model," or a kind of "schizophrenia" each seems to be incompatible with classical and Reformed Christology.[65]

---

62. On introspective and access consciousness, see Joseph Jedwab, "The Incarnation and Unity of Consciousness," 168–85.

63. Oliver D. Crisp, *God Incarnate: Explorations in Christology* (New York: T&T Clark, 2009), 156.

64. Senor, "Drawing on Many Traditions," 88–113.

65. Jedwab, "The Incarnation and Unity of Consciousness," 182 (nb. Jedwab does not ultimately advocate for this position). Tim Bayne, "The Inclusion Model of the Incarnation: Problems and Prospects," *Religious Studies* 37 (2001): 138. The charge of schizophrenia is made by Garrett DeWeese, who says that it seems less than desirable to attribute "to Jesus a condition that we would consider pathological in any other person" (Garrett J. DeWeese, "One Person, Two Natures: Two Metaphysical Models of the Incarnation," in *Jesus in Trinitarian Perspective*, ed. Fred Sanders and Klaus D. Issler [Nashville: B&H Academic, 2007], 132). Likewise P. T. Forsyth, *The Person and Place of Jesus Christ* (London: Independent Press, 1909), 319. John Macquarrie, *Jesus Christ in Modern Thought* (London: SCM Press, 1990), 167. Yet, others view an abnormal psychology as an inevitable consequence of abnormal ontology (Pawl, *Defense of Conciliar Christology*, 218).

Fourth, because of the classical affirmation of a simple God who does not discursively reason, conversations about the divine "mind" must be understood in strictly analogous, or anthropomorphic, terms. Because God's thought and action is noncompetitive and nondiscursive, language of two minds need not lead to two minds in conflict with one another in a schizophrenic way. So, to take a human analogue, the denial of discursive reasoning in God's knowing makes divine knowing more analogous to my dad discursively reasoning about baseball while simultaneously driving his daily route to work than it is to the psychology of schizophrenia or split personalities.[66] That is, my dad's nondiscursive reasoning about the route to work that he has taken for the last twenty years does not contradict, or fragment, his ability to discursively reason about baseball teams.

These minimal criteria open classical and Reformed Christology up to multiple options for accounts of Christ's mind(s). To name a few, something close to Morris' two minds could be compatible with the above; likewise, some version of Jedwab's Divine-human-sphere view (in which Christ has "two systems of powers, beliefs, and desires" [and intentions]) and potentially even some accounts of extended minds could meet the criteria.[67]

C. Anointed by the Spirit

The classical and Reformed Christology argument that Jesus exercised ordinary human agency toward immediate human effects, however, it must also include the times in which the Spirit endowed Jesus with unique capacities. It is therefore the activity of the Holy Spirit that allows classical and Reformed Christology to remain committed to the ordinary human agency alongside the biblical testimony of Christ's extraordinary human action (like knowing about Nathanael before meeting him [Jn 1:43-51]). These extraordinary capacities are not a necessary consequence of the hypostatic union, but the bestowal of grace upon the human nature by the Holy Spirit and the work of Christ's mediatorial office. Indeed, Turretin says that "the acts of the anointing were dispensed through intervals of time …. Thus, the Spirit of wisdom (with which he was anointed) restrained its own acts and did not at once pour forth its rays in all their fulness upon the intellect of Christ."[68]

When John says that Christ is given "the Spirit without measure," the Reformed insists this phrase does not suggest an infinite amount of grace is contained in Christ's

---

66. On the importance of analogical language for Christ's psychology, see Daley, *God Visible*, 276. Likewise see the caution by Davidson, "'Not My Will but Yours Be Done,'" 200.

67. Jedwab, "The Incarnation and Unity of Consciousness," 177; Anna Marmodoro, "The Metaphysics of the Extended Mind in Ontological Entanglements," in *The Metaphysics of the Incarnation*, ed. Anna Marmodoro and Jonathan Hill (Oxford: Oxford University Press, 2011), 205–27.

68. Turretin, *Institutes*, II:13.xiii.9.

5. Human Agency

human nature, because the finite cannot contain the infinite.[69] Owen describes the anointing of the Spirit as the means by which the humanity of Christ receives the "furniture" necessary to perform his mediatorial office from the Holy Spirit.[70]

The significance of the work of the Holy Spirit and Christ's human capacities comes to bear on Owen's exposition of the prophetic office in his commentary on Heb. 1:1-2. Owen adamantly defends the finite agency of Christ's humanity, saying that Christ did *not* have "in his human nature an absolutely infinite comprehension of all individual things, past, present, and to come ... but he was furnished with all that wisdom and knowledge which the human nature was capable of, both as to principle and exercise, *in the condition wherein it was*, without destroying its finite being and variety of conditions."[71] That is, the Spirit bestows grace upon the human nature of Christ in accordance with the capacity of that nature in its condition at certain stages of Christ's life. So the Spirit's gift of habitual grace corresponded proportionally to the age and capacity of Christ's human nature. For example, as an infant, Christ's human nature was perfectly grace-filled in proportion to the capacities and needs of an infant. This allows for a genuine increase in knowledge, without introducing culpable ignorance into Christ's mission.[72] We might say, therefore, that Christ grew in grace *as* he grew in stature.[73] Owen summarizes, "As the faculties of his mind were enlarged by degrees and strengthened, so the Holy Spirit filled them up with grace for actual obedience."[74] The grace that Christ experienced according to his human nature likewise corresponded to the necessity of his mediatorial action. Owen says that Christ was "filled with all that perfection of habitual grace and wisdom which was or could be necessary to the discharge of that whole duty which, as a man, he owed unto God."[75] That is, Christ received the grace he needed to fulfill his role as the mediator. For example, Christ needed to be without sin if he was to be a mediator for us, but he did not need to have comprehensive knowledge according to his human nature. So, while according to his divine nature, Christ "had an omnisciency of the whole nature and will of God, as the Father himself hath, because the same with that of the Father, their

---

69. Ibid., II:13.xii.3.; WJO, *Communion*, 2:61; *Christologia*, 1:93, 239; *Understanding the Mind of God*, 4:196; *Condescension of Christ*, 17:563; *Theologoumena* I.iii.6 (BT, 14–19). Trueman, *Claims*, 171; Tay, *Priesthood*, 65; Holmes, "Communicatio Idiomatum," 80.

70. WJO, *Pneumatologia*, 3:172, 173, 175, 204, 430; *Spirit as Comforter*, 4:392–3; Owen states that the "anointing" occurs in several stages: (1) conception, (2) baptism, (3) death (Jn 17:9); (4) ascension (Heb. 1:9) (4:392–3).

71. WJO, *Exposition of Hebrews*, 20:28; likewise, *Christologia*, 1:93; cf. Trueman, *Claims*, 173; Calvin, *Institutes*, II.xiv.2, 483–4; Willis, *Calvin's Catholic Christology*, 80–2.

72. Turretin, *Institutes*, II:13.xiii.4.

73. This is similar to what Spence says is the "grace appropriate to his receptivity" (*Incarnation and Inspiration*, 56) and what Trueman calls the "incremental grace" that the Holy Spirit endows (*John Owen*, 95).

74. WJO, *Pneumatologia*, 3:170; see Daniels, *Christology*, 295; Kapic, *Communion*, 87.

75. WJO, *Exposition of Hebrews*, 20:30.

will and wisdom being the same … by virtue of their oneness in the same nature,"[76] in his human nature Christ is the recipient of the Father's revelation. Owen says, "It was from the Father that he heard the word and learned the doctrine that he declared unto the church. This is asserted wherever there is mention made of the Father's sending, sealing, anointing, commanding, teaching him; of his doing the will, speaking the words, seeking the glory, obeying the commands of him that sent him."[77]

Therefore, we see here not a necessary communication of properties from the divine to the human (per Lutheranism), nor necessary maximal capacities of the humanity of Christ (per accounts of the beatific vision), but a gracious bestowal of the Holy Spirit upon the finite humanity of Christ by the Father in order that he might fulfill his mission as the theandric messiah.

II. Dependent

While the first section focused on the external perspective of christological action and Christ's human dependence upon the Spirit,[78] the following section focuses on the internal perspective and Christ's human dependence upon the Word. It is from this perspective that classical and Reformed Christology reinforces its commitment to the personal identity of the theandric mediator with the Logos and the prioritization of divine agency. While the above section distinguished itself from accounts of strong instrumentality (which claim that Christ's humanity possesses maximal human knowledge and the beatific vision), this section advocates for an account of weak instrumentality (i.e., the dependence and subsequence of human agency) that is also able to preserve the integrity of the humanity of Christ as ordinary and distinct. So in conjunction with the theandric unity established in Chapter 4 and the singular correspondence of Christ's two wills above, classical and Reformed Christology also insists that Christ's ordinary and distinct human agency is not independent agency nor does it prioritize human action. Instead, Christ's distinct and ordinary human agency is also dependent.

To some degree, this is typical of all human agency, since all humans are passive in their acquisition of many capacities. So this ought not to be alarming for any account of Christology that seeks to affirm the integrity of the humanity of Christ. However, Christ's human agency bears a unique relationship to the Son's divine agency because of the *sui generis* relationship of his human nature to his divine nature.[79] This subsection will argue that Christ's human agency is dependent

---

76. Ibid., 20:29.

77. Ibid., 3:28–9.

78. This mutual dependence of Christ's humanity on Word and Spirit builds upon the themes of dependence and compatibility in Christa L. McKirland, "Did Jesus Need the Spirit? An Appeal for Pneumatic Christology to Inform Christological Anthropology," *Perichoresis* 19 (2021): 43–61.

79. WJO, *Christologia*, 1:158, 228; see also *Glory of Christ*, 1:328.

upon his divine agency in terms of instrumental dependence (§A) and it argues for the coherence of this position with the previous commitments through the various perspectives on actions (§B). As such, classical and Reformed Christology is able to cohere with its commitment to the *an/enhypostatic* distinction and the affirmation of a single theandric agent.

A. Agency and Dependence: Instrumentality

The operational dependence of Christ's human agency is rooted in the ontological dependence of Christ's human nature (i.e., the *an/enhypostatic* distinction).[80] This means that conciliar christological unity is *not* derived from Christ's action but evidenced by it. However, we cannot stop with this ontological affirmation, but must also follow it to its operational implications.[81] As Thomas Joseph White rightly says, "It follows from this line of thinking [i.e., *an/enhypostatic*] that the human nature of Jesus (his body and soul) is an instrument of his person, in an analogical and unique sense of the term."[82] Classical and Reformed Christology embraces this as another point at which the operational mirrors the ontological. That is, the asymmetry in Christ's ontology is necessarily mirrored by the asymmetry of his operations.

The doctrine of the instrumentality of Christ's human nature has fallen under strong suspicion in a modern theological climate that presumes and defends Christ's humanity above all else.[83] For example, Hans Urs von Balthasar calls christological instrumentality the "most dangerous tendency of the whole patristic Christology."[84] Even Demetrios Bathrellos, who advocates for conciliar Christology and for "Monothelite terminology" within dyothelitism, says that "it is the person who is ... the subject of willing and acting. But if this is the person of the logos, then I'm not sure that this is sufficiently human" and that it "may overshadow and eventually undermine the completeness and integrity of Christ's humanity."[85] That is, Bathrellos worries that if the agent of christological action is the Logos and his humanity is the instrument by which the Logos performs human actions, then it

---

80. Barth, *CD* I/2, 163; see Ivor J. Davidson, "Theologizing the Human Jesus: An Ancient (and Modern) Approach to Christology Reassessed," *IJST* 3 (2001): 135.

81. It seems that many contemporary Reformed thinkers stop here. For example, in Michael Allen's articulation of the asymmetry between the two natures in Reformed Christology, he appeals to the preexistence of Christ's divine nature—rather than addressing an asymmetry in action (Allen, *Christ's Faith*, 124; likewise, Wellum, *God the Son Incarnate*, 336 appeals to the *extra Calvinisticum*).

82. White, *Incarnate Lord*, 113.

83. Poignantly illustrating this, Pannenberg states that if forced into an ultimatum, modern theology would "rather surrender the confession of his divinity than to doubt that he was really a man" (*Jesus*, 189).

84. Hans Urs von Balthasar, *Cosmic Liturgy: The Universe According to Maximus the Confessor*, trans. Brian E. Daley (San Francisco: Ignatius, 2003), 228.

85. Bathrellos, *Byzantine Christ*, 188, 53.

may be the case that Christ is insufficiently human. This aversion to the language of instrumentality is even seen among scholars and interpreters who are positively retrieving patristic and medieval sources which explicitly affirm instrumentality.[86]

However, we need not have such a strong reticence about this concept that was "commonplace" in ancient Christology.[87] First, the mere affirmation of instrumentality has not historically indicated the loss of genuine humanity; even Nestorius used the language of instrumentality.[88] Second, the language of instrumentality is *present*, although not *prominent*, in the classical and Reformed tradition. For example, Francis Turretin says that Christ's humanity is "instrumental" in Christ's operations "because he assumed it on account of operation and works by it."[89] Additionally, Jonathan Edwards describes the human nature as an "organ" of the divine actions of the Son.[90] Likewise, Vermigli and the *Synopsis of Purer Theology* affirm both the two-natured mediation of Christ and the instrumentality of his human nature.[91] More recently, both Michael Allen and John Webster affirm the use of instrumentality within Reformed Christology.[92] As such, the concept is present throughout the Reformed tradition. However, one striking illustration of its lack of prominence is the 2008 publication on *Peter Vermigli and the Outward Instruments of Divine Grace*, which gives nearly forty pages to Christology, yet only produces one explicit reference on the instrumentality of his human nature.[93] I contend that the lack of prominence of this concept within the Reformed tradition need not imply incompatibility, but rather evidences prioritization of one perspective of christological action over another. Finally, we need not be so reticent to recognize the category of instrumentality because it does not necessarily lead to viewing Christ as a "marionette."[94]

---

86. See the concern about "merely instrumental" by Williams and Abraham (*Christ the Heart of Creation*, 80; *Divine Agency and Divine Action*, 2:117).

87. Bathrellos, *The Byzantine Christ*, 93. John McGuckin calls this the "flagship" principle of Cyril's Christology (*Saint Cyril of Alexandria*, 186).

88. Nestorius, "Nestorius's First Sermon Against the Theotokos," in *The Christological Controversy*, trans. Richard A. Norris, SECT (Philadelphia: Fortress, 1980), 129; cf., Daley, *God Visible*, 185–7.

89. Turretin, *Institutes*, II:13.vi.6.

90. WJE, "Misc. no. 738," 18:364; see also "Misc. no. 1150," 20:521. Unfortunately (though perhaps indicative of the lack of prominence of this concept in the Reformed tradition), Seng-Kong Tan suggests that this indicates Edwards's distance from the Reformed tradition ("Trinitarian Action in the Incarnation," in *Jonathan Edwards as Contemporary: Essays in Honor of Sang Hyun Lee*, ed. Don Schweitzer [New York: Peter Lang, 2010], 127–50).

91. Vermigli, *Life, Letters, and Sermons*, 180; *Synopsis*, 2:109. For recent treatments, see also Oliver Crisp's employment of "ownership" (*God Incarnate*, 158).

92. Allen, *Christ's Faith*, 119; John Webster, "The Place of Christology in Systematic Theology," in *The Oxford Handbook of Christology*, ed. Francesca Murphy (New York: Oxford University Press, 2015), 617.

93. Zuidema, *Peter Martyr Vermigli*, 77.

94. Balthasar, *Cosmic Liturgy*, 228.

We find a careful, thorough, and influential account of instrumental action in Thomas Aquinas.[95] Aquinas distinguishes the way an "inanimate instrument" is moved (i.e., physical force, like a carpenter moving a saw), a living instrument with a sense appetite (e.g., a horse's sense appetites and a rider holding a carrot on a stick), and a rational animate instrument which is moved by the will (like a servant who wills to serve his master).[96] Christ's humanity is animate and rational, therefore most similar to that of a servant. While strong instrumentality imputes maximal human knowledge into the human nature of Christ and the beatific vision as a precondition for its use as an instrument, weak instrumentality allows the ordinary character of human capacities and powers to be preserved in the humanity of Christ.

The prudence of instrumentality is largely seen in its account of the unity of action. So unlike a servant or a rider (which are moved from outside themselves), Christ's humanity is moved "from within."[97] This is what Thomas calls a private instrument so that it is the agent's (i.e., the Logos') "very own." While anyone can operate an axe, a hand can only be operated by the one to whom it belongs.[98] Because of this "ownership" of the instrument, every action (and passion) of Christ according to this instrument is predicated of God the Son.[99] Just as anything that happens to my hand happens to me, so too must we say that anything that happens to Christ's human nature happens to God the Son, allowing us to affirm again that "one of the Trinity suffered in the flesh."

The affirmation of instrumentality (even in its weak version) protects against coincidental action—actions that occur simultaneously, yet without a shared cause—which I perceive to be an insufficiently unified account of christological action.[100] If instrumentality is wholesale rejected (i.e., every version and every perspective), then it seems that the human effects of Christ and the divine effects of Christ are merely coincidental, and if these acts are merely coincidental, then we will (A) have difficulty affirming God the Son as the agent of Christ's acts of salvation, (B) have little assurance that Christ will continue to bring about effects

---

95. This paragraph (and entire section) is informed by J. David Moser, "The Flesh of the Logos, Instrumentum Divinitatis: Retrieving an Ancient Christological Doctrine," *IJST* 23 (2021): 313–32.

96. Aquinas, *ST* III, Q.18, A.1, ad.2; Legge, *Trinitarian Christology of St Thomas Aquinas*, 190–202.

97. Aquinas, *ST* III, Q.18, A.1, ad.2; see Legge, *Trinitarian Christology of St Thomas Aquinas*, 200; Barnes, *Christ's Two Wills in Scholastic Thought*, 129.

98. Aquinas, *SCG* 4.41.11; see also Arcadi, *An Incarnational Model of the Eucharist*, 178.

99. For contemporary accounts of ownership, see Crisp, *The Word Enfleshed*, 113, 187; Arcadi, *Eucharist*, 178; Crisp, *God Incarnate*, 158.

100. "Coincidental action" I take to be two events which have independent causal histories (Lowe, *Personal Agency*, 28, 36). Lowe gives the example of a tile blown off a roof and a man walking underneath it as coincidental and contrasts this with a man walking through a tripwire that connects to the roof tile, causing it to fall as noncoincidental.

that are consistent with divine operations and character (i.e., Christ could sin according to his human nature), and (C) have a difficult time distinguishing Christ's human acts from our own. Most basically, my contention is that if Christ's human and divine effects lack any sort of a shared causal source (i.e., instrumentality), then Christ's human and divine effects are as unified and significant as the faithful-rooster's crow and the sunrise. With this account of weak instrumentality, we can reject the overdetermined causation of Christ's humanity as that of a video game character (i.e., strong instrumentality), but we must also reject the analogy of Christ's humanity as that of an automated arcade game video demonstration and my son's correlated movement of the joystick (on the assumption he's controlling the character) as merely coincidental.[101]

However, it might fairly be asked how such a position, which articulates the Son as the agent acting by this rational animate instrument, coheres with the classical and Reformed claim that Christ is a singular theandric agent. That is, if instrumentality implies that the Logos is the "primary agent" then classical and Reformed Christology has contradicted its central claim of theandric action according to distinct agencies. However, I would suggest that classical and Reformed christological agency can respond to this question by virtue of greater specification of the perspective that one takes on an action.[102]

B. Perspectives on Agency

Classical and Reformed Christology employs both internal and external perspectives on an action. It is through this understanding of perspectives that classical and Reformed Christology can affirm both the theandric action and the instrumental action of Christ. The concept of distinct perspectives on Christ and his actions has a strong precedent in the history of Christology and, therefore, finds an appropriate home in classical and Reformed Christology.[103] A similar conundrum is seen in Maximus, who affirms both the instrumentality and the self-movement of the humanity of Christ. Bathrellos says that we can solve

---

101. This analogy is provided in Daniel M. Wegner, *The Illusion of Conscious Will* (Cambridge, MA: MIT Press, 2002), 9–10.

102. It might be objected that this move departs from Owen. However, I think something similar to this change in perspective is occurring in Owen (albeit, implicitly) when he affirms that "all the moral operations of that nature are the acts of the person of the Son of God" (WJO, *Christologia*, 1:215).

103. The introduction of "perspectives" does not necessarily imply equal validity of all perspectives. There may be criteria (like biblical usage, contextual connotations, and coherence with other affirmations) by which we prioritize one perspective over another. For example, in Chapter 2 we discussed the unity of trinitarian action from the perspective of causality and the distinction of action from the perspective of *terminus*. One could argue that the New Testament defaults to the latter perspective and therefore can be understood as the default (although not exclusive) Christian view.

the knot of these two positions, which "seems to be inconsistent," by virtue of a distinct "point of view."[104] Likewise, Emery says that the "human action of Christ can be considered in two ways: (1) according to its proper form, and thus it differs essentially from his divine action; and (2) as an instrument of the divinity, and under this second aspect the human operation of Christ participates in the power (*virtus*) of the divine operation itself, as its instrument."[105] Additionally, several Thomists approach a similar apparent incongruity in Thomas Aquinas, that of the question of Christ's single and "second *esse*," by means of "two levels" or "two ways" or "two different aspects."[106] As such, an appeal to perspectives is not a weasel move to avoid contradiction but a precedented and traditional move.

So for classical and Reformed Christology, I propose that we name these two perspectives on christological action the "internal" and "external" perspectives. Externally, classical and Reformed Christology considers Christ as a single theandric mediator, executing his actions according to distinct capacities with their distinct effects. From the internal perspective, classical and Reformed Christology understands the Logos to be ontologically and operationally fundamental to Christ's being and acts through his rational animate internal instrument. We might imagine an example of internal and external perspectives on an action with the analogy of starting a car. A car is composed of both electrical (e.g., battery, ignition switch, spark plugs) and mechanical (e.g., pistons, crankshaft, valves) components. When you look at it from the outside, one could turn the key of a car and say that the "car" is "agent" of the act of starting and it produces distinctive immediate effects (e.g., headlights and a rumbling sound) that belong to either component due to the proper operations of that component. However, if you were to "look under the hood" of the vehicle (i.e., the internal perspective), you could see that the electrical component operationally precedes the mechanical by necessity. The pistons do not move if the ignition switch does not first draw on the battery's electrical power. This internal perspective shows how one nature (i.e., the electrical) can operationally precede another without violating the external perspective and without confusing the immediate effects of either operation within the singular event.[107] Therefore, this account of weak instrumental action is distinguishable from strong instrumental action insofar as the instrument retains ordinary and distinctly human capacities (agencies) that are the immediate principle of human operations. Therefore, classical and Reformed Christology's commitment to weak

---

104. Bathrellos, *The Byzantine Christ*, 165.

105. Emery, "Le Christ médiateur," 350–1.

106. See Riches, *Ecce Homo*, 174–5; Williams, *Christ the Heart of Creation*, 36; ST III, Q.2, A.4.

107. The car is an "agent" in a nontechnical sense (i.e., it does not "intend" anything). Additionally, for people who know cars, this analogy falls apart if pushed any farther because there is a mutual dependence between the electric and mechanical when the mechanical moves the alternator to recharge the battery (which would be most analogous to the *genus tapeinoticum*, in which the human nature communicates properties to the divine).

instrumentality is distinguished from the capacities of strong instrumentality (see Ch. 5 §I.A–B) and the effects of strong instrumentality (see Ch. 6 §II.A).

With these perspectives on christological action, we can now apply these perspectives to the previous chapter on trinitarian action and thereby appreciate the trinitarian character of Christ's action. For example, when we consider the perspective of triune causality and the internal perspective on christological agency, we see Christ's humanity as the animate rational instrument of his divinity, not independently caused by the Son alone but by the triune God.[108] That is, because Christ's human agency is causally dependent upon divine action (which is indivisibly triune), there is a triune causal shape to every act in Christ's life. When we consider the internal perspective in conjunction with the triune *terminus*, we can see that the accomplishment of this action properly terminates on the Son, and we can appropriate the perfection of this act to the Spirit and the orchestration of this act to the Father. Likewise, the internal perspective reminds us that Christ's humanity is not a distinct agent who performs basic actions apart from the divine agency of Christ.[109] Instead, the agency of Christ's humanity is dependent upon God. So, even under the perspective of causality (in which God is a single agent, putatively implying that natures are agents), classical and Reformed Christology can avoid the charge of Nestorianism.[110]

However, the more common perspective of classical and Reformed Christology is the external view of Christ as the theandric mediator. The external perspective can, likewise, affirm the triune causality and trinitarian *terminus* of christological action—i.e., Christ's acts are God's and they terminate upon the Son. Additionally, I would suggest that this prioritization of the external perspective is viable for classical and Reformed Christology because of (1) the soteriological emphasis on the mediator in both natures, (2) the negative connotation that instrumentality has in contemporary culture, and (3) the literal biblical claims which seem to hold both natures together with more symmetry in the one mediator (Acts 20:28; 1 Cor. 2:8; Lk. 1:31-32). Therefore, classical and Reformed Christology coheres with the operational implications of the *an/enhypostatic* distinction and the theandric agent by affirming both the instrumentality and dependence of the human agency of Christ (from the internal perspective) and yet prioritizing the distinct agencies united in the theandric mediator (from the external perspective).

---

108. The affirmation of triune causality here is contrary to Cross, *The Metaphysics of the Incarnation*, 218–30.

109. Contrary to Thielicke's claim of the humanity of Christ possessing "supreme originality and autonomy" (*The Evangelical Faith*, 2:321).

110. The requirement of the shift in perspective indicates that instrumentality and composite Christology, or "dual agency," are not as superficially compatible as is sometimes assumed and accepted without extended attention (e.g., Allen claims that "agency ... can proceed ... simultaneously and coextensively" while also affirming that the humanity of Christ is "instrumental", *Christ's Faith*, 113, 119).

III. Human Agency in Scripture: Hebrews 5:7-10

Having seen Christ's distinct and ordinary human agency and the compatibility of theandric action with the fundamental divine agency of Christ, this section will turn to the biblical testimony on Christ's human agency in order to evidence the coherence of classical and Reformed Christology with the ultimate authority of Scripture. Given the high quantity of potentially relevant material, Hebrews 5 will serve as a paradigmatic text as it articulates some of the earliest moments of Jesus' life alongside several "high christological" claims (e.g., Heb. 1:1-13), and it serves as a touch point for various contemporary interlocutors engaged below.[111] Specifically, this section will argue that Hebrews 5 applies "pressure" toward an account of Christ's ordinary and distinct human agency. As such it simultaneously applies pressure against accounts which maximize, or divinize, Christ's human agency (i.e., strong instrumentality) and those which deny the distinctiveness of Christ's human agency, humanizing Christ's divinity (i.e., kenoticists).

These two positions (i.e., strong instrumentality and kenoticism) have been theologically engaged above, yet the goal here is to show the biblical prudence of classical and Reformed Christology in relation to these options. Representing the humanization of divinity, John Stackhouse suggests that those who "take their theological cues particularly from the Bible" will see in Hebrews 5 that God "subtracted something from himself."[112] Likewise, advocating for a "Reformed version of Kenoticism," McCormack suggests, "What the man Jesus experiences, God experiences"—and, thereby, there is "a real communication of human 'attributes' to the Logos."[113] Conversely, the opposite position advocates for Christ's "deified humanity" in that his "human self-awareness is that of [i.e., identical to] the incarnate Word" and Christ has "immediate awareness" of "all things from the Father."[114]

It will be argued that the classical and Reformed view of Christ's human agency is distinct and ordinary through an examination of the rhetorical structure and function of the passage (§A) and then four key juxtapositions within the passage

---

111. Donald A. Hagner, "Son of God as Unique High Priest: The Christology of the Epistle to the Hebrews," in *Contours of Christology in the New Testament*, ed. Richard N. Longenecker (Grand Rapids: Eerdmans, 2005), 252; A. Katherine Grieb, "'Time Would Fail Me to Tell ... ': The Identity of Jesus Christ in Hebrews," in *Seeking the Identity of Jesus: A Pilgrimage*, ed. Beverly Roberts Gaventa and Richard B. Hays (Grand Rapids: Eerdmans, 2008), 212.

112. Stackhouse, "Jesus Christ," 149.

113. McCormack, "With Loud Cries," 50. McCormack's version of kenoticism is slightly distinct from the ontological, functional, and kryptic evaluated above. However, the relevant aspect here is that his account humanizes divinity and lacks distinction between Christ's two agencies.

114. White, *The Incarnate Lord*, 274, 271. Specifically of this text, McCall, "Son Though He Was," 148-9, suggests that a deified humanity is a plausible reading.

(§B–E). These "juxtapositions" between the divine identity of Christ and his very human actions evidence the distinctiveness of Christ's human agency and the biblical coherence of Christ's human agency with his divine identity and capacities.[115]

A. Rhetorical Structure and Pastoral Function of Heb. 5:7-10

Hebrews 5 is a literary touchstone for the letter, reaching back to the beginning of the letter (Heb. 1:5) with a quote of Ps. 2:7 ("You are my Son; today I have begotten you"; Heb. 5:5) and looking forward in the letter by announcing the Melchizedekian priesthood (7:1-28). This is all encapsulated within a dynamic discourse regarding faithful endurance to the point of suffering (a key theme of the book as a whole). As part of the exposition of the superiority of Christ's priesthood (4:14–8:2) and superior sacrifice (8:3–10:18), this passage (possibly an early creed or hymn)[116] is located within a section (4:15–5:10) that demonstrates the general conditions required of any priest (5:1-4), conditions which ultimately find their fulfillment in Christ.[117] Focusing especially on the solidarity of the priest with the people, this text shows that priests are "chosen from among people" to act on their behalf in relation to God, offering gifts and sacrifices (5:1).[118] They can "deal gently" (μετριοπαθεῖν) since they too experience weakness (5:2) and are appointed to their office by God. Christ, then, is presented as the one who ultimately fulfills these characteristics and this office through "his intense identification with the weakness of those he represents."[119]

---

115. These juxtapositions are similar to what Rowan A. Greer calls "double judgment" ("The Jesus of Hebrews and the Christ of Chalcedon," in *Reading the Epistle to the Hebrews: A Resource for Students*, ed. Eric F. Mason and Kevin B. McCruden, SBLRBS 66 [Atlanta: Society of Biblical Literature, 2011], 233). R. B. Jamieson argues for the centrality of paradoxical claims about Jesus' humanity and divinity in Hebrews (*The Paradox of Sonship: Christology in the Epistle to the Hebrews*, SCDS [Downers Grove, IL: IVP Academic, 2021]).

116. Egon Brandenburger, "Text und Vorlagen von Hebr. V 7-10: Ein Beitrag zur Christologie des Hebräerbriefs," *Novum Testamentum* 11 (1969): 191–8. This is especially likely of verses 7-9 based on the introductory relative pronoun (ὅς), participial style, and unique language (Theodor Lescow, "Jesus in Gethsemane bei Lukas und im Hebräerbrief," *ZNWKK* 58 [1967]: 215–17).

117. William L. Lane, *Hebrews 1–8*, WBC 47A (Dallas: Thomas Nelson, 1991), 124; see Gareth Lee Cockerill, *The Epistle to the Hebrews*, NICNT (Grand Rapids: Eerdmans, 2012), 230 for the chiasm. Luke Timothy Johnson, *Hebrews: A Commentary* (Louisville: Westminster John Knox, 2006), 137, lists twelve of these qualities.

118. F. F. Bruce emphatically says, "At no point can the objection be voiced that because He was the Son of God it was different, or easier for Him" (*The Epistle to the Hebrews*, NICNT [Grand Rapids: Eerdmans, 1990], 102).

119. Johnson, *Hebrews*, 144. See the emphasis on these in David M. Moffitt, *Atonement and the Logic of Resurrection in the Epistle to the Hebrews*, NovTSup (Boston: Brill, 2013), 193; Bruce, *Hebrews*, 122; Johnson, *Hebrews*, 137; Brian Small, *The Characterization of Jesus in the Book of Hebrews*, BIS 128 (Boston: Brill, 2014), 285.

The pastoral and theological purpose of this section (i.e., 5:1-10) portrays Christ as the one who suffers on behalf of the people so that he might be the model of faithful obedience and a sympathetic fellow traveler, both of which seem to require human agency.[120] Articulating Christ as our model of faithful obedience, Brian Small notes that although the language of imitation is not explicit in Chapter 5, here we have a "clear" place where the author "urged" believers to follow the example of Christ.[121] Particularly, it is Jesus' perseverance in the midst of suffering that serves as a model for our own perseverance.[122] Likewise, the author of Hebrews argues that through his weakness Christ empathizes with us, as one who has experienced similar trials (5:2) and is a sympathetic fellow traveler.[123] These experiences are so genuine that Calvin claims, "If Christ had been untouched by any sorrow, then no consolation would come to us from his sufferings."[124]

Yet the encouragement that the suffering hearer derives from this letter is rooted in a high degree of semblance between Christ's experiences and their own. Therefore, the pastoral function of the section itself seems to push toward viewing Christ's human capacities as ordinary and similar to ours. As such this text's purpose of presenting Christ as the sympathetic pilgrim who perseveres through weakness (even amid suffering) seems to push against the "extraordinary" accounts of Christ's human agency being "perfectly consummated as to the happiness of His soul" at all times by virtue of the beatific vision "from the instant of his conception."[125] Likewise, the author's presentation of Christ as a model of obedience and faithfulness seems to presuppose a strong degree of similitude between his capacity and means of obedience (i.e., dependence and prayer) and those of his readers.

While the function of the text pushes against deifying Christ's humanity, the following four juxtapositions detailed below evidence the contrast of Christ's divine identity with his surprising human operation. As such, they articulate Christ's distinct agencies.

---

120. Cockerill, *Hebrews*, 242 n. 62 lists these three characteristics of the section. See Lane's argument for Christ's humanity as the emphasis of this section (*Hebrews*, 223-4).

121. Small, *Characterization of Jesus*, 312; William R. G. Loader, *Sohn und Hoherpriester: Eine traditionsgeschichtliche Untersuchung zur Christologie des Hebräerbriefes*, WMANT 53 (Neukirchen-Vluyn: Neukirchener, 1981), 101.

122. David A. DeSilva, *Perseverance in Gratitude: A Socio-Rhetorical Commentary on the Epistle to the Hebrews* (Grand Rapids: Eerdmans, 2000), 191; cf. Moffitt, *Atonement*, 192-3.

123. See Amy L. B. Peeler, "With Tears and Joy: The Emotions of Christ in Hebrews," *Koinonia* 20 (2008): 12.

124. John Calvin, *The Epistle of Paul the Apostle to the Hebrews*, ed. David W. Torrance and T. F. Torrance, trans. William B. Johnston, Calvin's Commentaries (Grand Rapids: Eerdmans, 1963), 64.

125. Thomas Aquinas, *Commentary on the Epistle to the Hebrews*, trans. Chrysostom Baer (South Bend, IN: St. Augustine's, 2006), 117 (§260).

B. The One That Had Days Without Flesh Who Prays (5:7)

The first juxtaposition, verse 7, "In the days of his flesh, Jesus offered up prayers and supplications, with loud cries and tears, to him who was able to save him from death," represents a "long and complex clause" that "sketches in brief much of Hebrews' understanding of Jesus' faithful existence and therefore of his priestly identity."[126] In this verse, we see a juxtaposition between the divine identity of one who preexists his flesh and the human activity of one who offers prayers and tears (startling capacities for a pre-existent being).

The exalted phrase, "in the days of his flesh" (ἐν ταῖς ἡμέραις τῆς σαρκὸς αὐτοῦ), seems to be an unsettling opening to a "vivid description of the humanity of Christ."[127] The phrase implies both ontologically and qualitatively distinct periods of Christ's existence. Ontologically, the period of his assuming flesh (cf. Jn 1:14) implies that there was a "time" when he existed without flesh, "before" the incarnation.[128] Qualitatively (i.e., describing the "quality of life"), this phrase (and especially the usage σάρξ [flesh]) signifies the "human experience" and capacities of "frailties, weaknesses, and infirmities" (mirroring 5:2; cf. Ps. 78:39; 1 Cor. 15:50).[129] With the affirmation of this period of ontological flesh and qualitative experience, the implication is that this one agent has days *not* in the flesh with these capacities of frailty and weakness.

Notably, like the priests in 5:1 who "offer gifts" (προσφέρῃ δῶρά) and sacrifices for sin (cf. 5:3), Jesus offers (προσενέγκας) his prayers and supplications "toward the altar."[130] As an offering made with "loud cries and tears," these prayers are likely both for himself (i.e., in regard to his death as they are offered to "him who was able to save him from death") and for others.[131] Insofar as the prayers are for himself in faith, he reflects the act of the priests (who offer sacrifices for themselves [5:3]), yet in a superior way (i.e., Christ's prayers are not for his own sins).[132] Praying for

---

126. Johnson, *Hebrews*, 145.

127. Harold W. Attridge, *Hebrews: A Commentary on the Epistle to the Hebrews* (Philadelphia: Fortress, 1989), 148.

128. Moffitt, *Atonement*, 210. The word "before" is being used (at minimum) as an anthropomorphism for a being who exists outside of time (likewise, Attridge, *Hebrews*, 209–10).

129. Lane, *Hebrews*, 109; Attridge, *Hebrews*, 149; WJO, *Exposition of Hebrews*, 21:498; Cockerill, *Hebrews*, 242.

130. Craig R. Koester, *Hebrews* (New York: Yale University Press, 2001), 93; WJO, *Exposition of Hebrews*, 21:449.

131. The context of these prayers and supplications is highly debated (see, for example, August Strobel, *Der Brief an die Hebräer*, Das Neue Testament Deutsch 9/2 [Göttingen: Vandenhoeck & Ruprecht, 1991], 57–9). Yet beyond the "death directed" nature of the prayer (Attridge, *Hebrews*, 148), we will not enter into the discussion.

132. Small, *Characterization of Jesus*, 118. Contrary to those who claim he did not pray for himself (Mathias Rissi, "Die Menschlichkeit Jesu nach Hebr. 5, 7–8," *Theologische Zeitschrift* 11 [1955]: 40–2; Sonderegger, "The Sinlessness of Christ," 270; *ST* III, Q. 21, A.3).

oneself (i.e., unfolding one's will before God for a change in oneself) is an activity possible only for humans (since only humans can unfold a will distinct from God and only humans can change).[133] As such, we see the genuinely human activity of Christ that "underscores the utter dependence of the Son" in his humanity which he lives by faith.[134] The "loud cries and tears" likewise evidence that Christ experienced human life and suffering in a way that "poignantly demonstrates his solidarity with humanity."[135] It is this emotional expression and faithfulness which lead to his prayers being "heard because of his reverence" through the Father's raising of him "from death [i.e., the 'realm of the dead']" (cf. Ps. 15:10; 16:10; 40:11).[136] Christ's solidarity with humanity in suffering, faith, prayer, dependence, and the threat of death communicates the ordinariness of his human nature and capacities and thereby applies theological pressure against those who claim that Christ viewed the beatific vision in his humanity.[137]

C. The Forever-Priest Who Dies (5:6, 7d, 10)

Second, the *inclusio* of references to Christ's Melchizedekian priesthood in 5:6 and 5:10 ("priest forever"; 5:6) is juxtaposed with the death of this priest in 5:7.[138] This Melchizedekian theme is likely Hebrews' most unique contribution to New

---

133. Aquinas, *ST* III, Q.11, A.1.

134. Cockerill, *Hebrews*, 243. David M. Moffitt, "'If Another Priest Arises': Jesus' Resurrection and the High Priestly Christology of Hebrews," in *The Letter to the Hebrews: Critical Readings*, ed. Scott D. Mackie, TTCCRBS (New York: T&T Clark, 2018), 127, notes the role of faith in this text, especially as he compares Jesus to Moses in Heb. 11:19.

135. Small, *Characterization of Jesus*, 218.

136. That is, σώζειν ἐκ (Jn 12:27; 2 Cor. 1:10) rather than σώζειν ἀπο (more likely, "prevent from dying"; see Koester, *Hebrews*, 298). There is a large debate on how Christ was "heard." By affirming the resurrection element, I am following Moffitt, *Atonement*, 190; Loader, *Sohn und Hoherpriester*, 10, 99–104; Lane, *Hebrews*, 120. For a good summary and the "plethora" of difficulties in this text that "defy the ablest exegetes," see Neil R. Lightfoot, "The Saving of the Savior: Hebrews 5:7ff," *Restoration Quarterly* 16 (1973): 166–73.

137. McCall, "Son Though He Was," 148–9, provides three reasons why the beatific vision is consistent with Hebrews 5. I am not contesting any of McCall's reasons here (I agree with each one), but I disagree with his conclusion because the reasons provided here (i.e., the identification of Christ with the people, the act of praying, the loud cries and tears, and the pastoral function of this text) present an "obstacle" to claiming that Christ possesses the beatific vision.

138. The background material on Melchizedek abounds. I am taking a typological (though still historical) view of Melchizedek; see Gareth Lee Cockerill, "Melchizedek Without Speculation: Hebrews 7:1–25 and Genesis 14:17–24," in *A Cloud of Witnesses: A Theology of Hebrews in Its Ancient Contexts*, ed. Richard Bauckham et al., LNTS 387 (New York: T&T Clark, 2008), 128–44.

Testament Christology.[139] The quotation and employment of Ps. 110:4 ("you are a priest forever, after the order of Melchizedek") bring together some of the loftiest themes of Hebrews (kingship, priesthood, sonship; eternality).[140] These quotations, claims, and connections are significant because they connote the divine in both Jewish and Hellenistic cultures as "true God language" via qualities "inherent" to divinity (esp. eternality).[141]

The counterintuitively juxtaposed reality of this forever-priest is that he dies. The priest who is supposed to "remain" (Heb. 7:3; Jn 12:34) dies. Moffitt suggests that Christ was "appointed by God to serve in Melchizedek's eternal priestly order. Yet Jesus did in fact die."[142] Mortality is a capacity that neither Jews nor Greeks would have approved of being predicated of God.[143] However, in this text, we see Jesus crying out "to the one who is able to save *him* from death" (πρὸς τὸν δυνάμενον σῴζειν αὐτὸν ἐκ θανάτου) and therefore can locate Christ's prayers specifically in the context of his death.[144] Such a stark juxtaposition is not shirked by the author of Hebrews but embraced as a reality of the Son as the sympathetic high priest.

D. The Son Who Learns Obedience (5:8)

Third, the conjunction "although" (καίπερ) in verse 8 ("Although a son, he learned obedience through what he suffered") explicitly signals the juxtaposition between Christ as the "Son" and his experience of learning "obedience from what he

---

139. Richard Bauckham, "The Divinity of Jesus Christ in the Epistle to the Hebrews," in *The Epistle to the Hebrews and Christian Theology*, ed. Richard Bauckham et al. (Grand Rapids: Eerdmans, 2009), 19; Hagner, "Son of God," 256.

140. Notably, the language of "forever" recalls Heb. 1:8 and its claim of Christ: "Your throne, O God, is forever." For a defense of the vocative translation here, see Hagner, "Son of God," 251.

141. Bauckham, "Divinity of Jesus," 31, 35; Small, *Characterization of Jesus*, 170. This reading is influenced, but not determined, by the usage of Melchizedek and Ps. 110:4 in Heb. 7:3; for further support see Bauckham, "Divinity of Jesus," 29.

142. Moffitt, "If Another Priest Arises," 131. The use of Moffitt here might provoke the question of whether Jesus was a priest while on earth or not. Moffitt will say, "no" (ibid., 131–2; *Atonement*, 194–208); Owen will say, "yes" (WJO, *Exposition of Hebrews*, 22:514). However, as Peterson suggests (*Perfection*, 193), even if he is not yet appointed to his office, Christ is performing priestly functions.

143. Small, *Characterization of Jesus*, 161, shows the way in which Cicero contrasts mortality and divinity (linking the character of "age" exclusively with humanity). The transcendent God of the Old Testament is likewise eternal (e.g., Isa. 43:10-11; 44:6; 48:12-14).

144. Lane, *Hebrews*, 119, 120; see Cockerill, *Hebrews*, 243, on the relevance of the inclusion of the pronoun. See Mathias Rissi, *Die Theologie des Hebräerbriefs: Ihre Verankerung in der Situation des Verfassers und seiner Leser*, WUNT 41 (Tübingen: Mohr Siebeck, 1987), 79 on the connection between death and suffering in Hebrews.

suffered" (ἔμαθεν ἀφ' ὧν ἔπαθεν τὴν ὑπακοήν).¹⁴⁵ The title of sonship, already prominent in Hebrews (1:2, 5, 8; 3:6; 4:14; 5:5), carries "great emphasis on the majesty and grandeur" of Christ and indicates "the unique relationship that Jesus has with God."¹⁴⁶ The anarthrous noun phrase (ὢν υἱός; lit. "being Son") evidences the *quality* of Sonship, the kind which (presumably) would have excluded learning through suffering.¹⁴⁷ As Bauckham argues, the title carries "the eternal truth of his very being," rather than a messianic office which he is given in time that corresponds "to his antecedent status."¹⁴⁸

However, this Son paradoxically learns obedience through what he suffers.¹⁴⁹ Jamieson suggests, "The best explanation why it is surprising that the Son learns obedience through divine discipline is that 'Son' is a divine designation."¹⁵⁰ Despite the "dignity of his person," he was not "spared" the suffering that would bring about redemption.¹⁵¹ Since we do not want to affirm that Christ's learning implies a transition from disobedience to obedience, because Christ was and is without sin (Heb. 4:15; 1 Pet. 2:22), Christ's "learning" means endurance through a new and difficult experience.¹⁵² Disarmingly, this son "learns" through "suffering." Playing off the Greek tragedians, the author presents Christ as the hero who models obedience to the will of God in the midst of suffering perfectly, even to the point of death.¹⁵³

E. *The Source of Eternal Salvation Who Is Perfected (5:9)*

Fourth, Heb. 5:9 ("being made perfect, he became the source of eternal salvation to all who obey him") tells of how Christ experiences progression (i.e., is made perfect and became something else) yet is designated as the "source of *eternal* salvation"

145. Johnson, *Hebrews*, 147.

146. Cockerill, *Hebrews*, 247; Small, *Characterization of Jesus*, 179; Bauckham, "Divinity of Jesus," 18; DeSilva, *Perseverance in Gratitude*, 85; WJO, *Exposition of Hebrews*, 21:525.

147. Cockerill, *Hebrews*, 247.

148. Bauckham, "Divinity of Jesus," 21; John Webster, "One Who Is Son: Theological Reflections on the Exordium to the Epistle to the Hebrews," in *Epistle to the Hebrews and Christian Theology*, ed. Richard Bauckham et al. (Grand Rapids: Eerdmans, 2009), 82; Small, *Characterization of Jesus*, 99.

149. Lane, *Hebrews*, 121; Peeler, "Tears and Joy," 16. Eduard Riggenbauch says that these are starkly contrasted that they seem to be in contradiction with one another (*Der Brief an die Hebräer*, Kommentar zum Neuen Testament 14 [Leipzig: A. Deichert, 1913], 388–9).

150. Jamieson, *The Paradox of Sonship: Christology in the Epistle to the Hebrews*, 68.

151. WJO, *Exposition of Hebrews*, 21:525.

152. This aorist verb ἔμαθεν ("learned") is the hook upon which the preceding participles (προσενέγκας, εἰσακουσθείς, ὤν) all hang. See Jukka Thurén, "Gebet und Gehorsam des Erniedrigten (Hebr. V 7–10 noch einmal)," *Novum Testamentum* 13 (1971): 144 on prayer as a precondition for obedience.

153. Lane, *Hebrews*, 121; Johnson, *Hebrews*, 147; Calvin, *Hebrews*, 66.

(αἴτιος σωτηρίας αἰωνίου). These juxtaposed capacities of the one agent are true of him according to his distinct agencies. While this last phrase appears nowhere else in the New Testament, Isa. 45:17 promises "eternal salvation" (σωτηρίαν αἰώνιον LXX) that is brought by YHWH. Early Jewish interpreters, likewise, attribute this phrase to the activity of God.[154] Therefore, we might say that the efficacy of this eternal salvation presupposes Christ as the "eternal God," who brings eternal salvation and is himself its eternal source.[155] Further solidifying Christ's supremacy and dignity, the conclusion of verse 9 (where Christ is "obeyed") presupposes Christ as one with the authority to command and one to whom honor is shown, even after his earthly life.[156]

Being "perfected" (τελειωθείς), like learning obedience, does not imply moral imperfection for Christ, but a vocational completion of his official task, ultimately in his exaltation and session.[157] In the intercessory acts of his exaltation, and only then, can he "fulfill his vocational qualifications" and reach the "goal of the salvific process."[158] The requirement of temporal capacities seems counterintuitive and is thereby juxtaposed with the one who is a source of *eternal* salvation and has the authority to give commands. Gareth Cockerill holds both sides of this juxtaposition together when he summarizes Christ's work: "The eternal Son of God who was without defect has become 'perfected' as the Savior of humankind."[159]

F. Summary

I have argued that these four juxtapositions present Christ as the eternal Son who suffers, prays, learns, obeys, and ultimately dies. The passage depends on a level of continuity between Christ's suffering and the Christian's that pushes against the

---

154. See Grieb, "Time Would Fail," 202; for this claim in Philo, see Cockerill, *Hebrews*, 250.

155. Cockerill, *Hebrews*, 250; Johnson, *Hebrews*, 148.

156. Small, *Characterization of Jesus*, 205. Here Small says that Jesus has a "capacity for action" which "extends beyond the normal human life span." On the basis of capacities' relationship to natures, I would then say that Christ is here displaying a nature which "extends beyond the normal human." Herbert Braun, *An die Hebräer*, Handbuch zum Neuen Testament 14 (Tübingen: Mohr Siebeck, 1984), 147, illustrates the juxtaposition inherent to obeying the one who obeyed.

157. Kevin B. McCruden, "The Concept of Perfection in the Epistle to the Hebrews," in *Reading the Epistle to the Hebrews: A Resource for Students*, ed. Eric F. Mason and Kevin B. McCruden, SBLRBS 66 (Atlanta: Society of Biblical Literature, 2011), 213-15; David Peterson, *Hebrews and Perfection: An Examination of the Concept of Perfection in the Epistle to the Hebrews*, SNTSMS 47 (New York: Cambridge University Press, 2005), 35-7.

158. Small, *Characterization of Jesus*, 223; Attridge, *Hebrews*, 153; Peterson, *Hebrews and Perfection*, 96-103.

159. Cockerill, *Hebrews*, 248.

divinization of Christ's humanity, his beholding of the divine essence.[160] Christ's very human acts of praying for himself in the face of death, learning obedience, and yet faithfully enduring through suffering apply pressure toward an understanding of Christ's ordinary human agency.

These ordinary human capacities are prominent in this passage, yet contrary to Bruce McCormack, rather than constituting the divine identity of Christ, they are juxtaposed to it. Consequently, the degree to which Christ's divinity is humanized (as McCormack suggests) is the degree to which these juxtapositions lose their intended pastoral and theological value. If we allow Christ's deity to be "humanized," these claims are less rhetorically comprehensible and are less capable of encouraging Christians to run to "the throne of grace, that we may receive mercy and find grace to help in time of need" because we have such a great high priest (Heb. 4:16). Resisting such a reading are the claims of Heb. 5:7-10, whereby the human acts of Christ are vivid and rhetorically powerful claims intended to encourage the reader of Christ's sympathetic priesthood. As such, the text of Hebrews 5 pressures us toward viewing the humanity of Christ as ordinary and distinct, simultaneously pressuring the reader against the views that Christ's humanity is divinized or divinity humanized. The above, therefore, shows the coherence of a classical and Reformed understanding of Christ's human agency with the biblical testimony and the pastoral prudence of understanding Hebrews 5 in a classical and Reformed way.

IV. Theological and Pastoral Prudence

With the conciliar and biblical coherence of the classical and Reformed account of Christ's human agency presented, we now turn to theological and pastoral prudence in the implications of such an account. This section will illustrate two such benefits, Christ's sympathy *with* us and his obedience *for* us.

A. Christ as a Sympathetic Model to Imitate

In Jesus' distinct and dependent human agency, we have a high priest who is able to sympathize with us in our weakness and a prophet who teaches us the way of life with God perfectly. While some accounts present divine suffering as a devotional advantage,[161] classical and Reformed Christology presents Jesus as the sympathetic

---

160. For the rhetorical effects of this text, which depend on Christ's relatable and ordinary humanity, see Peeler, "Tears and Joy." Owen likewise considers the beatific vision to be an improbability, partially because of the strong claims of Hebrews 5 (*Exposition of Hebrews*, 21:518, 506).

161. Davis and Evans, "Conclusion," 321.

sufferer who knows *our* human suffering, not as a different kind of suffering (i.e., divine suffering) but "precisely as human pain ... as our pain."[162]

Likewise, Jesus provides for us a model of human dependence and life with God. Owen says that one reason "God sent his Son to take our nature upon him ... was that he might set us an example in our own nature, in one who was like unto us in all things, ... of that holy obedience which he requireth of us."[163] Elsewhere he calls Christ the "pattern to [which we] conform ourselves unto [while] under our infirmities" and he bids his readers, "Let him that would go to Christ, consider well how Christ went to God for him."[164] While we recognize the vocational distinction, the "unsubstitutably" historical location of Christ's human life,[165] and the *sui generis* character of Christ's hypostatic union that create discontinuity between his human life and ours, we look to Christ as our "prototype and example" of the Christian life.[166] So we do not seek to imitate Christ's divine operations, but exemplary human operations of faith, obedience, and love to the Father empowered by the Holy Spirit.

B. Christ's Obedience as Human

While Christ is *like us* so that we can be "for him" (e.g., imitation of Christ), we must not limit Christ human actions to the "Christological Pelagianism" of mere exemplary activity;[167] he is also *like us* in order that he might be "for us." Mirroring the Nazianzen ontological axiom, classical and Reformed Christology recognizes an operational precondition for Christ bringing us to God through an obedient *human* life and death.[168] As such, classical and Reformed Christology affirms Glenn Butner's claim: "If Christ had offered a divine obedience, he would not have healed the human will, and Christians' wills would not be healed when they participate in

---

162. Williams, *Christ the Heart of Creation*, 92. Calvin likewise says, "Whenever our troubles press us and torture us, we should cast our minds back to the Son of God who toiled under the same burdens," John Calvin, in *The Epistle of Paul the Apostle to the Hebrews*, ed. David W. Torrance and T. F. Torrance, trans. William B. Johnston, Calvin's Commentaries (Grand Rapids: Eerdmans, 1963), 64.

163. WJO, *Pneumatologia*, 3:510–11.

164. John Owen, *Exposition of the Hebrews*, 21:512, 501.

165. This phrase comes from Frei, *Identity of Jesus Christ*, 109.

166. WJO, *Christologia*, 1:171; see John B. Webster, "The Imitation of Christ," *Tyndale Bulletin* 37 (1986): 95–120; Christopher R. J. Holmes, *Ethics in the Presence of Christ* (New York: T&T Clark, 2012), 24 on the proper theological location of imitation of Christ and the christological danger of allowing "exemplarism" to dictate ethics.

167. Bathrellos, *The Byzantine Christ*, 21–2.

168. See this soteriological motivation for the Christology of Zwingli in Drake, *Flesh of the Word*, 12.

Christ's humanity."[169] So, while many modern theologians (both inside and outside the Reformed tradition) advocate for obedience as an act of Christ's divinity, it is my contention here that obedience is a human operation according to Christ's distinct human agency with pastoral and theological significance.

While there have been both modern and evangelical accounts of divine obedience presented,[170] these rarely conform to classical and Reformed commitments, and few interpreters concede that they meet these standards. However, Scott Swain and Michael Allen advocate for a version of obedience belonging to Christ's divine agency that seeks to inhabit classical and Reformed theology. Employing the concept of proper trinitarian action (see Ch. 4), Swain and Allen advocate for viewing the obedience of the Son as the "proper mode" of the Son's acts in the economy of salvation "whereby he enacts the undivided work of the Trinity."[171] They argue that the obedience of the Son is the proper economic entailment of the eternal generation of the divine Son. However, I suggest that it is more prudent to consider obedience as an immediate effect of Christ's human agency and that the alternative proposal (i.e., of obedience as a divine operation) lacks coherence with classical and Reformed Christology at two points.

(1) Swain and Allen claim that the "Son's distinctive *modus essendi* as the Father's only begotten determines his distinctive *modus agendi* as the Father's obedient emissary."[172] However, this determination seemingly removes the volitional character of the Son's actions (i.e., it is merely the determined mode of external operation), and obedience is a necessarily volitional category; as Thomas Goodwin says, "As our disobedience was free, so must his satisfaction be."[173] Further, if the obedience of the Son is not volitional, then one wonders about the adverse implications for atonement theories (e.g., might a "divine child abuse"

---

169. D. Glenn Butner, *The Son Who Learned Obedience: A Theological Case against the Eternal Submission of the Son* (Eugene, OR: Pickwick, 2018), 73.

170. This conclusion is shared by a diverse cast of theologians, even if they come to it for different reasons. For example, Balthasar *TD*, 5:236–9; *CD* IV/1, §59.1; Darren Sumner helpfully summarizes Barth's position ("Obedience and Subordination in Karl Barth's Trinitarian Theology," in *Advancing Trinitarian Theology: Explorations in Constructive Dogmatics*, ed. Oliver D. Crisp and Fred Sanders, LATC [Grand Rapids: Zondervan, 2014], 131); Bruce A. Ware, *Father, Son, and Holy Spirit: Relationships, Roles, and Relevance* (Wheaton: Crossway, 2005), 21; Wayne A. Grudem, *Systematic Theology: An Introduction to Biblical Doctrine*, 2nd ed. (Grand Rapids: Zondervan, 2020), 307–19.

171. Scott R. Swain and Michael Allen, "The Obedience of the Eternal Son: Catholic Trinitarianism and Reformed Christology," in *Christology Ancient & Modern: Explorations in Constructive Dogmatics*, ed. Oliver D. Crisp and Fred Sanders, LATC (Grand Rapids: Zondervan, 2013), 77. Likewise, Michael R. Allen, *Justification and the Gospel: Understanding the Contexts and Controversies* (Grand Rapids: Baker Academic, 2013), 77, 84 calls obedience a "personal property."

172. Swain and Allen, "Obedience of the Eternal Son," 81.

173. Thomas Goodwin, *Christ Our Mediator* (Lafayette, IN: Sovereign Grace, 2001), I.8.

argument be back in play?).¹⁷⁴ (2) If obedience is a proper action of the Son, then I wonder if there are adverse effects on the doctrine of revelation. That is, if the Son (and only the Son) is obedient, then does the obedience of Christ actually reveal anything about the divine nature, or is it merely revelatory of the relation of the Son?¹⁷⁵ It seems as though we could not speak of the "humility" of the divine nature, only the "humility" of the Son.

These inconsistencies are made even stronger when we consider the biblical evidence for obedience as an immediate effect of human agency. Returning to Hebrews 5, McCall observes, if obedience is "learned," then it cannot be necessary to an eternal relation.¹⁷⁶ This temporal locatedness and growth seem to indicate human agency, unlike the pure activity of the divine nature. Likewise, this obedience is learned through what he suffered (ἔμαθεν ἀφ' ὧν ἔπαθεν τὴν ὑπακοήν), a capacity which belongs exclusively to Christ's human nature.¹⁷⁷ Furthermore, in Heb. 10:5-10 Christ "came into the world" (εἰσερχόμενος εἰς τὸν κόσμον; 10:5) in order to "do your will, O God" (τοῦ ποιῆσαι ὁ θεὸς τὸ θέλημά σου; 10:7). Then, in verses 9 and 10, the author comments on this act of coming to do the will of God "through the offering of the body of Jesus Christ once for all" (Heb. 10:10). Several aspects of this verse must be noted: (1) Like the above, there is a connection between obedience and the suffering/death of Christ.¹⁷⁸ (2) Christ speaks this Psalm (40:6-8) when he has come into the world as a purpose statement for his mission in the world, rather than a declaration of something he

---

174. On the invalidity of "necessary obedience" and the significance of voluntary in the atonement for the Reformed tradition, see T. Robert Baylor, "'He Humbled Himself': Trinity, Covenant, and the Gracious Condescension of the Son in John Owen," in *Trinity Without Hierarchy: Reclaiming Nicene Orthodoxy in Evangelical Theology*, ed. Michael F. Bird and Scott Harrower (Grand Rapids: Kregel Academic, 2019), 185 n. 48, 190.

175. It might be objected that humility could parallel the property "love" as both personally proper and essential. However, the way in which Swain and Allen link obedience (and thereby humility) to the Son's personal generation makes it difficult for obedience to be an essential property.

176. McCall, "Son Though He Was," 145; McCall gives the analogy of a soldier who enlists in the army and obeys her commander. It is not that she was "disobedient" prior to enlisting but that she was not in the appropriate relationship to "obey" (ibid., 133; likewise, McCall, *Analytic Christology*, 116; Cockerill, *Hebrews*, 242).

177. This is true even if "suffered" is "a virtual synonym for 'died'" (Paul Ellingworth, *The Epistle to the Hebrews*, NIGTC [Grand Rapids: Eerdmans, 1993], 292), since dying is likewise (and even more obviously) a human capacity.

178. Peter T. O'Brien, *The Letter to the Hebrews*, PNTC (Grand Rapids: Eerdmans, 2010), 348; Richard N. Longenecker, *Studies in Hermeneutics, Christology and Discipleship*, NTM 3 (Sheffield: Sheffield Phoenix Press, 2006), 124–5 for the connection between obedience and Christ's death.

has always done or accomplished before and by his coming.[179] That is, if the Son (according to his divinity) was being obedient in every act in creation since the beginning of time, one would expect the obedience to precede and include the act of becoming incarnate, not be something that is *possible* because of the coming of Christ in the flesh.[180] (3) The expression "your will, O God" (ὁ θεὸς τὸ θέλημά σου; 10:7) is true of Christ according to his human nature since the Father is not "the God" of the Son.[181] Each of these components links the obedience of Christ in Hebrews 10 to Christ's human agency and human operation.

This construal of human obedience is not merely a biblical truism but is soteriologically significant for classical and Reformed Christology. For some parts of the Reformed tradition, the obedience of Christ fulfills the "covenant of works" which Adam failed to keep in the garden, being imputed to the believers as an "alien righteousness." For Calvin, we are justified "by the obedience of Christ" which "he performed ... in his human nature" (see also Ch. 3 §II.B.3).[182] Likewise, Jonathan Edwards says,

> If Christ had remained only in the divine nature, he would not have been in a capacity to have purchased our salvation .... For Christ merely as God was not capable either of that obedience or suffering that was needful. The divine nature is not capable of suffering, for it is impassable and infinitely above all suffering; neither is it capable of obedience to that law that was given to man.'Tis as impossible that one that is only God should obey the law that was given to man as 'tis that he should suffer man's punishment ... It was needful to answer the law that that nature should obey the law to which the law was given. Man's law could not be answered but by being obeyed by man.[183]

Edwards' claims evidence the significance of obedience as a capacity of the human nature and the significance of the human obedience of Christ as the fulfillment of the obedience which was supposed to be offered by the first humans. Butner summarizes what he calls a "widespread argument among Reformed theologians" by stating, "Only human beings are subject to the law, so only human beings can

---

179. Peterson, *Hebrews and Perfection*, 147, says that this claim seems to portray the attitude of one who has already come (i.e., not one who has been obedient simply in the act of coming).

180. This is relevant because Swain and Allen suggest that the obedience of the Son precedes the assumption of a human nature ("Obedience of the Eternal Son," 86).

181. This is supported by texts like Jn 20:17, in which Jesus speaks of God as "my God and your God." Jesus places himself alongside Mary as one who adores and worships "God," actions which are only true of Jesus according to his human nature.

182. Calvin, *Institutes*, III.xi.9. Meritorious obedience as a soteriological category certainly precedes the Reformed tradition (Adams, *Human Nature*, 96; Vidu, *Atonement, Law, and Justice*, 83–5), but it is particularly meaningful for the Reformed tradition.

183. WJE, *A History of the Work of Redemption*, 9:295–6.

obey the law and thereby fulfill the covenantal obligations of humanity, providing obedience that is the basis for our justification."[184]

While the covenant of works lacks contemporary consensus, I contend that even an alternative position like the New Perspective on Paul, which is frequently unsympathetic to the covenant of works,[185] views Christ's obedience as an operation of human agency. Rather than meritorious action, N. T. Wright suggests that Jesus accomplishes obedience to the "saving purpose of YHWH, the plan marked out for Israel" which they failed to bring about.[186] This fulfillment of the plan for human Israel is brought about by Christ, whose role is to retrace the failures "of Adam, a recapitulation or rerunning of the divine program for" humanity.[187] This occurs through Christ's lifelong "faith" and "faithfulness" to God, culminating in his death.[188] As such, even on this account the obedience of Christ is an operation of his humanity and, likewise, carries significant soteriological freight.

In Christ we can be confident of our status before God because Christ fulfills the covenant on our behalf. As the theandric mediator, it is because Christ has "obeyed God's voice" that he is the one who makes and keeps the promise "I will be your God" as well as the one who fulfills the other side of the promise, "you will be my people" (Jer. 7:23).

V. Conclusion

This chapter has argued that Christ possesses an ordinary and distinct human agency that is also dependent upon his divine agency. In contrast to those who attribute the beatific vision and maximal human knowledge to Christ, this chapter argued that Christ possesses finite knowledge by which he was nescient of certain things and by which he exercised faith by the power of the Holy Spirit. Additionally, from an internal perspective on christological agency, this chapter argued that Christ's human agency is dependent upon his divine agency in a way that mirrors the ontological claim of Christ's *an/enhypostatic* human nature. Therefore, according to this internal perspective, Christ's humanity can be

---

184. Butner, *The Son Who Learned Obedience*, 104.

185. While not a prominent advocate for the New Perspective, see the critique of the covenant of works as it pertains to obedience in Bradley G. Green, *Covenant and Commandment: Works, Obedience, and Faithfulness in the Christian Life*, NSBT (Downers Grove, IL: InterVarsity, 2014), 156–7.

186. N. T. Wright, "The Letter to the Romans: Introduction, Commentary, and Reflections," *NIB*, ed. Leander E. Keck (Nashville: Abingdon, 2002), 10:529.

187. Dunn, *Romans 1–8*, 297.

188. Luke Timothy Johnson, "Romans 3:21-26 and the Faith of Jesus," in *Contested Issues in Christian Origins and the New Testament: Collected Essays*, NovTSup 146 (Boston: Brill, 2013), 249.

considered an animate internal instrument. Then this chapter turned to Hebrews 5 and the juxtapositions between Christ's human actions and his divine identity to argue that Scripture here resists both the divinization of Christ's humanity and humanization of Christ's divinity. Finally, it addressed the topics of Christ's human agency as a model of ethical human living and the soteriological significance of his human obedience.

Chapter 6

THE THEANDRIC AGENT: UNITY AND DISTINCTION

Having treated the distinctions in Christ's divine and human agencies, we now turn to the unity of Christ as the theandric mediator. As an attempt to reflect the trinitarian foundation and the Reformed emphasis on the integrity of both natures, this chapter was saved until last. However, it seeks to serve as the pinnacle of the argument, tying together the classical and Reformed commitment to the one mediator Jesus Christ as fully God, fully man. The main thesis of this book is that the classical and Reformed understanding Christ as a single theandric agent who operates according to distinct agencies simultaneously is a coherent and prudent position. The previous two chapters established the content of these distinct agencies, this chapter will argue for Christ as a theandric agent who acts according to those distinct agencies simultaneously.

The chapter begins with the affirmation of the singularity of the one agent (§I), discusses the distinction of immediate effects in this agent's actions (§II), addresses potential charges of Nestorianism (§III), and finally illustrates the soteriological significance of Christ's theandric unity by examining his mediatorial role as priest (§IV).

I. The Theandric Unity of the Agent

The unity of christological action lies in the theandric unity of a singular agent. Here I seek to further extend and reinforce Owen's commitment to Christ as a single theandric agent by examining the Reformed view of Christ as theandric in his mediatorial activity, then articulating historic and contemporary precedents for this christological position, and finally illustrating the unity of the single theandric agent and the distinction of immediate effects with a historic analogy.

A. Christ, the Theandric Mediator in Reformed Christology

As seen in Chapter 3, Owen insists that Christ is the mediator in both natures. The Son becomes incarnate, taking humanity upon himself in order to mediate between both God and humanity. Owen draws attention to "the divine constitution of the person of Christ as God and man .... [by] that ineffable divine act ... whereby the person of the Son of God assumed our nature, or took it into a personal subsistence with himself."[1] Owen claims, "The divine and human nature in Christ have but one personal subsistence; and so are but one Christ."[2] Upon this theological substructure, Owen and classical and Reformed Christology often view "Christ" not merely as the Logos *simpliciter* but as the God-man who exists as a single subsistence in two natures and acts as a single theandric agent.

Historically, the Reformed tradition's commitment to Christ's mediation in both natures came to a polemical climax against the largely Roman Catholic position of Christ's mediation only according to his human nature in the confrontation with Francesco Stancaro.[3] Defending the medieval Catholic position against Peter Vermigli, John Calvin, and a Reformed synod at Pińczów, Stancaro claimed that Christ was a mediator only according to his human nature based on 1 Tim. 2:5 ("one mediator … the *man* Jesus Christ") and his concern that the Son (in his divine nature) would be subordinate to the Father if he mediated in both natures.[4] One synod member responded by throwing a Bible at Stancaro's head in order to "impress the word of God upon him."[5] However, the more fundamental Reformed response centered on the importance of the composition of Christ as both God and man and the unity of Christ's theandric actions. Calvin says, "Paul places before our eyes a complete person composed of two natures," and their "union is necessarily demanded by the office of mediator."[6]

---

1. WJO, *Christologia*, 1:224. Notice that Owen predicates the label "person" of the God-man, a move which will not be followed in this account but is indicative of the classical and Reformed commitment to viewing the mediator as theandric.

2. WJO, *Vindication*, 2:418; see also *Exposition of Hebrews*, 21:526.

3. For example, Calvin, *Institutes*, II.xii.2.

4. For example, *Synopsis* 2:113 and Turretin (*Institutes*, II:14.ii.2) both engage Robert Bellarmine "De Christo Mediator, lib. V," in *Disputationes de Controversiis Christianae Fidei adversus hujus temporis Haereticos*, 4 vols (1581–93). For the history of the Stancaro debate, see Joseph N. Tylenda, "Christ the Mediator: Calvin Versus Stancaro," *CTJ* 8 (1973): 5–16; Stephen Edmondson, *Calvin's Christology* (New York: Cambridge University Press, 2004), 14–39; Joseph N. Tylenda, "Controversy on Christ the Mediator: Calvin's Second Reply to Stancaro," *CTJ* 8 (1973): 141. For the Reformed position, see Ch. 3 §II.A.1 and for the Catholic position, see Augustine, *A Treatise on the Grace of Christ, and on Original Sin*, II.33 (*NPNF*[1] 5:248); *Confessions*, X.43; *City of God*, 9.15, 378; Brian Daley "A Humble Mediator: The Distinctive Elements in Saint Augustine's Christology," *Word and Spirit* 9 (1987): 100–17; *ST* III, Q.26, A.1–2.

5. For this story, see George Huntston Williams, *The Radical Reformation*, 3rd ed., SCES 15 (Kriksville, MO: Truman State University, 2000), 1029–31.

6. Tylenda, "Calvin's Second Reply," 148, 156. He even says that "the mediator is constituted from two natures" (156). In the *Institutes* Calvin says, "he who was the Son of God became the Son of man—not by confusion of substance, but by unity of person. For we affirm his divinity so joined and united with his humanity that each retains its distinctive nature unimpaired, and yet these two natures constitute one Christ" (II.xiv.1).

Specifically, Calvin appeals to the need for both human and divine activity in Christ for him to fulfill the priestly office (see §IV below) since Christ can only die as the sacrifice if he is a man and can only constitute a sacrifice of infinite value and efficacy if he is God.[7] Likewise, the two natures of Christ's mediatorial operations "are clearly joined in" Jesus' claim to "sanctify myself" (Jn 17:19). Calvin says, "To be sanctified belongs to flesh, and on the other hand, to sanctify belongs to God, but both are found only in the complete person."[8] For the Reformed, Christ the theandric God-man (not the Logos *simpliciter* or the human nature) is primarily viewed as the mediator between God and humanity.[9] Because of this emphasis on Christ as the mediator according to both natures, the Reformed can not only appreciate the distinction of both natures but can also insist on the unity of action in the single theandric agent.

For classical and Reformed Christology, the theandric mediator is the agent of all christological acts. Owen states, "The person of Christ is neither his divine nature nor his human"; instead "his person is the principal or only agent; which being God-man, all the actions thereof, by virtue of the communication of the properties of both natures therein, are theandrical."[10] Vermigli adds that it is this theandric mediator "from which actions proceed."[11] We see this manifested in the repeated fourfold christological affirmation (see Ch. 3 § II.A.3), of which the first two points claim: "(1.) The agent; and that is the person of Christ. (2.) The immediate principle by which and from which the agent worketh; and that is the natures in the person."[12]

Owen's fourfold affirmation is mirrored in form and content by Reformed theologians around the world. For example, the Italian Francis Turretin, Dutch Peter van Mastricht, German Heinrich Heppe, and American Charles Hodge (who

---

7. Tylenda, "Christ the Mediator," 13.

8. Tylenda, "Calvin's Second Reply," 150.

9. For additional affirmations, see Heppe, *Reformed Dogmatics*, 458–509; Lindholm, *Jerome Zanchi*, 79. It might be objected that this position is inconsistent with the frequent Reformed affirmation that the Son functions in the office of mediator "before" the incarnation (see in Bavinck, *RD*, 3:365; Calvin, *Institutes* II.xiv.iii; *WCF* 8.2) since the Son is not theandric before the incarnation. While this objection is not frequently noted, the appointment of Christ to the office of mediator as a component of the covenant of redemption allows us to see Christ's pre-incarnate mediation as theandric because it is always *incarnandus* (toward the incarnation and on the basis of it). The Father can, thereby, designate the Son as the mediator from the "beginning of time," knowing that the Son will be incarnate and that there is no situation in which the Son does *not* become incarnate. This is consistent with Owen's constructions above; it is also very similar to Vermigli's solution in *Life, Letters and Sermons*, 203–4, 209.

10. WJO, *Vindication of the Preceding Discourse*, 2:329.

11. Vermigli, *Life, Letters, and Sermons*, 201.

12. WJO, *Vindication* 2:433.

cites Owen explicitly) all employ this ordered affirmation.[13] As such, the classical and Reformed tradition affirms the theandric mediator, the God-man, as the agent of the acts of God incarnate, who in his singular acts brings about distinct immediate effects according to the capacities of each nature.[14]

A couple of explicit statements of this axiomatic formula will illustrate the claim. The Dutch *Synopsis of Purer Theology* states,

> In performing the duties of his office and all the things that go with it ... [one] nature shares and behaves in consort with the other nature ....Thus while each nature has its own operations (*energeiai*), the work that is completed by them (*apotelesma*) is a work of the one "God-and-man" (*theandrikos*).[15]

Zanchi likewise follows this formula: "(1) The Operator or the agent, (2) the principle of action according to which and through which the acts are performed, (3) [the kinds of] actions that are carried out and (4) the work or *Apotelesmata* that is performed."[16] While less formulaic, John Gill suggests that there is "A communion of operations in both natures, to the perfecting of the same work; which, therefore, may be called 'theandric,' or the work of the God-man; there being a concurrence of both natures in the performance of it; which, when done, is ascribed to his Person."[17]

Finally, Heppe names: (1) "the effective cause ... is the divine-human person of Christ; (2) the principles therein active are the two natures of Christ; (3) each of them produces its particular effect; (4) thereby the work so achieved,

---

13. Peter van Mastrict, *Theoretico-Practica Theologia*, V.iv.13 (1:540); Heppe, *Reformed Dogmatics*, 446; Turretin, *Institutes*, II.14.II.2; Charles Hodge, *Systematic Theology*, 2:458; Bavinck, *RD*, 3:306. See John of Damascus, "Orthodox Faith," III.15 (304/92/93).

14. See Bavinck, *RD*, 2:259 for the "Reformed idea" of "personal life"—i.e., emphasis on the person. More recently Bruce McCormack says of Barth that "the redeeming Subject is neither the Logos simpliciter nor the human Jesus simpliciter but the God-human in this divine human unity" ("With Loud Cries," 47).

15. *Synopsis*, 2:85.

16. Jerome Zanchi, *De Incornatione Filii Dei Libri Duo* (Heidelberg, 1593), 146; translation in Lindholm, *Jerome Zanchi*, 107. Notice that the plural ἀποτελέσματα is used (following John of Damascus, *Orthodox Faith*, III.15, 304/92/93 and Thomas Aquinas, *Scriptum super Sententiis: Magistri Petri Lombardi*, ed. Maria F. Moos and P. Mandonnet [Paris: Lethielleux, 1956], III, d.18, q.1 a.1 ad.1) yet the singular English word "work" is also used. Because of the strong connection between the singular agent and the fourth point, it seems that the Reformed lean toward the singularity of this final claim and uses of the plural (e.g., ἀποτελέσματα) ought to be taken as the manifold results that comprise a singular event. Special thanks to David Moser for his insights into the Damascene and Aquinas here.

17. John Gill, *A Complete Body of Doctrinal and Practical Divinity*, 2 vols (London: Winterbotham, 1796), 2.1.62. Likewise, see Ames, *Marrow*, I.18.22.

the *apotelesma*, is only a divine-human work."[18] He goes on to clarify the unity within the tradition on this point, suggesting that the concept of ἀποτέλεσμα "is already completed fixed" within the tradition and he quotes Sohnius's definition as representative: "a single personal work, (in which) distinct acts of the two natures concur and unite."[19]

We can restate these Reformed axiomatic statements according to their common enumeration and the present employment of the language of agency: (1) the single theandric agent, (2) the agency of each nature, (3) the immediate effects of the distinction operations of each nature, and (4) the unity of completed action. The first and the fourth claims are mutually supporting in that any completed event which Christ brings about is necessarily his action as the theandric mediator, deriving its significance from his mediatorial office as God and man.[20] Likewise, the second and third claims represent another emphasis of Reformed Christology: the preservation of the capacities and inclinations of either nature in the hypostatic union.[21] Since each nature preserves its own capacities and each nature is necessarily involved in every completed action of Christ, the third point indicates that there are distinct immediate effects of either nature in every completed action.

Therefore, for the Reformed, there is a single theandric agent (i.e., executor of intentional action) who brings about events according to his distinct capacities which produce distinct immediate effects. The emphasis on distinction in Reformed Christology follows from and is balanced by the emphasis on the unity of the theandric mediator and his completed events according to both natures. It is one agent who enacts two distinct powers (or capacities), producing distinct immediate effects in his singular acts. Rather than seeing either nature as an agent distinct from the other, classical and Reformed Christology predicates the label "agent" to the theandric mediator, the God-man.[22]

---

18. Heppe, *Reformed Dogmatics*, XVII.25, 445.

19. Ibid., citing Georg Sohnius, *Exeg. Conf. Aug.*, 246.

20. The *apotelesma theandrikon* is sometimes considered in conversations on the communication of attributes as a key component of Reformed Christology. See DLGTT, s.v. "communicatio idiomatum / communicatio proprietatum"; Heppe, *Reformed Dogmatics*, 433; *Synopsis*, 2:109 n. 10.

21. Further, see this emphasis in Zwingli's claim: "For as each nature is in him in its entirety, so each nature preserves its own character (as far as their boundaries are concerned). His humanity can no more reign than his divinity die—even though he who reigns is human, and he who dies is God" ("Friendly Exegesis, That Is, Exposition of the Matter of the Eucharist to Martin Luther," in *Selected Writings of Huldrych Zwingli*, ed. H. Wayne Pipkin and Edward J. Furcha, trans. H. Wayne Pipkin [Eugene, OR: Pickwick, 1984], 2:324).

22. Contra Thomas Flint, who calls the human nature of Christ "an agent with morally significant freedom" so that it "thinks and feels and acts" in distinction (and division) from the divine agent, the Son ("Should Concretists Part with Mereological Models," 69, 70).

Since neither nature is an agent that acts toward the other, then we might say that there cannot be an I-Thou relationship between Christ's two natures. Employing the example of loving God, Owen says, "But whatever is spoken of this nature concerning the love of God unto the man Christ Jesus, and of his love to God, it is *the person of the Father* that is intended therein."[23] Therefore, the Son according to his human nature ought not to be said to "love himself" but rather directs his love toward the person of the Father. Finally, Owen claims that the union consisted in "Καθ' ὁμωνυμίαν, by an *equivocal denomination*, the name of the one person, namely, of the Son of God, being accommodated unto the other, namely, the Son of man."[24] Minimally, this evidences Owen's insistence on speaking of the acts of Christ as accomplished by the one mediator and a rejection of the possibility of affections between the two natures within Christ so that there is no "I-thou" between them.[25]

B. Precedents for Theandric Unity: Historic and Contemporary

The presentation of the classical and Reformed view of Christ as the theandric mediator is supported by historic and contemporary precedents for this claim. Specifically, considering "Christ" as the composite or "end product" of the union between God and humanity has what one interpreter calls a "Catholic pedigree" and (I will add) a contemporary parallel.[26] What is further, these precedents either constitute the conciliar christological tradition or seek to be compatible with it, evidencing the plausibility and internal coherence of this classical and Reformed claim with its conciliar commitment.

The first precedent for viewing the agent as theandric is the early church's willingness to consider Christ in terms of the incarnate God-man, in conjunction with its affirmation of Christ as the Logos and Son of God. Looking back at the ecumenical councils there was fluidity to the referent of the *hypostasis* of Christ. That is, it was not always clear if the referent of the *hypostasis* was the Word himself or the end-product of the hypostatic union (the God-man). As Grillmeier notes, Chalcedon applied the word *hypostasis* "not to the one Logos-subject" but "to the

---

23. WJO, *Christologia*, 1:231.

24. Ibid., 1:232; earlier in *Christologia* (1:226) he gives the example of Isaiah 7 and 9 ("mighty God" and a "child born").

25. This means that while obedience belongs to Christ according to his human agency, I do not think that the Son (qua humanity) "obeys himself" in a proper way, as maintained by Thomas Aquinas (*ST* III, Q.20, A.2; White, *Incarnate Lord*, 303). Instead, obedience is "personal" so that the Son (qua humanity) obeys the Father.

26. Lindholm, *Jerome Zanchi*, 96. This is "contemporary" as in "today," not Owen's day.

final form of him who had assumed flesh."²⁷ Likewise, Christopher Beeley says, "The council does not define Christ primarily as the divine Son of God .... Instead ... Chalcedon makes its focus to be the incarnate Lord, who is to be conceived in a balanced way of being both divine and human ... which could suggest that he is equally composed of both."²⁸ Further, John of Damascus suggests that "we say that the term 'Christ' is the name of the person and that it is not used in a restricted sense, but as signifying what is of two natures" such that we can say he is "said to be of two natures and in two natures."²⁹

However, this balance does not deny that the Logos is a divine *hypostasis*. Instead, the practice of viewing the *hypostasis* either as the undivided "end-product of the incarnation" (emphasizing symmetry—what I will call the external perspective) or to the "second person of the Trinity" *simpliciter* (emphasizing asymmetry—the internal perspective) evidences that the concept and language of *hypostasis* was open and perspective-dependent for the Fathers.³⁰ They were comfortable viewing Christ from different perspectives and understanding his personhood on different "levels" of predication.³¹ There is a similar openness in the thought of Leontius (which is followed by Maximus), so that Leontius can refer to "one composite hypostasis (μία σύνθετος ὑπόστασις)."³² He does so, however, while recognizing that from the "level of natures" Christ is a composite *hypostasis*, and from the "personal level" Christ is the Logos.³³ Connecting the discussion of *hypostases* to

---

27. Aloys Grillmeier and Theresia Hainthaler, *Christ in Christian Tradition, Volume 2 Part 2: The Church of Constantinople in the Sixth Century*, trans. Pauline Allen and John Cawte (Philadelphia: Westminster John Knox, 1995), 277; cf. David Coffey, "The Theandric Nature of Christ," *TS* 60 (1999): 405–31; Jaroslav Pelikan suggests that Chalcedon was "not clear" on this question since both referents were used (*The Christian Tradition: A History of the Development of Doctrine, Vol. 1: The Emergence of the Catholic Tradition [100–600]* [Chicago: University of Chicago Press, 1971], 265).

28. Christopher A. Beeley, *The Unity of Christ: Continuity and Conflict in Patristic Tradition* (New Haven: Yale University Press, 2012), 282; cf. Anthony Baxter, "Chalcedon, and the Subject in Christ," *The Downside Review* 107 (1989): 1–21.

29. John of Damascus, "Orthodox Faith," III.3, 272.

30. The quoted language comes from Demetrios Bathrellos, who also notes this practice in the early church (*The Byzantine Christ*, 44).

31. Brian E. Daley, "'A Richer Union': Leontius of Byzantium and the Relationship of Human and Divine in Christ," *Studia Patristica* 24 (1993): 251–2.

32. Leontius, "Adversus Nestorianos," (PG 86:1496A); in Maximus see "Epistle 12," (PG 91:488B); "Epistle 13," (PG 91.525C); "Epistle 15," (PG 91.556D, 557D); Nicholas Madden, "Composite Hypostasis in Maximus Confessor," *Studia Patristica* 27 (1993): 176.

33. Bathrellos, *The Byzantine Christ*, 105–6; cf. 28–9. Likewise, on Thomas and the different ways of referring to "Christ," see Eleonore Stump, "Aquinas' Metaphysics of the Incarnation," in *The Incarnation: An Interdisciplinary Symposium on the Incarnation of the Son of God*, ed. Stephen T. Davis, Daniel Kendall, and Gerald O'Collins (New York: Oxford University Press, 2004), 206.

agency conversations, the applicability and transferability of this historic category into the focus of our study is evidenced by Brian Daley's description of *hypostases* as "individual agents" who "use" freedoms and "implement" choices.[34]

Following this historic precedent of considering Christ as theandric, there is also a contemporary parallel between classical and Reformed claims of the theandric agent and a formidable branch of analytic Christology.[35] Specifically, I contend that the "model-A" position parallels classical and Reformed Christology, evidencing the logical plausibility of Christ as a composite agent and providing a contemporary defense of the classical and Reformed position.

Premised upon largely conciliar affirmations, orthodox analytic Christology distinguishes between "model-T" Christology and "model-A" Christology. Thomas P. Flint helpfully describes model-T as the conception "of the incarnation as a case of a substance's gaining a part" so that the humanity of Christ becomes a part *of the Logos*.[36] Therefore, on model-T, "Christ" refers to *the Word* who has taken a human nature as a part of himself. Conversely, model-A refers to the composite Christ who is composed of the Son and his human nature as constituent parts. Flint says that "the composite thus formed *is* not the Son [simpliciter]. The Son remains one part of the composite entity that results from his assuming a human nature … [which] we call Christ."[37] We might analogically (although perhaps irreverently) imagine model-A as a Peanut M&M and model-T as a plain peanut that is dipped into melted chocolate immediately before consumption.[38] The Peanut M&M is a composite snack composed of the peanut (as a part) and the chocolate (as another part), so the label "snack" refers to the whole composite candy. With a chocolate-dipped peanut, the peanut itself is the referent of "snack" and the chocolate becomes a part of that snack.

While both positions have theological merits and claim to possess historical predecessors, neither is without its complications.[39] One difficulty with model-T is the seemingly necessary denial of divine simplicity. That is, if the divine Son is simple, then the Son cannot be composed of parts or pieces; yet, according to

---

34. Daley, *God Visible*, 211.

35. On a definition of analytic Christology see Richard Sturch, *The Word and the Christ: An Essay in Analytic Christology* (New York: Clarendon, 1991), 1–2. Lindholm notes a general connection and continuity between Reformed Christology and contemporary analytic Christology (*Jerome Zanchi*, 21, cf. 1).

36. Flint, "Should Concretists Part with Mereological Models," 71.

37. Ibid., 79.

38. The analogy of model-A as a peanut M&M owes credit to Kevin Wong.

39. See, for example, Oliver D. Crisp, "Compositional Christology without Nestorianism," in *The Metaphysics of the Incarnation*, ed. Anna Marmodoro and Jonathan Hill (New York: Oxford University Press, 2011), 45–66; Brian Leftow, "A Timeless God Incarnate," in *The Incarnation: An Interdisciplinary Symposium on the Incarnation of the Son of God*, ed. Stephen T. Davis, Daniel Kendall, and Gerald O'Collins (New York: Oxford University Press, 2002), 273–302; Flint, "Should Concretists Part with Mereological Models."

model-T, the human nature becomes a part of the Son. Another worry here is that the Logos becomes something new in the incarnation, calling immutability into question, and this new thing is the addition of a creature, calling divine aseity into question.

While model-A can affirm simplicity and immutability in a straightforward way, since the Son remains what he eternally is and the "change" is an addition outside of himself in the composition of the whole Christ, it runs into problems when it enters into discussions of action. This is particularly the case because of the putatively "closed" concept of "personhood" (i.e., an individual substance of a rational nature) as opposed to the more open concepts of *hypostasis* and agent.[40] Flint affirms, "Most proponents of Model-A" say that the composite "Christ" is not a *person*; instead, the "person" is God the Son.[41] When model-A addresses actions, it encounters what Oliver Crisp calls the "no person problem," which he describes as "one of the least satisfactory parts" of compositional Christology and is an area "in which more work needs to be done."[42] Crisp gives the example of Jesus weeping at Lazarus' tomb in order to illustrate this problem. He says that the composite Christ who cries at the tomb cannot be the person of the Son (since the Son is impassible) and cannot be the human nature of Christ (since the human nature is not a person). So it appears that "no person is the *subject* of the weeping."[43] While

---

40. Boethius, "A Treatise Against Eutyches and Nestorius," in *The Theological Tractates; The Consolation of Philosophy*, ed. H. F. Stewart, E. K. Rand, and S. J. Tester, LCL 74 (Cambridge, MA: Harvard University Press, 1973), 93. While one could opt for a more Lockean definition of personhood, the closed nature of the concept would remain the same. Additionally evidencing the closed nature of the concept of person is the applicability of the concept across contexts (i.e., triune persons, human persons share the same definition). Whereas, the semi-open concept of "agent" shifts as the context shifts (i.e., the definitional criteria for a triune agent-in-relation are not identical to those for a theandric agent nor are either identical to an exclusively human agent). This is true, as it is with all concepts, only in the language game that the classical and Reformed tradition is playing. Therefore, the point stands even if the concept of "person" is more open in other language games (e.g., medieval Eastern theology).

41. Flint, "Should Concretists Part with Mereological Models," 81; for the near unanimous denial of Christ as a "human person," see Alfred J. Freddoso, "Human Nature, Potency and the Incarnation," *F&P* 3 (1986): 29; Oliver D. Crisp, *Divinity and Humanity: The Incarnation Reconsidered*, CIT (New York: Cambridge University Press, 2007), 8 n. 13; Gordon, *Holy One*, 69.

42. Oliver D. Crisp, *The Word Enfleshed: Exploring the Person and Work of Christ* (Grand Rapids: Baker Academic, 2016), 116, 118.

43. Ibid., 115, emphasis mine. While Crisp does not explicitly notice this, I think Crisp has an even more significant problem on this account. Since Crisp seems as though he would be willing to say that "forgiving sins" is an act of the "person" of the Son, then the subject of forgiving sins would be putatively distinct from the subject of "weeping" (i.e., no person)—tilting toward Nestorianism.

Crisp's explicit "no person problem" will remain unaddressed, I propose a classical and Reformed response to this problem by moving away from the closed language of "person" and dealing instead with the semi-open concept of "agent."[44] If we make this move, classical and Reformed Christology views Christ as the theandric agent of the action performing the immediate effect of weeping according to his human agency.

C. Historic Analogy of Theandric Action

In order to illustrate the coherence and plausibility of a single theandric agent who performs actions with distinct effects according to distinct agencies, we turn to a historic christological analogy. While all analogies are merely partial, imperfect representations of the *sui generis* hypostatic union, several analogies have been offered throughout the tradition,[45] one historically prominent illustration of Christ's theandric action that is particularly helpful here is the image of a single fire-sword.[46] A fire-sword subsists first, and primarily, in an iron nature that then assumes a fire nature into subsistence with itself without giving up any of its iron-ness.[47] Each of these natures (fire-ness and iron-ness) might have subsisted within themselves and formed swords in their own right if they were not united

---

44. This is not to say that classical and Reformed Christology cannot respond to the no-person problem, but that is not my goal in this project.

45. On the very imperfect nature of christological analogies, see Donald Fairbairn, *Grace and Christology in the Early Church*, OECS (New York: Oxford University Press, 2006), 118. One of the most prominent is the body/soul analogy (Thomas G. Weinandy, "The Soul/Body Analogy and the Incarnation: Cyril of Alexandria," *Coptic Church Review* 17 [1996]: 59–66). While many thinkers historically used it to indicate the unity of action, it seems that the Reformed tradition often used it to distinguish between the immediate effects of the operations of the soul (e.g., thinking) and the operations of the body (e.g., digesting); see Hodge, *Systematic Theology*, 2:394–5; Calvin, *Institutes*, II.14.1; Turretin, *Institutes*, II:13.viii.1; WJO, *Pneumatologia*, 3:101, 420.

46. John of Damascus, "Orthodox Faith," III.15, 308; Maximus, "Disputatio," (*PG* 91:337D–340A). It should be noted that Owen appreciates the way this analogy communicates distinct effects and a singular "agent," but does not appreciate the way it implies separability and an accidental union (WJO, *Christologia*, 1:230). For the historical origins of this analogy, see Dmitry Biriukov, "The Topic of Penetration of Fire into Iron in Byzantine Christology," *Review of Ecumenical Studies* 11 (2019): 409–23.

47. Some employ this analogy to illustrate the communication of properties from one nature to the other (e.g., the iron is heated by the fire). However, this move is not followed by classical and Reformed Christology because of the emphasis on the integrity of either nature in the human. As such, the burning bush of Exod. 3:2 is probably more ontologically apt because the bush is not consumed and retains its properties (WJO, *Glory of Christ*, 1:311). However, the analogy of the sword will be used for our study of action because bushes do not really "do" much and would make an uneventful analogy.

together. An iron sword might have existed without the fire-ness united to it, and the fire-ness might have constituted a sword in its own right (e.g., Luke Skywalker's lightsaber, or Hiccup's sword in *How to Train Your Dragon*).[48] Yet, upon this composition of the fire-sword, it has two distinct natures with distinct capacities, to burn and to cut, within the single act (i.e., one swing) of the single agent (i.e., one sword). So, as the fire-sword swings through wood, it creates the immediate effect of cutting according to its iron nature and burning according to its fire nature. While this analogy is certainly imperfect—especially since it fails to preserve the inseparability of the union (since the two could be separated and exist independently) and it fails to appreciate the *sui generis* character of the hypostatic union (since other swords could be likewise heated up, implying a merely quantitative distinction between Christians and Christ)[49]—it is helpfully illustrative of the composition of the singular agent and the distinction of the various effects according to distinct capacities.

With this analogy in place, we might follow the Damascene's example of Jesus raising the little girl back to life: "Thus, the child's being taken by the hand and drawn up was an effect of His human operation, whereas her being restored to life was an effect of His divine operation. For the latter is one thing and the former another, even though they are inseparable in the theandric operation."[50]

II. Distinct Agencies and Distinct Effects

The previous section argued that classical and Reformed Christology considers Christ as a singular theandric agent to whom every action is attributed and that the execution of these actions is "in, with, and through the full agency of his [Christ's] human and divine natures."[51] This subsection will argue that, in the unity of these

---

48. The claim that Christ's humanity *could* have existed apart from the assumption is an important feature for the affirmation of Christ's genuine humanity. However, whether Christ's human nature *would* have existed apart from the assumption will not be addressed here (see Richard Cross, *The Metaphysics of the Incarnation: Thomas Aquinas to Duns Scotus* [New York: Oxford University Press, 2005], 240).

49. Conversely, Oliver Crisp sees this parallel as a virtue of the analogy rather than a vice (*Divinity and Humanity*, 24–5). On Owen and the inseparability of the hypostatic union, see WJO, *Pneumatologia*, 3:160–1. Note that the inseparability here is not merely willed (i.e., that the Son *will* not be separated from the humanity) but that the humanity of Christ *could not* be separated from the Son yet still exist.

50. John of Damascus, "Orthodox Faith," III.15, 309.

51. Abraham, *Divine Agency*, 2:114. Abraham affirms a single agent in divine and human agency of Christ through Maximus. While Abraham's chapter is helpful as it addresses Maximus' and the Nestorian concern that lingers with dyothelitism (and, for Abraham, two minds Christology), this section seeks to elaborate upon the distinction of those agencies, its consequences, and the possibility of unity therein.

actions, each agency of Christ brings about distinct immediate effects (§II.A), yet these distinct agencies (bringing about distinct immediate effects) are executed by the single agent simultaneously (§II.B). As such, classical and Reformed Christology will be presented in relation to accounts of strong instrumentality (which unifies the effects) and parallelism (which distinguishes Christ's actions). As Reformed christological agency navigates these contemporary positions its biblical and theological prudence will be conveyed.

A. Distinct Effects

As evidenced in the Reformed axiom, and illustrated by the analogy of theandric action, there are distinct effects in any given singular theandric act of Christ. So, while the fire-sword moving horizontally through wood is a single action, each nature of the fire-sword produces distinct immediate effects. This claim is significant when Reformed Christology affirms both theandric mediation and the distinct capacities of either nature. That is, if each nature preserves its inherent properties and remains without change and without confusion in the incarnation, then the fundamental capacities of those natures must also be without change and without confusion.[52] Connecting the ontology of Christ to operations, Brian Daley rightly claims that natures define the "limits and possibilities for action."[53] Therefore, Christ's distinct natures imply distinct capacities (i.e., agencies) which bring about distinct immediate effects.[54] After an articulation of the way in which classical and Reformed Christology formulates the distinct immediate effects, this position will be related to an account of strong instrumentality whereby Christ's human operations participate in his divinity to a maximal degree and bring about effects as a new theandric energy.

The strong attribution of distinct effects is common in the Reformed tradition. Owen claims that since the divine nature "had neither change nor shadow of turning … it acts suitably unto itself; it acts nothing but what becomes it and is proper unto the divine nature."[55] Likewise, the *Synopsis* states that "each nature of Christ performs its own role in the work required to fulfill that task, and it does

---

52. Tylenda, "Calvin's Second Reply," 150.

53. Daley, *God Visible*, 267.

54. The plurality and distinction of agencies runs contrary to Matthew R. Crawford's affirmation of "the single agency and personhood of Jesus in whom divinity and humanity are united" (*Cyril of Alexandria's Trinitarian Theology of Scripture*, OECS [New York: Oxford University Press, 2014], 65). Notice that throughout this project we have not spoken of a personal agency or dual agency. Personal agency would imply there was one agency. Likewise, dual agency may imply that there are two parts, or aspects, of a single agency. Dual agency is perhaps similar to "dual nature," a phrase we might be able to say with sufficient nuance, but the potential for misunderstanding is high and deleterious.

55. WJO, "Condescension of Christ," 17:566.

so jointly, not separately, and yet not jumbled together but distinctly."[56] While this phraseology will be questioned below, the minimal judgment is the distinction between effects (and "role") that are accomplished "jointly ... [and] distinctly." While every action belongs to the person of Christ (like every property), we can also see that certain *effects* are "proper" to either agency (like properties are proper to either nature).[57] Likewise, Herman Bavinck claims that "Scripture and the church ... view the natures as being united in such a way that in the one divine-human work each nature does the thing that belongs to it."[58]

Stephen Holmes connects the affirmation of distinct effects (what he calls distinct operations in the one person) to the Reformed account of the communication of attributes. He says,

> Each nature preserves its own properties; each nature operates in the one person according to its essential properties; and yet every act of Christ is an act of the person, not of one of the natures .... However, and finally, the possibility of any particular action might be determined by reference to one or both of the natures, and so one form of possible predication concerning the incarnate Son is to follow Leo and speak improperly, although not without reason, of particular actions belonging to particular natures.[59]

The classical and Reformed predication of the distinct effects of the theandric mediator's singular acts is rooted in a Reformed version of the communication of attributes.[60] Developed in contrast to Lutheran Christology, the communication of attributes is often understood to comprise up to four *genera* (with the first two shared by both Reformed and Lutherans, and the first three agreed to by most Lutherans).[61] The first (*genus idiomaticum*) is a fairly non-controversial claim that whatever can be predicated of either nature is true of Christ's person. The second (*genus apotelesmata*) means that Christ's actions are acts of his person and that his person subsists in two natures, taken by the Reformed to mean that Christ performs every action in both natures which produce effects that are proper to

---

56. *Synopsis*, 2:109.

57. Jason Zuidema, *Peter Martyr Vermigli (1499-1562) and the Outward Instruments of Divine Grace*, Reformed Historical Theology 4 (Göttingen: Vandenhoeck & Ruprecht, 2008), 76.

58. Bavinck, *RD*, 3:315.

59. Holmes, "Communicatio Idiomatum," 81. See the connection between distinct ontology and distinct operations in Christ by Turretin, *Institutes*, II:13.vii.14–15.

60. Riches says that this theologoumenon has been "characteristically neglected" in modern theology (*Ecce Homo*, 6). For a monograph treating the topic in the Reformation, see Cross, *Communicatio Idiomatum*.

61. For the standard treatment of the *genera* in Lutheran theology, see Martin Chemnitz, *The Two Natures in Christ*, trans. J. A. O. Preus (St. Louis: Concordia, 1971), 157–413.

each.⁶² The third (*genus majestaticum*) is a uniquely Lutheran claim in which the humanity of Christ receives a real communication of divine attributes because of the intimacy of the union. So, importantly, the humanity of Christ can become ubiquitous by virtue of its union with an omnipresent divine nature. The fourth (*genus tapeinoticum*), the converse of the third *genus*, states that the divine nature receives human properties. However, both traditional Lutheran and Reformed Christologies reject this reciprocity.⁶³

While each of these is important, the Reformed affirmation and expansion of the second *genus* and the Reformed rejection of the third are notable for this project. The second *genus* is expanded by Huldrych Zwingli into the concept of *alloiosis*: "A linguistic device by means of which we can speak of the person of Christ as having done a thing, when we really mean that he had done a thing according to his human or his divine nature, respectively."⁶⁴ So, for example, Zwingli says that when we say "Christ went away" (cf. Jn 14:26), "Christ" is a reference to "Christ in his human nature" since it is only proper to his human nature to be spatially located.⁶⁵ Luther, supposing that this divides the person of Christ, calls this doctrine the "devil's mask."⁶⁶ Specifically, Lutherans worry that because of the affirmation of distinct effects and the denial of the third *genus*, Reformed theology "excludes the human nature from all official acts, the performance of which requires omnipotence, omniscience, and omnipresence."⁶⁷ Schmid says, "For the infinite value of Christ's merit cannot be a reality, unless performed by an organ participating in the infinite

---

62. See Cross, *Communicatio Idiomatum*, 23; whereby he characterizes this category as implying that both "natures have a causal role in the activity."

63. Chemnitz, *The Two Natures in Christ*, 246; for a defense of this claim in Luther, see David J. Luy, *Dominus Mortis: Martin Luther on the Incorruptibility of God in Christ* (Minneapolis: Fortress, 2014), 34, 51. Lutheran Leopoldo Sanchez suggests a different fourth *genus* (*genus pneumatikon*) which articulates the role of the Holy Spirit in the communication of grace to the humanity of Christ (*Receiver, Bearer, and Giver of God's Spirit: Jesus' Life in the Spirit as a Lens for Theology and Life* [Eugene, OR: Pickwick, 2015], 148).

64. Oliver D. Crisp, "Incarnation," in *The Oxford Handbook of Systematic Theology* (New York: Oxford University Press, 2007), 171. For a more elaborate definition and defense of Zwingli's use of the term, see Drake, *Flesh of the Word*, 71–4.

65. Drake, *The Flesh of the Word*, 68. William Peter Stephens, *Theology of Huldrych Zwingli* (New York: Oxford University Press, 1986); Richard Cross, "Alloiosis in the Christology of Zwingli," *JTS* 47 (1996): 105–22; see Franz Pieper, *Christian Dogmatics* (St. Louis: Concordia, 1950), 2:137. See Robert W. Jenson, "Triune Grace," in *The Gift of Grace: The Future of Lutheran Theology*, ed. Niels Henrik Gregersen et al. (Minneapolis: Fortress, 2005), 24 for a summary of Lutheran critiques.

66. *WA* 26:319; *LW* 37:218.

67. Pieper, *Christian Dogmatics*, 2:273.

power of God."⁶⁸ The classical and Reformed response is not to deny human activity but to distinguish between the immediate effects of either agency in the single action. Most relevantly for the Lutheran discussion, classical and Reformed Christology does not give up distinct effects, but instead (1) affirms the constancy and simultaneity of both agencies and (2) affirms the dignity of actions on the basis of the operator (i.e., the affirmation of the *apotelesma* being dependent upon Christ's theandric mediation, not on the immediate effect of either agency).

One point of connection between this account of distinct effects and contemporary Christology comes from contemporary Lutheran Ian McFarland and his use of the Dionysian claim that Christ does human things divinely and divine things humanly.⁶⁹ Beyond McFarland, this is often paired with the concept of instrumentality (what I am calling strong instrumentality) whereby an instrument takes on the power of the principal agent, like swinging an axe takes on the powers of its operator.⁷⁰

McFarland suggests that if we are to affirm the unity of the person of Christ and his full humanity, we must avoid the "Leonine temptation," referring to Leo's claim that "each form [nature] does in a communion with the other that activity which it possesses as its own."⁷¹ Additionally, both historians (like Harnack) and theologians (like Jenson) have become concerned that the Leonine principle "turns the [two] natures of Christ into subjects of action."⁷² Instead, McFarland insists that since the divine nature is invisible, transcendent, and imperceivable, any perceivable change is accomplished by his human nature. So that when Jesus performs miracles "the divine power of the Holy Spirit [is] operative in his human nature in the same way

---

68. Heinrich Schmid, *The Doctrinal Theology of the Evangelical Lutheran Church*, trans. Charles A. Hay and Henry E. Jacobs, 2nd ed. (Philadelphia: Lutheran Publication Society, 1889), 312–13.

69. Andrew Hofer, "Dionysian Elements in Thomas Aquinas's Christology: A Case of the Authority and Ambiguity of Pseudo-Dionysius," *The Thomist* 72 (2008): 409–42.

70. See Aquinas, *ST* III, Q.64. A.5. Theophil Tschipke, *L'humanité du Christ comme instrument de salut de la divinité*, trans. Philibert Secrétan, Studia Friburgensia 94 (Fribourg: Academic Press Fribourg, 2003), 156–62.

71. See the documents at Constantinople III (Tanner, *Decrees*, 1:129). Ian A. McFarland, "Spirit and Incarnation: Toward a Pneumatic Chalcedonianism," *IJST* 16 (2014): 149; McGuckin, *Saint Cyril of Alexandria*, 236.

72. Bathrellos, *The Byzantine Christ*, 176; for Adolf von Harnack, *History of Dogma*, trans. Neil Buchanan (Boston: Little, Brown, 1898), 4:205–6; Aloys Grillmeier, *Christ in the Christian Tradition: From the Apostolic Age to Chalcedon (451)*, trans. John Bowden (Louisville: John Knox, 1975), 1:536; Jenson, *Systematic Theology*, 1:131–2. For the historical discussion of this phrase, see Bathrellos, *The Byzantine Christ*, 184–6, 195–6, and Hovorun, *Will, Action and Freedom*, 21–2; cf. Riches, *Ecce Homo*, 81–2 for the potential solution within Leo that allows him to be understood as internally coherent; and see "Orthodox Faith," III.15, 309–10 for John of Damascus' appropriation of the phrase.

as in any other human being who performs miracles."[73] But Jesus' human nature so intimately participates in the energy (what McFarland defines as "characteristic modes of operation"; or, we might call agency) of the divine nature that "then there is no human activity of Jesus that is not also divine."[74] McFarland then appeals to Pseudo-Dionysius in the historic articulation of Christ's human acts done divinely and divine acts done humanly.[75] Appealing to Dionysius, Thomas Aquinas "holds that Christ's humanity was the instrumental efficient cause of salvation, [so] that Christ *secundum quod homo* (according as a human being) could produce a divine effect."[76] Therefore, Thomas can affirmingly quote Dionysius, "What is of man He works beyond man."[77] The consequence of this is the indistinguishability of effects whereby "no difference of any kind can be perceived" because, as Gregory of Nyssa says, humanity has been "mixed with the all-powerful Godhead ... like a drop of vinegar mingled in the boundless sea .... As all those characteristics that can be seen to be associated with what is mortal have been transformed into the characteristics of the Godhead."[78] Aaron Riches suggests that this means that the divine action of the Logos is "without separation" and "synergistically 'one'" with the natural energy of his human being.[79]

While classical and Reformed christological agency appreciates the unity of the singular action that the above allows, classical and Reformed Christology insists that distinct immediate effects are the consequence of the preservation of the integrity of both natures in the hypostatic union. So while the theandric agent brings about singular acts that are both divine and human, his distinct divine

---

73. McFarland, *Word Made Flesh*, 89 n. 45.

74. Ibid., 90.

75. Pseudo-Dionysius Areopagita, *Corpus Dionysiacum II*, ed. Günther Heil and Adolf Martin Ritter, Patristische Texte und Studien 36 (New York: De Gruyter, 1991), 161.

76. Corey Ladd Barnes, *Christ's Two Wills in Scholastic Thought: The Christology of Aquinas and Its Historical Contexts* (Toronto: PIMS, 2012), 2; Legge, Trinitarian Christology of St Thomas Aquinas, 191.

77. Aquinas, *ST* III, Q.19, A.1, ad.1. Christology is, like the Eucharist, then a case in which human agencies can produce divine effects (Reginald Lynch, OP, *The Cleansing of the Heart: The Sacraments as Instrumental Causes in the Thomistic Tradition*, Thomistic Ressourcement [Washington, DC: Catholic University of America Press, 2017], 121–4).

78. Gregory of Nyssa, "To Theophilus," in *Anti-Apollinarian Writings*, trans. Robin Orton, Fathers of the church: A New Translation 131 (Washington, DC: Catholic University of America Press, 2015), 267. For the soteriological significance of this claim, see Miguel Brugarolas, "Christological Eschatology," in *Greoggry of Nyssa's Mystical Eschatology*, ed. Giulio Maspero, Miguel Brugarolas, and Illaria Vigorelli, SP 101 (Leuven: Peeters, 2021), 36.

79. Riches, *Ecce Homo*, 145. Again, this claim is close to the classical and Reformed position, but notably distinct. For the Reformed, the energy (or agency) of Christ is not singular (as Riches suggests) but distinctly divine and human, executed by the singular theandric agent in a singular action (which is dependent upon the person, not either agency).

and human operations produce distinct immediate effects. Therefore, classical and Reformed Christology departs from a strict version of Dionysius's claim that Jesus does human things divinely and divine things humanly.[80] Instead, classical and Reformed Christology attributes those operations which belong properly to divinity to Christ according to his divine agency and those which belong properly to his humanity to his human agency.

In order to demonstrate the immediacy and proper predication of particular operations to either agency, we may turn to Luke 5 and observe that the perceivable sounds of Jesus' voice are the immediate effects of his human nature, yet the forgiveness of sins is an immediate effect of the divine nature, for "who can forgive sins but God alone?" (Lk. 5:21). As Zanchi says, "To forgive sins was a proper action to the divine nature, but to say [the words with human lips]: 'Thy sins be forgiven thee' was proper to the human nature."[81] This is, emphatically, not to suggest that Christ's natures independently act or constitute distinct agents, but as von Mastrict says, "these works proceed from the person of the God-man by the distinct effectiveness of both natures."[82] Likewise, when Jesus says that he sanctifies himself (Jn 17:19), he is here executing a divine prerogative that belongs properly and immediately to his divine agency. Finally, Christ petitions the Father for the "glory which I had with you before the world existed" (Jn 17:5). Such a desire and request for divine glory is only proper to divinity and therefore is not proper to "human activity."[83]

Nor does classical and Reformed Christology claim that these divine operations are exactly like other human miracles.[84] When ordinary humans perform the act of healing, a second agent is introduced, in Scripture this is often explicitly recognized through their acts of prayer or deference to the power of the Lord (Jas 5:14). For example, Daniel petitions the mercy of the Lord to interpret Nebuchadnezzar's dream because he knows that "no wise men, enchanters, magicians, or astrologers can show to the king the mystery … but there is a God in heaven who reveals mysteries" (Dan. 2:27-28). With the miracles and healings that the prophets and apostles perform, the agency (i.e., capacity to bring an event about) does not belong to that agent, but to God.[85] So Paul "heals" as an instrument of God working *through*

---

80. See McFarland, *Word Made Flesh*, 94 for a contemporary employment of this principle. Yet, McFarland nuances the claim that each energy remains distinct. Further, his pursuit of humanity "mirroring" divinity is similarly achieved below in the discussion of simultaneity.

81. Giroloma Zanchi, *Confession of the Christian Religion, Studies in the History of Christian Traditions*, ed. Luca Baschera and Christian Moser (Boston: Brill, 2007), XI.9, 211–12.

82. As cited in Heppe, *Reformed Dogmatics*, 445–6.

83. See Tylenda, "Calvin's Second Reply," 154–5.

84. Contrary to McFarland, "Spirit and Incarnation," 157.

85. I think this is true even on a continuationist's view of 1 Cor. 12:9. Even if someone has the "gift(s) of healing(s)," they do not seemingly have the capacity to bring about that event whenever they intend.

him (Acts 19:11-12). However, these features are not true of Jesus. When Jesus performs a miracle there is not an additional agent named nor does the agency to perform the miracle lie outside of himself. For example, Jesus, the theandric agent, performs the single act of walking on the water, defying the natural laws of gravity and buoyancy as the immediate effect of his divine agency and moving his feet in front of the other according to his human agency. Yet Peter's act of walking on the water (a similar human operation) requires the introduction of a second agent from whom he asks for help (i.e., notice his petition Κύριε … κέλευσόν [Mt. 14:28]), indicating that he does not possess the capacity to perform the action himself. Finally, we see this in the prophets who proclaimed, "thus says the Lord" (Isa. 37:6) and the apostles who worked "in the name of Jesus of Nazareth" (Acts 3:6); yet Jesus proclaims, "I say unto you" (Mt. 5:21-48) and heals to manifest his own authority (Mt. 9:6). These operations indicate that this one agent possesses the capacity and executes the prerogatives of divinity within himself.

The classical and Reformed insistence on distinct immediate effects, therefore, indicates that the Dionysian expression is, minimally, in need of nuance. It need not be totally rejected because the singular acts that the theandric agent performs are both divine and human. So there can be an "improper" sense in which the Dionysian expression is stated in classical and Reformed Christology—improper because human effects are immediately derived from human operations, but the human operations of Christ are simultaneously accompanied by divine operations in the one act of the theandric mediator.[86] So when the Reformed make this affirmation, it is much more like John of Damascus's statement (employing the historic analogy):

> Thus, while we speak of the cut burn and the burnt cut of the red-hot knife, we nevertheless hold the cutting to be one operation and the burning another, the one belonging to one nature and the other to the other—the burning to the fire and the cutting to the steel. In the very same way, when we speak of one theandric operation of Christ, we understand the two operations of His two natures: the divine operation of the divinity and the human operation of the humanity.[87]

The nuance provided to the Dionysian expression might be illustrated using another well-known patristic claim, but suggesting that a classical and Reformed account might modify Cyril's claim that the Word, the one patient, "suffered impassibly" and suggest that the Word, the one agent, "touched incorporeally."[88]

---

86. Contra the Nestorian charge against Reformed theology from Robert W. Jenson, "How Does Jesus Make a Difference," in *Essentials of Christian Theology*, ed. William C. Placher (Louisville: Westminster John Knox, 2003), 200.

87. John of Damascus, "Orthodox Faith," III.19, 323/132/33. Similarly, Austin Farrer, "Very God and Very Man," in *Interpretation and Belief*, ed. Charles C. Conti (London: SPCK, 1976), 126.

88. Cyril of Alexandria, *Scholia on the Incarnation of the Only-Begotten*, LFC 47, trans. P. E. Pusey (Oxford: J. H. Parker, 1881), 232 says "suffered without suffering."

Cyril's claim is reduplicated to mean the one person "suffered" according to his human nature while remain impassible according to his divine nature. This claim can be reduplicated to mean that the one agent touched as an immediate effect of one nature (which possesses the capacity to touch) and yet remained incorporeal according to his divine nature.

Finally, in order to supplement the above historical and biblical defense of distinct effects of Christ's distinct natures, I will demonstrate the dogmatic value of this affirmation, specifically as it pertains to the triune God's indivisible operations by problematizing alternatives. If one denies the distinct effects of Christ's actions while also affirming the indivisible operations of the triune God, then it seems that she has two options: (A) include Christ's human operations in the indivisible operations of God or (B) strictly limit Christ's incarnate acts to his humanity and exclude them the indivisible operations of God.

As an example of "option A," Adonis Vidu (leveraging a Thomistic account of instrumentality) suggests that for Christ "every active response ... is to be predicated of the whole Godhead" because "all divine persons share the one efficient divine causality that moves the human nature of Christ."[89] Therefore, Christ's human intentional actions (such as speaking, seeing, walking, and eating) "are always instrumentalized human operations" and thereby acts of every divine person. However, without nuance it seems that Vidu's account leads to peculiar claims about Christ's actions that, in this account, belong properly to the Son. For example, it seems to follow that for Vidu, the whole Trinity speaks the words "the Father and I are one" and "my God, my God, why have you forsaken me." That is, if every human operation is strictly included in indivisible operations, then these human effects (i.e., speaking) must belong to the Father and Spirit as much as the Son.[90]

---

89. Adonis Vidu, The *Same God Who Works All Things: Inseparable Operations in Trinitarian Theology* (Grand Rapids: Eerdmans, 2021), 212, 209; cf. 213–14. Vidu's relationship with the Leonite principle above is complex. He disapproves of its rigidity of predication early in the volume (ibid., 80), then cites it, seemingly approvingly, immediately before affirming Pseudo-Dionysius (209).

90. I'm not convinced that my critique here evidences substantial differences as much as discrepancies in the langue of action, agential predication, and causality. It seems to me that it could be possible to speak about agential involvement in ways that do not primarily concern efficient causality, but are more transparent to the biblical text. This difference in agential predication and efficient causality can be illustrated with a less-than-hypothetical-example at my house: my twelve-year-old daughter developed an elaborate slide in our house down two flights of stairs using sleeping bags and a mountain of couch cousins. So when my three-year-old son wholeheartedly took the plunge and ended up breaking the railing of the stairs; he (the 3 y/o) is the efficient cause of the broken railing, but my older daughter is more proximately the agent of intentionally causing the event—and the one responsible for fixing it. It's not that Vidu and I would narrate this story differently, but that his focus on efficient causality orients in one way while my focus on agency orients it in another.

However, if "option B" is followed and Christ's incarnate acts are exclusively human operations and the human effects are excluded from indivisible operations,[91] then events such as Christ's healings, the transfiguration, and forgiveness of sins do not include the activity of the Father and Spirit. The exclusivity of the human activity of Christ might include empowerment by the Spirit (e.g., the human nature supernaturally led and enabled), however it would exclude the operational unity of Christ's acts with the Father.

B. Simultaneous Operations

The second claim of this section is that the distinct operations of these natures (bringing about distinct effects) occur simultaneously (i.e., concurrently, not in alternation). Concurrent operations build upon the unity of the theandric agent and an understanding of noncompetitive divine and human action, that divine and human action are not a zero-sum game.[92] Noncompetitive divine and human action is a theological consequence of the Creator-creature distinction, and especially, divine simplicity.[93] Since God is not a "part of the metaphysical furniture of the universe,"[94] a being among beings, he does not have to compete for ontological and operational space as finite agents do.[95] Consequently, God's actions are not in competition with human actions, so that particular occurrences can be predicated (in some sense) to both God and creatures (e.g., Gen. 50:20; Phil. 2:12). When added to the account of theandric action provided thus far, noncompetitive action means that the singular acts of Christ can be predicated of the one agent and classical and Reformed Christology can affirm *concursus* without fear of allowing distinct effects to imply distinct agents or requiring Christ to alternate between natures in his actions.[96]

---

91. This position might be considered an extreme version of McFarland's described above; however, McFarland's commitment to the unity of the triune God and the identity of Jesus as God excludes his explicit position from this critique (see especially, *Word Enfleshed*, 90). This position is likely most occupied by those who advocate for a kind of primacy attributed to the humanity of Christ (see esp. some of the Spirit Christology positions in Chapter 4 and below).

92. For a recounting of modernity's tendency to see divinity and humanity as necessarily in competition, see Riches, *Ecce Homo*, 142. For a theological defense of this claim, see Tanner, *Jesus, Humanity and the Trinity*, 4.

93. See the way this informs, and is established by, Christology in Williams, *Christ the Heart of Creation*, xii, 120, *passim*.

94. This turn of phrase belongs to Stanley M. Hauerwas, *Disrupting Time: Sermons, Prayers, and Sundries* (Eugene, OR: Wipf & Stock, 2004), 208.

95. Williams, *Christ the Heart of Creation*, 12.

96. This seems to be the underlying concern behind Katherine Sonderegger's rejection of *concursus* in favor of the affirmation that Christ's acts were God's doing to the exclusion of human agency ("The Sinlessness of Christ," in *Theological Theology: Essays in Honour of John Webster*, ed. David R. Nelson and Justin Stratis [New York: T&T Clark, 2015], 275). However, this dichotomy seems unnecessary if concursus is plausible and christological unity is ontologically and operationally rooted in the single theandric agent.

However, notice that here *concursus* and simultaneity are logically subsequent to the ontological and operational unity of the theandric agent rather than being the unifying principle of christological action. This is pertinent because *concursus* by itself is not a sufficient unifying principle for Christology.[97] *Concursus* is used to articulate divine and human action in other theological neighborhoods, all of which include multiple agents (e.g., providence, prayer, Scripture).[98] So, if *concursus* is used to explain the acts of multiple agents, then it alone is insufficient to establish conciliar christological unity; and if one attempts to ground unity primarily in *concursus*, then Nestorianism will not be far behind. Christology may be illustrative of (and even foundational for) divine and human *concursus* and non-competitive action, yet Christology involves the predication of actions to a single agent so *concursus* cannot (independently) establish the unity of Christ's actions, nor can Christ's actions serve as the paradigm for all divine and human action without strong recognition of *sui generis* character of christological action.[99] Therefore, while this account agrees with the use of *concursus* in modern Christologies,[100] it does not want to place the burden of unity upon this principle.

---

97. In contrast to this, *concursus* is proposed as an alternative to the communication of attributes by Telford Work, "Jesus' New Relationship with the Holy Spirit and Ours," in *Christology, Ancient and Modern: Explorations in Constructive Dogmatics*, ed. Oliver Crisp and Fred Sanders, LATC (Grand Rapids: Zondervan, 2013), 171–83.

98. E.g., Austin Farrer, *Scripture, Metaphysics, and Poetry: Austin Farrer's the Glass of Vision, with Critical Commentary*, ed. Robert MacSwain, ASTIA (Burlington: Ashgate, 2013), 36; A. N. S. Lane, "B. B. Warfield on the Humanity of Scripture," *Vox Evangelica* 16 (1986): 77–94; Christopher C. Green, *Doxological Theology: Karl Barth on Divine Providence, Evil, and the Angels*, TTCSST (New York: T&T Clark, 2011), 58–91.

99. Likewise, Katherine Sonderegger, *Systematic Theology: The Doctrine of God, Volume 1* (Minneapolis: Fortress, 2015), xix. Moves from the hypostatic union to providence, the sacraments, and Scripture abound, some with more attention than others to the discontinuity between christological and two-agent dual agency. George Hunsinger, *How to Read Karl Barth: The Shape of His Theology* (New York: Oxford University Press, 1991), 185–224; George Hunsinger, *The Eucharist and Ecumenism: Let Us Keep the Feast*, CIT (New York: Cambridge University Press, 2008), 162–5; Timpe, "Cooperative Grace, Cooperative Agency," 233; Stephen E. Fowl, "Scripture," in *The Oxford Handbook of Systematic Theology*, ed. John Webster, Kathryn Tanner, and Iain Torrance (New York: Oxford University Press, 2007), 345–61. Paul T. Nimmo, "Karl Barth and the Concursus Dei—A Chalcedonianism Too Far?," *IJST* 9 (2007): 58–72 makes an argument against a "Chalcedonian pattern," particularly in Barth, the most similar to the argument here appearing on 65–6.

100. E.g., Tanner, *God and Creation*, 90–104; Vanhoozer, *Remythologizing Theology*, 169; Tanner, *Jesus, Humanity and the Trinity*, 20–1, 44–5; Allen, *Christ's Faith*, 113; Barth helpfully includes the preceding, accompanying, and following aspects of divine action in its concurrence with human action (*CD* III/3, 90–154; IV/1, 40; IV/2, 753).

John of Damascus represents an early defender of simultaneity and concurrence of operations in Christ's singular actions. Upon the foundation of dyothelitism (Ch. 3 §I.B.3), John of Damascus says that while Christ has "two natural wills and two natural operations, ... He is one and the same who wills and acts naturally according to both natures .... And we say that He wills and acts in each, not independently, but in concert [ἡνωμένος]. 'For in each form He wills and acts in communion with the other.'"[101] Based on the theandric unity of Christ, the Damascene says, "All the actions of each form [i.e., nature] at all times belonged to one Person, [yet] we nevertheless in no way confuse these things which were done inseparably .... Therefore, Christ acts through each of His natures and in Him each nature acts in communion with the other."[102]

For the classical and Reformed tradition this means that the single theandric agent brings about distinct immediate effects of his two distinct agencies concurrently. Summarizing Reformed christological action, Ivor Davidson suggests, "In the redemptive action of Christ both natures cooperated perfectly, participating together in his mediatorial work in accordance with their respective properties."[103] Francis Turretin elaborates upon this position by distinguishing between the efficient cause (i.e., the theandric mediator) and the exciting causes from which operations come (i.e., either capacity): "Although the efficient cause of the operations of Christ is one alone, still the exciting cause is twofold—the divinity and humanity. The work upon which both exciting (*egergema*) causes exert their power is one, but the action (*energeia*) is twofold."[104] Here, although in a different language (i.e., I am referring to actions as singular and operations as plural), it is the judgment in Turretin that there is one event, one completed action, but two operations (*energeia*) from two principles (*egergema*) occurring simultaneously. Further, William Ames suggests that the two natures in Christ are

> concurring unto the same operations; so that they are performed together by each nature, but according to their own distinct properties. Hence it comes to pass that all the doings and sufferings of Christ are referred properly to his person as the proper Terminum, bound of them; although some are properly to be referred to the one, some to the other nature, as to their beginning and proper respects.[105]

Unified simultaneity is, therefore, a feature of the execution of a single theandric agent. It is because Christ is a single theandric agent who acts singularly that he (necessarily) simultaneously produces distinct immediate effects. Therefore,

---

101. John of Damascus, "Orthodox Faith," III.14, 296; quoting Leo, *Epistle* 28.4 (PG 54.768B).

102. John of Damascus, "Orthodox Faith," III.15, 311; citing Leo Epistle 28.4 (PL 54.768B); cf. *OF* III.19, 321–2/128–31 for the use of "proper" operations in either nature.

103. Davidson, "Christ," 458.

104. Turretin, *Institutes*, II:13.vii.15.

105. Ames, *Marrow*, I.18.22.

classical and Reformed Christology resists articulating christological action in terms of cloistered parallelism or alternating agency.

What I am calling cloistered parallelism distributes actions exclusively to one nature or the other. This is maybe most commonly seen in accounts which subscribe to the language of "two-narratives" Christology, "two … subjects," "two I's," and "two agents." If each nature constitutes a subject, or agent (with its own "narrative" and "self"), then it seems to divide the execution of actions into one nature or another and cloister the other nature off from involvement in that action.[106] This kind of account could utilize noncompetitive action; however, it would seem to ground christological unity in *concursus* (unlike classical and Reformed Christology) instead of the theandric agent with *concursus* as a secondary manifestation. For example, Richard Swinburne provides the analogy of a "divided mind" whereby, "In performing some actions, the agent is acting on one system of belief and not guided by beliefs of the other system" such that "different actions would be done in the light of different systems."[107] Likewise, Richard Cross introduces a distinction between causal and predicative agency, the former referring to causal origin, the latter referring to the subject of predication. Cross applies this distinction to Christ, saying that the human actions of Christ belong to the humanity of Christ by virtue of causal agency and only to the Word by virtue of predication as the Word is the subsistence of the human nature.[108] While Cross comes close to Turretin and the Reformed position, without the affirmation of a single "efficient cause … Christ" (the God-man) so that the theandric God-man is both the causal agent and the predicative subject of every human and divine effect of Christ it seems that Cross has opened the door to two distinct actions (divine and human) which are executed in parallel by two distinct "subjects" (i.e., agents).[109] Other examples of collective agency are sometimes (seemingly unwittingly) a consequence of attempts to affirm the genuine humanity of Christ. Commonly theologians will refer to Christ as a

---

106. James William McClendon, Jr., *Systematic Theology* 2:247–9, 276; Richard A. Norris, "Introduction," in *The Christological Controversy*, ed. Richard A. Norris, SECT (Minneapolis: Fortress, 1980), 24; Thomas Weinandy, *Jesus: Essays in Christology*, FRSCTP (Ave Maria, FL: Sapientia, 2014), 266–78; Cross, *The Metaphysics of the Incarnation*, 319; Charles M. Stang, "The Two 'I's of Christ," 529–47; Flint, "Should Concretists Part with Mereological Models," 69, 70.

107. Swinburne, *Christian God*, 201–2.

108. Cross, *The Metaphysics of the Incarnation*, 226. Likewise, Léon Seiller says that Christ's human actions belong to the Word not causally but predicatively (*L'activité humaine du Christ selon Duns Scot*, Études de Science religieuse 3 [Paris: Éditions Franciscaines, 1944], 55).

109. Cross explicitly affirms two subjects, although he does not address "two agents" anywhere. For a critique of Cross and the historical stream he aligns himself with, see Riches, *Ecce Homo*, 216–17; likewise, Jonathan Hill, "Introduction," in *The Metaphysics of the Incarnation*, ed. Anna Marmodoro and Jonathan Hill (New York: Oxford University Press, 2011), 2.

"human agent" and as a "divine agent" (or either one) without showing how Christ can be both while not being two agents.[110] Representative of this move is Rowan Williams' claim that Jesus, who is the "supremely and perfectly human agent … is also the perfectly divine agent."[111] Likewise, Flint suggests that viewing Christ's human nature "as an agent with morally significant freedom" allows us to "take seriously the claim that Christ was 'a man like us in all things but sin.'"[112]

Likewise, simultaneity resists an understanding of Christ's divine and human actions in an alternating form, like a nozzle on a garden hose that can be flipped on or off.[113] David Brown illustrates the perceived prominence of this view, calling it the dominant assumption "through most of the course of Christian history."[114] This view has adherents from the Reformed tradition as well. Appealing to the concept of consciousness, William Shedd says that there is an "alternation in the self-consciousness of Christ, according as the human and divine natures advanced or retreated."[115] These operations, he says, are like the human mind which experience radically distinct things from one moment to the next (e.g., happiness and sadness).[116] Often as a consequence of this view, Christ's default mode of operating is human agency as the operational "center of gravity" with

---

110. Abraham, *Divine Agency*, 2:113; White, *Incarnate Lord*, 119; Allen, *Christ's Faith*, 138-9; Charles Hodge, *Systematic Theology* (Grand Rapids: Eerdmans, 1981), 2:379; McCormack, "With Loud Cries," 47. David VanDrunen claims that the Son *as God* is the "agent of creation and providence" over all creatures, and *as Christ* is the "agent of redemption, and thereby rules over the church" ("The Two Kingdoms Doctrine and the Relationship of Church and State in the Early Reformed Tradition," *Journal of Church and State* 49 [2007]: 750; cf. *Natural Law and the Two Kingdoms: A Study in the Development of Reformed Social Thought* [Grand Rapids: Eerdmans, 2010], 180).

111. Williams, *Christ and Creation*, 165.

112. Flint, "Should Concretists Part with Mereological Models," 69.

113. For example, Hans Schwarz articulates the way that Christ chose to employ the divine will at certain points but not others (*Christology* [Grand Rapids: Eerdmans, 1998], 159).

114. David Brown, *Divine Humanity: Kenosis and the Construction of a Christian Theology* (Waco, TX: Baylor University Press, 2011), 178-9. While I do not agree with Brown's historical claim here, I do think it is reflective of modern perceptions of classical Christology and therefore must be engaged.

115. William G. T. Shedd, *Dogmatic Theology*, 3 vols (New York: Charles Scribner's Sons, 1880-94), 3:392. Notice how the principles of operations are *competitively* advancing and retreating as in a zero-sum game. Likewise, Meyendorff critiques John Knox for positing a shifting, or bouncing back and forth, from divinity to humanity: "His [Christ's] person is … imagined as containing constantly shifting levels of divinity and humanity, depending upon his acting, either as God or as man" ("New Life in Christ: Salvation in Orthodox Theology," *TS* 50 [1989]: 487).

116. Shedd, *Dogmatic Theology*, 2:321.

the occasional interruption of divinity.[117] This position may be seen in an earlier interpretation of John Owen's Spirit Christology and is advocated for implicitly and explicitly in contemporary literature.[118] For example, Brian Leftow, when considering how Christ was tempted, says that the "Son voluntarily foreswore use of His distinctively divine powers .... Everything He did, we could do, in much the same way."[119] This drawing from exclusively human power is a pattern in Christ's human life, he says, "save perhaps in working certain miracles" (i.e., interruptions of divinity in Christ's otherwise human actions).[120] The proximity of this position to the classical and Reformed attribution of immediate effects to distinct principles of operation (i.e., agency) is notable. However, the alternating agency view believes that the ascription of an operation to his human agency excludes the agency of his divine nature in that action entirely, while classical and Reformed Christology seeks to appeal to unified simultaneity.[121] So it seems that on this alternating agency position, one act of Christ is more or less divine than the next. Yet, classical and Reformed Christology views the theandric mediator's actions as an "unbroken completeness of the human [and divine] activity."[122]

We might summarize the distinct effects yet concurrent operation in the words of the *Synopsis*, "In performing the duties of his office and all the things that go with it ... [one] nature shares and behaves in consort with the other nature .... Thus while each nature has its own operations (*energeiai*), the work that is completed by them (*apotelesma*) is a work of the one 'God-and-man' (*theandrikos*)."[123]

---

117. John Webster, *Word and Church: Essays in Christian Dogmatics I* (New York: T&T Clark, 2001), 128 names this position in order to critique it.

118. It is for something close to this reason that John Webster is concerned about the "adoptionist potential" of Evangelical biblical studies ("Jesus Christ," in *The Cambridge Companion to Evangelical Theology*, ed. Timothy Larsen and Daniel J. Treier [Cambridge: Cambridge University Press, 2007], 58).

119. Brian Leftow, "Tempting God," *F&P* 31 (2014): 23.

120. Ibid. Likewise, Bruce A. Ware, *The Man Christ Jesus: Theological Reflections on the Humanity of Christ* (Wheaton: Crossway, 2012), 118; Gerald F. Hawthorne, *The Presence and the Power: The Significance of the Holy Spirit in the Life and Ministry of Jesus* (Dallas: Word, 2003), 113.

121. It is on this front where we might note Calvin's unfortunate (i.e., minimally, imprecise and improper) claim that it was necessary that "the human nature should act separately according to its peculiar character" and that the divinity was "silent" in those acts (*A Harmony of the Gospels: Matthew, Mark and Luke*, ed. David W. Torrance and Thomas F. Torrance, trans. A. W. Morrison, Calvin's New Testament Commentaries [Grand Rapids: Eerdmans, 1972], 3:98–9).

122. Williams, *Christ and Creation*, 33.

123. *Synopsis*, 2:85.

So the single theandric agent brings about distinct immediate effects through his distinct agencies which operate concurrently. There is no cloistering of actions or periods of time off to one agency or the other since both natures concurrently operate in every theandric action.

III. Objection! The Charge of Nestorianism

Having made a positive argument for the unity and distinction of classical and Reformed christological agency, it is worth engaging one of the most common charges of incoherence brought against the Reformed tradition: Nestorianism.[124] This error of dividing the person of Christ has been a favorite accusation hurled at the Reformed by their opponents for centuries and is the concern of many contemporary theologians as well.[125] This error may be the likeliest inconsistency (given its conciliar commitment) of Reformed Christology because of its close attention to distinctions; yet I contend that Nestorianism need not be the inevitable error of classical and Reformed Christology.[126] We might subdivide the charge of Nestorianism into two related, but distinct, objections of incoherence. The first objection is that the two agencies of Christ constitute two agents (§A), while the second grants that the theandric mediator is one agent then questions whether this introduces a fourth agent (in addition to the Father, Son, and Holy Spirit) into God's actions (§B).

A. Do Two Agencies Imply Two Agents?

The charge of Nestorianism against classical and Reformed Christology is potentially fatal to this project because it would mean that it fails to cohere with its conciliar criterion. In order to evaluate this accusation rightly, we must first define it. Nestorianism is frequently treated in terms of ontological descriptions of Christ (i.e., does the label "God" apply to Christ while in the womb of Mary such that she is called the *Theotokos* [God-bearer]?). Hereby any descriptions of an ontological predicate *grammatically* attributable to Christ will be considered under the question of "ontological Nestorianism."[127] However, this question

---

124. For a few historical examples, see Cross, *Communicatio Idiomatum*, 33–5.

125. For the "tendency toward Nestorianism in modern Christology," see White, *Incarnate Lord*, 113. For a zinger from Luther to Zwingli, see *LW*, 37:212–13.

126. Brian Daley says that Nestorianism is frequently associated with analytical thinking and precision regarding Christ and his actions (Daley, *God Visible*, 16, 179), which are largely considered as virtues in and Reformed Christology.

127. See the emphasis on subjects and verbs in Daley, *God Visible*, 192; George Kalantzis, "Is There Room for Two?: Cyril's Single Subjectivity and the Prosopic Union," *St Vladimir's Theological Quarterly* 52 (2008): 99; Weinandy, *Does God Suffer?*, 179 n. 11; Donald Davidson notes a similar pattern in philosophy ("Agency," 44). See the nuance between grammatical and ontological subjects, which I am extending to action here, in John Behr, *The Nicene Faith: True God of True God*, The Formation of Christian Theology 2 (Crestwood, NY: St. Vladimir's Press, 2004), 228.

requires an additional inquiry into "act Nestorianism." So if avoiding "ontological Nestorianism" requires a single subject of distinct predicates ("one and the same Christ" is "truly God and truly man"), then avoiding "act Nestorianism" requires a single agent of distinct actions. The charge of act Nestorianism may be seen in David Luy's critique of Zwingli, whereby the Reformer "eschews the unity of Christ and speaks as if divinity and humanity act as their own discrete subjects."[128] If the *Theotokos* formula of Chalcedon is the litmus test for ontological or grammatical Nestorianism, the *theopaschite* affirmation in Constantinople II ("One of the Trinity suffered in the flesh") is the litmus test for determining "act Nestorianism."[129] So, as Cyril of Alexandria says against Nestorius (in ontological terms), "All the sayings contained in the Gospels must be referred to a single person."[130]

Avoiding "act Nestorianism" not only is a necessity in order to cohere with the conciliar commitment of classical and Reformed Christology but is also necessary for classical and Reformed Christology to cohere with the authority of Scripture. So we must not only affirm the *theopaschite* formula, but also recognize that all the actions contained in the Gospels refer to a single agent. For instance, Christ is the one who can claim both to be "before Abraham" (Jn 8:58) and have grown up in Nazareth (Mt. 13:57) in the first century. Christ is the one who prays in the garden and is the one to whom Christians pray (Acts 7:56, 60; 1 Cor. 16:22; 2 Cor. 12:8, 9; Rev. 22:20).[131] Additionally, the one who says "the Father and I are one" (Jn 10:30) must be the same agent who claims that "the Father is greater than I" (Jhn 14:28).

I contend that classical and Reformed Christology has the resources to avoid the pitfall of act Nestorianism and to remain coherent with its conciliar and biblical commitment. Classical and Reformed Christology's response is a wholehearted embrace of the acts of Christ as accomplished by the single theandric agent. As Owen claims, "Whatever acts are ascribed unto him [Christ], however immediately performed, in or by the human nature, or in and by his divine nature, they are all the acts of that one person, in whom are both these natures."[132] Further, he says

---

128. Luy, *Dominus Mortis*, 125. Drake directly responds to this charge in Zwingli, seeking to acquit Zwingli of Nestorianism (*Flesh of the Word*, 71-4).

129. This follows Thomas Weinandy's insistence that the councils' fundamental commitment being expressed as the "one and the same 'who'" of Christ's incarnate acts ("The Doctrinal Significance of the Councils of Nicaea, Ephesus, and Chalcedon," in *The Oxford Handbook of Christology*, ed. Francesca Murphy [New York: Oxford University Press, 2015], 560).

130. Tanner, *Decrees*, 1:55-7.

131. For prayer as an act directed to Jesus in Owen, see WJO, *Christologia*, 1:112-13; *Vindiciæ Evangelicæ*, 12:246. I recognize that some of these prayers are to the "Lord." However, "Lord" refers to Jesus in several places in the New Testament (Capes, *Divine Christ*, 111-50), and each of the texts used here references Jesus (or the Son of man) explicitly in the surrounding context, making Jesus the likely referent.

132. WJO, *Vindication*, 2:415. For more on the "immediacy" qualifier, see Ch. 3 §II.B.2.

that "all the operations and works of Christ, as mediator, are theandrical."¹³³ So there is one executor of the completed action who works by means of two distinct agencies.¹³⁴

With a single theandric agent having two distinct agencies, classical and Reformed Christology can affirm that every action of Christ, regardless of its immediate principle, is an action of the theandric agent. Therefore, it can affirm with Constantinople II that "one of the Trinity suffered in the flesh." That is, the theandric agent was bruised and beaten in his nature that has the capacity to suffer. Taking a few additional examples: As stated above, in his one act of walking on water (Mt. 14:26), the theandric mediator defies the natural laws of gravity and buoyancy as the immediate effect of his divine agency and moves his feet in front of the other according to his human agency. It is not that his walking on the water is an act of one nature to the exclusion of the other.¹³⁵ Likewise, in eating the supper with his disciples (Matt 26:26–9), the one theandric agent performs the act of lifting up the bread and chewing it as an immediate effect of one capacity and declaring this supper to be an expansion of the Passover as the immediate effect of another.¹³⁶ While the distinct capacities of Christ may be the immediate principle of a particular effect, every action of Christ is an act of the one theandric mediator, the one agent.¹³⁷ Therefore, it is not that either nature or agency "accomplishes" actions, since it is the theandric agent who performs actions "by means of" both capacities.¹³⁸

---

133. WJO, *Vindication of the Preceding Discourse*, 2:329.

134. This mirrors Gregory of Nazianzus' formulation of Christ as two "whats" (ἄλλο καὶ ἄλλο) but not two "whos" (ἄλλος καὶ ἄλλος) (*On God and Christ*, 157). Owen references this distinction (without citation) in WJO, *Vindiciæ Evangelicæ*, 12:231.

135. Historically this is true because of the Aristotelian commitment to actions belong to subjects (see Aquinas ST I, Q. 39, A. 5, ad. 1; Oakes, *Infinity Dwindled to Infancy*, 140–8).

136. See Darrell L. Bock, "Jesus From the Earth Up: Thinking About Jesus' Humanity in the Canon," in *Who Do You Say I Am?: On the Humanity of Jesus*, ed. George Kalantzis, David Capes, and Ty Kieser (Eugene, OR: Cascade, 2020) on Jesus' divine prerogative in the institution of the Lord's supper.

137. As such, this position corresponds well with the adverbial modification of the single subject rather than nominalizing each nature as a subject, even if the emphasis on this account is elsewhere (see J. David Moser, "Tools for Interpreting Christ's Saving Mysteries in Scripture: Aquinas on Reduplicative Propositions in Christology," *SJT* 73 [2020]: 294).

138. Therefore, when the councils attribute actions to natures, I consider these "improper" way of predication or (relatedly) elliptical description. Similar to the way that Acts 20:28 improperly predicates "blood" of "God" (i.e., improper because the divine nature does not have blood), an action may improperly be predicated of a nature. It may also be an elliptical description. We can refer to an action as belonging to a part, but this is merely a re-description of the action. For example, we can say that the ball broke the glass (making the ball the subject of the action); however, this is an elliptical way of re-describing the action: "my son threw the

To illustrate the pastoral benefit and coherence of classical and Reformed Christology, we might ask: How did the theandric mediator endure temptation or stay faithful through suffering? Since these are categories and capacities (i.e., temptation and suffering) which belong to his human agency, to appeal to Christ's divine agency is a category mistake. It would be like asking how the iron of the fire-sword made it through the rain without being extinguished, since being extinguished is a category that pertains to the fire-ness of the fire-sword and therefore will be answered in fire-ness terms. Certainly, the iron-ness was involved in its journey through the rain, but the immediate capacity in question is the fire-ness. Therefore, we likewise can understand the God-man's temptations as real temptations according to his human capacity (since he is not able to be tempted according to his divine [Jas 1:13]) without attributing the action (i.e., whole event) to his human agency exclusively. Therefore, this act is not Nestorian, nor does it deny the conciliar affirmation of two principles of operation, since classical and Reformed Christology is not saying that the human nature itself overcame temptation but that the theandric mediator, by means of his human capacity empowered by the Holy Spirit, intentionally overcame temptation. Likewise, we are not saying that Christ's divine agency was absent, only that this particular immediate effect (i.e., overcoming temptation) belongs to his human agency. There are several effects that Christ may have been bringing about according to his divine agency in this act (e.g., infusing grace into the human nature to enable it to be the holy means by which he overcomes sin). Therefore, classical and Reformed Christology can affirm distinct immediate effects as the consequences of distinct agencies without falling into act-Nestorianism.

B. Four Agents of Divine Action?

Because of the above response, we can be confident that the agent who says, "I thirst" is the same as the one who declared, "Before Abraham was, I am."[139] Yet there is another Nestorian question looming here: Is the agent who says, "I am the first and the last" in Rev. 22:13 the same agent-in-relation to whom we appropriate the declaration "I am the first and I am the last" in Isa. 44:6 (see also

---

ball toward the house and caused the glass window to break." It is therefore more appropriate to say that "my son" is the agent and not "the ball." Likewise, when Chalcedon encourages the reader to "consider what nature it was that hung, pierced with nails, on the wood of the cross" (Tanner, *Decrees*, 81), it is an elliptical way of saying that the theandric mediator, according to his human nature, hung on the cross. I think that either of these ways of understanding the councils is preferable to Pawl's claim of a "robust predicate," whereby a nature can be said to be "doing something" (Pawl, *In Defense of Extended Conciliar Christology*, 28) because the improper and elliptical interpretations make the extraordinary (and incomplete) way of referring to Christ more obvious and explicit than "robust predicate."

139. Oakes says that a failure to preserve the unity of these two agents results in "Nestorian schizophrenia" (*Infinity Dwindled to Infancy*, 143).

Heb. 11:26; Jude 5)?[140] That is, it seems that the agent who speaks in Isaiah and saves the people of Israel (i.e., the divine Son) has properties and capacities that make him nonidentical to the agent who performs the action of laying down his head to sleep (i.e., the theandric mediator). However, if they are not identical, and if the theandric mediator is an agent, then it seems that classical and Reformed Christology has introduced a new agent into the Trinity (i.e., a fourth agent).[141] Bathrellos calls this "a huge and intractable problem, which must be confronted," and yet, he admits that "neither Maximus nor any of the other post-Chalcedonians succeeded in offering an absolutely satisfactory" account.[142]

Thus, in order to avoid this charge, this subsection will seek to (1) point to the ontological and operational foundation of the theandric mediator in classical and Reformed Christology, (2) present the significance of divine aseity and immutability for this conversation, and (3) define the contexts of the conversation clearly so that the term "agent" from the perspective of one context does not violate the predication of three agents from another perspective.

First, classical and Reformed Christology roots the ontology of the incarnation in the *an/enhypostatic* distinction.[143] And since operations mirror ontology, we can attribute ontological and operational priority to the divine identity and agency of Christ. Human agency in all people is dependent upon divine agency insofar as it is created by God and enabled by God. How much more so is Christ's human agency dependent upon and enabled by divine agency when Christ's humanity subsists in a divine person?[144] Building on an analogy from Katherin Rogers, we might note

---

140. This problem is similarly pertinent to our reading of Owen, especially since Spence argues that the "person of the incarnate Christ was not to be identified without qualification with the eternal Son" (*Incarnation and Inspiration*, 34, see also 100) but that they must be distinguished, a distinction he considers to be "essential to the gospel" [76]. Likewise, Spence denies that the Son is "the single subject" of Christ's actions (Spence, "Christ's Humanity and Ours," 96). So, while Owen does not explicitly address this question, it seems that the solution below, which is based on Owen's thought above, would be sufficient to get Owen out of the problem.

141. Tanner, *Decrees*, 1:116, 114. This is not merely a logical concern but also a pastoral one. If Christ and the Son are distinct agents, then it seems that (to riff off a Torrance phrase) there is not only a "God behind the back of Jesus" but also a "Son behind the back of Jesus" (Thomas F. Torrance, *Christian Doctrine of God, One Being Three Persons* [New York: T&T Clark, 2001], 243). A similar critique of "Antiochene Christology" is leveled by Robert Jenson, *Systematic Theology*, 1:126.

142. Bathrellos, *Byzantine Christ*, 46, 115.

143. It might be objected that Christ's theandric action fails to mirror the ontology of the *an/enhypostatic* union. However, recalling Owen's distinction between the "incarnation" (i.e., the act of the Son assuming an anhypostatic human nature) and the "hypostatic union" (the post-assumption state of affairs), we might say that the external perspective mirrors the more symmetrical hypostatic union and the internal perspective mirrors the more asymmetrical *an/enhypostatic* distinction.

144. Bathrellos, *Byzantine Christ*, 170.

that when my son is playing a hockey video game, the character that he is playing is an agent who is not identical to him (i.e., my son is not composed of digital pixels, nor is he skating in Canada like his video game character).[145] However, my son is fundamental to that character so that if that agent does something (e.g., score a goal), my son can rightly say, "I scored a goal." Likewise, the second divine agent-in-relation is determinative for the identity and action of the theandric agent. As Brian Leftow, reflecting a model-A conviction, says, "The Son is not identical with Jesus Christ. The Son is instead just part of Jesus Christ, the part which determines who Christ is."[146] Similarly, since the iron sword is fundamental to the fire-sword, the pre-fire sword can be identified as the same agent as the fire-sword even though they are not perfectly identical (i.e., one has the property "hot to the touch" while the other does not).

Second, we must note how divine immutability relates to Christ's actions. As stated in Chapters 2 and 3, the change that is brought about in the incarnation is on the side of the creature rather than God. Therefore, while this objection seems to raise a question about the relationship between the Logos before the incarnation and the Logos after the incarnation, there can be no "before" or "after" for an eternal God. Instead (under the condition of a fallen world), the Word is timelessly *incarnandus*, not that his flesh is eternal or that there is no *logos asarkos*, but that the Word did not *temporally* precede the plan to actualize the hypostatic union c. 4 BCE.[147] Therefore, the change in the incarnation is not a real change in the Son, but a change on the side of the creature and in the way that other creatures view that agent. Analogously, at one point in time, my (now) oldest daughter was an only child. When my second daughter was born, there was no essential change in my oldest because the youngest was the one who experienced the change. This change, however, implies a change in the names that we predicate of her, so we might start calling her "Sissy" or "big sis" and the capacities that she has (e.g., playing catch with her sister). Yet "Sissy" and the (previously) "only child" are the same agent, even if they do not have the exact same properties.

Finally, we must define the perspectives and contexts under consideration.[148] This point may be the most fundamental in discussions concerning this objection. For example, Bruce McCormack raises a version of this objection when he raises a concern about the compatibility of claims to theandric action and composite

---

145. Katherin A. Rogers, "The Incarnation as Action Composite," *F&P* 30 (2013): 251.

146. Leftow, *Timeless God Incarnate*, 290.

147. For an even stronger version than this in Shedd, see Crisp, *Revisioning Christology*, 76-7. This distinction is most prominent in discussion of Barth's treatment of the Logos and election. See George Hunsinger, "Election and the Trinity: Twenty-Five Theses on Theology of Karl Barth," in *Trinity and Election in Contemporary Theology*, ed. Michael T. Dempsey (Grand Rapids: Eerdmans, 2011), 96-7; George Hunsinger, *Reading Barth with Charity: A Hermeneutical Proposal* (Grand Rapids: Baker Academic, 2015), 51-60. See McFarland, *Word Made Flesh*, 85 for a helpful discussion on the Son, eternality, and time.

148. Zanchi makes a similar move to solve this problem (see Lindholm, *Jerome Zanchi*, 97).

consideration (which supports greater mutuality) and the an/enhypostatic character of the incarnation with the accompanying claims of instrumentality (which supports the prioritization of Christ's divinity and divine personhood). For McCormack these are mutually exclusive options and, he argues, that we should opt for the articulation of Christ as a theandric "composite." Further he suggests that the "post-Chalcedonian elaboration of the *anhypostasia* of the human 'nature' of Christ" led to (and continues to lead to) "the suppression of a feature of the New Testament witness to Jesus Christ that ought to have been obvious to all, viz. that Jesus was a human individual and, as such, a rational agent of spontaneously willed activity with his own 'act of being.'"[149]

Yet, McCormack's view of the incapability of these positions neglects the distinct perspectives that the tradition has regularly employed when addressing this question and his focus on "personhood" does not retain the benefits of the semi-open nature of agency language (see Ch. 6 §I.B). Therefore, rather than viewing it as an inconsistency in the tradition, classical and Reformed Christology exercises the distinct internal and external perspectives on this question. Without such a move, an insistence on defining triune agents as independent producers of distinct actions and maintaining the same context (and, thereby, definition of agent), it would seem possible that the theandric agent (as a producer of actions) would be considered a fourth member of this community.[150]

However, the triune God is not three causally independent agents. Instead, the triune God is three agents-in-relation from the perspective of an action's *terminus* (a distinct perspective from the one taken in our account of the theandric mediator as an agent). Therefore, when we ask "who walked on water?" the answer, when we take the external perspective, is "the theandric mediator." However, if we take the perspective of "causality," we could say "God." If we take the perspective of termination, we could ask, "Which divine person walked on water?" and answer, "The Son." Therefore, because of the various perspectives and the semi-openness of the concept of agency, when we name the theandric mediator with the three agents-in-relation, we no more name four agents than naming "Father, Son, Holy Spirit, Jesus, and God" names five agents.

So by means of the single theandric agent, classical and Reformed Christology avoids the charge that two agencies implies two agents. Likewise, through the *an/enhypostatic* distinction, the immutability of God, and the perspectives on divine action, classical and Reformed Christology avoids adding a fourth agent to the Trinity. As such, classical and Reformed christological agency coheres with its commitment to biblical authority and the affirmation of conciliar Christology. What is more, the evasion of act-Nestorianism evidences one of the pastoral benefits of classical and Reformed Christology: we can have confidence that "the Father himself loves" us and that we will "have peace" (Jn 16:27, 33) because

---

149. McCormack, *Humility of the Eternal Son*, 158–9; likewise, 118–20, 155, 157.

150. This claim may suggest a potential incoherence between social Trinitarianism and a Reformed view of the theandric mediator.

the Son who "came from the Father ... into the world" is the same agent as the theandric mediator who leaves the world and goes before the Father to intercede on our behalf (Jn 16:28).

IV. Pastoral and Theological Significance: Theandric Priestly Action

In order to further defend the theological prudence of the classical and Reformed presentation of Christ as a theandric mediator who executes singular action according to distinct agencies by which he simultaneously bring about distinct immediate effects, we turn to the locus in which Owen most accentuated Christ's theandric mediation: the priestly role of Jesus.

In his commentary on Heb. 9:14, Owen follows the "learned author" in stating that "in the discharge of his priestly office he acts as God and man in one person" so that "the person whose acts they are is God and man, and acts as God and man, in each nature suitably unto its essential properties."[151] Here we see both the singularity of the theandric agent and distinct agency of each nature. Apart from such an affirmation, Owen insists that we are not able to understand the claims that God purchased his church with his own blood (Acts 20:24) or that the Lord of glory was crucified (1 Cor. 2:8). He claims,

> The sum is, that the person of Christ is the principle of all his mediatory acts; although those acts be immediately performed in and by virtue of his distinct natures, some of one, some of another, according unto their distinct properties and powers. Hence are they all theandrical; which could not be if he were not a priest in both natures.[152]

The importance of the single theandric agent and the distinct agencies of Christ is seen clearly in Owen's account of the pinnacle of Christ's priestly activity, his sacrifice on the cross. Owen understands the biblical claim that "he sacrificed himself" (citing Eph. 5:2, Heb. 1:3, 9:14, 25, 26, 7:27) to mean that Christ (the theandric agent) sacrifices his human nature.[153] Owen says, "'He,' in the first place, as it is spoken of the sacrificer, denotes the person of Christ, and both natures

---

151. WJO, *Exposition of Hebrews*, 23:295; on Christ's priestly office in general, see *Vindiciæ Evangelicæ*, 12:408; see also *Exposition of Hebrews*, 2:469; Cleveland, "Covenant," 139. This role of Christ as the mediating priest has been called a "major focus" and "something of a preoccupation" of Owen's work (Tay, *Priesthood*, 48; Trueman, *Claims*, 187).

152. WJO, *Exposition of Hebrews*, 23:295; "Wherefore he was so far a mediator and priest in both his natures, as that whatever he did in the discharge of those offices was the act of his entire person; whereon the dignity and efficacy of all that he did depend" (*Exposition of Hebrews*, 23:296). Likewise, see Tylenda, "Calvin's Second Reply," 149.

153. On the significance of human agency and dyothelitism on the cross, see his work on Heb. 10:7 (WJO, *Vindiciæ Evangelicæ*, 12:431–2; *Exposition of Hebrews*, 23:468–74).

therein; 'himself,' as the sacrificed, is only the human nature of Christ, wherein and whereof that sacrifice was made. He makes the atonement actively, as the priest; himself passively, as the sacrifice."[154] Notice that the "sacrificer" is the "person" in "both natures." That is, the theandric agent sacrifices and the "wherein and whereof" of the human operation is the nature that possesses the proper capacity.

Owen is particularly attentive to the implications of this for the nature of salvation. He is specifically concerned that if the sacrifice (i.e., Christ's human nature) was finite, then its value must also be finite.[155] Owen's response evidences the importance of his christological foundation in the *an/enhypostatic* human nature and the unity of the theandric agent. He claims that the infinite value of Christ's sacrifice arose "from the dignity of his person, his deity giving sustentation unto his human nature in the sacrifice of himself."[156] Insistent on the theandric nature of every action, he articulates the divine operation of Christ's theandric act of sacrificing himself as "giving sustentation." Owen says, "Though the thing sacrificed was but finite, yet the person sacrificing was infinite, and the ἀποτέλεσμα of the action follows the agent, that is, our mediator, Θεάνθρωπος [theanthropos],—whence the sacrifice was of infinite value."[157] That is, the "agent" of the sacrifice is the theandric mediator and the significance of the event follow from his singular theandric act. Elsewhere, Owen says, "For by reason of the indissoluble union of both his natures, his person became the principle of all his mediatory acts, and from thence had they their dignity and efficacy."[158] As a contemporary example, we might say that the significance of the actions of the Queen of England is derived from the dignity of her person. Therefore, she might move her hand in a particular way across a piece of paper while holding a pen (i.e., sign her name) and that action would carry significant weight, even though the immediate principle (i.e., her hand) did not accomplish anything dignified in itself nor was her hand motion necessarily any different than anyone else's hand motion, but because of the dignity of her person and the context of the action the event was composed of several distinct immediate effects (e.g., putting ink to paper, ratifying a law, banning trophy hunting).

Bringing together the unity of the single agent and diversity of capacities, Owen places these words in the mouth of Jesus in order to bring hope to the church: "I will put myself into thy condition. I will undergo and bear that burden of guilt and punishment which would sink thee eternally into the bottom of hell. I will pay that which I never took; and be made *temporally* a curse for thee, that thou mayest attain unto *eternal* blessedness."[159]

---

154. WJO, *Vindiciæ Evangelicæ*, 12:431.
155. Bruce McCormack calls this the "problem of equivalency" ("With Loud Cries," 51).
156. WJO, *Pneumatologia*, 3:176.
157. WJO, *Vindiciæ Evangelicæ*, 12:431–2.
158. WJO, *Pneumatologia*, 3:176. Owen adamantly maintains the "indissolubility" of the hypostatic union (WJO, *Exposition of Hebrews*, 20:484–5; see Daniels, *Christology*, 303–6).
159. WJO, *Glory of Christ*, 1:341–2; cf., *Christologia*, 1:40.

V. Summary

This chapter has argued that the unity of the single agent lies in Christ's ontological and operational composition as the single theandric mediator. As such, classical and Reformed Christology rests upon the Reformed emphasis on Christ as the mediator in both natures. Such an understanding of composition finds precedents in both historic and modern orthodox Christologies. As the God-man, this one agent performs singular actions according to his distinct agencies by which he simultaneously produces distinct effects. The distinction in these immediate effects reflects the integrity of each nature, their capacities, and the distinct agencies therein. Because of the distinction in immediate effects, classical and Reformed Christology distinguishes itself from accounts which posit uniformity of operational effects and because of the simultaneity of operations, classical and Reformed Christology distinguishes itself from accounts which only posit parallel agency or an alternation of agency. Insofar as the unity of Christ's simultaneous operations are rooted in the theandric agent, the distinct agencies do not constitute distinct agents. Therefore, classical and Reformed christological agency is shown to be coherent with the biblical and conciliar prohibition against act-Nestorianism. Finally, the theological and pastoral significance of classical and Reformed Christology was illustrated through Owen's account of the priestly office of Christ. We might summarize this chapter by quoting Owen's commitment to Christ the priest and the "concurrent actings" of the two natures while upholding the singularity of the theandric agent: "wherever there is mention of Christ's offering himself, it relates principally to the person, God-man, who offered."[160]

---

160. Phrase from WJO, *Exposition of Hebrews*, 23:314; longer quote from *Vindiciæ Evangelicæ*, 12:431.

Chapter 7

CONCLUSION

The preceding work has judged classical and Reformed christological agency to be logically coherent and theologically prudent. It sought to defend its logical coherence by attending to the testimony of John Owen and then examining the *prima facie* liabilities of specific claims in the account. It sought to articulate its theological prudence in conversation with various other contemporary accounts of christological action.

I. Summary

The project began by raising awareness of the prominence of the agency word-group in contemporary accounts of christological operations, highlighting the accompanying need for clarity. This introduction established the criteria for classical and Reformed theology and profiled a key witness for the tradition, John Owen. Classical and Reformed Christology was characterized as a tradition that is committed to the ultimate authority of Scripture, the "ministerial" authority of the ecumenical councils, classical Trinitarianism, and Reformed christological emphases. With these commitments established, the introduction noted possible incongruities of classical and Reformed Christology when articulated in terms of agency. Specifically, it raised questions of trinitarian and christological action, noting contemporary positions that address such questions.

From this foundation, Chapters 2 and 3 provided the testimony of John Owen through a nuanced interpretation of his understanding of trinitarian and christological action. Both chapters reflected the structural influence of ontology upon the articulation of trinitarian and christological operations. Chapter 2 argued for understanding Owen within a classical trinitarian framework, articulating the essential unity and personal distinction of the triune God in classical ways. This framework affirmed the simplicity and pure act of the divine nature that included the unity of the divine attributes, understood by Owen in a christologically oriented mode. Because of this essential unity, God possesses one understanding, one will, and one power. Yet distinction exists in the personal relations of origin (begottenness and spiration). This ontological foundation of unity and distinction is mirrored by the operational unity and distinction of divine action. For Owen the singularity of the divine essence and attributes establishes a singularity of agency and operation. In every divine action toward creation, the triune God acts indivisibly so that God (from the perspective of causality) can be considered a single agent. Yet the distinct relations of the divine persons are also mirrored in the operations of the triune God through the divine missions and appropriated acts. From the perspective of the *terminus* of an action, classical and Reformed theology can understand the three persons as distinct agents-in-relation. In spite of Owen's occasional lack of technical imprecision, throughout this chapter the description of Owen's classical and Reformed trinitarian theology defended itself against interpretations of Owen that attribute strong trinitarian distinction (i.e., something like proto-social Trinitarianism) and others that accuse him of internal theological inconsistency.

Chapter 3 carried forward many of these same themes into its articulation of Owen's testimony regarding classical and Reformed christological ontology and operations: the trinitarian shape of Owen's Christology, his consistent adherence to conciliar and traditionally Reformed Christology (in spite of modern interpretations to the contrary), and his continued technical imprecision. Specifically, Chapter 3 presented Owen's understanding of the assumption of an *anhypostatic* human nature as a trinitarian act which terminates upon the Son. As a consequence of this hypostatic union, Owen follows the conciliar commitment to two sets of natural properties in Christ (including two wills) and the Reformed rejection of a humanized deity (i.e., kenoticism) and a divinized humanity (i.e., the ubiquity of Christ's human nature). Owen then follows through with these ontological commitments in the realm of christological operations. Central to his (and a classical and Reformed) account is the doctrine of christological mediation according to both natures. As such, Owen understands Christ as a single theandric agent who operates in two distinct agencies. This draws from the conciliar affirmation of distinct principles of operation and allows Owen to distinguish between immediate effects of either agency. Building on the previous chapter, this chapter drew attention to the trinitarian shape of Owen's Christology and argued that it remains consistent with the commitments of classical and Reformed Christology.

The final three chapters brought Owen's testimony regarding classical and Reformed Christology into conversation with adjacent contemporary accounts and conversations. Chapters 4 and 5 further specified the divine and human agencies of Christ (respectively). Within both, the importance of the perspective on an action is emphasized and the centrality of Scripture is upheld. Chapter 5 argues for the trinitarian and simple divine agency of Christ in classical and Reformed Christology. In contrast to some accounts of Spirit Christology, this chapter argued that the execution of Christ's acts as a single agent is able to be predicated properly of the Son. Yet this predication of Christ's acts to a single divine agent need not imply that God is three independent agents (as many accounts of social Trinitarianism suggest). Instead, from the perspective of causality, the triune God acts in his singular agency to produce indivisible actions. As such, classical and Reformed Christology is able to appreciate the role of the Holy Spirit in Christology, identifying the Spirit as both the *terminus* of the application of divine operations by Christ and the *terminus* of the application of divine operations upon Christ's humanity. This divine agency is also, necessarily, simple and in pure act. The Son does not "empty himself" of properties or scale back his capacities. Instead, he constantly operates according to his simple divine agency. Further, an exposition of Romans 5 supported these conclusions by showing that Christ's acts are filial and in necessary distinction from his human operations. As such, Christians have the confidence that the agent who gave up his life on the cross is none other than God the Son, manifesting the indivisible love of all three divine persons.

Chapter 5 articulated and defended the ordinary, distinct human agency of Christ. Specifically, it argued in contrast to those who suggest that Christ beheld the divine essence in his humanity and possessed maximal human knowledge while on earth. Instead, it was argued that Christ possessed finite knowledge and nescience of some things, allowing him to exercise faith by the power of the Holy Spirit. Yet Christ's ordinary, distinct human agency is also dependent upon his divine agency in a way that operationally mirrors the *an/enhypostatic* distinction. As such, the chapter introduced the internal perspective by which the humanity of Christ is considered an animate internal instrument of the divine Son. This ordinary and distinct human agency is then reflected in the various juxtapositions present in Hebrews 5. Accordingly, the theological and pastoral value of Christ's human agency includes the imitation of Christ and christological human obedience.

Chapter 6 specifically articulated the theandric unity of Christ the mediator as a single agent operating according to distinct agencies. It argued for the precedent of christological composition within historic and contemporary christological accounts. The chapter articulated the two agencies of the mediator as necessarily distinct, yet simultaneously executed by the single theandric agent. According to these conclusions classical and Reformed Christology demonstrated its ability to resolve the *prima facie* liability of two agencies: Nestorianism. Additionally, the prudence of a single theandric agent acting in two distinct agencies was illustrated through Owen's understanding of the priestly work of Christ.

This project has sought to display the logical coherence and theological prudence of classical and Reformed Christology in terms of agency. It was argued that this account of classical and Reformed Christology maintained its commitment to Scripture, the ecumenical councils, classical Trinitarianism, and the integrity of Christ's humanity. Materially, classical and Reformed Christology argues that Christ is predominantly viewed as a single theandric agent who acts according to his two agencies, by which he simultaneously brings about distinct immediate effects in his singular actions.

This conclusion was reached by drawing from the thought of John Owen as an exemplar of both classical and Reformed thinking. Additionally, it provided clarity in agency terminology and attended to the trinitarian and broader christological implications of specific predications of agency language. A core tenet of classical and Reformed christological agency is the affirmation of distinct perspectives on the basis of agency as a semi-open and context-dependent concept. According to these distinct perspectives, classical and Reformed Christology is able to appreciate the trinitarian unity of God's indivisible acts, the distinction between the divine persons as agents-in-relation in trinitarian activity, and the fundamental character of divine agency in christological operations.

II. Liabilities and Proximate Positions

With this verdict and these perspectives in place, it should be clear how classical and Reformed Christology avoids its *prima facie* liabilities and relates to other proximate positions. The trinitarian liabilities are accounted for through the unity of indivisible divine operations, proper action, and appropriations. The christological liabilities are accounted for through the singular theandric action and immediate effects of distinct agencies.

Regarding the trinitarian liabilities specifically, predicating the label "agent" of Christ need not imply that the triune God is three independent agents, as it superficially appeared. The circumvention of this conclusion is rooted in classical and Reformed theology's claim that all three agents-in-relation cause divine operations in Christ (not the Son alone). The second liability was the implication that ascribing the efficacy of divine action to the Spirit implies that the Spirit is the one on whom the execution of incarnate acts terminates. However, it was argued on the basis of indivisible operation, proper action, and appropriations that the Son is the one to whom we predicate the execution of christological acts and the Spirit is the one to whom we appropriate the perfection and application of those operations. Finally, the divine nature need not be emptied of its capacities, nor could it be, in order for Christ to operate humanly because of Christ's distinct and simple divine agency operating concurrently with his distinct, noncompetitive human agency.

Classical and Reformed Christology avoids these *prima facie* liabilities and is able to maintain internal coherence with each of its commitments. Additionally, classical and Reformed Christology's prudence is evidenced through its relation to the contemporary proximate positions. At multiple points classical and Reformed Christology intersects each of these contemporary positions, yet none fully encapsulate the account herein. In conversation with social Trinitarianism, it was argued that classical and Reformed theology adheres to the singularity of divine agency, causality, and operation, rather than three distinct agents of distinct actions. Yet, in continuity with social models of the Trinity, classical and Reformed theology is able to distinguish between divine persons on the basis of acts terminating properly on the Son, and appropriately upon the Father, Son, and Holy Spirit, given the personal mode of action of each divine person.

Likewise, by virtue of the above distinctions, classical and Reformed Christology does not predicate proper acts to the Holy Spirit or attribute the execution of the acts of Christ to the Spirit as some Spirit Christologies do. However, classical and Reformed Christology is able to appreciate the activity of the Holy Spirit as a distinct agent-in-relation while affirming the proper filial action of Christ.

As the final proximate position of theology proper, kenoticism can be both appreciated for its concern to maintain Jesus' genuine human operations and materially avoided because of its claim that Christ's divine agency is quantitatively lessened. Instead of accomplishing an articulation of genuine humanity through kenosis or krypsis, classical and Reformed christological agency accounts for Christ's human activity by the simultaneous yet distinct operations of divine and human agencies. These simultaneous yet distinct operations of Christ's two agencies are undivided by virtue of their singular execution and action by the singular theandric agent.

When in conversation with contemporary christological claim, classical and Reformed Christology is also seen to be coherent and prudent. So parallelism shares a view of simultaneous distinct agencies with classical and Reformed Christology. Yet, rather than merely appealing to *concursus*, sequestering complete actions off to either nature, or proposing alternative agency, classical and Reformed Christology views Christ's distinct agencies as those by which the singular theandric agent brings about distinct immediate effects in a single action.

While the preceding question reflects the external perspective on christological actions, from the internal perspective it might be suggested that classical and Reformed Christology is a version of strong instrumentality. Indeed, the two positions share an affirmation of the priority of divinity and the proper predication of the execution of christological actions to the Son. Unlike strong instrumentality, however, classical and Reformed Christology prioritizes another perspective, and even from the internal perspective, the classical and Reformed understanding does not adhere to the communication of the Son's power to the instrument (i.e., proportionality) that many proponents of strong instrumental accounts hold to.

Having clarified its avoidance of certain liabilities and its relation to certain proximate positions, we can identify topics for future research related to a classical and Reformed account of christological agency.

III. Future Research

Although the coherence and prudence of classical and Reformed christological agency have been demonstrated, plenty of work remains to be done within Reformed Christology. First, perhaps most obviously, agency must be related to other prominent classical christological categories. For example, while "power," "will," "nature," and "person" here have been employed and paralleled at points, classical and Reformed Christology would benefit from extended treatments on the relationship between agency and these other categories. Likewise, other (more modern) terms could benefit from increased clarity in relation to classical and Reformed Christology (e.g., the divine and/or human "I" of the Son/Christ, modern understandings of "consciousness," and the concept of "personality").[1]

---

1. This is not to suggest that such terms have received no clarifying attention (e.g., Rowan Williams, "Person and Personality in Christology," *Downside Review* 94 [1976]: 253–60), but that these could use additional extended treatments.

Within the category of agency there are, additionally, several lingering questions and areas of future research. There is likely fruitful work to be done on the question of how other contexts of divine and human agency connect to christological action. While classical and Reformed Christology strongly affirms the *sui generis* character of divine and human action in Christ, might there still be connections between christological action and divine and human agency in spheres such as sanctification and providence?[2]

Broader Reformed theology may also benefit from conversations with christological agency. This is particularly true for the Reformed emphasis on the integrity of Christ's human nature. So, there remain questions on the similarities and dissimilarities between Christ's experience of human agency and the Christian's. Likewise, the Reformed doctrine of monergism in regeneration seems uniquely positioned to be compared with, and mutually illuminated by, christological dyothelitism.

Additionally, an epistemological question lingers around classical and Reformed Christology's understanding of divine action: What criteria can be used to name distinct immediate effects of divine operations in Scripture, particularly operations that both natures are capable of (e.g., loving and knowing)? This question might lead to a close reading of several other biblical texts and may further add to the biblical foundation of classical and Reformed Christology.

Finally, several questions revolve around the human agency of Christ, particularly its relation to our own human agency. Perhaps the most interesting of these questions involves the definition and continuity of human agency (both Jesus' and the Christian's) in the eschaton. That is, does Jesus gain maximal human knowledge in the eschaton, and will we? What impact does the answer have on our conception of agency in that context?

IV. Closing Statement

This project has sought to bring greater clarity to the christological concept of agency and to classical and Reformed christological operations. It has articulated the logical coherence of the classical and Reformed commitments to Scripture, the conciliar Christology, classical Trinitarianism, and particular Reformed christological emphases. Further, it demonstrated the prudence of classical and Reformed christological agency through its capacity for theological contribution

---

2. Michael Horton, "'Let the Earth Bring Forth ... ': The Spirit and Human Agency in Sanctification," in *Sanctification: Explorations in Theology and Practice*, ed. Kelly M. Kapic (Downers Grove, IL: InterVarsity, 2014), 127–49; Ross Hastings, "Divine and Creational Agency in Asymmetric Compatibilism: A Barthian Option," in *Divine Action and Providence: Explorations in Constructive Dogmatics*, ed. Oliver D. Crisp and Fred Sanders, LATC (Grand Rapids: Zondervan Academic, 2019), 115–36; Kathryn Tanner, *Christ the Key* all represent attempts in this direction.

to the academy and pastoral benefit to the church. With Owen, I recognize that Christology's ultimate goal is not logical coherence or terminological precision. Instead, the final goal of an account of Christology is the presentation of the "Glory of Christ"—that we might behold him and thereby be made like him. As Owen says, "The great end of the description given of the person of Christ, is that we may love him, and thereby be transformed into his image."[3] So as we leave the topic of christological agency, I hope that we do so with more than mere conceptual clarity, but also with a transformative and sanctifying vision of the mediator who acts on our behalf and reveals the triune God to us.

---

3. WJO, *Christologia*, 1:27.

BIBLIOGRAPHY

Abraham, William J. *Divine Agency and Divine Action, Volume I: Exploring and Evaluating the Debate*. New York: Oxford University Press, 2018.

Abraham, William J. *Divine Agency and Divine Action, Volume II: Soundings in the Christian Tradition*. New York: Oxford University Press, 2018.

Adams, Marilyn McCord. *What Sort of Human Nature? Medieval Philosophy and the Systematics of Christology*. The Aquinas Lectures. Milwaukee: Marquette University Press, 1999.

Alfaro, Sammy. *Divino Compañero: Toward a Hispanic Pentecostal Christology*. Eugene: Wipf & Stock, 2010.

Allen, R. Michael. *The Christ's Faith: A Dogmatic Account*. T&T Clark Studies in Systematic Theology. New York: T&T Clark, 2009.

Allen, R. Michael. *Justification and the Gospel: Understanding the Contexts and Controversies*. Grand Rapids: Baker Academic, 2013.

Allen, R. Michael. *Reformed Theology*. Doing Theology. New York: T&T Clark, 2010.

Alston, William P. "Divine and Human Action." In *Divine and Human Action: Essays in the Metaphysics of Theism*, edited by Thomas Morris, 257–80. Ithaca: Cornell University Press, 1988.

Alvarez, Maria, and John Hyman. "Agents and Their Actions." *Philosophy* 73 (1998): 219–45.

Anatolios, Khaled. *Retrieving Nicaea: The Development and Meaning of Trinitarian Doctrine*. Grand Rapids: Baker Academic, 2011.

Anscombe, G. E. M. *Intention*. Cambridge: Harvard University Press, 1957.

Anselm of Canterbury. "Why God Became Man." In *The Major Works*, edited by Brian Davies and G. R. Evans, 260–356. OWC. New York: Oxford University Press, 1998.

Aquinas, Thomas. *Commentary on the Epistle to the Hebrews*. Translated by Chrysostom Baer. South Bend: St. Augustine's, 2006.

Aquinas, Thomas. *Commentary on the Gospel of John: Chapters 1–5*. Edited by Daniel Keating and Matthew Levering. Translated by Fabian R. Larcher and James A. Weisheipl. Thomas Aquinas in Translation. Washington, DC: Catholic University of America Press, 2010.

Aquinas, Thomas. *Commentary on the Gospel of John: Chapters 6–12*. Edited by Daniel Keating and Matthew Levering. Translated by Fabian R. Larcher and James A. Weisheipl. Thomas Aquinas in Translation. Washington, DC: Catholic University of America Press, 2010.

Aquinas, Thomas. *Compendium of Theology*. Translated by Richard J. Regan. New York: Oxford University Press, 2009.

Aquinas, Thomas. *De Unione Verbi Incarnati*. Edited by Roger W. Nutt. Dallas Medieval Texts and Translations 21. Bristol: Peeters, 2015.

Aquinas, Thomas. *Scriptum super Sententiis: Magistri Petri Lombardi*. Edited by Maria F. Moos and P. Mandonnet. 4 vols. Paris: Lethielleux, 1956.

Aquinas, Thomas. *The Summa contra Gentiles*. Translated by the English Dominican Fathers. 4 vols. London: Burns Oates, 1924–9.

Aquinas, Thomas. *Summa Theologiæ*. 61 vols. London: Blackfriars, 1963–81.
Arcadi, James M. *An Incarnational Model of the Eucharist*. CIT. New York: Cambridge University Press, 2018.
Asselt, Willem J. Van, and Eef Dekker. "Introduction." In *Reformation and Scholasticism: An Ecumenical Enterprise*, edited by Willem J. Van Asselt and Eef Dekker, 11–44. TSRPRT. Grand Rapids: Baker Academic, 2001.
Attridge, Harold W. *Hebrews: A Commentary on the Epistle to the Hebrews*. Philadelphia: Fortress, 1989.
Audi, Robert. "Intending." *Journal of Philosophy* 70 (1973): 387–403.
Augustine. *Answer to Faustus, A Manichean*. Edited by Roland Teske. The Works of Saint Augustine: A Translation for the 21st Century I/20. Brooklyn: New City, 2007.
Ayres, Lewis. *Augustine and the Trinity*. Cambridge: Cambridge University Press, 2010.
Ayres, Lewis. *Nicaea and Its Legacy: An Approach to Fourth-Century Trinitarian Theology*. New York: Oxford University Press, 2006.
Balthasar, Hans Urs von. *Cosmic Liturgy: The Universe According to Maximus the Confessor*. Translated by Brian E. Daley. San Francisco: Ignatius, 2003.
Balthasar, Hans Urs von. *Theo-Drama: Theological Dramatic Theory*. Translated by Graham Harrison. 5 vols. San Francisco: Ignatius, 1988–2003.
Bankston, Will. "The Responsiveness of Pure Actuality: Unmediated Agency, Linguistic Potentiality and the Divine Accommodation of Speech Acts." *IJST* 21 (2019): 290–313.
Barclay, John M. G., and Simon J. Gathercole, eds. *Divine and Human Agency in Paul and His Cultural Environment*. TTCBS. New York: T&T Clark, 2008.
Barnes, Corey Ladd. *Christ's Two Wills in Scholastic Thought: The Christology of Aquinas and Its Historical Contexts*. Toronto, CA: Pontifical Institute of Medieval Studies, 2012.
Barnes, Michel René. *The Power of God: Δύναμις in Gregory of Nyssa's Trinitarian Theology*. Washington, DC: Catholic University of America Press, 2001.
Barrett, Matthew, and Michael A. G. Haykin. *Owen on the Christian Life: Living for the Glory of God in Christ*. Wheaton: Crossway, 2015.
Bartel, Timothy W. "Like Us in All Things, Apart from Sin?" *Journal of Philosophical Research* 16 (1991): 19–52.
Barth, Karl. *Church Dogmatics*. Edited by G. W. Bromiley and T. F. Torrance. 4 vols. In 14 parts. Edinburgh: T&T Clark, 1956–75.
Barth, Karl. *Der Römerbrief—Zweite Fassung 1922*, vol. 47 *Karl Barth Gesamtausgabe, Abteilung II. Akademische Werke*, edited by Cornelis van der Kooi and Katja Tolstaja. Zürich: Theologischer Zürich, 2008.
Barth, Karl. *Die kirchliche Dogmatik*. 13 vols. Zürich: Theologischer, 1948–67.
Barth, Karl. *Karl Barth's Table Talk*. Edited by John D. Godsey. Richmond: John Knox, 1962.
Barth, Markus, and Helmut Blanke. *Colossians: A New Translation with Introduction and Commentary*. Translated by Astrid B. Beck. AB 34B. New York: Doubleday, 1994.
Bathrellos, Demetrios. *The Byzantine Christ: Person, Nature, and Will in the Christology of St. Maximus the Confessor*. OECS. New York: Oxford University Press, 2004.
Bauckham, Richard. "The Divinity of Jesus Christ in the Epistle to the Hebrews." In *The Epistle to the Hebrews and Christian Theology*, edited by Richard Bauckham, Daniel R. Driver, Trevor A. Hart, and Nathan MacDonald, 15–36. Grand Rapids: Eerdmans, 2009.
Bauckham, Richard. *God Crucified: Monotheism and Christology in the New Testament*. Grand Rapids: Eerdmans, 1999.
Bauckham, Richard. *Gospel of Glory: Major Themes in Johannine Theology*. Grand Rapids: Baker Academic, 2015.

Bauckham, Richard. *Jesus and the God of Israel: God Crucified and Other Studies on the New Testament's Christology of Divine Identity*. Grand Rapids: Eerdmans, 2008.

Bavinck, Herman. *Reformed Dogmatics*. Edited by John Bolt. Translated by John Vriend. 4 vols. Grand Rapids: Baker Academic, 2003–8.

Baxter, Anthony. "Chalcedon, and the Subject in Christ." *The Downside Review* 107 (1989): 1–21.

Baylor, T. Robert. "A Great King above All Gods: Dominion and Divine Government in the Theology of John Owen." PhD diss., University of St Andrews, 2016.

Baylor, T. Robert. "'He Humbled Himself': Trinity, Covenant, and the Gracious Condescension of the Son in John Owen." In *Trinity without Hierarchy: Reclaiming Nicene Orthodoxy in Evangelical Theology*, edited by Michael F. Bird and Scott Harrower, 165–93. Grand Rapids: Kregel Academic, 2019.

Bayne, Tim. "The Inclusion Model of the Incarnation: Problems and Prospects." *Religious Studies* 37 (2001): 125–41.

Beeke, Joel R., and Mark Jones. *A Puritan Theology: Doctrine for Life*. Grand Rapids: Reformation Heritage, 2012.

Beeley, Christopher A. *The Unity of Christ: Continuity and Conflict in Patristic Tradition*. New Haven, CT: Yale University Press, 2012.

Belt, Henk van den, Andreas J. Beck, William den Boer, and Riemer A. Faber, eds. *Synopsis Puioris Theologiae/Synopsis of a Purer Theology: Latin Text and English Translation Volume 2 Disputations 24–42*. Translated by Riemer A. Faber. SMRTTS 8. Boston: Brill, 2016.

Blaauw, Corné. "'An Holy and Beautiful Soul': Jonathan Edwards on the Humanity of Christ." *JES* 6 (2016): 16–30.

Blowers, Paul M. "Maximus the Confessor and John of Damascus on Gnomic Will (γνώμη) in Christ: Clarity and Ambiguity." *Union Seminary Quarterly Review* 63 (2012). 44–50.

Bock, Darrell L. "Jesus from the Earth Up: Thinking About Jesus' Humanity in the Canon." In *Who Do You Say I Am?: On the Humanity of Christ*, edited by George Kalantzis, David Capes, and Ty Kieser. Eugene: Cascade, 2020.

Boethius, "A Treatise against Eutyches and Nestorius." In *The Theological Tractates; The Consolation of Philosophy*, edited by H. F. Stewart, E. K. Rand, and S. J. Tester, 2–128. LCL 74. Cambridge, MA: Harvard University Press, 1973.

Bonhoeffer, Dietrich. *Berlin, 1932–1933*. Edited by Larry L. Rasmussen. Translated by Isabel Best and David Higgins. DBWE 12. Minneapolis: Fortress, 2009.

Brandenburger, Egon. "Text und Vorlagen von Hebr. V 7–10: Ein Beitrag zur Christologie des Hebräerbriefs." *Novum Testamentum* 11 (1969): 190–224.

Braun, Herbert. *An die Hebräer*. Handbuch zum Neuen Testament 14. Tübingen: Mohr Siebeck, 1984.

Brock, Rita Nakashima. *Journeys by Heart: A Christology of Erotic Power*. New York: Crossroad, 1988.

Brown, David. *Divine Humanity: Kenosis and the Construction of a Christian Theology*. Waco, TX: Baylor University Press, 2011.

Bruce, F. F. *Romans: An Introduction and Commentary*. Tyndale New Testament Commentaries. Downers Grove, IL: IVP Academic, 1985.

Bruce, F. F. *The Epistle to the Hebrews*. NICNT. Grand Rapids: Eerdmans, 1990.

Bryant, Herschel Odell. *Spirit Christology in the Christian Tradition: From the Patristic Period to the Rise of Pentecostalism in the Twentieth Century*. Cleveland, TN: CPT, 2015.

Burger, Hans. *Being in Christ: A Biblical and Systematic Investigation in a Reformed Perspective*. Eugene: Wipf & Stock, 2009.

Butner, D. Glenn. *The Son Who Learned Obedience: A Theological Case against the Eternal Submission of the Son*. Eugene: Pickwick, 2018.

Calvin, John. *The Epistle of Paul the Apostle to the Hebrews*. Edited by David W. Torrance and T. F. Torrance. Translated by William B. Johnston. Calvin's Commentaries. Grand Rapids: Eerdmans, 1963.

Calvin, John. *A Harmony of the Gospels: Matthew, Mark and Luke*. Edited by David W. Torrance and Thomas F. Torrance. Translated by A. W. Morrison. Calvin's New Testament Commentaries. Grand Rapids: Eerdmans, 1972.

Calvin, John. *Institutes of the Christian Religion*. Edited by John T. McNeil. Translated by Ford Lewis Battles. 2 vols. LCC. Louisville: Westminster John Knox Press, 1960.

Capes, David B. *The Divine Christ: Paul, the Lord Jesus, and the Scriptures of Israel*. Acadia Studies in Bible and Theology. Grand Rapids: Baker, 2018.

Carson, D. A. *Divine Sovereignty and Human Responsibility: Biblical Perspective in Tension*. Grand Rapids: Baker, 1994.

Carson, D. A. *The Gospel According to John*. PNTC. Grand Rapids: Eerdmans, 1991.

Chemnitz, Martin. *The Two Natures in Christ*. Translated by J. A. O. Preus. St. Louis: Concordia, 1971.

Chun, Young-Ho. "The Trinity in the Protestant Reformation: Continuity within Discontinuity." In *The Cambridge Companion to the Trinity*, edited by Peter C. Phan, 128–48. New York: Cambridge University Press, 2011.

Claunch, Kyle. "The Son and the Spirit: The Promise of Spirit Christology in Traditional Trinitarian and Christological Perspective." PhD diss., Southern Baptist Theological Seminary, 2017.

Clayton, Philip. *Adventures in the Spirit: God, World, Divine Action*. Minneapolis: Fortress, 2008.

Cleveland, Christopher. *Thomism in John Owen*. Burlington: Ashgate, 2013.

Cleveland, Kendall. "The Covenant of Redemption in the Trinitarian Theology of John Owen." PhD diss., University of St Andrews, 2016.

Coakley, Sarah. *Powers and Submissions: Spirituality, Philosophy and Gender*. Challenges in Contemporary Theology. Oxford: Blackwell, 2002.

Coakley, Sarah. "What Does Chalcedon Solve and What Does It Not? Some Reflections on the Status and Meaning of the Chalcedonian 'Definition.'" In *The Incarnation: An Interdisciplinary Symposium on the Incarnation of the Son of God*, edited by C. Stephen Davis, Daniel Kendall, and Gerald O'Collins, 143–63. New York: Oxford University Press, 2002.

Cockerill, Gareth Lee. "Melchizedek without Speculation: Hebrews 7:1-25 and Genesis 14:17–24." In *A Cloud of Witnesses: A Theology of Hebrews in Its Ancient Contexts*, edited by Richard Bauckham, Daniel Driver, Trevor Hart, and Nathan MacDonald, 128–44. LNTS 387. New York: T&T Clark, 2008.

Cockerill, Gareth Lee. *The Epistle to the Hebrews*. NICNT. Grand Rapids: Eerdmans, 2012.

Coffey, David. "The Theandric Nature of Christ." *Theological Studies* 60 (1999): 405–31.

Constantineanu, Corneliu. *The Social Significance of Reconciliation in Paul's Theology: Narrative Readings in Romans*. LNTS. New York: T&T Clark, 2010.

Cooper, John W. *Panentheism: The Other God of the Philosophers: From Plato to the Present*. Grand Rapids: Baker Academic, 2006.

Cooper, Tim. "The State of the Field: 'John Owen Unleashed: Almost.'" *Conversations in Religion and Theology* 6 (2008): 226–57.

Crawford, Matthew R. *Cyril of Alexandria's Trinitarian Theology of Scripture*. OECS. New York: Oxford University Press, 2014.

Crisp, Oliver D. "Compositional Christology without Nestorianism." In *The Metaphysics of the Incarnation*, edited by Anna Marmodoro and Jonathan Hill, 45–66. New York: Oxford University Press, 2011.

Crisp, Oliver D. *Divinity and Humanity: The Incarnation Reconsidered*. CIT. New York: Cambridge University Press, 2007.

Crisp, Oliver D. *God Incarnate: Explorations in Christology*. New York: T&T Clark, 2009.

Crisp, Oliver D. "Incarnation." In *The Oxford Handbook of Systematic Theology*, 160–75. New York: Oxford University Press, 2007.

Crisp, Oliver D. *Revisioning Christology: Theology in the Reformed Tradition*. Burlington: Routledge, 2011.

Crisp, Oliver D. *The Word Enfleshed: Exploring the Person and Work of Christ*. Grand Rapids: Baker Academic, 2016.

Crisp, Oliver D., and Kyle C. Strobel. *Jonathan Edwards: An Introduction to His Thought*. Grand Rapids: Eerdmans, 2018.

Cross, Richard. "Alloiosis in the Christology of Zwingli." *The Journal of Theological Studies* 47 (1996): 105–22.

Cross, Richard. *Communicatio Idiomatum: Reformation Christological Debates*. CPHST. New York: Oxford University Press, 2019.

Cross, Richard. "The Incarnation." In *The Oxford Handbook of Philosophical Theology*, edited by Thomas P. Flint and Michael C. Rae, 452–75. New York: Oxford University Press, 2011.

Cross, Richard. *The Metaphysics of the Incarnation: Thomas Aquinas to Duns Scotus*. New York: Oxford University Press, 2005.

Cyril of Alexandria. "Third Letter to Nestorius (Ep. 17)." In *Select Letters*, edited by Lionel R. Wickham, 12–33. OECT. New York: Clarendon, 1983.

Daley, Brian E. "'A Richer Union': Leontius of Byzantium and the Relationship of Human and Divine in Christ." *Studia Patristica* 24 (1993): 239–65.

Daley, Brian E. "Christ and Christologies." In *Oxford Handbook of Early Christian Studies*, edited by Susan Ashbrook Harvey and David G. Hunter, 886–905. New York: Oxford University Press, 2008.

Daley, Brian E. *God Visible: Patristic Christology Reconsidered*. CPHST. New York: Oxford University Press, 2018.

Daley, Brian E. "The Persons in God and the Person of Christ in Patristic Theology: An Argument for Parallel Development." In *The Mystery of the Holy Trinity in the Fathers of the Church the Proceedings of the Fourth Patristic Conference, Maynooth, 1999*, edited by D. Vincent Twomey and Lewis Ayres, 9–36. Portland: Four Courts, 2007.

Daley, Brian E. "The Word and His Flesh: Human Weakness and the Identity of Jesus in Patristic Christology." In *Seeking the Identity of Jesus: A Pilgrimage*, edited by Beverly Roberts Gaventa and Richard B. Hays, 251–69. Grand Rapids: Eerdmans, 2008.

Daniels, Richard. *The Christology of John Owen*. Grand Rapids: Reformation Heritage, 2004.

Davidson, Donald. "Actions, Reasons, and Causes (1963)." In *Essays on Actions and Events*, 3–20. New York: Oxford University Press, 2001.

Davidson, Donald. "Agency (1971)." In *Essays on Actions and Events*, 43–62. New York: Oxford University Press, 2001.

Davidson, Ivor J. "'Not My Will but Yours Be Done': The Ontological Dynamics of Incarnational Intention." *IJST* 7 (2005): 178–204.

Davidson, Ivor J. "Theologizing the Human Jesus: An Ancient (and Modern) Approach to Christology Reassessed." *IJST* 3 (2001): 129–53.

Davis, C. Stephen. "Metaphysics of Kenosis." In *The Metaphysics of the Incarnation*, edited by Anna Marmodoro and Jonathan Hill, 114–33. New York: Oxford University Press, 2011.

Davis, Stephen T. "Is Kenosis Orthodox?" In *Exploring Kenotic Christology: The Self-Emptying of God*, edited by C. Stephen Evans, 112–38. New York: Oxford University Press, 2006.

Davis, Stephen T. "Perichoretic Monotheism: A Defense of a Social Theory of the Trinity." In *Trinity: East/West Dialogue*, 35–52. Studies in Philosophy and Religion 24. Dordrecht: Kluwer Academic, 2003.

Davis, Stephen T., and C. Stephen Evans. "Conclusion: The Promise of Kenosis." In *Exploring Kenotic Christology: The Self-Emptying of God*, edited by C. Stephen Evans, 313–21. New York: Oxford University Press, 2006.

Del Colle, Ralph. *Christ and the Spirit: Spirit-Christology in Trinitarian Perspective*. New York: Oxford University Press, 1994.

Del Colle, Ralph. "Incarnation and the Holy Spirit." *Spirit and Church* 2 (2000): 199–229.

DeSilva, David A. *Perseverance in Gratitude: A Socio-rhetorical Commentary on the Epistle to the Hebrews*. Grand Rapids: Eerdmans, 2000.

DeWeese, Garrett J. "One Person, Two Natures: Two Metaphysical Models of the Incarnation." In *Jesus in Trinitarian Perspective*, edited by Fred Sanders and Klaus D. Issler, 114–53. Nashville: B&H Academic, 2007.

Dixon, Philip. *Nice and Hot Disputes: The Doctrine of the Trinity in the Seventeenth Century*. New York: T&T Clark, 2003.

Dorner, Isaac August. *History of the Development of the Doctrine of the Person of Christ*. 5 vols. Edinburgh: T&T Clark, 1897.

Duby, Steven J. *Divine Simplicity: A Dogmatic Account*. T&T Clark Studies in Systematic Theology. New York: T&T Clark, 2014.

Dunn, James D. G. *Christology in the Making: A New Testament Inquiry into the Origins of the Doctrine of the Incarnation*. Grand Rapids: Eerdmans, 1996.

Dunn, James D. G. "Rediscovering the Spirit (1)." In *The Christ and the Spirit Volume 2: Pneumatology*, 44–61. Grand Rapids: Eerdmans, 1998.

Dunn, James D. G. *Romans 1–8*. WBC 38A. Nashville: Thomas Nelson, 1988.

Edmondson, Stephen. *Calvin's Christology*. New York: Cambridge University Press, 2004.

Edwards, Jonathan. *A History of the Work of Redemption*. Edited by John Frederick Wilson. The Works of Jonathan Edwards, vol. 9. New Haven: Yale University Press, 1989.

Eglinton, James. *Bavinck: A Critical Biography*. Grand Rapids: Baker Academic, 2020.

Eisenbaum, Pamela Michelle. *Paul Was Not a Christian: The Original Message of a Misunderstood Apostle*. New York: Harper One, 2009.

Ellingworth, Paul. "'Like the Son of God': Form and Content in Hebrews 7:1–10." *Biblica* 64 (1983): 255–62.

Ellingworth, Paul. *The Epistle to the Hebrews*. NIGTC. Grand Rapids: Eerdmans, 1993.

Ellis, Brannon. *Calvin, Classical Trinitarianism, and the Aseity of the Son*. New York: Oxford University Press, 2012.

Emery, Gilles. "Le Christ médiateur: L'unicité et l'universalité de la médiation salvifique du Christ Jésus suivant Thomas d'Aquin." In *Christus, Gottes schöpferisches Wort: Festschrift für Christoph Kardinal Schönborn*, edited by George Augustin, Maria Brun, Erwin Keller, and Markus Schulze, 337–55. Freiburg: Herder, 2010.

Emery, Gilles. "The Personal Mode of Trinitarian Action in Saint Thomas Aquinas." *The Thomist* 69 (2005): 31–77.
Emery, Gilles. *The Trinitarian Theology of Saint Thomas Aquinas*. New York: Oxford University Press, 2010.
Entwistle, F. R. "John Owen's Doctrine of Christ." In *Puritan Papers: Volume 2, 1960–1962*, edited by J. I. Packer. Phillipsburg, NJ: P&R, 2001.
Eschner, Christina. "'Die Hingabe des einzigen Sohnes "für" uns alle': Zur Wiederaufnahme des Steben-'für'-Motivs aus Röm 5,6–8 in Röm 8,32." In *Letter to the Romans*, edited by Udo Schnelle, 659–78. BETL 226. Leuven: Peeters, 2009.
Eschner, Christina. *Gestorben und hingegeben "für" die Sünder: die griechische Konzeption des Unheil abwendenden Sterbens und deren paulinische Aufnahme für die Deutung des Todes Jesu Christi*. WMANT 122. Neukirchen-Vluyn: Neukirchener, 2010.
Evans, C. Stephen. "Kenotic Christology and the Nature of God." In *Exploring Kenotic Christology: The Self-Emptying of God*, edited by C. Stephen Evans, 190–217. New York: Oxford University Press, 2006.
Fairbairn, Donald. *Grace and Christology in the Early Church*. OECS. New York: Oxford University Press, 2006.
Farrer, Austin. *Scripture, Metaphysics, and Poetry: Austin Farrer's the Glass of Vision, with Critical Commentary*. Edited by Robert MacSwain. Ashgate Studies in Theology, Imagination and the Arts. Burlington: Ashgate, 2013.
Farrer, Austin. "Very God and Very Man." In *Interpretation and Belief*, edited by Charles C. Conti, 126–37. London: SPCK, 1976.
Fee, Gordon D. *Pauline Christology: An Exegetical-Theological Study*. Peabody: Hendrickson, 2007.
Ferguson, Sinclair B. "John Owen and the Doctrine of the Person of Christ." In *John Owen: The Man and His Theology*, edited by Robert W. Oliver. Phillipsburg: P&R, 2002.
Ferguson, Sinclair B. *John Owen on the Christian Life*. Carlisle: Banner of Truth, 1987.
Feser, Edward. *Scholastic Metaphysics: A Contemporary Introduction*. Heusenstamm: Editions Scholasticae, 2014.
Fesko, J. V. *The Covenant of Redemption: Origins, Development, and Reception*. RHT 35. Göttingen: Vandenhoeck & Ruprecht, 2015.
Fesko, J. V. "The Doctrine of Scripture in Reformed Orthodoxy." In *A Companion to Reformed Orthodoxy*, edited by Herman J. Selderhuis, 249–64. BCCT 40. Boston: Brill, 2013.
Flint, Thomas P. "Should Concretists Part with Mereological Models of the Incarnation." In *The Metaphysics of the Incarnation*, edited by Anna Marmodoro and Jonathan Hill, 67–87. New York: Oxford University Press, 2011.
Forsyth, P. T. *The Cruciality of the Cross*. Eugene: Wipf and Stock, 1997.
Forsyth, P. T. *The Person and Place of Jesus Christ*. London: Hodder and Stoughton, 1909.
Fowl, Stephen E. "Scripture." In *The Oxford Handbook of Systematic Theology*, edited by John Webster, Kathryn Tanner, and Iain Torrance, 345–61. New York: Oxford University Press, 2007.
Freddoso, Alfred J. "Human Nature, Potency and the Incarnation." *F&P* 3 (1986): 27–53.
Frei, Hans W. *The Identity of Jesus Christ: The Hermeneutical Bases of Dogmatic Theology*. Expanded and updated. Eugene: Cascade, 2013.
Gathercole, Simon J. *Defending Substitution: An Essay on Atonement in Paul*. Acadia Studies in Bible and Theology. Grand Rapids: Baker Academic, 2015.
Gathercole, Simon J. "The Trinity in the Synoptic Gospels and Acts." In *The Oxford Handbook of the Trinity*, edited by Gilles Emery and Matthew Levering, 55–68. New York: Oxford University Press, 2011.

Giles, Kevin. *Jesus and the Father: Modern Evangelicals Reinvent the Doctrine of the Trinity*. Grand Rapids: Zondervan, 2006.

Goetz, Ronald. "The Suffering God: The Rise of a New Orthodoxy." *Christian Century* 103 (1986): 385–9.

Goldman, Alvin I. *Theory of Human Action*. Englewood Cliffs, NJ: Prentice-Hall, 1970.

Gondreau, Paul. *The Passions of Christ's Soul in the Theology of St. Thomas Aquinas*. Beiträge zur Geschichte der Philosophie und Theologie des Mittelalter. Münster: Aschendorff, 2002.

Goodwin, Thomas. *Christ Our Mediator*. Layfayette, IN: Sovereign Grace, 2001.

Goodwin, Thomas. *The Work of the Holy Ghost in Our Salvation*. Works of Thomas Goodwin 6. Edinburgh: Banner of Truth, 1979.

Gordon, James R. *The Holy One in Our Midst: An Essay on the Flesh of Christ*. Minneapolis: Fortress, 2016.

Gorman, Michael J. *The Death of the Messiah and the Birth of the New Covenant: A (Not So) New Model of the Atonement*. Eugene: Cascade, 2014.

Green, Christopher C. *Doxological Theology: Karl Barth on Divine Providence, Evil, and the Angels*. T&T Clark Studies in Systematic Theology. New York: T&T Clark, 2011.

Greer, Rowan A. "The Jesus of Hebrews and the Christ of Chalcedon." In *Reading the Epistle to the Hebrews: A Resource for Students*, edited by Eric F. Mason and Kevin B. McCruden, 231–49. SBL Resources for Biblical Studies 66. Atlanta: Society of Biblical Literature, 2011.

Gregory Of Nyssa, "An Answer to Ablabius: That We Should Not Think of Saying There Are Three Gods." In *Christology of the Later Fathers*, edited and translated by Cyril C. Richardson, 256–68. LCC. Louisville: Westminster John Knox, 1954.

Gregory Of Nyssa, "To Theolphilus." In *Anti-Apollinarian Writings*, translated by Robin Orton, 259–70. Fathers of the Church: A New Translation 131. Washington, DC: Catholic University of America Press, 2015.

Gribben, Crawford. *John Owen and English Puritanism: Experiences of Defeat*. OSHT. New York: Oxford University Press, 2016.

Grieb, A Katherine. "'Time Would Fail Me to Tell … ': The Identity of Jesus Christ in Hebrews." In *Seeking the Identity of Jesus: A Pilgrimage*, 200–14. Grand Rapids: Eerdmans, 2008.

Grillmeier, Aloys. *Christ in the Christian Tradition: From the Apostolic Age to Chalcedon (451)*. Translated by John Bowden. Vol. 1. Louisville: John Knox, 1975.

Grillmeier, Aloys. *Christ in the Christian Tradition: From the Council of Chalcedon (451) to Gregory the Great (590–604)*. Translated by John Cawte and Pauline Allen. 2 vols. Louisville: Westminster John Knox.

Grillmeier, Aloys, and Theresia Hainthaler. *Christ in Christian Tradition, Volume 2 Part 2: The Church of Constantinople in the Sixth Century*. Translated by Pauline Allen and John Cawte. Philadelphia: Westminster John Knox, 1995.

Grudem, Wayne A. "Biblical Evidence for the Eternal Submission of the Son to the Father." In *The New Evangelical Subordinationism? Perspectives on the Equality of God the Father and God the Son*, edited by Dennis W. Jowers and H. Wayne House, 223–61. Eugene: Pickwick, 2012.

Grudem, Wayne A. *Systematic Theology: An Introduction to Biblical Doctrine*. 2nd ed. Grand Rapids: Zondervan, 2020.

Gunton, Colin. *Father, Son and Holy Spirit: Toward a Fully Trinitarian Theology*. New York: T&T Clark, 2003.

Gunton, Colin. "Forward." In *In the Likeness of Sinful Flesh: An Essay on the Humanity of Christ*. Scholars' Editions in Theology. New York: T&T Clark, 2006.

Gunton, Colin. *Theology through the Theologians: Selected Essays 1972–1995*. New York: T&T Clark, 2003.

Gunton, Colin. "Two Dogmas Revisited: Edward Irving's Christology." *JST* 41 (1988): 359–76.

Habets, Myk. *The Anointed Son: A Trinitarian Spirit Christology*. Eugene: Wipf & Stock, 2010.

Habets, Myk. "Spirit Christology: The Future of Christology." In *Third Article Theology: A Pneumatological Dogmatics*, edited by Myk Habets, 207–32. Minneapolis: Fortress, 2016.

Haga, Joar. *Was There a Lutheran Metaphysics? The Interpretation of Communicatio Idiomatum in Early Modern Lutheranism*. Refo500. Göttingen: Vandenhoeck & Ruprecht, 2012.

Hagner, Donald A. "Son of God as Unique High Priest: The Christology of the Epistle to the Hebrews." In *Contours of Christology in the New Testament*, edited by Richard N. Longenecker, 247–67. Grand Rapids: Eerdmans, 2005.

Hanson, R. P. C. *The Search for the Christian Doctrine of God: The Arian Controversy, 318–381*. Grand Rapids: Baker Academic, 2006.

Harnack, Adolf von. *History of Dogma*. Translated by Neil Buchanan. 7 vols. Boston: Little, Brown, 1895–1900.

Harris, Murray J. *Jesus as God: The New Testament Use of Theos in Reference to Jesus*. Grand Rapids: Baker Academic, 1992.

Harris, Murray J. *Second Epistle to the Corinthians*. NIGTC. Grand Rapids: Eerdmans, 2005.

Hart, David Bentley. *The Experience of God: Being, Consciousness, Bliss*. New Haven, CT: Yale University Press, 2013.

Hastings, Ross. "Divine and Creational Agency in Asymmetric Compatibilism: A Barthian Option." In *Divine Action and Providence: Explorations in Constructive Dogmatics*, edited by Oliver D. Crisp and Fred Sanders, 115–36. LATC. Grand Rapids: Zondervan Academic, 2019.

Hastings, Ross. "'Honouring the Spirit': Analysis and Evaluation of Jonathan Edwards' Pneumatological Doctrine of the Incarnation." *IJST* 7 (2005): 279–99.

Hauerwas, Stanley M. *Disrupting Time: Sermons, Prayers, and Sundries*. Eugene: Wipf & Stock, 2004.

Hawthorne, Gerald F. *The Presence and the Power: The Significance of the Holy Spirit in the Life and Ministry of Jesus*. Dallas: Word, 2003.

Hector, Kevin W. "Barth and Theological Method." In *Blackwell Companion to Karl Barth*, edited by George Hunsinger and Keith L. Johnson, 1: 83–108. 2 vols. New York: Blackwell, 2020.

Hector, Kevin W. *The Theological Project of Modernism: Faith and the Conditions of Mineness*. OSAT. New York: Oxford University Press, 2015.

Helm, Paul. *Calvin: A Guide for the Perplexed*. New York: T&T Clark, 2008.

Heppe, Heinrich. *Reformed Dogmatics*. Edited by Ernst Bizer. Translated by G. T. Thomson. Eugene, OR: Wipf & Stock, 2007.

Hill, Jonathan. "Introduction." In *The Metaphysics of the Incarnation*, edited by Anna Marmodoro and Hill, Jonathan, 1–19. New York: Oxford University Press, 2011.

Hill, Wesley. *Paul and the Trinity: Persons, Relations, and the Pauline Letters*. Grand Rapids: Eerdmans, 2015.

Hodge, Charles. *Systematic Theology*. 3 vols. Grand Rapids: Eerdmans, 1981.

Hofer, Andrew. "Dionysian Elements in Thomas Aquinas's Christology: A Case of the Authority and Ambiguity of Pseudo-Dionysius." *The Thomist* 72 (2008): 409–42.

Holmes, Christopher R. J. *Ethics in the Presence of Christ*. New York: T&T Clark, 2012.

Holmes, Christopher R. J. *The Holy Spirit*. NSD. Grand Rapids: Zondervan, 2015.

Holmes, Stephen R. "Classical Trinitarianism and Eternal Functional Subordination: Some Historical and Dogmatic Reflections." *SBET* 35 (2017): 90–104.

Holmes, Stephen R. *The Quest for the Trinity: The Doctrine of God in Scripture, History and Modernity*. Downers Grove, IL: IVP Academic, 2012.

Holmes, Stephen R. "Reformed Varieties of the Communicatio Idiomatum." In *The Person of Christ*, edited by Stephen R. Holmes and Murray A. Rae, 70–86. New York: T&T Clark, 2005.

Holmes, Stephen R. "'Something Much Too Plain to Say': Towards a Defence of the Doctrine of Divine Simplicity." *NZSTR* 43 (2001): 137–54.

Hornsby, Jennifer. "Agency and Action." In *Agency and Action*, edited by John Hyman and Helen Steward, 1–24. Royal Institute of Philosophy Supplement 55. New York: Cambridge University Press, 2004.

Horton, Michael. "'Let the Earth Bring Forth …': The Spirit and Human Agency in Sanctification." In *Sanctification: Explorations in Theology and Practice*, edited by Kelly M. Kapic, 127–49. Downers Grove, IL: InterVarsity, 2014.

Horton, Michael. *Lord and Servant: A Covenant Christology*. Louisville: Westminster John Knox, 2005.

Horton, Michael. *Rediscovering the Holy Spirit: God's Perfecting Presence in Creation, Redemption, and Everyday Life*. Grand Rapids: Zondervan, 2017.

Hovorun, Cyril. *Will, Action and Freedom: Christological Controversies in the Seventh Century*. Medieval Mediterranean 77. Boston: Brill, 2008.

Hunsinger, Deborah van Deusen. "The Master Key: Unlocking the Relationship of Theology and Psychology." *Inspire* 5 (2001): 20–2.

Hunsinger, George. *The Eucharist and Ecumenism: Let Us Keep the Feast*. Current Issues in Theology. New York: Cambridge University Press, 2008.

Hunsinger, George. *How to Read Karl Barth: The Shape of His Theology*. New York: Oxford University Press, 1991.

Hunsinger, George. "Justification and Mystical Union with Christ: Where Does Owen Stand?" In *The Ashgate Research Companion to John Owen's Theology*, 199–214. Burlington: Ashgate, 2012.

Hurtado, Larry W. *One God, One Lord: Early Christian Devotion and Ancient Jewish Monotheism*. Philadelphia: Fortress, 1988.

Hyman, John, and Helen Steward, eds. *Agency and Action*. Royal Institute of Philosophy Supplement 55. New York: Cambridge University Press, 2004.

Jamieson, R. B. *The Paradox of Sonship: Christology in the Epistle to the Hebrews*. Studies in Christian Doctrine and Scripture. Downers Grove, IL: IVP Academic, 2021.

Jedwab, Joseph. "The Incarnation and Unity of Consciousness." In *The Metaphysics of the Incarnation*, edited by Anna Marmodoro and Jonathan Hill, 168–85. New York: Oxford University Press.

Jenkins, Skip. *A Spirit Christology*. Ecumenical Studies. New York: Peter Lang, 2018.

Jenson, Robert W. "How Does Jesus Make a Difference." In *Essentials of Christian Theology*, edited by William C. Placher, 191–205. Louisville: Westminster John Knox, 2003.

Jenson, Robert W. *Systematic Theology: Volume 1: The Triune God*. New York: Oxford University Press, 2001.

Jenson, Robert W. *The Triune Identity: God according to the Gospel*. Philadelphia: Fortress Press, 1982.

Jenson, Robert W. "Triune Grace." In *The Gift of Grace: The Future of Lutheran Theology*, edited by Niels Henrik Gregersen, Bo Holm, Ted Peters, and Peter Widmann, 17–30. Minneapolis: Fortress, 2005.

Jenson, Robert W. "You Wonder where the Spirit Went." *Pro Ecclesia* 2 (1993): 296–304.

John of Damascus, "Orthodox Faith." In *Saint John of Damascus: Writings*, translated by Frederic H. Chase Jr, 165–406. The Fathers of the Church: A New Translation 37. Washington DC: Catholic University of America Press, 1958.

Johnson, Elizabeth A. *Consider Jesus: Waves of Renewal in Christology*. New York: Crossroad, 1990.

Johnson, Keith E. "The Work of the Holy Spirit in the Ministry of Jesus Christ: A Trinitarian Perspective." *TJ* 38 (2017): 147–67.

Johnson, Luke Timothy. *Hebrews: A Commentary*. Louisville: Westminster John Knox, 2006.

Johnson, Luke Timothy. "Romans 3:21–6 and the Faith of Jesus." In *Contested Issues in Christian Origins and the New Testament: Collected Essays*, 241–54. NovTSup 146. Boston: Brill, 2013.

Jones, Mark. *Why Heaven Kissed Earth: The Christology of the Puritan Reformed Orthodox Theologian, Thomas Goodwin (1600–1680)*. Reformed Historical Theology 13. Göttingen: Vandenhoeck & Ruprecht, 2010.

Jones, Paul Dafydd. *The Humanity of Christ: Christology in Karl Barth's Church Dogmatics*. New York: T&T Clark, 2008.

Junius, Franciscus. *A Treatise on True Theology with the Life of Franciscus Junius*. Translated by David C. Noe. Grand Rapids: Reformation Heritage, 2014.

Kalantzis, George. "Is There Room for Two?: Cyril's Single Subjectivity and the Prosopic Union." *St Vladimir's Theological Quarterly* 52 (2008): 95–110.

Kapic, Kelly, M. "The Spirit as Gift: Explorations in John Owen's Pneumatology." In *The Ashgate Research Companion to John Owen's Theology*, edited by Kelly Kapic and Mark Jones, 113–40. Burlington: Ashgate, 2012.

Kapic, Kelly, M. *Communion with God: The Divine and the Human in the Theology of John Owen*. Grand Rapids: Baker Academic, 2007.

Kapitan, Tomis. "The Incompatibility of Omniscience and Intentional Action: A Reply to David P. Hunt." *Religious Studies* 30 (1994): 55–66.

Kärkkäinen, Veli-Matti. *Holy Spirit and Salvation: Sources of Christian Theology*. Louisville: Westminster John Knox Press, 2010.

Kärkkäinen, Veli-Matti. "The Spirit of Life: Moltmann's Pneumatology." In *Jürgen Moltmann and Evangelical Theology: A Critical Engagement*, edited by Sung Wook Chung, 126–51. Eugene: Pickwick, 2012.

Käsemann, Ernst. *Commentary on Romans*. Grand Rapids: Eerdmans, 1980.

Kay, Brian K. *Trinitarian Spirituality: John Owen and the Doctrine of God in Western Devotion*. Studies in Christian History and Thought. Eugene: Wipf & Stock, 2008.

Keating, Daniel. "Thomas Aquinas and the Epistle to the Hebrews: 'The Excellence of Christ.'" In *Christology, Hermeneutics, and Hebrews: Profiles from the History of Interpretation*, edited by Jon C. Laansma and Daniel J. Treier, 84–99. LNTS 423. New York: T&T Clark, 2012.

Keith, Chris. *Jesus' Literacy: Scribal Culture and the Teacher from Galilee*. LNTS 413. New York: T&T Clark, 2011.

Kelly, J. N. D. *Early Christian Doctrines*. Rev. ed. New York: HarperCollins, 1978.

Kelsey, David H. "Human Being." In *Christian Theology: An Introduction to Its Traditions and Tasks*, 141–67. Philadelphia: Fortress, 1982.
Kieser, Ty. "The Holy Spirit and the Humanity of Christ in John Owen: A Re-Examination." *IJST* 25 (2023): 93–113.
Kieser, Ty. "Is the Filioque an Obstacle to a Pneumatologically Robust Christology? A Response from Reformed Resources." *JRT* 12 (2018): 394–412.
Kieser, Ty. "John Owen as Proto-Social Trinitarian? Reinterpreting Owen and Resisting a Recent Trend." *SJT* 74:3 (2021): 222–34.
Kirk, J. R. Daniel. *A Man Attested by God: The Human Jesus of the Synoptic Gospels*. Grand Rapids: Eerdmans, 2016.
Kistemaker, Simon. *Exposition of the Second Epistle to the Corinthians*. NTC. Grand Rapids: Baker, 1997.
Knox, John. *The Humanity and Divinity of Christ: A Study of Pattern in Christology*. New York: Cambridge University Press, 1967.
Koester, Craig R. *Hebrews*. New York: Yale University Press, 2001.
Kolb, Robert, and Timothy J. Wengert, eds. "Formula of Concord (1577)". *The Book of Concord: The Confessions of the Evangelical Lutheran Church*, translated by Charles P. Arand, Eric Gritsch, Robert Kolb, William Russell, Ames Schaaf, Jane Strohl, and Timothy J. Wengert, 481–660. Minneapolis: Fortress, 2000.
Kooi, Cornelis Van Der. "On the Identity of Jesus Christ: Spirit Christology and Logos Christology in Converse." In *Third Article Theology: A Pneumatological Dogmatics*, edited by Myk Habets, 193–206. Minneapolis: Fortress, 2016.
Kreitzer, Larry Joseph. *Jesus and God in Paul's Eschatology*. BACBS 19. New York: Bloomsbury Academic, 2015.
Krimmer, Heiko. *Römerbrief*. Bibel-Kommentar 10. Neuhausen-Stuttgart: Hänssler, 1983.
Kušnieriková, Michaela. *Acting for Others: Trinitarian Communion and Christological Agency*. Emerging Scholars. Minneapolis: Fortress, 2017.
LaCugna, Catherine Mowry. *God for Us: The Trinity and Christian Life*. New York: Harper, 1991.
Lane, William L. *Hebrews 1–8*. WBC 47a. Dallas: Thomas Nelson, 1991.
Laub, Franz. *Bekenntnis und Auslegung: Die paränetische Funktion der Christologie im Hebräerbrief*. Biblische Untersuchungen 15. Regensburg: F. Pustet, 1980.
Law, David R. "Le kénotisme luthérien et anglican: les christologies de Gottfried Thomasius et Frank Weston." *Études théologiques et religieuses* 89 (2014): 313–40.
Leftow, Brian. "Tempting God." *F&P* 31 (2014): 3–23.
Leftow, Brian. "A Timeless God Incarnate." In *The Incarnation: An Interdisciplinary Symposium on the Incarnation of the Son of God*, edited by Stephen T. Davis, Daniel Kendall, and Gerald O'Collins, 273–302. New York: Oxford University Press, 2002.
Legge O. P., Dominic. *The Trinitarian Christology of St Thomas Aquinas*. New York: Oxford University Press, 2017.
Lescow, Theodor. "Jesus in Gethsemane bei Lukas und im Hebräerbrief." *Zeitschrift für die neutestamentliche Wissenschaft* 58 (1967): 215–39.
Letham, Robert. *The Holy Trinity: In Scripture, History, Theology, and Worship*. Phillipsburg: P&R, 2004.
Letham, Robert. "John Owen's Doctrine of the Trinity in Its Catholic Context." In *The Ashgate Research Companion to John Owen's Theology*, edited by Kelly Kapic and Mark Jones, 185–98. Burlington: Ashgate, 2012.
Letham, Robert. "The Trinity between East and West." *JRT* 3 (2009): 42–56.

Lightfoot, Neil R. "The Saving of the Savior: Hebrews 5:7ff." *Restoration Quarterly* 16 (1973): 166–73.

Lim, Paul C. H. *Mystery Unveiled: The Crisis of the Trinity in Early Modern England*. OSHT. New York: Oxford University Press, 2012.

Lindholm, Stefan. *Jerome Zanchi (1516–90) and the Analysis of Reformed Scholastic Christology*. RHT 37. Göttingen: Vandenhoeck & Ruprecht, 2016.

Liston, G. "A Chalcedonian Spirit Christology." *Irish Theological Quarterly* 81 (2016): 74–93.

Lloyd, R. Glynne. "The Life and Work of the Reverend John Owen D.D. the Puritan Divine, with Special Reference to the Socinian Controversies of the Seventeenth Century." PhD diss., The University of Edinburgh, 1942.

Loader, William R. G. *Sohn und Hoherpriester: Eine traditionsgeschichtliche Untersuchung zur Christologie des Hebräerbriefes*. Neukirchen-Vluyn: Neukirchener, 1981.

Loke, Andrew Ter Ern. *A Kryptic Model of the Incarnation*. ANCTRTBSS. Burlington: Ashgate, 2014.

Loke, Andrew Ter Ern. "On the Use of Psychological Models in Christology." *Heythrop Journal* 58 (2017): 44–50.

Lonergan, Bernard J. F. *The Incarnate Word*. Edited by Robert M. Doran and Jeremy D. Wilkins. Translated by Charles C. Hefling. Collected Works of Bernard Lonergan, 8 vols. Toronto: University of Toronto Press, 2016.

Long, D. Stephen. *The Perfectly Simple Triune God: Aquinas and His Legacy*. Minneapolis: Fortress, 2016.

Longenecker, Richard N. *Studies in Hermeneutics, Christology and Discipleship*, NTM 3. Sheffield: Sheffield Phoenix, 2006.

Louth, Andrew. *St. John Damascene: Tradition and Originality in Byzantine Theology*. OECS. New York: Oxford University Press, 2002.

Lowe, E. J. *Personal Agency: The Metaphysics of Mind and Action*. New York: Oxford University Press, 2008.

Luy, David J. *Dominus Mortis: Martin Luther on the Incorruptibility of God in Christ*. Minneapolis: Fortress, 2014.

Lynch, O.P., Reginald. *The Cleansing of the Heart: The Sacraments as Instrumental Causes in the Thomistic Tradition*. Thomistic Ressourcement. Washington, DC: Catholic University of America Press, 2017.

Madden, Nicholas. "Composite Hypostasis in Maximus Confessor." *Studia Patristica* 27 (1993): 175–97.

Maillard, Pierre-Yves. *La vision de Dieu chez Thomas d'Aquin: une lecture de l'In Ioannem à la lumière de ses sources augustiniennes*. Bibliothèque Thomiste 53. Paris: Vrin, 2001.

Marmodoro, Anna. "The Metaphysics of the Extended Mind in Ontological Entanglements." In *The Metaphysics of the Incarnation*, edited by Anna Marmodoro and Jonathan Hill, 205–27. Oxford: Oxford University Press, 2011.

Marshall, Bruce D. "Christ and the Cultures: The Jewish People and Christian Theology." In *The Cambridge Companion to Christian Doctrine*, edited by Colin E. Gunton, 81–100. New York: Cambridge University Press, 1997.

Marshall, Bruce D. "Ex Occidente Lux? Aquinas and Eastern Orthodox Theology." *Modern Theology* 20 (2004): 23–50.

Marshall, Bruce D. *Trinity and Truth*. Cambridge: Cambridge University Press, 2010.

Marshall, Bruce D. "The Unity of the Triune God: Reviving an Ancient Question." *The Thomist* 74 (2010): 1–32.

Marshall, I. Howard. "The Meaning of 'Reconciliation.'" In *Unity and Diversity in New Testament Theology: Essays in Honor of George E. Ladd*, 117–32. Grand Rapids: Eerdmans, 1978.

Martin, Ralph P. *Reconciliation: A Study of Paul's Theology*. Atlanta: John Knox, 1981.

Maston, Jason. *Divine and Human Agency in Second Temple Judaism and Paul: A Comparative Study*. WUNT 2/297. Tübingen: Mohr Siebeck, 2010.

Mastrict, Peter van. *Theoretico-Practica Theologia*. 2 vols. Utrecht: W. van de Water, 1724.

McCall, Thomas H. "Relational Trinity: Creedal Perspective." In *Two Views on the Doctrine of the Trinity*, edited by Jason S. Sexton, 113–37. CBT. Grand Rapids: Zondervan Academic, 2014.

McCall, Thomas H. "Son Though He Was, He Learned Obedience: The Submission of Christ in Theological Perspective (in Dialogue with Thomas Aquinas and Karl Barth)." In *Listen, Understand, Obey: Essays on Hebrews in Honor of Gareth Lee Cockerill*, edited by Caleb Friedeman, 131–53. Eugene: Pickwick, 2017.

McCall, Thomas H. *Which Trinity? Whose Monotheism? Philosophical and Systematic Theologians on the Metaphysics of Trinitarian Theology*. Grand Rapids: Eerdmans, 2010.

McClendon, James William. *Doctrine: Systematic Theology Vol. 2*. Nashville: Abingdon, 1986.

McCormack, Bruce L. "Karl Barth's Christology as a Resource for a Reformed Version of Kenoticism." *IJST* 8 (2006): 243–51.

McCormack, Bruce L. "The Actuality of God: Karl Barth in Conversation with Open Theism." In *Engaging the Doctrine of God: Contemporary Protestant Perspectives*. Grand Rapids: Baker Academic, 2008.

McCormack, Bruce L. "'With Loud Cries and Tears': The Humanity of the Son in the Epistle to the Hebrews." In *The Epistle to the Hebrews and Christian Theology*, edited by Richard Bauckham, Daniel Driver, Trevor Hart, and Nathan MacDonald, 37–68. Grand Rapids: Eerdmans, 2009.

McCruden, Kevin B. "The Concept of Perfection in the Epistle to the Hebrews." In *Reading the Epistle to the Hebrews: A Resource for Students*, edited by Eric F. Mason and Kevin B. McCruden, 209–29. SBL Resources for Biblical Studies 66. Atlanta: Society of Biblical Literature, 2011.

McDonald, Suzanne. *Re-imaging Election: Divine Election as Representing God to Others and Others to God*. Grand Rapids: Eerdmans, 2010.

McFarland, Ian A. "Spirit and Incarnation: Toward a Pneumatic Chalcedonianism." *IJST* 16 (2014): 143–58.

McFarland, Ian A. *The Word Made Flesh: A Theology of the Incarnation*. Louisville: Westminster John Knox, 2019.

McFarland, Ian A. "'Willing Is Not Choosing': Some Anthropological Implications of Dyothelite Christology." *IJST* 9 (2007): 3–23.

McGrath, Alister E. *Christian Theology: An Introduction*. 5th ed. Malden: Wiley-Blackwell, 2011.

McGrath, James F. *The Only True God Early Christian Monotheism in Its Jewish Context*. Urbana: University of Illinois Press, 2009.

McGraw, Ryan M. *A Heavenly Directory: Trinitarian Piety, Public Worship and a Reassessment of John Owen's Theology*. Göttingen: Vandenhoeck & Ruprecht, 2014.

McGraw, Ryan M. *John Owen: Trajectories in Reformed Orthodox Theology*. New York: Palgrave Macmillan, 2017.

McGraw, Ryan M. "Seeing Things Owen's Way: John Owen's Trinitarian Theology and Piety in Its Early-Modern Context." In *John Owen between Orthodoxy and Modernity*,

edited by Willem van Vlastuin and Kelly M. Kapic, 189–204. BCCT 39. Boston: Brill, 2019.
McGuckin, John Anthony. *Saint Cyril of Alexandria and the Christological Controversy.* Crestwood: St. Vladimir's Seminary, 2010.
McMaken, W. Travis. "Definitive, Defective or Deft?: Reassessing Barth's Doctrine of Baptism in Church Dogmatics IV/4." *IJST* 17 (2015): 89–114.
Mele, Alfred R. "Intention." In *Blackwell Companion to Philosophy of Action*, edited by Timothy O'Connor and Constantine Sandis, 108–13. Malden: Blackwell, 2010.
Meyendorff, John. *Christ in Eastern Christian Thought.* Crestwood: St. Vladimir's Seminary, 1987.
Meyendorff, John. "New Life in Christ: Salvation in Orthodox Theology." *Theological Studies* 50 (1989): 481–99.
Michaels, J. Ramsey. *The Gospel of John.* NICNT. Grand Rapids: Eerdmans, 2010.
Moffitt, David M. *Atonement and the Logic of Resurrection in the Epistle to the Hebrews.* Supplements to Novum Testamentum 141. Boston: Brill, 2013.
Moffitt, David M. "'If Another Priest Arises': Jesus' Resurrection and the High Priestly Christology of Hebrews." In *The Letter to the Hebrews: Critical Readings*, edited by. Scott D. Mackie, 124–35. T&T Clark Critical Readings in Biblical Studies. New York: T&T Clark, 2018.
Moltmann, Jürgen. *The Crucified God: The Cross of Christ as the Foundation and Criticism of Christian Theology.* Translated by R. A. Wilson and John Bowden. Minneapolis: Fortress, 1993.
Moltmann, Jürgen. *The Spirit of Life: A Universal Affirmation.* Translated by Margaret Kohl. Minneapolis: Fortress, 1992.
Moltmann, Jürgen. *The Trinity and the Kingdom: The Doctrine of God.* Translated by Margaret Kohl. Minneapolis: Fortress, 1993.
Moltmann, Jürgen. *The Way of Jesus Christ: Christology in Messianic Dimensions.* Translated by Margaret Kohl. Minneapolis: Fortress, 1995.
Moo, Douglas. *The Letter to the Romans.* 2nd ed. NICNT. Grand Rapids: Eerdmans, 2018.
Morris, Leon. *The Epistle to the Romans.* PNTC. Grand Rapids: Eerdmans, 1988.
Morris, Leon. *The Gospel According to John.* NICNT. Grand Rapids: Eerdmans, 1971.
Morris, Thomas. *The Logic of God Incarnate.* Ithaca: Cornell University Press, 1986.
Mortimer, Sarah. *Reason and Religion in the English Revolution: The Challenge of Socinianism.* New York: Cambridge University Press, 2014.
Muller, Richard A. "A Note on 'Christocentrism' and the Imprudent Use of Such Terminology." *WTJ* 68 (2006): 253–60.
Muller, Richard A. *Divine Will and Human Choice: Freedom, Contingency, and Necessity in Early Modern Reformed Thought.* Grand Rapids: Baker Academic, 2017.
Muller, Richard A. *Post-Reformation Reformed Dogmatics: The Rise and Development of Reformed Orthodoxy.* 4 vols. Grand Rapids: Baker Academic, 2003.
Muller, Richard A. "Sources of Reformed Orthodoxy: The Symmetrical Unity of Exegesis and Synthesis." In *A Confessing Theology for Postmodern Times*, edited by Michael S. Horton, 43–62. Wheaton, IL: Crossway, 2000.
Nazianzus, St. Gregory of. *On God and Christ: The Five Theological Orations and Two Letters to Cledonius.* Translated by Lionel Wickham. PPS 23. Crestwood: St. Vladimir's Seminary, 2002.
Need, Stephen W. *Truly Divine and Truly Human: The Story of Christ and the Seven Ecumenical Councils.* Peabody: Hendrickson, 2008.

Nestorius. "Nestorius's First Sermon against the Theotokos." In *The Christological Controversy*, translated by Richard A. Norris, 123–34. Sources of Early Christian Thought. Philadelphia: Fortress, 1980.

Nimmo, Paul T. "Karl Barth and the concursus Dei—A Chalcedonianism Too Far?" *IJST* 9 (2007): 58–72.

Norris, Richard A., ed. *The Christological Controversy*. Sources of Early Christian Thought. Minneapolis: Fortress, 1980.

Oakes S. J., Edward T. *Infinity Dwindled to Infancy: A Catholic and Evangelical Christology*. Grand Rapids: Eerdmans, 2011.

Oberman, Heiko. "Extra Dimension in the Theology of Calvin." *The Journal of Ecclesiastical History* 21 (1970): 43–64.

O'Brien, Peter T. *The Letter to the Hebrews*. PNTC. Grand Rapids: Eerdmans, 2010.

O'Connor, Timothy. *Persons and Causes: The Metaphysics of Free Will*. New York: Oxford University Press, 2000.

O'Connor, Timothy. "Reasons and Causes." In *A Companion to the Philosophy of Action*, edited by Timothy O'Connor and Constantine Sandis, 129–38. Malden: Blackwell, 2010.

Ortlund, Gavin. "Divine Simplicity in Historical Perspective: Resourcing a Contemporary Discussion." *IJST* 16 (2014): 436–53.

Owen, John. *Biblical Theology: The History of Theology from Adam to Christ*. Translated by Stephen Westcott. Grand Rapids: Reformation Heritage, 1994.

Owen, John. *The Works of John Owen*. Edited by William H. Gould. 24 vols. Edinburgh: Johnston & Hunter, 1850–5.

Owen, Paul. "Jesus as God's Chief Agent in Mark's Christology." In *Mark, Manuscripts, and Monotheism: Essays in Honor of Larry W. Hurtado*, edited by Chris Keith and Dieter Roth, 40–57. LNTS 528. New York: T&T Clark, 2015.

Packer, J. I. "Forward." In *From Heaven He Came and Sought Her: Definite Atonement in Historical, Biblical, Theological, and Pastoral Perspective*, edited by David Gibson and Jonathan Gibson, 13–16. Wheaton, IL: Crossway, 2013.

Pannenberg, Wolfhart. *Jesus: God and Man*. Translated by Lewis L. Wilkins and Duane A. Priebe. Philadelphia: Westminster, 1968.

Pannenberg, Wolfhart. *Systematic Theology*. Translated by Geoffrey W. Bromiley. 3 vols. Grand Rapids: Eerdmans, 1991–1998.

Patterson, Patrick D. M. "By Thine Agony and Bloody Sweat: A Dogmatic Description of the Double Agencies of Christ-A Modest Proposal." PhD diss., University of Toronto, 2013.

Pawl, Timothy. *In Defense of Conciliar Christology: A Philosophical Essay*. OSAT. New York: Oxford University Press, 2016.

Pawl, Timothy. *In Defense of Extended Conciliar Christology: A Philosophical Essay*. OSAT. New York: Oxford University Press, 2019.

Peeler, Amy L. B. "With Tears and Joy: The Emotions of Christ in Hebrews." *Koinonia* 20 (2008): 12–26.

Pelikan, Jaroslav. *The Christian Tradition: A History of the Development of Doctrine, Vol. 1: The Emergence of the Catholic Tradition (100–600)*. Chicago: University of Chicago Press, 1971.

Peppiatt, Lucy. "Life in the Spirit: Christ's and Ours." In *The Christian Doctrine of Humanity: Explorations in Constructive Dogmatics*, edited by Oliver Crisp and Fred Sanders, 165–81. LATC. Grand Rapids: Zondervan, 2018.

Peterson, David. *Hebrews and Perfection: An Examination of the Concept of Perfection in the Epistle to the Hebrews*. SNTSMS 47. New York: Cambridge University Press, 2005.
Peterson, Erik. *Der Brief an die Römer*. Ausgewählte Schriften 6. Würzburg: Echter, 1997.
Pieper, Franz. *Christian Dogmatics*. 4 vols. St. Louis: Concordia, 1950-7.
Plantinga, Alvin. *The Nature of Necessity*. New York: Oxford University Press, 1974.
Plantinga Jr., Cornelius. "Social Trinity and Tritheism." In *Trinity, Incarnation, & Atonement: Philosophical & Theological Essays*, edited by Ronald J. Feenstra and Cornelius, Plantinga Jr., 21-47. Notre Dame: University of Notre Dame Press, 1989.
Porter, Stanley E. *Καταλλάσσω in Ancient Greek Literature, with Reference to the Pauline Writings*. Estudios de filología Neotestamentaria 5. Cordoba: Ediciones El Almendro, 1994.
Pseudo-Dionysius Areopagita. *Corpus Dionysiacum II*. Edited by Günther Heil and Adolf Martin Ritter. Patristische Texte und Studien, Band 36. New York: De Gruyter, 1991.
Radde-Gallwitz, Andrew. "The Holy Spirit as Agent, Not Activity: Origen's Argument with Modalism and Its Afterlife in Didymus, Eunomius, and Gregory of Nazianzus." *Vigiliae Christianae* 65 (2011): 227-48.
Rahner, Karl. "Chalkedon—Ende oder Anfang." In *Das Konzil von Chalkedon: Geschichte und Gegenwart*, edited by Aloys Grillmeier and Heinrich Bacht. 3 vols. Würzburg: Echter Verlang, 1954.
Rahner, Karl. "Current Problems in Christology." In *Theological Investigations Volume I: God, Christ, Mary and Grace*, translated by Cornelius Ernst, 149-200. New York: Crossroad, 1982.
Rahner, Karl. *Foundations of Christian Faith: An Introduction to the Idea of Christianity*. Translated by William V. Dych. New York: Seabury, 1978.
Rahner, Karl. "Theos in the New Testament." In *Theological Investigations Vol. 1: God, Christ, Mary and Grace*, translated by Cornelius Ernst, 79-148. Baltimore: Helicon, 1961.
Rahner, Karl. *The Trinity*. Translated by Joseph Donceel. Milestones in Catholic Theology. New York: Crossroad, 1997.
Rees, Thomas, trans. *The Racovian Catechism*. Lexington: American Theological Library Association, 1962.
Rehnman, Sebastian. *Divine Discourse: The Theological Methodology of John Owen*. Texts and Studies in Reformation and Post-Reformation Thought. Grand Rapids: Baker Academic, 2002.
Reid, Thomas. "93. To James Gregory." In *The Correspondence of Thomas Reid*, edited by Paul Wood. EETR 4. Edinburgh: Edinburgh University Press, 2002.
Reid, Thomas. *Essays on the Active Powers of Man*. Edited by Knud Haakonssen and James A. Harris. EETR 7. University Park: Penn State University Press, 2010.
Richardson, Christopher. "The Passion: Reconsidering Hebrews 5:7-8." In *The Letter to the Hebrews: Critical Readings*, edited by Scott D. Mackie, 108-23. T&T Clark Critical Readings in Biblical Studies. New York: T&T Clark, 2018.
Richardson, Neil. *Paul's Language about God*. Journal for the Study of the New Testament Supplement Series 99. Sheffield: Sheffield Academic, 1994.
Riches, Aaron. *Ecce Homo: On the Divine Unity of Christ*. Interventions. Grand Rapids: Eerdmans, 2016.
Riggenbach, Eduard. *Der Brief an die Hebräer*. Kommentar zum Neuen Testament 14. Leipzig: A. Deichert, 1913.
Rippee, Ryan. "John Owen on the Work of God the Father." *PRJ* 8 (2016): 86-103.

Rissi, Mathias. "Die Menschlichkeit Jesu nach Hebr. 5, 7-8." *Theologische Zeitschrift* 11 (1955): 28-45.
Rissi, Mathias. *Die Theologie des Hebräerbriefs: Ihre Verankerung in der Situation des Verfassers und seiner Leser*. WUNT 41. Tübingen: Mohr Siebeck, 1987.
Rogers, Katherin A. "The Incarnation as Action Composite." *F&P* 30 (2013): 251-70.
Rowe, Christopher Kavin. "Biblical Pressure and Trinitarian Hermeneutics." *Pro Ecclesia* 11 (2002): 295-312.
Ruben, David-Hillel. "Cambridge Actions." In *A Companion to the Philosophy of Action*, edited by Timothy O'Connor and Constantine Sandis, 82-9. Malden: Blackwell, 2010.
Russell, Norman. *The Doctrine of Deification in the Greek Patristic Tradition*. New York: Oxford University Press, 2006.
Sanchez M., Leopoldo A. *Receiver, Bearer, and Giver of God's Spirit: Jesus' Life in the Spirit as a Lens for Theology and Life*. Eugene: Pickwick, 2015.
Schleiermacher, Friedrich. *Christian Faith: A New Translation and Critical Edition*. Edited by Catherine L. Kelsey and Terrence N. Tice. Translated by Terrence N. Tice, Catherine L. Kelsey, and Edwina Lawler. 2 vols. Louisville: Westminster John Knox, 2016.
Schnabel, Eckhard J. *Der Brief des Paulus an die Römer: Kapitel 1-5*. HTANT. Witten: SCM Brockhaus, 2015.
Schreiner, Thomas R. *Romans*. BECNT. Grand Rapids: Baker Academic, 1998.
Schweitzer, Don. *Contemporary Christologies: A Fortress Introduction*. Minneapolis: Fortress, 2010.
Schwöbel, Christoph. *God: Action and Revelation*. Studies in Philosophical Theology. Kampen: Kok Pharos, 1992.
Schwöbel, Christoph. "Reformed Traditions." In *The Cambridge Companion to the Summa Theologiae*, edited by Philip McCosker and Denys Turner, 319-42. New York: Cambridge University Press, 2016.
Seifrid, Mark A. *The Second Letter to the Corinthians*. PNTC. Grand Rapids: Eerdmans, 2014.
Seiller, Léon. *L'activité humaine du Christ selon Duns Scot*. Études de Science religieuse 3. Paris: Éditions Franciscaines, 1944.
Senor, Thomas. "Drawing on Many Traditions: An Ecumenical Kenotic Christology." In *The Metaphysics of the Incarnation*, edited by Anna Marmodoro and Jonathan Hill. New York: Oxford University Press, 2011.
Shedd, William G. T. *Dogmatic Theology*. 3 vols. New York: Charles Scribner's Sons, 1888-1894.
Small, Brian. *The Characterization of Jesus in the Book of Hebrews*. Biblical Interpretation Series 128. Boston: Brill, 2014.
Sonderegger, Katherine. *Systematic Theology: The Doctrine of God, Volume 1*. Minneapolis: Fortress, 2015.
Sonderegger, Katherine. "The Sinlessness of Christ." In *Theological Theology: Essays in Honour of John Webster*, edited by David R. Nelson and Justin Stratis, 267-75. London: T&T Clark, 2015.
Spence, Alan. "Christ's Humanity and Ours: John Owen." In *Persons, Divine and Human: Kings College Essays in Theological Anthropology*, edited by Christoph Schwöbel and Colin Gunton, 74-97. Edinburgh: T&T Clark, 1991.
Spence, Alan. *Incarnation and Inspiration: John Owen and the Coherence of Christology*. New York: T&T Clark, 2007.
Spence, Alan. "John Owen and Trinitarian Agency." *SJT* 43 (1990): 157-73.

Sprinkle, Preston M. *Paul and Judaism Revisited: A Study of Divine and Human Agency in Salvation*. Downers Grove, IL: IVP Academic, 2013.

Sprinkle, Preston M., and Stephen Westerholm. *Paul and Judaism Revisited: A Study of Divine and Human Agency in Salvation*. Downers Grove, IL: IVP Academic, 2013.

St. Maximus the Confessor. *On the Cosmic Mystery of Jesus Christ*. Translated by Paul M. Blowers and Robert Louis Wilken. Popular Patristics Series 25. Crestwood: St. Vladimir's Seminary, 2003.

Stackhouse Jr., John G. "Jesus Christ." In *The Oxford Handbook of Evangelical Theology*, edited by Gerald R. Mcdermott, 146–57. New York: Oxford University Press, 2010.

Stang, Charles M. "The Two 'I's of Christ: Revisiting the Christological Controversy." *Anglican Theological Review* 94 (2012): 529–47.

Starke, John. "Augustine and His Interpreters." In *One God in Three Persons: Unity of Essence, Distinction of Persons, Implications for Life*, edited by Bruce A. Ware and John Starke, 155–72. Wheaton: Crossway, 2015.

Stauffer, Ethelbert. "θεός, θεότης, ἄθεος, θεοδίδακτος, θεῖος, θειότης." In vol. 3 of *TDNT*, edited by Gerhard Kittel and Gerhard Friedrich, translated by Geoffrey W. Bromiley, 65–123. Grand Rapids: Eerdmans, 1964–76.

Stephens, William Peter. *Theology of Huldrych Zwingli*. New York: Oxford University Press, 1986.

Stover, Dale A. "The Pneumatology of John Owen: A Study of the Role of the Holy Spirit in Relation to the Shape of a Theology." PhD diss., McGill University, 1967.

Strobel, August. *Der Brief an die Hebräer*. Das Neue Testament Deutsch. Göttingen: Vandenhoeck & Ruprecht, 1991.

Strong, Augustus Hopkins. *Systematic Theology: A Compendium*. Valley Forge, PA: Judson, 1907.

Stump, Eleonore. *Aquinas*. London: Routledge, 2005.

Stump, Eleonore. "Aquinas' Metaphysics of the Incarnation." In *The Incarnation: An Interdisciplinary Symposium on the Incarnation of the Son of God*, edited by Stephen T. Davis, Daniel Kendall, and Gerald O'Collins, 197–220. New York: Oxford University Press, 2004.

Stump, Eleonore, and Norman Kretzmann. "Absolute Simplicity." *F&P* 2 (1985): 353–82.

Sturch, Richard. *The Word and the Christ: An Essay in Analytic Christology*. New York: Clarendon, 1991.

Sumner, Darren O. "Obedience and Subordination in Karl Barth's Trinitarian Theology." In *Advancing Trinitarian Theology: Explorations in Constructive Dogmatics*, edited by Oliver D. Crisp and Fred Sanders, 130–45. LATC. Grand Rapids: Zondervan, 2014.

Swain, Scott R., and Michael Allen. "The Obedience of the Eternal Son: Catholic Trinitarianism and Reformed Christology." In *Christology Ancient & Modern: Explorations in Constructive Dogmatics*, edited by Oliver D. Crisp and Fred Sanders, 74–95. LATC. Grand Rapids: Zondervan, 2013.

Swinburne, Richard. *The Christian God*. New York: Oxford University Press, 1994.

Swinburne, Richard G. "What Is so Good about Having a Body?" In *Comparative Theology: Essays for Keith Ward*, edited by T. W. Bartel, 134–42. London: SPCK, 2003.

Tan, Seng-Kong. "Trinitarian Action in the Incarnation." In *Jonathan Edwards as Contemporary: Essays in Honor of Sang Hyun Lee*, edited by Don Schweitzer, 127–50. New York: Peter Lang, 2010.

Tanner, Kathryn. *Christ the Key*. New York: Cambridge University Press, 2010.

Tanner, Kathryn. *God and Creation in Christian Theology*. Minneapolis: Fortress, 2005.

Tanner, Kathryn. *Jesus, Humanity and the Trinity*. Minneapolis: Fortress, 2001.

Tanner, Kathryn. "The Trinity as Christian Teaching." In *The Oxford Handbook of the Trinity*, edited by Gilles Emery and Matthew Levering, 349–58. New York: Oxford University Press, 2011.

Tanner, Norman P., ed. *Decrees of the Ecumenical Councils*. Vol. 1. Washington, DC: Georgetown University Press, 1990.

Tay, Edwin E. M. *The Priesthood of Christ: Atonement in the Theology of John Owen (1616–1683)*. Studies in Christian History and Thought. Milton Keynes: Paternoster, 2014.

Taylor, Charles. *Sources of the Self: The Making of the Modern Identity*. New York: Cambridge University Press, 1989.

Thielicke, Helmut. *The Evangelical Faith*. 3 vols. Edinburgh: T&T Clark, 1974–82.

Thompson, Thomas R. "Nineteenth-Century Kenotic Christology: The Waxing, Waning, and Weighing of a Quest for a Coherent Orthodoxy." In *Exploring Kenotic Christology: The Self-Emptying of God*, 74–111. New York: Oxford University Press, 2006.

Thompson, Thomas R., and Cornelius Plantinga Jr. "Trinity and Kenosis." In *Exploring Kenotic Christology: The Self-Emptying of God*, edited by C. Stephen Evans, 165–89. New York: Oxford University Press, 2006.

Thurén, Jukka. "Gebet und Gehorsam des Erniedrigten (Hebr. V 7–10 noch einmal)." *Novum Testamentum* 13 (1971): 136–46.

Tilling, Chris. *Paul's Divine Christology*. Grand Rapids: Eerdmans, 2015.

Timpe, Kevin. "Cooperative Grace, Cooperative Agency." *EJPR* 7 (2015): 223–45.

Torrance, Alan J. "Is Love the Essence of God?" In *Nothing Greater, Nothing Better: Theological Essays on the Love of God*, edited by Kevin J. Vanhoozer, 114–37. Grand Rapids: Eerdmans, 2001.

Torrance, Thomas F. *Christian Doctrine of God, One Being Three Persons*. New York: T&T Clark, 2001.

Treier, Daniel J. "Incarnation." In *Christian Dogmatics: Reformed Theology for the Church Catholic*, edited by Michael Allen and Scott R. Swain, 216–42. Grand Rapids: Baker Academic, 2016.

Treier, Daniel J. "'Mediator of a New Covenant': Atonement and Christology in Hebrews." In *So Great a Salvation: A Dialogue on the Atonement in Hebrews*, edited by Jon C. Laansma, George H. Guthrie, and Cynthia Long Westfall, 105–19. LNT 516. New York: T&T Clark, 2019.

Trueman, Carl R. *John Owen: Reformed Catholic, Renaissance Man*. Burlington: Routledge, 2007.

Trueman, Carl R. "Patristics and Reformed Orthodoxy: Some Brief Notes and Proposals." *SBJT* 12 (2008): 52–60.

Trueman, Carl R. *The Claims of Truth: John Owen's Trinitarian Theology*. Carlisle: Paternoster, 1998.

Tschipke, Theophil. *L'humanité du Christ comme instrument de salut de la divinité*. Translated by Philibert Secrétan. Studia Friburgensia 94. Fribourg: Academic Fribourg, 2003.

Turretin, Francis. *Institutes of Elenctic Theology*. Edited by James T. Dennison. Translated by George Musgrave Giger. 3 vols. Phillipsburg: P&R, 1992.

Turretin, Francis. *Institutio Theologiæ Elencticæ*. 3 vols. New York: Robert Carter, 1847.

Tweeddale, John W. *John Owen and Hebrews: The Foundation of Biblical Interpretation*. T&T Clark Studies in English Theology. T&T Clark, 2019.

Tylenda, Joseph N. "Christ the Mediator: Calvin Versus Stancaro." *Calvin Theological Journal* 8 (1973): 5–16.

Tylenda, Joseph N. "Controversy on Christ the Mediator: Calvin's Second Reply to Stancaro." *Calvin Theological Journal* 8 (1973): 131–57.
Ursinus, Zacharias. *The Commentary of Dr. Zacharias Ursinus on the Heidelberg Catechism*. Translated by G. W. Williard. Columbus: Scott & Bascom, 1851.
VanDrunen, David. *Natural Law and the Two Kingdoms: A Study in the Development of Reformed Social Thought*. Grand Rapids: Eerdmans, 2010.
VanDrunen, David. "The Two Kingdoms Doctrine and the Relationship of Church and State in the Early Reformed Tradition." *Journal of Church and State* 49 (2007): 743–63.
Vanhoozer, Kevin J. *Biblical Authority after Babel*. Grand Rapids: Brazos, 2016.
Vanhoozer, Kevin J. "Foreword." In *Communion with the Triune God*, edited by Kelly M. Kapic and Justin Taylor, 11–14. Wheaton, IL: Crossway, 2007.
Vanhoozer, Kevin J. *Remythologizing Theology: Divine Action, Passion, and Authorship*. CSCD. New York: Cambridge University Press, 2010.
Vanhoozer, Kevin J. "The Spirit of Light After the Age of Enlightenment: Reforming/Renewing Pneumatic Hermeneutics via the Economy of Illumination." In *Spirit of God: Christian Renewal in the Community of Faith*, edited by Jeffrey W. Barbeau and Beth Felker Jones, 149–67. Downers Grove, IL: IVP Academic, 2015.
Vanhoozer, Kevin J., and Daniel J. Treier. *Theology and the Mirror of Scripture: A Mere Evangelical Account*. Studies in Christian Doctrine and Scripture. Downers Grove, IL: IVP Academic, 2015.
Velde, Dolf te. *The Doctrine of God in Reformed Orthodoxy, Karl Barth, and the Utrecht School: A Study in Method and Content*. SRT 25. Boston: Brill, 2013.
Venema, Hermann. *Translation of Hermann Venema's Inedited Institutes of Theology*. Translated by Alexander W. Brown. Edinburgh: T&T Clark, 1850.
Vermigli, Peter Martyr. *Life, Letters, and Sermons*. Edited by John Patrick Donnelly. Translated by John Patrick Donnelly. PML 5. Kirksville, MO: Trueman State University Press, 1999.
Vidu, Adonis. "Ascension and Pentecost." In *Being Saved: Explorations in Human Salvation*, edited by Marc Cortez, Joshua R. Farris, and S. Mark Hamilton, 102–23. London: SCM, 2018.
Vidu, Adonis. *Atonement, Law, and Justice: The Cross in Historical and Cultural Contexts*. Grand Rapids: Baker Academic, 2014.
Vidu, Adonis. "Opera Trinitatis Ad Extra and Collective Agency." *EJPR* 7 (2015): 27–47.
Vidu, Adonis. "The Place of the Cross Among the Inseparable Operations of the Trinity." In *Locating Atonement: Explorations in Constructive Dogmatics*, edited by Oliver D. Crisp and Fred Sanders, 21–42. LATC. Grand Rapids: Zondervan, 2015.
Vidu, Adonis. "Trinitarian Inseparable Operations and the Incarnation." *JAT* 4 (2016): 106–27.
Vlastuin, Willem van, and Kelly Kapic, eds. *John Owen between Orthodoxy and Modernity*. SRT 39. Boston: Brill, 2019.
Vidu, Adonis. "Introduction, Overview and Epilogue." In *John Owen between Orthodoxy and Modernity*, edited by Willem van Vlastuin and Kelly M. Kapic, 3–34. SRT 39. Boston: Brill, 2018.
Ward, Timothy. *Words of Life: Scripture as the Living and Active Word of God*. Downers Grove, IL: IVP Academic, 2009.
Ware, Bruce A. *Father, Son, and Holy Spirit: Relationships, Roles, and Relevance*. Wheaton: Crossway, 2005.
Watson, Francis. "The Triune Divine Identity: Reflections on Pauline God-Language, in Disagreement With J. D. G. Dunn." *JSNT* 23 (2001): 99–124.

Watson, Thomas. *A Body of Divinity*. Carlisle: Banner of Truth, 1983.
Webster, John. *Confessing God: Essays in Christian Dogmatics II*. New York: Bloomsbury T&T Clark, 2005.
Webster, John. *God without Measure: Working Papers in Christian Theology: Volume 1: God and the Works of God*. New York: Bloomsbury, 2016.
Webster, John. *Holiness*. Grand Rapids: Eerdmans, 2003.
Webster, John. *Holy Scripture*. CIT. New York: Cambridge University Press, 2006.
Webster, John. "One Who Is Son: Theological Reflections on the Exordium to the Epistle to the Hebrews." In *Epistle to the Hebrews and Christian Theology*, edited by Richard Bauckham, Daniel R. Driver, Trevor A. Hart, and Nathan MacDonald, 69–94. Grand Rapids: Eerdmans, 2009.
Webster, John. "The Imitation of Christ." *Tyndale Bulletin* 37 (1986): 95–120.
Webster, John. "The Place of Christology in Systematic Theology." In *The Oxford Handbook of Christology*, edited by Francesca Murphy, 611–27. New York: Oxford University Press, 2015.
Webster, John. *Word and Church: Essays in Christian Dogmatics*. New York: T&T Clark, 2001.
Wegner, Daniel M. *The Illusion of Conscious Will*. Cambridge, MA: MIT Press, 2002.
Weinandy, Thomas G. *Does God Suffer?* Notre Dame: University of Notre Dame Press, 2000.
Weinandy, Thomas G. *Jesus Becoming Jesus: A Theological Interpretation of the Synoptic Gospels*. Washington, DC: Catholic University of America Press, 2018.
Weinandy, Thomas G. "Jesus' Filial Vision of the Father." *Pro Ecclesia* 13 (2004): 189–201.
Weinandy, Thomas G. *The Father's Spirit of Sonship: Reconceiving the Trinity*. Eugene: Wipf & Stock, 2011.
Weinandy, Thomas G. "The Soul/Body Analogy and the Incarnation: Cyril of Alexandria." *Coptic Church Review* 17 (1996): 59–66.
Wellum, Stephen J. *God the Son Incarnate: The Doctrine of Christ*. Foundations of Evangelical Theology. Wheaton: Crossway, 2016.
Wessling, Jordan. "Christology and Conciliar Authority: On the Viability of Monothelitism for Protestant Theology." In *Christology, Ancient and Modern: Explorations in Constructive Dogmatics*, edited by Oliver D. Crisp and Fred Sanders, 151–70. LATC. Grand Rapids: Zondervan Academic, 2013.
White, Thomas Joseph. *The Incarnate Lord: A Thomistic Study in Christology*. Washington, DC: Catholic University of America Press, 2015.
Williams, George Huntston. *The Radical Reformation*. 3rd ed. Sixteenth Century Essays and Studies 15. Kriksville, MO: Truman State University, 2000.
Williams, Rowan. *Christ the Heart of Creation*. London: Bloomsbury Continuum, 2018.
Willis, E. David. *Calvin's Catholic Christology: The Function of the So-Called Extra Calvinisticum in Calvin's Theology*. Studies in Medieval and Reformation Thought 2. Leiden: Brill, 1966.
Witherington III, Ben. "The Trinity in the Johannine Literature." In *The Oxford Handbook of the Trinity*, edited by Gilles Emery and Matthew Levering, 69–79. New York: Oxford University Press, 2011.
Wittman, Tyler R. "The End of the Incarnation: John Owen, Trinitarian Agency and Christology." *IJST* 15 (2013): 284–300.
Wolter, Michael. *Der Brief an die Römer: Teilband 1: Röm 1–8*. EKK VI/1. Neukirchen-Vluyn: Patmos, 2014.

Wolterstorff, Nicholas. *Divine Discourse: Philosophical Reflections on the Claim that God Speaks*. New York: Cambridge University Press, 1995.

Work, Telford. "Jesus' New Relationship with the Holy Spirit and Ours." In *Christology, Ancient and Modern: Explorations in Constructive Dogmatics*, edited by Oliver Crisp and Fred Sanders. LATC. Grand Rapids: Zondervan, 2013.

Wright, N. T. "Jesus and the Identity of God." *Ex Auditu* 14 (1998): 42–56.

Wright, N. T. "The Letter to the Romans: Introduction, Commentary, and Reflections." In *The New Interpreter's Bible*, edited by Leander E. Keck, 10:393–770. Nashville: Abingdon, 2002.

Yeago, David S. "The New Testament and the Nicene Dogma: A Contribution to the Recovery of Theological Exegesis." *Pro Ecclesia* 3 (1994): 152–64.

Zuidema, Jason. *Peter Martyr Vermigli (1499–1562) and the Outward Instruments of Divine Grace*. Reformed Historical Theology 4. Göttingen: Vandenhoeck & Ruprecht, 2008.

INDEX

Abraham, William 4, 10, 10 n.49, 183 n.51
accordion effect 15
act Nestorianism 146, 199, 201, 204, 207
agency language 3–5, 7, 40, 44, 204, 211
agent-causality model 11–12, 16
Allen, R. Michael 25 n.123, 37, 137 n.9, 151 n.81, 152, 167, 168 n.175, 169 n.180
alloiosis 186
Alvarez, Maria 13, 16
an/enhypostatic 41, 72–3, 119–20, 120 n.69, 121–2, 134, 151, 156, 170, 202, 202 n.143, 204, 206, 211
Apollinarianism 20, 39, 147
apotelesma 80, 87 n.125, 88–9, 99, 176–7, 187, 197
apotelesma theandrikon 87, 177 n.20
appropriated actions 109–14
appropriations 36, 53, 62–4, 66, 109–10, 133
Aquinas, Thomas 23–4, 29, 61, 68, 107, 153, 155, 188
Augustine 29, 105–6

Bach, Kent 121 n.72
Balthasar, Hans Urs von 1, 151
Barth, Karl 1 n.4, 6 n.29, 35, 42, 131–3, 176 n.14
Bathrellos, Demetrios 151, 154–5, 179 n.30, 202
Bauckham, Richard 163
Bavinck, Herman 23, 26, 31, 136 n.7, 139, 144, 185
Beeley, Christopher 179
Blowers, Paul M. 144 n.47, 144 n.51
Brown, David 117, 196
Bruce, F. F. 125, 158 n.118
Butner, D. Glenn 166–7, 169–70

Calvin, John 23, 24 n.121, 26, 73, 110, 142, 159, 169, 174–5, 174 n.6
Capes, David B. 129 n.92

causality, perspective of 57, 65, 97, 103, 105–6, 109, 133, 156, 210
Chalcedon 1, 5–6, 18–21, 36, 38–9, 102, 111, 178–9, 199, 201 n.138, 202, 204
Christologia 66, 91
christological agency 2, 2 n.7, 8, 17–18, 31–4, 37, 42–3, 67, 71, 79, 101–2, 106, 116, 119, 122, 154, 156, 170, 184, 188, 198, 204, 207, 209, 211, 213–15
Christ's human nature 24–6, 40–1, 71, 72 n.37, 76, 95, 101, 108, 113, 120–1, 136, 149, 151, 153, 168, 183 n.48, 196, 206, 210, 214
classical Trinitarianism 22–4, 47, 53, 103, 106, 108, 116, 133, 209, 211, 214
Claunch, Kyle 112
Cleveland, Christopher 33, 45 n.9, 70 n.25, 78–9
coarse-grained theory 13–15
Cockerill, Gareth 164
coherence 3, 31, 34, 42, 102–3, 106, 114–15, 120–4, 135–6, 141, 151, 182
Communion 21–2, 60, 74 n.51, 87–8, 88 n.127, 89, 176, 187
concursus 193, 193 n.97, 195
constant agency 118–22
Constantinople II 1, 19–20, 199–200
Constantinople III 19, 54, 54 n.66, 91–2, 94, 120, 133
counting acts 13 n.60
Creator-creature distinction 47, 192
Crisp, Oliver D. 116, 119–20, 121 n.71, 181–2, 181 n.43
Cross, Richard 115 n.54, 195, 195 n.109
Cyril of Alexandria 19–20, 190–1, 199

Daley, Brian E. 5, 135, 180, 184, 198 n.126
Daniels, Richard 49 n.33
Davidson, Donald 15, 142 n.41, 143
Davidson, Ivor, J. 1 n.4, 131 n.109, 142, 142 n.41, 143, 194

Davis, Stephen T. 103, 117
death of Christ 124, 129–31, 168
Death of Death 57–9
DeWeese, Garrett 147 n.65
distinct capacities 20–2, 90, 92, 155, 177, 183–4, 200
distinct effects 184–92
distinguishing acts 13 n.60
divine agency 103, 114–15
    appropriated actions 109–14
    constant agency 118–22
    distinctly 129–31
    proper actions and personal modes 106–9
    in Scripture 122–4
    shared 127–8
    simple agency 115–18
    singular 103–6, 124–6
divine missions 61–2
divine passibility and limitation 37–8
divine simplicity 9 n.43, 10, 22–4, 46, 48–50, 49 n.35, 50, 52, 65 n.127, 102, 114, 116–18, 122, 133, 180, 192
Dorner, Isaac August 136 n.6
Drake, K. J. 25 n.124, 140 n.25, 199 n.128
Dunn, James 125, 125 n.86
dyothelitism 78–9, 141–2, 146, 151, 183 n.51, 194, 214

Eck, John 137 n.11
Edwards, Jonathan 31, 152, 169
Emery, Gilles 102, 108 n.30, 109, 155
Ephesus 19–20
Evans, William B. 25 n.123
extra calvinisticum 25, 75–6, 116–19, 122, 133, 140 n.25

Ferguson, Sinclair B. 71 n.29, 74 n.51, 80 n.92
filial divine agency 37, 41, 59, 66, 89, 109, 112–13, 123–4, 127–8, 211–12
fine-grained theory 13–14
Flint, Thomas P. 5, 177 n.22, 180–1, 196
Forsyth, P. T. 131
Frei, Hans 8

Gaine, Simon Francis 138 n.17, 140 n.30
Gathercole, Simon J. 3 n.13
Gill, John 176
Goodwin, Thomas 167

Gorman, Michael 125
gospel of John 1
Gregory of Nazianzus 20, 200 n.134
Gregory of Nyssa 110, 188
Grillmeier, Aloys 178–9
Gunton, Colin 32, 41 n.195

Habets, Myk 79 n.88
Hawthorne, Gerald F. 112, 116
Hebrews 5 138 n.19, 157–8, 161 n.137, 165, 165 n.160, 168, 171, 211
Heppe, Heinrich 87
Hodge, Charles 6
Holmes, Stephen 79 n.88, 185
The Holy Spirit 11, 24, 26, 30, 35–7, 45, 50–2, 55–9, 55 n.71, 61, 63–4, 65 n.127, 67, 71–2, 80 n.91, 86, 90, 94, 96–8, 102–3, 106, 109–14, 116, 119 n.64, 133, 135–6, 141, 148–50, 166, 170, 186 n.63, 187, 201, 210–12
human activity 25, 37, 160–1, 187–9, 192, 213
human agency
    desires and will 141–8
    finite knowledge 136–41
    Holy Spirit 148–50
    instrumentality 151–4
    obedience 166–70
    perspectives 154–6, 154 n.103
    priest 161–2
    in scripture 157–8
    sympathetic model 165–6
Hyman, John 13, 16
hypostasis 83, 179–80
hypostatic union 69–70

identity 19–20, 19 n.82, 126–8, 150, 158–60, 165, 171, 202–3
immediacy 92–6, 189
indivisible operations 33, 55–7, 65–6, 71, 97 n.13, 104, 114, 191–2, 212
instrumental action 41, 153–5
instrumentality 151–4
internal coherence 2 n.8, 18, 43, 101, 178, 212

Jenkins, Skip 114 n.48
Jenson Robert 5
John of Damascus 87, 179, 190, 194
Johnson, Elizabeth A. 3 n.14, 39

Kapic, Kelly 33 n.158
Kärkkäinen, Veli-Matti 37
Kelsey, David 7–8
kenotic/kenoticism 38, 115, 115 n.50, 116, 116 n.58, 117–19, 117 n.59, 122, 130, 132–3, 157, 157 n.113, 210, 213
Kent, Clark 116
Kieser family
  daughter(s) 89, 110, 121 n.71, 127–8, 143–4, 191 n.90, 203
  son(s) 16, 19 n.82, 154, 200 n.138, 203
  wife 11, 19, 121
krypsis 119–22, 120 n.69, 134, 213
kryptic 115, 119–21, 133

Leftow, Brian 116, 197
Leo the Great 19, 21, 21 n.93
Letham, Robert 60 n.99
Logos Christology 36, 37 n.172
Loke, Andrew 119
Lowe, E. J. 16, 153 n.100

magnet 57–8, 107–8, 110
Maximus the Confessor 19, 22, 183 n.51
McCall, Thomas H. 34 n.159, 35 n.162, 104, 138 n.19, 161 n.137, 168, 168 n.176
McCormack, Bruce 5, 33 n.158, 37, 157, 157 n.113, 165, 176 n.14, 203–4, 206 n.155
McDonald, Suzanne 137 n.12
McFarland, Ian A. 39 n.182, 105 n.18, 146 n.59, 187–8, 189 n.80, 192 n.91
McGrath, Alister E. 114 n.49
McGraw, Ryan M. 49 n.35, 76 n.64, 139 n.23
mediator, ontology of (Owen) 68–9
  an/enhypostatic 72–4
  assumption and hypostatic union 69–70
  communication of attributes 74–5
  essential properties (dyothelitism) 78–9
  humanity 77
  one person 69
  son's assumption 70–1
  spirit, role of 71–2
  two natures 75–7
mediator, operations of (Owen) 79–80
  distinct agencies 89–90
  Holy Spirit 96–8

human agency 96–8
immediacy 92–6
principium quod/quo 86–9, 88 n.127, 89 n.128
principles 90–2
single agent 80
Son and mediator 85–6
theandric agent 80–4, 82 n.100
Meyendorff, John 196 n.115
Michaels, J. Ramsey 105 n.16
ministerial authority 17 n.76, 19 n.80, 209
model-A Christology 180–1
model-T Christology 180–1
Moffitt, David M. 162, 162 n.142
Moltmann, Jürgen 35, 35 n.163, 112
Moo, Douglas 124
Morris, Leon 105 n.16, 125
Morris, Thomas 146 n.61
Moser, J. David 153 n.95
Mosser, Carl 35 n.162
Muller, Richard 30, 60

Nestorianism 19–20, 38, 40, 72–3, 88–9, 137 n.11, 145, 146 n.61, 156, 173, 193, 198–201, 204, 207, 211

O'Connor, Timothy 12 n.51, 12 n.54, 16–17
one will 47–8
Owen, John 27, 28 n.136, 29 n.140, 29 n.143, 31 n.151, 33 n.158. *See also* mediator, ontology of (Owen); mediator, operations of (Owen)
  especial impression 61–2
  historical location 27–8
  indivisible operations 33, 55–7, 65–6, 71, 97 n.13, 104, 114, 191–2, 212
  pneumachristology 97
  principle of operation 54–5
  testimony 28–33
  trinitarian and christological action 30–1
  Vindication of the Doctrine of the Trinity 52, 99

Pannenberg, Wolfhart 151 n.83
parallelism 38–40, 39 n.184, 184, 195, 213
pastoral prudence 131–3
Patterson, Patrick D. M. 40
Pauline 4, 122–3, 130

Peanut M&M 180
Pneumatologia 56, 61, 64, 97, 113
prima facie liabilities 33–42, 101, 209, 211–12
principium quod/quo 80, 86–9, 88 n.127, 89 n.128
proper actions 106–9, 113, 168, 189, 212
prudence 3, 3 n.9, 31, 34, 42–3, 99, 101–3, 101 n.1, 106, 115, 119, 131, 134–6, 153, 157, 165, 184, 205, 209, 211–14

Radde-Gallwitz, Andrew 65 n.127
Rahner, Karl 39, 39 n.187, 114 n.48, 143 n.43
reconciliation 79, 123, 129–31
Reid, Thomas 16
restriction 119, 121 n.71
reverse proportionality 6, 8, 33
Riches, Aaron 188
Rom. 5:10 126, 130

Schmid, Heinrich 186–7
Schnabel, Eckhard J. 124 n.81
Schwarz, Hans 196 n.113
Schwöbel, Christoph 5
Scotus, Duns 29
Seiller, Léon 195 n.108
Senor, Thomas 116 n.58, 147
Shedd, William 196
simple agency 115–18
simplicity and pure act 45–6
simultaneous operations 192–8
singular agency 53–4, 103–6, 124–6
social trinitarianism 34–5, 34 n.159–34 n.160, 35 n.162, 103–6, 212
Sola Scriptura 17, 26–7, 146
Spence, Alan 32, 73 n.45, 74 n.51, 85 nn.114–15, 87 n.123, 107 n.24, 119 n.64, 202 n.140
Spirit Christology 36–7, 36 n.169, 37, 37 n.172, 107, 109, 111, 114, 197, 210, 212
spirit, role of 71–2
Stancaro, Francesco 174
strong instrumentality 40–1, 150, 153–4, 156–7, 184, 187, 213
Swain, Scott 167, 168 n.175, 169 n.180
Swinburne, Richard 8, 195

sword 22, 182–4, 182 n.47, 201, 203
Synopsis of Purer Theology 152, 176, 184–5, 197

Tanner, Kathryn 7
Tan, Seng-Kong 152 n.90
Tay, Edwin 68 n.3, 98
terminus 44, 58–9, 59 n.90, 63–4, 66, 70, 70 n.25, 85 n.115, 97, 102–3, 105–9, 112–14, 154 n.103, 156, 204, 210–11
theandric unity
    analogy 182–3
    historic and contemporary 178–82
    mediator 173–8
theopaschite formula 20, 34, 38, 199
Thielicke, Helmut 40 n.188
totus Christus 80 n.92
triune God 11, 27, 34, 36, 42, 44–5, 51–3, 65–6, 125–6, 132–4, 156, 191, 204, 209–10, 212, 215
    appropriations 62–4
    begotten of the father 50
    distinct agents-in-relation (plural) 64–5
    divine agents-in-relation 58–9
    divine attributes 46–7
    divine missions 61–2
    divine relations and persons 49–50
    father and the son *(filioque)* 50–1
    indivisible operations 55–7
    one will 47–8
    operations *ad extra* and *ad intra* 59–61
    principle of operation 54–5
    simplicity and pure act 45–6
    singular agency 53–4
    triune agent (singular) 57–8
    triune persons 48–9
    unity of 45
Trueman, Carl R. 29, 29 n.143, 44 n.3, 44 n.5, 51, 56, 60, 60 n.97
Turretin, Francis 23–4, 87–9, 98–9, 105, 139, 148, 152, 175–6, 194–5
Tylenda, Joseph N. 174 n.6

Ursinus, Zacharias 108

VanDrunen, David 196 n.110
Vermigli, Peter Martyr 152, 175, 175 n.9

Vidu, Adonis 7, 10, 102, 191, 191 n.89
Vindication 52, 87–9, 99
Vindiciæ Evangelicæ 44 n.5, 47
Vlastuin, Willem van 33 n.158

Webster, John 131 n.108, 152, 197 n.118
Weinandy, Thomas G. 8 n.40, 199 n.129
Wellum, Stephen 6
Westminster Confession 23

White, Thomas Joseph 141, 145–6, 151
Williams, Rowan 6, 139 n.24, 196
Williams, Scott 34 n.160
Wright, N. T. 132, 170

YHWH 23, 125–7, 132, 164, 170

Zanchi, Jerome 176, 189, 203 n.148
Zwingli, Huldrych 186

www.ingramcontent.com/pod-product-compliance
Lightning Source LLC
Chambersburg PA
CBHW051519230426
43668CB00012B/1668